Contemporary Latin American Cultural Studies

Contemporary Latin American Cultural Studies

Edited by Stephen Hart
Professor of Hispanic Studies,
University College London, UK

and Richard Young
Professor of Spanish and Latin American Studies,
University of Alberta, Canada

A member of the Hodder Headline Group
LONDON
Distributed in the United States of America by
Oxford University Press Inc., New York

First published in Great Britain in 2003 by
Arnold, a member of the Hodder Headline Group,
338 Euston Road, London NW1 3BH

http://www.arnoldpublishers.com

Distributed in the United States of America by
Oxford University Press Inc.,
198 Madison Avenue, New York, NY10016

© 2003 Arnold

All rights reserved. No part of this publication may be reproduced or
transmitted in any form or by any means, electronically or mechanically,
including photocopying, recording or any information storage or retrieval
system, without either prior permission in writing from the publisher or a
licence permitting restricted copying. In the United Kingdom such licences
are issued by the Copyright Licensing Agency: 90 Tottenham Court Road,
London W1T 4LP.

The advice and information in this book are believed to be true and
accurate at the date of going to press, but neither the authors nor the publisher
can accept any legal responsibility or liability for any errors or omissions.

British Library Cataloguing in Publication Data
A catalogue record for this book is available from the British Library

Library of Congress Cataloging-in-Publication Data
A catalog record for this book is available from the Library of Congress

ISBN 0 340 80821 7 (hb)
ISBN 0 340 80822 5 (pb)

1 2 3 4 5 6 7 8 9 10

Typeset in 10 on 12½pt Sabon by Phoenix Photosetting, Chatham, Kent
Printed and bound in Malta

What do you think about this book? Or any other Arnold title?
Please send your comments to feedback.arnold@hodder.co.uk

Contents

List of contributors *ix*

Introduction 1
Stephen Hart and Richard Young

PART 1   LATIN AMERICA AND CULTURAL STUDIES

1 Cultural studies and revolving doors 12
Néstor García Canclini

2 Cultural studies and literary criticism at the cross-roads of value 24
Beatriz Sarlo

3 The place of literature in cultural studies 37
William Rowe

4 *Adiós*: a national allegory (some reflections on Latin American Cultural Studies) 48
John Beverley

PART 2   CULTURAL ICONS

5 Contesting the cleric: the intellectual as icon in modern Spanish America 62
Nicola Miller

6 Cultural myths and Chicana literature: a field in dispute 76
María Cristina Pons

7 Recontextualizing violence as founding myth: *La sangre derramada* by José Pablo Feinmann 90
Rita De Grandis

8 Eva Perón: one woman, several masks 102
Lidia Santos

PART 3   CULTURE AS SPECTACLE/COMMODITY

9 The spectacle of identities: football in Latin America   116
   Eduardo P. Archetti

10 Modernity, modernization and melodrama: the bolero in Mexico in the
   1930s and 1940s   127
   Vanessa Knights

11 Stars: mapping the firmament   140
   John King

12 *Los globalizados también lloran*: Mexican *telenovelas* and the
   geographical imagination   151
   Laura Podalsky

13 Local(izing) images: Montevideo's televisual praxis   167
   Victoria Ruétalo

14 The young and the damned: street visions in Latin American cinema   177
   Geoffrey Kantaris

PART 4   CULTURE, HEGEMONY AND OPPOSITION

15 Identity, politics and *mestizaje*   192
   Amaryll Chanady

16 Brazilian cinema: reflections on race and representation   203
   Robert Stam

17 Of silences and exclusions: nation and culture in nineteenth-century
   Colombia   215
   Patricia D'Allemand

18 *Testimonio* and its discontents   228
   Francesca Denegri

19 Nicomedes Santa Cruz and the vindication of Afro-Peruvian culture   239
   Martha Ojeda

20 Queering Latin American popular culture   253
   David William Foster

PART 5   CULTURAL PRACTICES

21 Food in Latin America   268
   Mike González

22	**Capoeira culture: an impertinent non-Western art form** Floyd Merrell	**278**
23	**Mama Coca and the Revolution: Jorge Sanjinés's double-take** Stephen Hart	**290**
24	**Buenos Aires and the narration of urban spaces and practices** Richard Young	**300**

References — **313**

Index — **341**

List of contributors

Eduardo P. Archetti is Professor of Social Anthropology at the University of Oslo. His main publications are *Guinea Pigs: Food, Symbol and Conflict of Knowledge in Ecuador* (1997), *Masculinities: Football, Polo and the Tango in Argentina* (1999), and *El potrero, la pista y el ring: las patrias del deporte argentino* (2001). He has recently edited, jointly with Noel Dyck, *Sport, Dance and Embodied Identities* (2003). He is working on a comparative analysis of dance, music and sport in Argentina, Cuba and Brazil.

John Beverley is a Professor and current chair of the Department of Hispanic Languages and Literatures at the University of Pittsburgh, Pennsylvania, USA. His most recent books include an edited collection, *From Cuba* (2003), *Subalternity and Representation* (1999), and *Una modernidad obsoleta* (1998). A new book, *The Politics of Truth: On Testimonio*, is forthcoming from the University of Minnesota Press. He was a member of the Latin American Subaltern Studies Group.

Amaryll Chanady is Professor of Comparative Literature and departmental chair at the University of Montreal. Her main publications are *Latin American Identity and Constructions of Difference* (1994) and *Entre exclusion et inclusion: La symbolisation de l'Autre dans les Amériques* (1999).

Patricia D'Allemand is Senior Lecturer in Latin American Literature and Culture in the Department of Hispanic Studies at Queen Mary, University of London. Currently researching into nationalist discourses in nineteenth-century Colombia, she has published widely, particularly in cultural theory and history of ideas, and is author of *Latin American Cultural Criticism: Re-Interpreting a Continent* (2000).

Rita De Grandis is Associate Professor of Spanish American Literature and Comparative Literature at the University of British Columbia. She teaches in the Department of French, Hispanic and Italian Studies and the Program of Latin American Studies. Her areas of specialization include modern and contemporary Latin American literature, literary theory, cultural and gender criticism. She is the author of *Polémica y estrategias narrativas en America*

Latina (1993), and co-editor of *Questioning Hybridity in the Americas* (with Zilà Bernd, 1999). She was also the invited editor of a Special Issue on 'María Luisa Bemberg: entre lo político y lo personal', *Revista de Canadiense de Estudios Hispánicos* (2002); 'Relaciones entre cine y literaturas hispánicas,' ANCLAJES, *Revista del Instituto de Análisis Semiótico del Discurso* (2000); and a Special Issue on 'Eva Perón: Variations on a Myth,' *Canadian Association of Latin American and Caribbean Studies* (1999). She has published numerous articles in refereed journals in Canada, Argentina, Chile, Brazil, Cuba, Peru, Puerto Rico, Spain, the United States and Israel.

Francesca Denegri, a freelance writer now living in Lima, taught Latin American literature for a number of years at University College London. She has published *El abanico y la cigarrera: la primera generación de mujeres ilustradas en el Perú* (1996), a testimonial text, *Soy Señora: testimonio de Irene Jara* (2000), as well as numerous articles on Peruvian literature. She is currently preparing a study on Flora Tristan.

David William Foster is Regents' Professor of Spanish, Interdisciplinary Humanities, and Women's Studies at Arizona State University. His most recent publications include *Violence in Argentine Literature: Cultural Responses to Tyranny* (University of Missouri Press, 1995); *Cultural Diversity in Latin American Literature* (University of New Mexico Press, 1994); *Contemporary Argentine Cinema* (University of Missouri Press, 1992); and *Gay and Lesbian Themes in Latin American Writing* (University of Texas Press, 1991). He is also the editor of *Sexual Textualities: Essays on Queer/ing Latin American Writing* (University of Texas Press, 1997), *Buenos Aires: Perspectives on the City and Cultural Production* (University of Florida Press, 1998), and *Contemporary Brazilian Cinema* (University of Texas Press, 2000). In 1989, Foster was named the Graduate College's Outstanding Graduate Mentor, and in 1994 he was named the Researcher of the year by the Alumni Association.

Néstor García Canclini is one of Latin America's leading commentators on contemporary culture. He is Director of the Program on Urban Culture at the Universidad Autónoma Metropolitana in Mexico City and has also taught at universities in Latin America, North America and Europe. His books have won international awards and have been translated into several languages. Among his most significant publications are *Culturas híbridas: estrategias para entrar y salir de la modernidad* (1990), *Consumidores y ciudadanos: conflictos multiculturales de la globalización* (1995), and *La globalización imaginada* (1999).

Mike González is Senior Lecturer in Hispanic Studies at the University of Glasgow. He was editor (with Daniel Balderston and Ana María López) of the *Routledge Encyclopedia of Contemporary Latin American and Caribbean*

Culture (2001) and (with Daniel Balderston) of the *Routledge Encyclopedia of Latin American Literature* (forthcoming 2004). His other publications include *The Gathering of Voices: The Poetry of 20th Century Latin America* (1992) and the forthcoming *Being Intercultural: Modern Languages and the Future of Higher Education* (with Alison Phipps) to be published in 2003. He has written for the theatre and is a regular broadcaster with BBC Radio.

Stephen Hart is Professor of Hispanic Studies at University College London, England. He is co-editor of the Critical Guides series and commissioning editor of *Tamesis*. His main publications are *White Ink* (1993), *A Companion to Spanish American Literature* (1998), and *César Vallejo: autógrafos olvidados* (2003). He is currently working on a companion to Latin American cinema.

Geoffrey Kantaris is Senior Lecturer in Latin American Culture in the Department of Spanish and Portuguese, University of Cambridge, and Deputy Director of the Centre of Latin American Studies. His current research is on contemporary urban cinema from Colombia, Argentina and Mexico, and he has published several articles in this area. He is also the author of *The Subversive Psyche* (Oxford University Press), on post-dictatorship women's writing from Argentina and Uruguay.

John King is Professor of Latin American Cultural History at the University of Warwick. He has authored and edited some ten books on Latin American cinema, literature and cultural history. His most recent publications include *Magical Reels: A History of Cinema in Latin America* (expanded edition, London 2000); co-edited with Sheila Whitaker and Rosa Bosch, *An Argentine Passion: The Life and Work of Maria Luisa Bemberg* (London, 2000); (ed.) *The Cambridge Companion to Modern Latin American Culture*, Cambridge 2003. He is currently completing a monograph study of the Mexican cultural journal *Plural*, 1971–1976.

Vanessa Knights is a lecturer in Hispanic Studies at the Centre for Gender and Women's Studies, University of Newcastle upon Tyne, England. She is on the editorial board of the *Journal of Popular Music History*. Her main publications are *The Search for Identity in the Narrative of Rosa Montero* (1999) and *A New History of Spanish Writing 1939 to the 1990s*, co-authored with Chris Perriam, Michael Thompson and Susan Frenk (2000). She is currently working on a study of the bolero in Cuba, Mexico and Puerto Rico and co-editing two volumes, one on popular music and national identity and one on music in the television series *Buffy the Vampire Slayer*.

Floyd Merrell is Professor of Latin American Cultures and Literatures, Semiotic Theory, and Comparative Literature at Purdue University, West Lafayette, Indiana, USA. His most recent works include *Complementing Latin*

American Borders (Purdue University Press, 2003), *The Mexicans: A Sense of Culture* (Westview Press, CO, 2003), and *Sensing Corporeally: Toward a Posthuman Understanding* (University of Toronto Press, 2003).

Nicola Miller is Reader in Latin American History in the Department of History, University College, London, UK. She is a co-editor of the *Bulletin of Latin American Research*. Her main publications are *Soviet Relations with Latin America, 1959–1987* (1989) and *In the Shadow of the State: Intellectuals and National Identity in Twentieth-Century Spanish America* (1999). She is currently working on intellectuals and modernity in Latin America.

Martha Ojeda is Assistant Professor of Spanish and French at Transylvania University, Lexington, KY, USA, where she received the Bingham Award for Excellence in Teaching in 2002. Her research focuses on Afrohispanic literature and culture, particularly Afroperuvian literature. Her main publication is *Nicomedes Santa Cruz: ecos de África en Perú* (2003). She is currently working on a second book on Nicomedes Santa Cruz for the Afro-Romance Writers Series.

Laura Podalsky is an Assistant Professor at Ohio State University. She is the author of *Specular City: The Transformation of Culture, Consumption, and Space after Perón* (Temple University Press, 2003) and her essays on Latin American film and culture have been published in journals such as *Archivos de la Filmoteca, Cinemas*, and *Screen,* as well as in anthologies such as *Visible Nations* (University of Minnesota Press, 2000) and *Mediating Two Worlds* (BFI, 1993). She is currently working on a book on Latin American film, the politics of affect, and the contemporary public sphere.

María Cristina Pons is Assistant Professor of Latin American Literature at the University of California, Los Angeles (UCLA). Her main publications are *Memorias del olvido* (Siglo XXI, 1996), and *Más allá de las fronteras del lenguaje* (UNAM, 1998). She has also published several articles on diverse authors such as Cortázar, Piglia, Monsiváis, del Paso, Saer, and Soriano, as well as on the Argentinean historical novel (*Historia de la literatura argentina*, Emecé 2000). She is currently working on cultural myths, and co-editing two books, *Delirios de grandeza: los mitos argentinos: memoria, identidad y cultura,* and *Neoliberalism and Literature in Latin America*.

William Rowe is Anniversary Professor of Poetics at Birkbeck College. He is the author of eight books, among them *History and the Inner Life: Contemporary Poets of Latin America* (Oxford University Press, 2000), and is preparing a book on César Vallejo to be published by the University of San Marcos, Lima.

Victoria Ruétalo is Assistant Professor of Spanish and Latin American Studies at the University of Alberta in Canada. She has published articles in *Studies in Latin American Popular Culture* and *Quarterly Review of Film and Video* on Cultural Studies in the southern cone. She is currently working on a book titled *An Aesthetic in Ruins: Cultural Production in Post-Dictatorship Uruguay and Argentina*.

Lidia Santos is Associate Professor of Brazilian and Latin American Literature at Yale University. She is the author of Kitsch tropical: los medios en la literatura y el arte de America Latina (2001), awarded the 2003 prize from the LASA Brazil Section in the category 'Brazil in Comparative Perspective'. She is co-author of *Ritualidades latinoamericanas: un acercamiento interdisciplinario* and *Passions du Passe: recyclages de la memoire et visages de l'oubli* (2000). As a writer, she received the Guimarães Rosa Prize awarded by Radio France Internationale in 1992 and published *Flauta e cavaquinho* (1989) and *Os Ossos de esperanca* (1994). Work in progress includes: *Tears for Export: Soap Operas* and *Literature in Latin America and Brazil: Cosmopolitan Nation*.

Beatriz Sarlo is Professor of Culture and Literature at the University of Buenos Aires. She has taught in the United States (Berkeley, Columbia, Maryland), and has been Simón Bolívar Professor of Latin American Studies, in Cambridge, UK. Her books in English include *Borges: A Writer on the Edge* (1993) and *A Peripheral Modernity* (2001). Her latest book is *Pasión y excepción* (2003).

Robert Stam is Professor of Film Studies at New York University. He is the author of twelve books on cinema and cultural studies, most recently *Unthinking Eurocentrism: Multiculturalism and the Media* (with Ella Shohat, 1994) and *Tropical Multiculturalism* (1997). Forthcoming from Blackwell are three books on literature and cinema.

Richard Young is Professor of Spanish and Latin American Studies at the University of Alberta. His publications include *Octaedro en cuatro tiempos: texto y tiempo en un libro de Cortázar* (1993) and the edited volumes *Latin American Postmodernisms* (1997) and *Music, Popular Culture, Identities* (2002). He edited *Revista Canadiense de Estudios Hispánicos* from 1996 until 2003.

Introduction
Stephen Hart and Richard Young

The study of culture in Latin America has – for understandable reasons – been distinct from the practice of Cultural Studies in other countries. Unlike the British model which has often focused on broadening the terms of reference,[1] Latin American culture has more often than not been seen in terms of dilemmas, contestation and crisis, as the aptly named collection of essays has it: *On Edge: The Crisis of Contemporary Latin American Culture* (Yúdice et al., 1992). In a lecture given in Caracas on 15 May 1975 Alejo Carpentier argued that his generation was the first to view itself historically as an 'hombre-Historia-del-siglo-XX' (twentieth-century-Historical-man; 1981, p. 80), which led to a fundamental questioning about personal identity ('who am I?' Carpentier sees his generation asking itself; ibid.), and in turn to the realization that Latin American history was 'different from all other histories in the whole world' (ibid., p. 81). Latin America, as Carpentier went on to argue, has been a 'theatre of the most sensational collision of ethnicities to have ever occurred since the world began: the Indian, the black, the European' (ibid.). This new awareness of cultural difference, reflected in Carpentier's comments in 1975, had already been born at the dawn of the twentieth century in the context of the consolidation of national cultures, and was, furthermore, accompanied by a sense that Latin American culture had finally emerged from the colonial cage that required that it be no more than an inferior version of the European master copy. A number of crucial studies published in the opening decades of the twentieth century seem to bear out Carpentier's hypothesis. José Carlos Mariátegui's *Siete ensayos de interpretación de la realidad peruana* (Seven Interpretive Essays on Peruvian Reality, 1928; English translation 1971), for example, had presciently called for a greater role for the Indian in Peru's national and cultural space, while Fernando Ortiz's *Contrapunteo cubano del tabaco y el azúcar* (Cuban Counterpoint: Tobacco and Sugar, 1940; English translation 1947) had used two Cuban products – tobacco and sugar – to produce a new vision of how cultures intermingled in the New World; culture is not produced by acculturation, Ortiz argued, but rather by a complex interpenetrative process of transculturation.[2]

It was in 1971, however, that the tide truly turned; in that year Roberto Fernández Retamar published *Calibán* (Caliban), a no-holds-barred attack on the discourse of colonialism which – from the early days of the Spanish invasion in 1492 right up until the new imperialism of the United States after World War II – had consistently portrayed the Amerindian native as a monstrous, unlettered cannibal. Retamar turned the civilization/barbarism paradigm upside down, promoting the Caliban so vilified in Shakespeare's *The Tempest* as a new symbol of authentic Latin American culture. Retamar's anti-colonialist gesture also had deep implications for the way in which literature should be interpreted. In the Introduction to his *Para una teoría de la literatura hispanoamericana* (Towards a Theory of Spanish American Literature), published four years later, Retamar described the need in Latin America:

> for our literature to be approached in terms of its own specificity, so that it does not succumb to the orthopaedic treatment ['ortopedia' in the original Spanish] based on concepts modelled on other bodies, other realities; it should not be treated colonially but reflected upon according to its true nature. (1975, p. 1)

Ángel Rama's *Transculturación narrativa en América Latina* (Narrative Transculturation in Latin America, 1982), given that it uses a home-grown theory (transculturation) to promote understanding of a new brilliant generation of Latin American writers (the Boom), seems in retrospect to have been a perfect response to Fernández Retamar's rally call. Rama's masterpiece, *La ciudad letrada* (The Lettered City, 1984; English translation 1996), published posthumously, traces the links between lettered culture, state power and urban life in Latin America from the early days of the colonies up to the present day, and can arguably be seen as the matrix text of Latin American Cultural Studies, influencing a generation of later scholars.[3]

Is the notion of a home-grown Latin American cultural critique, however, a utopian delusion? Is it not the case, as books such as *What is Cultural Studies?*, edited by John Storey (1998), and *The Cultural Studies Reader*, edited by Simon During (1999) take for granted, that Cultural Studies were born and grew up in the English-speaking countries of the world. In *Latin American Cultural Criticism* (2000), Patricia D'Allemand makes a good case for tracing a coherent, self-contained genealogy of Latin American cultural criticism via the works of José Carlos Mariátegui, Ángel Rama, Alejandro Losada, Antonio Cornejo Polar and Beatriz Sarlo, and implicitly raises the question of the interface between cultural criticism produced *outside* as opposed to *inside* Latin America, an antagonism to which Alberto Moreiras has anxiously referred (2001, pp. 6–11). This issue is not restricted solely to Latin American Studies and it is, indeed, a burning issue in contemporary Spanish criticism, as José M. del Pino and Francisco la Rubia Prado's recent study *El hispanismo en los Estados Unidos* (Hispanism in the United States, 1999) pertinently demonstrates; while Hispanism in Spain relies on philological methods which are rooted in positivism, Spanish criticism in the United States is methodologically more pluralistic, and the two discourses are growing further and further apart as the years go by (1999, p. 9). Anecdotal evidence suggests a similar divisiveness exists within Latin American Studies. David William Foster has noted that 'when one travels in Latin America, it is difficult to escape the impression that one's subject of study back home in the office, the classroom, the library, have little to do with the actual processes of cultural production and consumption in the societies themselves' (1992, p. 35). When asked about the role of Cultural Studies in Argentina, Beatriz Sarlo, for example, made the following comment:

> In Argentina we do not call it 'Cultural Studies'. What is more, with Carlos Altamirano we have set up an MA outside the university and we've called it 'Sociology of Culture and Cultural Analysis', not 'Cultural Studies' – which is a term that has been put into mass circulation by the US academy. (1997b, p. 90)

Julio Ortega has suggested, for his part, that Cultural Studies is seen in some Latin American circles as 'another dominating Anglo-Saxon current' (1995, p. 224).

If the small informal survey held at the annual meeting of the Association of Hispanists of Canada held in Edmonton, Alberta, in 2000 is anything to go by, it is clear that scholars in Canada are in two minds about whether Cultural Studies is a positive development; while broadly in favour of Cultural Studies (70 per cent were in favour, 20 per cent sat on the fence, and 10 per cent were opposed), half of those surveyed regarded the concomitant fragmentation of the canon with some regret (20 per cent of those surveyed saw this fragmentation as something 'negative' but 'inevitable', another 20 per cent saw it as 'negative' and 'not inevitable' and a futher 10 per cent as 'here but not necessarily to stay').[4]

There are other problems too. One of the dangers of cultural studies, as Michael Green warned in 1995, is that it could become 'a complete post-disciplinary mish-mash' (1995, p. 227), or simply take on what English or some other subject left out, as Francis Mulhearn has suggested (quoted in Green, 1995, p. 227). Given the above, it is pertinent for us to ask the question once more: what is Latin American Cultural Studies and what methodologies are practised in its pursuit? On what projects are those who undertake cultural studies engaged? Are they political, intellectual, critical, or simply pedagogical?

It is clear that Latin American Cultural Studies covers a vast array of research activities and methodologies and it will be possible to offer only a small survey of the various trends in what follows. First, it is important to recall that a branch of Latin American Cultural Studies has offered a new home for what might be called feminist cultural criticism. A key role in this transition was played by Jean Franco's work; her *Plotting Women: Gender and Representation* (1989) used Sor Juana and La Malinche in order to offer a more gendered edge to the concept of Latin American cultural identity, while her more recent study, *The Decline and Fall of the Lettered City: Latin America in the Cold War* (2002), traces the gradual demise of the traditional notion of literature alongside that of lettered culture. The selection of her work found in *Critical Passions: Selected Essays* (1999), demonstrates how the fields of literature, popular culture and women's studies have overlapped in innovative ways. Other pioneering works ought to be mentioned in this context such as *Women, Culture, and Politics in Latin America* (1990), edited by Emilie Bergmann *et al.*, which offers a new gendered vision of Latin American literary culture and political life, and has separate studies on not only important literary figures such as Sor Juana, Alfonsina Storni and Victoria Ocampo, but also traces a new history of women's involvement in print culture via women's periodicals in the nineteenth and twentieth centuries. These and other studies such as Francine Masiello's wide-ranging *The Art of Transition: Latin American Culture and Neoliberal Crisis* (2001), may legitimately be seen in the context of the transformation of a constant motif – the recuperation of women's lives, writings and culture – within a broader intellectual framework.

One recognizably new offshoot of cultural studies has been the focus on popular culture. In *Memory and Modernity: Culture in Latin America* (1989), for example, William Rowe and Vivian Schelling studied, evaluated and thereby promoted popular forms of culture – as distinct from official forms of culture – which had been subalternized in the past. Other works in which popular culture has become the central focus include Eva P. Bueno and Terry Caesar's *Imagination Beyond Nation: Latin American Popular Culture* (1998), and Shelly Godsland and Anne M. White's *Cultura popular: Studies in Spanish and Latin American Popular Culture* (2002); a helpful survey is provided by Bermúdez (2003). Monographs on topical aspects of Latin American popular culture are now a regular feature on mainstream UK publishers' booklists, as Chris Taylor's readable *The Beautiful Game: A Journey Through Latin American Football* (1998), suggests. Jean Franco, in her essay 'What's in a Name?' (1999, pp. 169–80), however, offers some words of caution about this new trend.

Given the turn against literary studies understood in a traditionalist sense that this interest in popular culture has engendered – in recent years, as Moreiras puts it, 'high literature has suffered a drastic loss of cultural capital' (2001, p. 209) – there has, nevertheless, been a noticeable rise of interest in liminal literary production such as testimonial writing.[5] Some indication of the centrality of *testimonio* to cultural studies is suggested by the wealth of important theoretical studies on the genre, including, by way of sample, George Yúdice, '*Testimonio* and Postmodernism' (1991); John Beverley, 'The Margin at the Center: On *Testimonio*' (1993b); Brett Levinson, 'Neopatriarchy and After: *I, Rigoberta Menchú* as Allegory of Death' (1996); the response by Gordon Brotherston, 'Regarding the Evidence in *Me llamo Rigoberta Menchú*' (1996); Moraña, 'El boom del subalterno' (1997a); Francesca Denegri (2000), and Elzbieta Sklodowska (2003, especially pp. 102–4). A more jaundiced take on the whole issue is provided by Jon Beasley-Murray, 'Towards an Unpopular Cultural Studies: The Perspective of the Multitude' (2002).

Another piece of the jigsaw which has played a crucial role in the evolution of Latin American Cultural Studies has been subaltern studies; the 'Founding Statement' of the Latin American Subaltern Studies Group originally based in Pittsburgh is reproduced in *The Postmodernism Debate in Latin America* (Beverley *et al.*, 1995, pp. 135–46), and a sophisticated reading which treats the principal issues appears in John Beverley's *Subalternity and Representation: Arguments in Cultural Theory* (1999).[6] Pointing in a similar direction, approaches to culture have also delved into historiography and, in valorizing the Indian subaltern, they have adopted a more historically informed stance. In his trail-blazing work, *Escribir en el aire: ensayo sobre la heterogeneidad socio-cultural en las literatuas andinas* (1994), Antonio Cornejo Polar showed that cultural discourse in the Andes – from the works of El Inca Garcilaso de la Vega right up to the present day – had never been unitary and was always based on a conflict between different languages – Spanish and Quechua – and between different discursive modes – typically the oral versus the scriptural.[7] Ana Pizarro, in her *De ostras y caníbales: ensayos sobre la cultura latinoamericana* (1994), for example, combines a careful historiography of the Conquest and its immediate aftermath with individual essays on important thinkers such as Bartolomé de las Casas, Andrés Bello and Ángel Rama. In his major work, *The Darker Side of the Renaissance: Literacy, Territoriality, and Colonization* (1995), Walter Mignolo explodes the myth of knowledge and literacy as harbingers of 'Enlightenment', exposing instead the insidious ways in which the colonialist project in the Americas sought to keep the Amerindian subaltern enthralled in darkness. Peter Beardsell provides a historically inflected analysis of the cultural relationship between the Old and New Worlds in *Europe and Latin America: Returning the Gaze* (2000).

As a counter-balance, perhaps, to the interest in the Amerindian, the popular and the subaltern, a number of recent studies in the field have focused on modernity. Here a key role has been played by Beatriz Sarlo's work. Her ground-breaking study in intellectual history, *Una modernidad periférica: Buenos Aires, 1920 y 1930* (1988), ranges widely over various fields, from tango to poetry, novels and architecture, in order to produce a more problematized sense of the make-up of modernity in early twentieth-century Argentina. A related crucial concern of Sarlo's has also been to assess the transformation of the role of the intellectual in contemporary Argentina. In *Escenas de la vida posmoderna: intelectuales, arte y videocultura en la Argentina* (1994; English translation 2001), Sarlo identifies three dominant trends brought about by the demise of traditional literary culture and the emergence of various forms of artistic media: (1) the neo-liberal becomes a commentator on the ever-burgeoning culture industry; (2) the neo-populist intellectual is absorbed by the 'ruins' of popular culture; while (3) the critical intellectual focuses on the more testing task of elucidating social and aesthetic values within contemporary culture.[8] A related issue has been that of mass culture, and here the key text is Néstor García Canclini's *Culturas híbridas* (1990; English translation 1995). The collection of essays, *Las industrias culturales en la integración latinoamericana*, edited by Néstor García Canclini and Carlos Juan Moneta (1994), focuses on the tension within culture when placed in the context of globalization; the production, marketing and selling of cultural products such as films, *telenovelas*, TV programmes, videos, and music CDs are all grist to the mill. Canclini's more recent work, as in *La globalización imaginada* (1999a), has focused on the ways in which culture has been transformed as a result of commercial liberalization, typified by international economic treaties such as the North American Free Trade Agreement (NAFTA); see also his important essay, 'Políticas culturales e integración norteamericana: una perspectiva desde México' (1996). Another key figure is Carlos Monsiváis; in *Mexican Postcards* (1997a) and *Aires de familia: cultura y sociedad* (2000b), for example, Monsiváis ranges widely across various disciplines, interrogating the emergence of modernity, the interplay between Latin American cinema and Hollywood, and the creation of cultural identity via TV and popular culture.

Two other important voices within this dialogue should be mentioned: Jesús Martín-Barbero has analysed the ways in which the mass media interact with everyday life creating a play of resistances and seductions in the formation of cultural identies (see in particular his *Communication, Culture and Hegemony: From the Media to Mediations*, 1993) while George Yúdice has focused on the social web underlying the fabrication of culture, and particularly the linkages between culture and contemporary civil society; see in particular his essays, 'Estudios culturales y sociedad civil' (1994), and 'Civil Society, Consumption, and Governmentality in an Age of Global Restructuring' (1995). A seminal space within the analysis of modernity has been occupied by film studies, and here the reader is referred to John King's foundational *Magical Reels: A History of Cinema in Latin America* (1990), as well as visual culture (for a sample, see Baddeley and Fraser, 1989; and Noble, 2003). Modernity also offers a central focus in Vivian Schelling's edition of essays, *Through the Kaleidoscope: The Experience of Modernity in Latin America* (2000), which homes in on Brazilian culture in the main.

Perhaps the most fraught area in the field of Latin American Cultural Studies has been the interface between cultural studies and postmodernism. *The Postmodernism Debate in Latin America*, edited by John Beverley, Michael Aronna and José Oviedo (1995), focuses on the fiercely contested territory lying somewhere between Cultural Studies and postmodernism. Of particular interest is the essay in this collection by Nelly Richard which signals distrust of the portrayal of Latin America in terms of the exotic Other: 'Celebrating difference as exotic festival … is not the same as giving the subject of this difference the right to negotiate its own conditions of discursive control' (1995, p. 221). Two excellent recent studies which express reservations about

Anglo-American readings of postmodernism are Santiago Colás's *Postmodernity in Latin America* (1994) and Richard Young's *Latin American Postmodernisms* (1997). For a helpful discussion of the overlap between postcolonial theory and Latin American Cultural Studies, the reader is referred to Peter Hulme, 'La teoría poscolonial y la representación de la cultura en las Américas' (1996) and John Kraniauskas, 'Hybridity in a transnational frame: Latin Americanist and postcolonial perspectives on cultural studies' (2000).

Despite the various trends within the broad parameters of Latin American Cultural Studies listed above – and the list is by no means exhaustive – it should be underlined that Latin American Cultural Studies cannot be described as a discipline as such, given that it is irreducibly interdisciplinary and evokes a wide gamut of technologies and methodologies in order to create its discourse. For a sample of its interdisciplinarity, the reader is referred to Ramón de la Campa's 'Postmodernism and revolution: a Central American case study' (1995), a thoughtful essay which intersperses political with literary readings of a number of texts, ranging from Rigoberta Menchú's *testimonio* to Che Guevara's memoirs, and Borges's *Ficciones*; Nicola Miller's *In the Shadow of the State: Intellectuals and the Quest for National Identity in Twentieth-Century Spanish America* (1999) which effectively charts that territory between politics and literature; and Antonio Benítez Rojo's *The Repeating Island: The Caribbean and the Postmodern Perspective* (1992) which has recourse to chaos theory in the insightful analysis of Caribbean culture.

Cultural studies books clearly do not follow a set formula. Neil Larsen's *Reading North by South: On Latin American Literature, Culture and Politics* (1995), for example, offers a series of probing *marxisant* readings of varied cultural manifestations ranging from the Boom novel to football in Argentina, complemented by a series of individual readings of the work of significant critics such as John Beverley, Roberto Schwarz, Doris Sommer, Roberto González Echeverría and William Rowe. The introductory essay draws attention to the divide between the North American academy and Latin America (1995, p. 13), and the essay on 'The Cultural Studies Movement and Latin America' (1995, pp. 189–96) highlights the pitfalls involved when progressive US intellectuals fall prey to trendy images of Latin American culture (1995, p. 196). We find a similar style of presentation in Roberto Schwarz's work; using the nineteenth-century novelist, Machado de Assis, as a cornerstone of his analysis, this Brazilian critic has evolved a complex theory of the cultural relationship between Europe and Brazil based on the notion of 'misplaced ideas'; see his collection of essays, *Misplaced Ideas: Essays in Brazilian Culture* (1992).

The important point about these new readings is that each in its own way opens up new avenues of understanding of Latin American culture. It should be stressed, though, that the above summary offers simply a sample of the various voices within Latin American Cultural Studies. A richer, more textured picture can be gained by studying the historical evolution of the various organs which have published works in this field. An important voice in Latin America for cultural studies, for example, has been provided over the years by *Revista de Crítica Cultural* (Santiago, Chile) edited by Nelly Richard, along with its monograph series, Cuarto Propio, and by the Estudios Culturales series published by Beatriz Viterbo Editora in Buenos Aires, Argentina. An important forum for cultural studies in the United States has been provided by the *Revista Iberoamericana* (Pittsburgh) edited by Mabel Moraña, and by the *Revista de Crítica Literaria Latinoamerica*, previously published in Lima, and now edited by Raúl Bueno Chávez, from Dartmouth College. In Britain a significant forum for Latin American Cultural Studies has been provided by the *Journal of Latin American Cultural Studies* (London), edited by John Kraniauskas, and the new Centre for Latin American Cultural Studies based in Manchester.[9]

The present volume explores in greater detail some of the issues touched on in recent encyclopaedias of Latin American culture (such as Standish, 1995–6; and Balderston *et al.*, 2000) and it has some important similarities with the collection of essays, *Contemporary Spanish Cultural Studies*, edited by Barry Jordan and Rikki Morgan-Tamosunas (2000). Like the editors of that volume, we approach Latin American Cultural Studies as, to quote their words, 'a significant new field concerned primarily with the study of how cultural meanings and thus identities get sedimented and organized through cultural practices and relations of power' (2000, p. 8). But, although there is room for dialogue in cultural studies between Spain and Latin America, especially in the emerging field of Trans-Atlantic Studies, there are significant differences between the present book and the earlier one on Spain with respect to the range of subjects and how these are treated. In particular, some of the chapters we have included here touch on issues that are either exclusively relevant for Latin America or are addressed in ways that understandably recognize its historical and cultural specificity: its colonial history and postcolonial dilemmas; the formation of its national cultures; the co-existence and intermingling of different races and ethnicities, and the different practices that have resulted in areas such as everyday life, food, or the diverse products of the entertainment and culture industries. Even the notion of cultural studies itself evokes different reactions depending on whether it is considered from the perspective of the study of culture in Spain or in Latin America.

We have collected 24 chapters in total and have organized them in the following pages in five Parts. Part 1 is devoted to aspects of the theory and practice of cultural studies and includes chapters that, in addition to considering the nature of cultural studies as a critical practice, also focus on some of the controversies that have come to surround it when it is pursued with respect to culture in Latin America. The chapters in Part 2 analyse cultural icons in Latin America, in particular the ways in which narratives of the past or important historical and cultural figures have been iconized as images of identity that have been incorporated into notions of nationality and statehood. Part 3 contains chapters focusing on activities and forms of expression such as football, music, *telenovelas*, television, and film, which are often considered as popular culture in that they embody the notion of culture as spectacle or commodity and are circulated or promoted by culture industries. In Part 4 elements of popular culture, specifically film and cartoons, are also discussed in two of the chapters, but the Part as a whole is more immediately concerned with questions of hierarchy and hegemony and how these are formulated and contested in various forms of cultural expression and practice in relation to official and non-official cultures, social inclusion and exclusion, and issues in gender, race and ethnicity. Finally, the chapters in Part 5 highlight different rituals and practices that are not only a part of the routines and cycles of everyday life in Latin America but are, in some cases, such as food and Brazilian *capoeira*, examples of what is sometimes considered to be most idiosyncratically Latin American.

Unlike recent dictionaries and encyclopaedias, the present volume does not attempt to identify and describe the many facets of Latin American culture systematically. We offer instead an eclectic set of chapters, each of which contains a study of a specific cultural condition or phenomenon related, for the most part, to a particular country or community. Readers interested in more general historical commentaries on politics and society, or precise forms of cultural expression, such as literature, music or cinema, might consult other texts, such as Philip Swanson's *Companion to Latin American Studies* (2003). Each chapter has been contributed by a specialist, but is directed to general readers, to students and other specialists on Latin America. Quotations from texts not originally written in English are provided, and the notes attached to each essay, as well as the references at the end of the book, also contribute to the accessibility of the subject. Although not an encyclopaedia, students and the general reader will find, nonetheless, that *Contemporary Latin American Cultural Studies* is a comprehensive introduction to the study of culture in Latin America that not only offers detailed analyses of specific cultural phenomena but also highlights issues of contemporary concern and the methods by which they are studied.

NOTES

1. The best example is Raymond William's famous tripartite definition of culture as outlined in his essay, 'The Analysis of Culture', the first consisting of 'the best that has been thought and written in the world', the second consisting of 'documentary culture', that is 'the body of intellectual and imaginative work, in which, in a detailed way, human thought and experience are variously recorded', and the third, which is the 'social' definition according to which culture 'is a description of a particular way of life, which expresses certain meanings and values not only in art and learning but also in institutions and ordinary behaviour' (1961, pp. 57–8).
2. For more on the theory of transculturation and its ramifications in anthropological, cultural and literary studies, see Pratt (1992), MacDougall (1998), and Berry and Epstein (1999).

3   For more discussion of the influence of Rama on later scholars, see the volume devoted to his work, *Ángel Rama y los estudios latinamericanos*, ed. Mabel Moraña (1997b), and Gollnick (2003, pp. 110–13).
4   There is a similar divide in British Hispanism; see Smith (1989), Jordan (1990), Reed (1992), and Hart (1993).
5   In Britain, booksellers – a good indication on the ground as to where the discipline has been going in recent years – draw attention to the following trends: there are more sales of modern Spanish fiction, Latin American writers, and women writers, whereas 'Medieval Studies is dead, [and] Golden Age authors are still going, but decreasingly so' (Anja Louis, Head of Spanish at Grant & Cutler Booksellers Ltd, London, in an e-mail message to Stephen Hart on 29 April 2000). This change in fortunes has been felt most acutely in Britain in the decline in the study of pre-1700 literature. In a recent article, Jonathan Thacker, a British Golden-Age specialist, pertinently asks if the *comedia* specialists have, 'like the silk worm, built the house in which they will die' (1999, p. 16).
6   For more discussion of subaltern studies, see Hart (1999) and Rodríguez (2000).
7   For further discussion on the notion of heterogeneity in Antonio Cornejo Polar's version of cultural studies, see Mabel Moraña (1995), Mazzotti and Zevallos (1996), Schmidt-Welle (2002) and Higgins (2003). Similar in some respects to the work of Antonio Cornejo Polar, Martin Lienhard, particularly in his study, *La voz y su huella: escritura y conflicto étnico-cultural en América latina 1492–1988* (1991), focuses on the epistemological schisms operating at the centre of Andean culture.
8   Sarlo's position has not been without its critics though. See William Rowe's chapter in this volume (especially p. 41) as well as Alberto Moreiras's argument that Sarlo adopts a too Manichean distinction between cultural studies and literary studies along the axis of aesthetic value (Moreiras, 2001, pp. 250–63).
9   For more information on the Centre for Latin American Cultural Studies at the University of Manchester, see the website http//www.art.man.ac.uk/Lacs

PART 1

Latin America and cultural studies

1

Cultural studies and revolving doors

Néstor García Canclini

1

How is it possible to determine, at this point, what is meant by cultural studies? In books with those terms in their title we find re-interpretations of the history of literature; debates on what is happening to culture and politics as they take over familiar institutions or free themselves from dictatorships; critiques of the weaknesses of the humanities and social sciences; polemics on the correct or politically most productive explanation of Derrida and Deleuze, Lacan and Laclau; on modernism and postmodernism, and globalization and its opponents: the subaltern, the postcolonial and the post-western. The list does not end here, and to enumerate it would serve only to exhaust our perplexity.

It would seem that something is happening with cultural studies today similar to what was happening 20 years ago with Marxism, when it was not clear whether it was still in one of the forms appropriated by the state or in its Althusserian, neo-Gramscian or guerrilla versions, until the demolition of the Berlin Wall made these distinctions less rigid. Some critics have implied that perhaps cultural studies was successful as a substitute for Marxism. However, the conditions in which the insufficiencies of cultural studies, social sciences and the humanities are raised are now different.

We need to talk about the reformulation of cultural studies in order to locate them among changes that are taking place without the noise of falling walls. Hence, I shall make some references to transformations that are different from those we perceived in 1989 and, of course, different from those that 30 or 40 years ago moved Raymond Williams, Roland Barthes, and others to undertake *transdisciplinary readings* on *the hidden connections between culture, economy and power*. If these characteristics still define the project of cultural studies, as they did back then, the problem is not one of choosing the correct or politically more effective interpretation of that legacy, but of discovering the roles of culture in the present stage of capitalism. My resources for re-thinking this question come above all from Latin America, but I shall take into account that one of the differences of the current moment is that we can no longer enclose ourselves in national or regional cultures.

2

One of the key tasks is to locate this quest in today's redistribution of power in communications and the academic world. As we move from the twentieth to the twenty-first century, four forces predominate in the international administration of the image of what is considered 'Latin American': (a) *Spanish publishing groups*, ultimately subordinated to European megacorporations (Bertelsmann, Planeta) and complemented in part by communications conglomerates (Prisa, Telefónica, and Televisión Española); (b) *several US communications corporations* (CNN, Time Warner); (c) *Latin American Cultural Studies*, concentrated in US universities and with small complementary enclaves in Canada and Europe; and (d) *cultural studies in Latin America* understood in the broad sense as the heterogeneous production of specialists in cultural, literary and scientific-social processes, whose exchanges are intense, but less institutionalized than those of US Latin Americanists. There is a fifth player, namely governments in Latin America and their cultural policies, but it is not easy to justify their place among the predominant forces on account of their diminished participation with respect to strategic trends in cultural development.

The rate of participation of audiovisual companies in relation to intellectual production is still low. A more extensive analysis would have to consider the current reconfiguration of images of Latin America in CNN journalism, the entertainment products distributed by Time Warner, Televisa, and Globo, and the distribution of recorded disks by the large corporations and other players in communications, who move their investments among written, audiovisual and digital media. Here I will be concerned above all with the recomposition of academic and publishing power.

Spanish publishers, who control the market for books in Spanish with a ratio of seven to three in relation to the total for Mexico City, Buenos Aires and the rest of Latin America, see the continent as a creator of literature and as an area of expansion of their Spanish clientele. They rarely publish cultural, sociological or anthropological studies by Latin Americans and, when they do, their affiliates in Argentina, Chile, Colombia or Mexico limit their circulation to the country of origin. Save for a few medium-sized publishers based in Barcelona, Mexico City and Buenos Aires, such as Fondo de Cultura Económica, Paidós and Gedisa, the international image of Latin America that has been created has been that of a provider of narrative fiction, not of social and cultural thought, to which only a domestic interest is attributed for the country that generates it.

The Latin Americanists in the United States and specialists in cultural studies, who pay attention not only to Latin American literature but also to socio-cultural research, must be recognized. More books by Roger Bartra, Jesús Martín Barbero, Beatriz Sarlo and ten other thinkers from Latin America are translated into English, taught in their universities and discussed in journals in that language than in Spanish universities and publications. But the cultural studies of the English-speaking world are devoted more to interpretations pronounced by authors from Latin America than to the socio-cultural and economic processes of the continent. As an exacerbation of the textualism of cultural studies, above all in the US, notions of the popular, the national, hybridization, and the modernity and postmodernity of Latin Americans are hotly debated, while the cultural and social movements to which such concepts allude are rarely studied. It has become more stimulating to confront authors from the south with those from the north than to work with them both in order to renew our view of high culture and the media, the disenchantment with the transitions to democracy, the war in Colombia and neighbouring places, or the recomposition of geo-politics and culture between the US and Latin America.

3

The textualizing tendencies of cultural studies has generalized introspective practices. Cultural Studies began as an emergency exit. For decades, the disciplines were reached by special doors, depending on whether you wished to enter Language and Literature, Philosophy, Anthropology or History. The spaces and subjects not reached in this way were grouped as area studies: there were departments of Spanish and Portuguese, French or Italian, Chinese, or African religions. Over time, interdisciplinarity, migrations, mass communication, and other disorders of the world made the walls that separated departments porous. Then came Cultural Studies, and also Latin American Cultural Studies, which are not the same as Anglo-American Cultural Studies, although they have a parallel transdisciplinary vocation. Entering by the door to philosophy, they found ways to Anthropology and discovered that what was being learned in Literature, Economics or Sociology served to get them into other buildings, even if it was by the windows.

The Cultural Studies that opened those emergency exits today seems at times like a revolving door. This does not mean that there are no changes while it is turning. You can enter a Derridian and come out a Homi Bhabhian, start out a logocentrist and take a turn towards deconstruction, go from the textual analysis of the door to the debate on the performativity of its hinges. What usually puts a stop to this compulsive circularity is that it is practised in conference papers and thus cannot last longer than 15 or 20 minutes.

4

In order to explain this better, it is necessary to differentiate between Cultural Studies and its different forms. One of these is the movement that brought together the – at times epistemological, at times generational – confrontations with the routine and the deafness in the humanities disciplines and the social sciences; research undertakings that reveal the connections of culture with power, of economic injustices with those in gender, of art with the cultural industries. All of that continues to thrive and gives uneven results, to be found in a few books rather than in journals. Frequently, the transversality of this non-discipline that is Cultural Studies was the key to a renewed exploration of culture: reading a literary text with the instruments of sociology, studying folk crafts or music as processes of communication, wondering about the stylistic resources with which a social scientist constructs an argument.

By saying that these studies constitute a non-discipline I am referring to the fact that they are formed by departing from the theoretical orthodoxies and routines of thought with which specialists customarily research such subjects. Cultural Studies progressed thanks to its irreverence with respect to the exclusivity of the segmentation of intellectual property, although this should not be taken to be synonymous with a disregard for science. The best specialists in Cultural Studies have learned to understand culture within a particular discipline: Raymond Williams, Jean Franco, and Beatriz Sarlo studying literature in order to turn later to intellectual history; David Morely and Jesús Martín Barbero undertaking research in communications in order to explain that the media are not to be understood except as belonging to cultural practices. Their works were produced by taking a field of knowledge seriously and by feeling at some moment a sense of unease similar to what we experience today in relation to gated communities.

From the eighteenth to the twentieth century, the structuring of disciplinary fields was like tracing streets and organizing autonomous territories at a time when it was necessary to defend the specificity of each branch of knowledge in relation to theological and philosophical totalizations. But the disciplines took on this urban task enthusiastically and, for security reasons, began to close streets and prevent them from being used for the purpose for which they were originally built: free circulation and passage from one district to another. Cultural Studies is an attempt to re-open avenues and pathways, and prevent them from becoming the private extension of a few houses.

I have recalled the disciplinary origin of some noteworthy specialists because it is sometimes thought that doing cultural studies does not require working the data with discipline and rigour. In fact, more data needs to be acquired, the statistics that those who study literature do not usually deal with or, alternatively, the narratives and metaphors that economists and sociologists use without problematizing them, need to be taken seriously. The task of cultural studies is not improved by substituting data with intuition, nor by getting away with an essay instead of developing a systematic enquiry. What gives them greater openness and intellectual density is daring to deal with connected issues that were not previously considered together when discussing a particular subject. Why do certain novelists, in addition to experimenting with rhetorical devices, do so from a position of ethnicity or gender? What makes the consumption of soap operas different when they are received in a metropolitan country or in one of the periphery, and in the context of stronger or weaker local traditions?

We know that over the years Cultural Studies also became the formula of a market-oriented academy according to which those initial undertakings, although still barely systematized, were converted into master's and doctoral degrees, or subaltern, postcolonial and post-disciplinary canons, whereby knowledge was sometimes confused with access to academic tenure and at other times with the impossibility of obtaining it. In one way or another, by combining the hegemonic and ill-reputed sides of things, Cultural Studies offered a repertoire of quotable authors and authorized quotations, euphoric politicizations with no recipient, and a show of erudition in which the transnational never abandoned its local demeanour. In short, a self-corralled abundance. For this reason some volumes devoted to Cultural Studies convey the feeling that to work in this field is like going around in a revolving door.

I am not proposing to retrieve the initiative of the original movement, that of the Birmingham group, for example. The world has changed too much these past 30 years for that to be realistic. In fact, dozens of authors, daring ideas, and a few research undertakings that remained faithful to that origin by going along other paths have kept the project alive. I could mention the example of a few innovators, such as Stuart Hall and George Yúdice, but when I try to lengthen the list there come to mind authors who are almost never mentioned in the Citation Index of Cultural Studies conferences, people like John Berger, and texts that do not pretend to be cultural studies, like those of Norbert Lechner, for example. There are also some young researchers, both from Latin America and the US, who have read all there is to know about the study of culture, but whose goal in life is not to develop cultural studies, or to assert the politically and epistemologically correct. These are dissenting enquiries that raise or lower the gaze on current challenges to research in a different way: they speak of the different conditions under which culture is made when the success and failures of neoliberalism have modified what was understood as power and as a symbolic world.

5

In the 1990s, the debate focused on connecting and differentiating Latin American Cultural Studies and Cultural Studies in Latin America. A level of theoretical exchange was achieved that was at times productive and made it possible to understand better the various forms of intellectual practice in the US and Latin America (Beverley, Mato, Mignolo) and its different modes of moving between academia, politics and esthetic research (Achugar, Moreiras, Richard). Although these authors illuminate north/south socio-cultural relations, the bibliography identified overall as studies in culture or cultural studies has little to do with the socio-economic, political and communicational bases of recent cultural transformations. That is to say, the transformations in which the place of the protagonists is occupied by the transnational players previously cited as re-organizers of the image and conditions of existence of what is considered to be Latin American.

Cultural studies and Latin American studies in the 1980s and 1990s were linked to revolutionary movements that had reached their end or were discredited, or to social-democratic 'alternatives' in the processes of democratization, having failed as economic, social and cultural projects. Now we can only count on such points of reference in innovative social movements (Zapatismo in Mexico, Sem Terra in Brazil, human rights groups elsewhere), which are significant movements for confronting indigenous issues, extreme poverty and the historical effects of dictatorship, but which are insufficient as substitutes or to generate decisive change in the decadent party system. Thus, the absence of consistent players able to confront the processes of denationalization and transnationalization at a macro level (at Seattle, Davos and São Paulo it was only possible to make out a protest movement, not a programme) leaves with weak social support what in cultural studies was a strategic project. Here I can only point out a question that requires greater consideration.

Placing ourselves at this new stage requires returning to a key historical feature of cultural studies: the development of empirically based socio-cultural theory in order to understand the evolution of capitalism critically; not the assertion of politically correct positions, but *the tense relationship between a utopian imaginary, that is only partly political, and an intellectual and empirical exploration that sometimes goes along with it and sometimes contradicts it*. While neither the utopian imaginary nor the intellectual exploration of the 1960s or the 1980s may be repeated today, no philological restoration of the foundational moment is possible either; it is not a matter of suturing a wounded tradition.

In order to avoid such distractions, it is appropriate to focus on the *tension* between what the utopian imaginary and the intellectual exploration might be today: for example, the tension that occurs *between the promises of global cosmopolitanism and the loss of national projects*. What is new in this conflict? To what disciplines or to what kind of not specifically cultural knowledge is it necessary to link the study of culture?

In 1950, when Octavio Paz wrote in *The Labyrinth of Solitude* (Spanish original, 1950, English editions, 1961, 1985) that Mexicans felt themselves to be contemporary with all people for the first time, television and video did not yet exist, let alone the words that represent new forms of intercultural communication: compact disk, diskette, scanner, the Internet, cellular phone and TV shopping. We could never have been as cosmopolitan then as we are now, as contemporary with many cultures, and all without travelling. Suffice it to see how young people combine the new forms of neighbourhood territorialization such as graffiti with transnational musical and television messages.

But this stage also brings a loss of national projects. Until a few years ago we spoke of French, Italian and US cinema, of Mexican crafts and muralism, and Spanish or Argentinean literature. Those distinctions serve more as an historical evocation than to identify what is filmed, painted and written today. For similar reasons, nations are ceasing to be political players and even less as markers for locating cultural production. Those who decide what is produced and who also distribute it are called CNN, Sony and Time Warner. Even when they retain names of nationality – America on Line, Telefónica de España – their offices and their stock capital do not depend on one country in particular.

In the age of information, what is the most valuable property in the world worth owning? Jeremy Rifkin replied:

> Radio frequencies – the electromagnetic spectrum – in the age of wireless communication an ever greater quantity of human communication and commercial activity will be conveyed along them. Our personal computers, electronic diaries, wireless, internet, mobile phones, locators, radios and televisions all depend on the spectrum of radio frequencies to send and receive messages, photos, audio files, data. (2001, p. 9)

And Rifkin shows that this spectrum, treated as 'common property' (others say it is the new inheritance of humanity), is no longer controlled by nations or governments, but by those commercial corporations that administer almost all the airwaves. Even the US, Rifkin adds, is giving up its capacity to regulate communications within its territory.

While writing a new Introduction to *Culturas híbridas* (2001) a few months ago, I wondered about the economic bases of this deconstruction of nations. Let me mention a few: above all, the loss of financial control through the disappearance of a national currency in Ecuador and El Salvador, or through the inflexible pegging of currency to the dollar in Argentina. Even where national currencies subsist, the emblems they carry no longer represent a capacity to negotiate prices and wages or internal and external debts in a sovereign manner. The same is true of the economy and the economy of symbolic culture that circulates within their territories.

In the twentieth century, between the 1940s and the 1960s, the creation of publishing companies in Argentina, Brazil and Mexico, as well as some in Colombia, Chile, Peru, Uruguay and Venezuela led to 'import substitution' in the field of literary culture that was decisive for the development of education and the formation of modern nations and democratic citizens. In the past three decades, the majority of publishers have gone bankrupt or have sold their catalogues to Spanish publishing houses, which were then bought out by French, Italian and German companies. The new owners of Babel are called Bertelsmann, Planeta and Vivendi, now the major producers of books in Latin America, Europe, and in the US also, ever since Bertelsmann acquired Random House.

In Argentina the transnationalization of telecommunications, begun more than ten years ago, handed over most of the culture industries to foreign companies. The advantages yielded by their investments are not reciprocated in North American or European markets. Argentinean producers, like many Peruvians, Venezuelans and Mexicans, prefer to become managers for Telefónica de España, AET or CNN.

Today's cosmopolitanism and the new dependencies cannot be understood with the vocabulary of the age when we spoke of imperialism and nation. Although those words have not lost their usefulness, as much as we need the vocabulary that designates the new objects – compact disk, diskette, telemarketing – we also need the words from the new dictionary of a transnational economy – external debt, dumping, stand-by loans, recession, risk country – that express the relationships among the most widely differing participants in entirely new ways. And, of course, the semantic arbitrariness with which economists use those terms is of enormous interest for cultural studies and social psychology. With singular adherence to the formulas of depression, it is said that the health of an economy depends on there being no inflation, on interest rates not rising, and on there being no increase in consumption. When the negative indicators are at their greatest, disasters appear for the majority of people, such as a rise in unemployment. But those 'secondary' signs do not worry economists, who are able to find the positive side to such dispiriting facts. If a country is losing ground, they say it had *negative growth* or *slowed down* for that year or decade. If there is inflation, instead of correcting economic organization, they change the name of the currency: in Brazil they changed it to the *real*, keeping the imaginary correspondence of the money to the facts, although the uselessness of that linguistic manoeuvre is exposed when within a few months the currency has lost 140 per cent of its value.

In order not to remain just at the fringe of the linguistic game, it is relevant for cultural studies to understand how those turns of speech, those disconcerting ways of telling the story, are related to the unequal access of countries to expansion in economics and communications. The US retains 55 per cent of world earnings generated through cultural products, the European Union 25 per cent, Japan and Asia receive 15 per cent, and Ibero-American countries only 5 per cent. The most notorious of economic disadvantages, namely that of Latin America, resulting from low investment by our governments in science, technology and the industrial production of culture, conditions the poor global competitiveness and the limited distribution of the majority of films, videos and disks to the interior of each country alone.

To the weakness of production in publishing should be added – save for Brazil and Mexico – our poor participation in audiovisual markets. In a study undertaken at the beginning of the 1990s, Rafael Roncagliolo showed that, although internal cultural production in Latin America was poor, the spread of televisions and video cassette players and audiovisual consumption placed us above various European countries. However, that opulence has declined and comparisons with respect to advanced technologies that give access to quality information and cultural innovations are even more unfavourable. While, in the US, 539 of every 10,000 persons possess a fax machine, there are 480 in Japan, 34 in Uruguay, and 11 in Chile. As for televisions, the US has 805 for every 1,000 inhabitants and France 589, while for peripheral countries with a high level of production in television sets, such as Mexico and Brazil, it is 219 and 220 respectively (UNESCO, *World Culture Report*, 1998, pp. 46, 107). It is customary to expect that the Internet will democratize access to the national and international public spheres, but less than 2 per cent of Latin Americans have access to the World Wide Web, as opposed to 23.3 per cent in the US and 6.9 per cent in the remaining countries of the Organization for Economic Development and Cooperation (Trejo Delarbe, 1999, p. 122). The richest 20 per cent of the population monopolizes 93.3 per cent of access to the Internet and has at its disposition, in the case of readers of English, 70 per cent of the hosts, the sites from which information is disseminated, which in Spanish do not amount to 2 per cent.

How is it possible to continue to pursue cultural studies without analysing the consequences of these processes of concentration of resources? It is not that research into literature or cinema should no longer work with texts or that they should decipher their intrinsic meanings and even assess their specific esthetic value more carefully than usual when it comes to cultural studies. But while they are concerned with the processes of reception, it is also relevant to consider, along with the texts and the ideological debates that frame them, the unequal accumulation of cultural property, the lack of symmetry in regional access to information and entertainment, or the possibility that each culture constructs its own image and understands those of others. How the new conditions of symbolic production and circulation modify ways of reading, watching cinema or chatting by Internet is part of the discursive sense of society. How can we limit ourselves to talking about literary texts if those who produce them treat them as publishing products? What can we gather about music and films if they are selected and marketed as the disk of the week or as merchandise for multi-screen theatres?

6

Latin American and US studies are now appearing that endeavour to understand the cultural and economic logic of the current dependence of Latin

America on the US, the increasing 'latinization' of the latter, and the subordination of both to transnational entities that are not headquartered exclusively in any country. But few studies go beyond description in order to develop critical projects in the style initially conceived by cultural studies. This is a result, in part, of the conditions under which we produce knowledge and, in a separate context, critical thought. In Latin America ritual laments about the Americanization of language and consumption are heard, but we have no cultural economists who study the interaction of global business with symbolic production, nor do we have more than four or five research groups devoted to the distribution of Spanish-speaking music, cinema, television, and literature in US society. Unless the actions of universities and governments are re-directed, we will arrive at the summit on the Free Trade Area of the Americas in 2005 with as little information about the potential of our cultural and communications resources as when Mexico signed the North American Free Trade Agreement.

In this respect, the task of Latin Americanist and Interamerican associations dedicated to the social sciences and the humanities is still pending. Do CLACSO (Consejo Latinoamericano de Ciencias Sociales), FLACSO (Facultad Latinamericana de Ciencias Sociales), FELAFACS (Federación Latinoamericana de Facultades de Comunicación Social), and LASA (Latin American Studies Association) have nothing to say about the opportunities and risks of competition over telecommunications in Latin America between Telefónica de España and AET, between Spanish banks (Bilbao Vizcaya and Santander) and City Bank? With their takeovers of the last two years in Mexico, those three banks have acquired 83 per cent of the national banking system and therefore the power of decision concerning to whom and for what they are going to lend money, what their cultural foundations would do with the historic monuments and works of art that form part of their economic assets, whom they will support, or how they will restrict artistic and scientific development.

It would be useful for us to have in Latin America somewhat more than the 40 or 50 specialists on those matters who are poorly paid by their universities and are without appropriate libraries or the document services of their own governments accessible for research purposes. These Latin American experts, with access to the Internet and a trip or two now and then to US libraries, are renewing the hypotheses with which to understand what is happening. But the scope of the research requires an infrastructure different from that of public institutions in Latin America. The possibilities of our having political impact would be different if, in addition to meeting for a while with northern researchers at two Interamerican conferences a year, the institutions that organize them destined funds for joint north–south research and sponsored independent studies of the significance of the purchase of banks along with their assets in cultural and scientific foundations, television companies and Internet portals, recording and publishing companies.

What will all this mean for Latin American audiences and for migrants in other Latin American countries, in the US and in Canada? It may be supposed that such an Interamerican policy concerning knowledge would not only benefit the creators, intellectuals and consumers in this continent (i.e., in Latin America), but also the 35 million speakers of Spanish who live in the US. We would be able to intervene in a consistent manner in regional and world forums where the Latin American ministers of culture and telecommunications are usually silent. We would perceive the potential of the children of Cuban, Salvadoran and Mexican farmers and merchants who are becoming doctors, university professors and lawyers in the US. It would occur to us how to influence the class of middlemen and the English-speaking institutions that, after 2005, outside this continent, are going to take many more decisions than those that are currently adopted concerning the war in Colombia, unemployment, human rights, and information in the cities of Latin America.

Just as we will not escape underdevelopment without substantial increases in investment in science and technology, we cannot hope that the voices and images conveying what is Latin American can be anything other than the magical realism spread by European publishers and our social decay filmed for the newsreels of CNN or Hollywood films on drug trafficking unless we change the interaction between cultural research and policies on culture and communications.

All of this relocates the classic agenda of cultural studies. Let me conclude with an example, a core issue in the dialogue between Latin Americans and Latin Americanists: the question of diversity. Affirmative action continues to be important in the areas of ethnicity and gender, but even there it is restricted as long as we are not able to study and invent new ways to affirm cultural diversity with respect to economic-symbolic transnationalization. We know that these claims must seek to reduce social inequality, but we shall not be successful unless we can count on information and a cultural power, not necessarily equivalent to, but able to confront what is held by transnational players. I do not know how cultural studies can be significantly renewed if we do not begin at the very least with the idea that this is our horizon, even if it seems too wide.

7

Perhaps this tension between the promises of global cosmopolitanism and the loss of national projects does not seem so different from those that inspired undertakings like those of Raymond Williams when he worked within his own country on the conflicts of his time. They are similar and they differ, in that globalized modernity is still modernity. It does not abandon capitalism but exaggerates it. Today we operate in another landscape that is like an explosion of the previous one. In this explosive expansion of technologies and economies, of cultural repertoires and consumer offers, in this outbreak of markets and cities, projects and public spaces have been lost, but fragments and splinters remain, picked up by social and cultural movements. To use an image by Alessandro Barrico, their trajectories leave graffiti in which we look for meaningful figures. Cultural studies is the attempt to find the sense of the traces inscribed by those surviving fragments.

DEDICATION

This chapter is dedicated to Ana María.

NOTE ON THE TEXT

Translation by Richard Young. The original Spanish version of this chapter is to appear in *Nuevo Texto Crítico*.

2

Cultural studies and literary criticism at the cross-roads of value

Beatriz Sarlo

The title of my chapter alludes to a cross-roads: a place where paths meet and where they diverge, where decisions are taken, where a connection is established or broken. And at this cross-roads I find a question: what makes a discourse socially significant? What value do our discourse and our practices possess in contemporary society? If the answer to this question didn't concern us, the impasse at the cross-roads would disappear. Certainly the question as to the social impact that a discourse possesses merits consideration. Who can say what is socially significant if we live, as Lyotard pointed out some time ago, in 'clouds of sociability' characterized by different evaluative and linguistic environments?[1] Cultural studies argues that it is possible to look at these diffuse, unstable environments (which produce what we nowadays call society) and find significance in certain practices based on their quantity (for example, how many thousands of individuals are watching a TV programme) or their quality (for example, a video seen by no more than a few hundred people can be important because it crystallizes an issue which, by virtue of a self-generated cycle, is considered to be an important one). Any discussion about the impact of symbolic practices proves at the very least that little is really known about the meaning of our discourse or that of the media in the public domain, and that we're on shaky ground.

Nevertheless, these questions, and the approximate answers given to these questions, were not always so vague. In Latin America at the beginning of the twentieth century literary criticism was a socially significant activity. The influential role it played in the creation of a modern public domain is recognized not only by historians who have a perspective on the process and who can point to things that the *dramatis personae* of the original drama probably missed, but was also glimpsed at that time. The debates about literature and national culture which occurred in the first two decades of the twentieth century galvanized the intellectual community of the time; they spilled out into the public sphere, magnetizing politicians and statesmen. Plans about national identity, state policies about immigration and ethnic minorities were put forward. National literature became a socially significant topic and, unlike at the threshold of this century, it elicited interest in more than just academic or writers' circles. The debate about national literature was crucial in Argentina at the end of the nineteenth and beginning of the twentieth century, it was influential in plans for educational reform and it delineated a space in which artists, the state élite, administrators and an important sector of the emerging middle class interacted in a lively, polemical fashion. The debate, encouraged initially by dilettantes, opened out onto issues which were important to a non-literary audience and influenced administrators as well as those drafting state policy. Literature and literary criticism were socially significant because they were considered, like the history and language of a nation, to be at the heart of a Republican education. Thus, at the dawn of the twentieth century, literary criticism left its mark on public discourse and its views had to be taken into account at the time when, as far as the state was concerned, the cultural blueprint for the country's future was being drawn up.

Allow me to give another example. When we look at Latin American magazines and newspapers from the 1960s and beginning of the 1970s (including the late 1950s) it is clear that the debate about the political and ideological justification for aesthetic value and, in particular, literary value, took off with such intensity that it shows how weighty a topic it was for the New Left scene. Something socially significant was at stake in those theories which posited a connection between literary and revolutionary practice. Almost all the writers of that period had to make some pronouncement about this connection which was central to the epistemology of the New Left. Those debates were socially significant whatever we think about the political events which framed them. Many things happened in the years following the climax and eventual defeat of the Revolution. In many instances, as occurred in Argentina, aesthetic renewal was condemned along with the Left Wing avant-garde. But going beyond politics, it also culminated in the re-writing of culture by the mass media, especially the audio-visual media, which were beginning to dominate at the time. It was then that we entered the dawn of the mass media age in which we still live.

I am convinced that art focused on the public domain has already reached its apogee, even though the conflicts run as deep nowadays as they did in the past. These conflicts, in any case, are different and, as is only natural, demand different responses. In the past 10 or 15 years cultural studies has emerged as an appropriate solution to the dynamics of this new landscape. Without wishing to force the comparison, I would say that social movements and cultural studies were extremely functional fellow-travellers leading, on the one hand, to the transition to democracy and, on the other, to the demise of modern totalizing systems. What is more, while literary criticism became more and more technical and lost influence with the man in the street (for whom it has frankly become like reading hieroglyphics),[2] cultural studies was put forward as a way out of this double impasse: creating a new space in the public domain as well as offering a discourse which was less hermetic than literary criticism.

THE SOCIAL REDEMPTION OF LITERARY CRITICISM VIA CULTURAL ANALYSIS

Let us briefly examine a few aspects of the situation outlined above. First, the hegemony of the audio-visual mass media. It is well known that we're moving towards and within a 'video-sphere' and that the public sphere as well as public political domains can be seen nowadays as part of a larger electronic arena. Technological changes are irreversible. We live in cyberspace even though vast minorities in Latin America still have to face gigantic obstacles in order to be assimilated as citizens within a new cultural and political sphere which is as extensive as it is stratified. Reading and writing are still the key to deciphering the written word even if the latter is no longer written on paper and has become virtual, flowing freely around that ring which we call the Internet, rolling around the world like a gigantic ball of text, or gliding without a page or a beginning or an ending around computer screens. It is true that cyberspace requires a new type of reading. But even if in the future non-alphabetic texts are included in encyclopaedias, significant texts will carry on being written texts. No amount of technological daydreaming can deny this obvious fact.

Nevertheless, the place of discourse, the way it is used and produced, is changing. And, within discourse, literature too is changing. Sophisticated citizens in the cyber-nations of the future will be connected, or are already connected, to a massive flow of writing, images and sounds. Literature, philosophy and history, understood in terms of genre, float and mutate within the dense cloud of hypertext which surrounds the planet (dense in addition because of the frequency with which stupidity and whim are considered part and parcel of freedom, anti-institutionalism and the free production of cultural goods). In any case one's personal opinion about these developments is irrelevant given their unstoppability (my own viewpoint is a rather sceptical one precisely because I am a good cyber-citizen and know its language reasonably well).

Let us look at the change which seems to me to be the most spectacular as well as the most profound: reading. This simple act which we take for granted – given the socio-economic cost caused by illiteracy in our societies – will have to be completely re-invented. Reading is going through a transformation. We will perhaps be the last generation of traditional readers. Reading is a costly activity in terms of the skills and time it requires. The decipherment of a written 'surface' demands an intense act of concentration for a relatively long period of time. We look at the text and we look *into* the text. We observe the reading matter intensely and extensively, we are *in* the text and *with* the text. Even while we may profess belief in a negative metaphysics which teaches us that the written word no longer possesses a depth which can be reached by delving into it, and that no totality exists which can be reconstructed from a mass of fragments, we're experts in deep reading who, paradoxically, recognize the futility of a metaphysics with pretensions to 'depth'. These 'sophisticated' activities which we carry out on texts have always been very different from those carried out by the general public, although something about the ordered nature of the operation as well as its intensity provides the basis for a common ground between intellectual and non-intellectual reading practices.

Let us address this question one more time. This common ground has been eroded. Reading, within the 'video-sphere', is absolutely necessary but it is evolving in different ways. Intensity is the preserve of other types of discourse (such as *live rock* which is experienced in an extremely intense way). Reading in cyberspace puts a premium on speed and the ease with which you can surf from one surface to another. In the past we used to walk on our texts; in the not so distant future we will glide over them, surfing their fractal maps. The future of literary criticism in a world where the place of literature has changed, and will continue to change even more rapidly, cannot be understood within the framework of the debates which took place some 30 or 40 years ago. The international academy has noticed how things have been developing and has planned out its own responses to them. The growing popularity of cultural studies and cultural analysis, which provides employment for hundreds of literary critics who have re-tooled themselves, is one such response.

Cultural Studies has existed in England as a discipline since around the middle of the 1960s. Gathering around Richard Hoggart and Stuart Hall in Birmingham and Raymond Williams, a solitary figure in Cambridge, a small nucleus of academics raised a number of audacious questions which, at that time, did not elicit the slightest interest from literary critics in England or elsewhere in the world.[3] But suddenly Raymond Williams, a figure whom literary critics mentioned little or not at all, became famous. This spectacular change cannot be explained without taking into account the challenge that literary criticism was facing in terms of the cultural transformations which I have tried to delineate above. A reasonably similar set of circumstances led to the gradually increasing impact of Walter Benjamin who stopped being read as a critic and a thinker in order to become – without his planning it – the forerunner of academic studies about urban culture, something quite different from those philosophical readings which, earlier on, had led to the work of architectural historians such as Manfredo Tasfuri or philosophers such as Cacciari. Something similar occurred in the US academy with Pierre Bourdieu, whose work did not reach the aristocratic purview of literary criticism until the 1980s.[4] Thus, in the space of a few years, many critics discovered that their discipline needed something new, something different, something pluralist and something culturalist.

This movement towards cultural studies gave rise to *the social redemption of literary criticism via cultural analysis*. It was a path followed in many countries almost at the same time. On the other hand, literary studies were beginning to exert an influence on some disciplines which, initially, were quite resistant to change such as History and Anthropology which, during this period, also absorbed the so-called 'linguistic turn'. Things were going in various directions at the time: literary criticism was looking for help from cultural studies (which only a few years before had been seen as too sociological), while History was courting literary criticism in search of new methodologies and a new sensibility in order to read texts in a more sophisticated way. Each discipline was negotiating with its adjacent discipline, discovering what it lacked and hoping that its neighbour could offer it something it needed. This unpretentious metaphor is used here in an attempt to describe the state of things that my audience knows only too well. These cross-fertilizations have a more sophisticated name – 'postmodern epistemologies' – and their presence is very obvious in the subjects which capture the academy's interest in Latin America and the United States nowadays.

I do not intend here to strike up a polemic with this tendency which, furthermore, is the villain in a tale of decadence invented by the rabidly anti-relativistic and anti-culturalist Right. Cultural studies has a legitimacy which to me seems obvious. Nevertheless I should pause briefly to analyse the reasons why cultural studies cannot solve the problems faced by literary criticism. Those questions we face as literary critics have not been answered as a result of the merger between literary criticism and cultural studies, nor have the problems disappeared as a result of our reincarnation as cultural analysts. To mention but three: the relationship between literature and the symbolic realm of the social world (which cultural studies tends to take for granted, although a large part of Raymond Williams's work investigates this theoretical question); the specific characteristics of literary discourse, an issue which is simplified when viewed solely from the perspective of the literary establishment (literature is defined by the literary establishment at every historic juncture and in every cultural space); and the dialogue between literary and social texts (which we cannot carry on solving simply by canonizing Bakhtin as the only patron saint in this regard).[5] These issues properly belong to the discipline of literary criticism and it is important not to ignore them simply because, until recently, they were not in fashion or because they do not elicit sophisticated, passionate debates nowadays.

But even these theoretical dilemmas can be swept under the carpet if we accept that there is something that literary criticism cannot blandly share out among other disciplines. This is the question of value; I refer to aesthetic value. This problem is as important for literary criticism as is the wider question of values in contemporary society. We learned our lesson. We professed relativism to be the touchstone of our multicultural convictions. But the consequences of extreme relativism were thrown back at us by right-wing anti-relativists when they accused us of destroying not only the male, white, western canon but literature itself. In order to enter this debate without a moralist's bad faith we should recognize openly that literature is valuable not because all texts are identical and because they can all be 'culturally' explained, but rather because, on the contrary, they are all different and are resistant to a boundless sociocultural interpretation. There is always 'something' left over when we explain literary texts in social terms and this 'something' is crucial. It is not an inexpressible essence, but rather a site of resistance, the force of a meaning which stays in the text and yet varies with the passing of time. To put it a different way: men and women are equal, but texts are not. The equality of people is a necessary given (it is the philosophical basis underlying democratic liberalism). Saying all texts are equal is the equivalent of suppressing those qualities which make them valuable. Literary criticism needs to re-address the question of value if it seeks, in overcoming the straitjacket of over-technical language, to speak about issues which are not inscribed within the territory of other social disciplines. The great literary critics of this century (from Benjamin to Barthes, from Adorno to Lukács, from Auerbach to Bakhtin) have been masters of this debate about values.[6] Literature is socially significant because that 'something' which we capture with great difficulty stays in the text and can be re-activated once the text has exhausted its other social functions.

I wonder if we're communicating this simple fact to students and readers alike: we're attracted to literature because it is a high-impact discourse, a discourse which is in a state of tension because of the conflict between – and fusion of – aesthetic and ideological realms. I wonder if we repeat as frequently as we should that we study literature because it affects us in a special way as a result of the density of its form and meaning. I wonder if we will be able to say these things without being pedantic or elitist or hypocritical or conservative.

THE DEBATE ABOUT VALUE AND THE CANON

Perhaps we're living through the final years of literature such as it has been understood up until now. Novels and films may be condemned to disappear within the flow of video-sphere. I'm not suggesting that narrated 'stories' will stop being shown on TV or at the cinema, but rather that films, such as they were invented in the twentieth century, may have come to the end of the road, apart from a handful of producers and a minority group within the general public. It might happen in the future that hypertext will not only be a comfortable way of managing footnotes or different levels of information, but it may also become a new paradigm of the syntax which over the centuries literature has moulded and changed.

We do not yet know what developments will occur in the next few decades.

The openness of literary criticism towards cultural analysis had positive consequences in that it increased the remit of the discourses and practices which it could now analyse. But the time to take stock has arrived. Literary criticism as a separate discipline should not disappear and be swallowed up within the flow of 'all things cultural'. Nobody wants to be the last, self-satisfied priest of the higher arts. Nevertheless we cannot let go – without also losing a sense of perspective – of this unique type of discourse which is still with us (literature). Literature is extremely complex and its complexity has proved, until now, that it was attractive (and indispensable) for varying sections of the reading public. Values are very much at stake here. And it is a good thing that it is not only the traditionalists who are saying this. It was a bad move to be defensive, thereby seeming to admit implicitly that only the conservative critics or the traditionalist intellectuals were in a position to address a problem which is as central to political theory as it is to literary theory. The debate about values was the big debate at the turn of the century.

The challenge is to see if we are able to imagine new ways of assessing values which (although it may seem contradictory) are simultaneously pluralist, relativistic, formalist and not based on a conventional approach. A relativistic perspective contends that values vary according to cultural contexts. According to relativism we should read texts in their contexts and judge them based on the strategies they use in order to solve the questions which those contexts consider to be appropriate. In this way the debate about values is always a 'textualized' discussion. From a transcultural perspective values are relative within the global space in which cultures are equal (in the same way that citizens are equal). But not all of the values within one given culture (this issue has already been addressed by Habermas)[7] merit the same degree of esteem if they are viewed from an extra-cultural context. Values are relative but they do differ. And for each culture values are not seen as relative from an intra-textual point of view. Cultures can be respected and, at the same time, differentiated.

Relativism demands that cultures are understood internally in terms of their own history and dynamics. However, when cultures come into contact with each other (and in a globalized world cultures are involved in an uninterrupted flow of contact and conflict), values become crucial to the debate. For example, the values of a macho culture based on servile work are no longer respectable when viewed from the perspective of a republican culture which is geared towards citizenship and which views the sexes in egalitarian terms. From an internal point of view, the more traditional a culture is, the more its members are inclined to demand a culture which is founded substantially on values. And thus we arrive at the second problem. Are values entirely based on convention even in those cultures which have passed all the tests of modernization and modernity? When we claim that a pluralist and democratic culture is better suited to the interests and options of its members than a culture which is founded on theological principles (for example, with regard to women's rights or the writer's right to express his/her views), we are constructing an argument which is not simply a rhetorical one. In some respect it touches on issues which have nothing to do with convention (if this word is preferred to 'substance'): we choose freedom when faced with the theological order, the best option when faced with beliefs which are presented as natural or which are imposed on us by the force of a tradition which is not always symbolic.

Cultural studies develops arguments which cannot ignore the question of values. If it ignores them, it runs the risk of becoming a sociology of subaltern culture which is more inclined to listen to salsa music or watch TV than evaluate educational institutions, political discourse or popular uses of high culture. As a basis for theoretical consistency, neither relativism nor sociology nor populism will do. I believe that literary criticism and cultural studies need each other. Literary studies might make a contribution to cultural studies by addressing a number of polemical questions. The literary and artistic canon, what is taught and how it is taught, is one of these questions. I wonder: is the literary canon intolerable because it's male, white and western, and, if so, would the answer be to broaden and diversify it? Or are we opposed to the very idea of devising and accepting a canon? Or would we only accept a canon if, before proclaiming its existence, we could agree to a constitutional pact about the terms in which it might be revised, let's call it a canon subject to unlimited and periodic modifications? Or to put it another way: do we believe that there are great works of literature which are significant despite other ideological considerations? If we accept this, then the question of values inevitably emerges. If we do not accept this idea, are we prepared to renounce our right to appropriate a cultural tradition and, above all, are we prepared to renounce on behalf of others to whom we would thereby not pass on this tradition in schools and universities because we think that the tradition is itself not politically correct?

Cultural studies is nowadays like a fortress set against a canonic view of literature. We live among the ruins of Foucault's revolution.[8] We learned that where there was discourse there was also power, and the consequences of this assumption cannot be underestimated. We could not go on talking about texts without examining the power relationships which underlay them and (at the same time) which they imposed with the efficiency of a war machine. A few years later French sociology of the intellectual camp established another principle: where there is discourse there is also a struggle for intellectual legitimization. Finally, Michel de Certeau corrected the early Foucault:[9] if it was true that where there was discourse there was also power, at the same time those in a subordinate position invented reading strategies which implied active responses to canonic texts, and these were responses which could contradict what the texts meant for other readers or what they meant for their authors. Cultural studies followed the intellectual meanderings brought together by these various ideas which, let's be clear about this, do not exactly lead naturally to a discussion about the canon but rather to its refutation.

However, the question could be expressed (as Gayatri Spivak suggests) from the point of view of the right to a cultural heritage.[10] Traditional (or classic) texts possess a *sustained* meaning which varies according to one's reading expectations, giving rise to a hermeneutic space which is rich and varied. Collections of great works were established according to different hierarchies which canonic practice formulated over time; can these collections provide the basis for a programme which is sensitive to cultural differences? And can they be read as devices offering excellent hermeneutical opportunities for the creation of new meanings and the discussion of old ones? Literary criticism raises not only questions of literary texts but also elicits demands in the strong sense of the term: these are things which a text should create, things which readers want to create with a text. What is at stake here, it seems to me, is not the continuation of a specialized activity, which works with literary texts, but rather our rights, and the rights of other sectors of society including the subaltern classes and all types of minorities, within the overall framework of our cultural heritage. This implies new connections with texts of the past in a fruitful process of migration; texts move from their original epochs, and ancient texts occupy new symbolic landscapes.

As an academic discourse which seeks to remain aloof from controversy, literary criticism needs only transfer its procedures to the recently upgraded scriptural cyberspace of the future and thereby invent (as is already happening) the new critical instruments needed to interpret hypertext. Literary criticism could also change itself into the academic study of the *mortal remains of literature*. This metamorphosis would simply make it disappear as a discourse produced in that value-laden intersection between academic and non-academic practices. I am not sure, though, that literary criticism as a public discourse, as a socially significant discourse, could solve its problems with such a simple gesture. Alternatively cultural studies could intervene and help literary studies and obtain some reward as a result. Aesthetics is not very popular among cultural analysts because cultural analysis is heavily relativistic and has inherited the relativistic perspective pertaining in the sociology of culture and popular culture studies. However, the question of aesthetics cannot be ignored without something significant being lost. That is because, if we ignore aesthetics, we will be losing that very object of study which cultural studies is trying to construct (as an object within culture which is different from that understood in anthropological terms). If there is an object of study for cultural studies, it is culture defined in a way which differs from the classical anthropological definition. It is important to recall (Hannah Arendt once wrote) that art and culture are not the same thing.[11]

The difficulty we face is that we are no longer certain in which respects (whether pertaining to form or content) art constitutes a unique expression of culture with a dimension which can be defined separately from other cultural practices. Thus, once more, the issue which concerns us is the extent to which we can identify the specific dimension of art as that element which tends to be overlooked from a culturalist perspective and which inspires cultural studies, even though cultural studies has up until now been ultra-relativistic as far as the formal and semantic texture of a work is concerned. We also face another paradox: it could also be argued that cultural studies is perfectly equipped to examine everything within the symbolic realm of the social world *except* art. I know that this statement may appear exaggerated. However, we all know that we feel uncomfortable when our object of study is art.

Let me provide some personal input at this point. Whenever I was on committees, along with European and American colleagues, judging videos and films, we had difficulties in establishing a common ground for making decisions: the non-Latin American judges looked at the Latin American videos with sociological eyes, pointing to their social or political merits and ignoring their discursive problems. I personally was inclined to judge the videos from an aesthetic point of view, relegating their social and political impact to a secondary position. The non-Latin Americans behaved liked cultural analysts (and occasionally like anthropologists) while I took on the role of art critic. It was difficult to reach a conclusion because we were talking different languages. A young Argentine film director had a similar experience during a European film festival. He showed his film (which was a highly sophisticated version of one of Cortázar's short stories)[12] but the critics at the festival told him that this type of film was European territory, and that they expected something more political from a Latin American film.

Everything seems to suggest that we Latin Americans should produce works which are suitable for cultural analysis whereas Others (basically Europeans) have the right to create works which are suitable for art criticism. The same might be said of women and the lower social classes: they are expected to produce cultural objects while white men produce art. This is a racist point of view even if it is held by people affiliated with the international left. But this racism is not only something which can be blamed on them. We suffer from the same thing as well. We must demand the right to 'art theory' and its analytical methods. We ought also to initiate a discussion about the definition of our field: the discipline of cultural studies will be completely legitimate once we manage to separate it from anthropology (from which we have learned so much), and a separation requires a re-definition of objects of study as much as a discussion about values.

If we do not see any difference between pop, jazz or rock music, we will be making a mistake. If we do not see the difference between a crude political film and a film by Hugo Santiago or Raúl Ruiz, we will be making a mistake. If we do not see any difference between a TV clip of Brazilian MTV and Caetano Veloso, we will be making a mistake. If we do not see the difference between Silvina Ocampo and Laura Esquivel, we will be making a mistake.[13] In every one of these cases there is a difference in terms of form and content which should be discerned via perspectives which are not always those used by cultural studies. Silvina Ocampo is different from Laura Esquivel even if one admits that Esquivel's ideas about women are politically correct. They are different because there is an extra factor in Ocampo which is totally absent from Esquivel. Art has to do with this extra factor. And the social meaning of a work of art in an historical perspective depends on this extra factor, as it is dependent on its audience if we simply consider it in terms of its present impact (or only in terms of its marketability).

Sometimes I feel that the cultural studies canon is established by the market, which is not a better source of authority than an elitist academic. A culture is also formed with texts whose impact is specifically limited to a minority. Stating this is not the same as pandering to elitism; it is simply recognizing the manner in which cultures function, as gigantic translation machines whose cultural materials do not need to pass a popularity test at every point in time. Although along pathways which only God knows about, these cultural materials may have popular appeal in the future. Inspired by the generous encouragement of cultural studies, I feel we are ignoring our own past as literary critics. Many of us come from Roland Barthes, and Walter Benjamin, just as Hoggart came from Auden's poetry,[14] and Williams never abandoned the field of English literature. We have a right to both worlds.

The great public debate nowadays revolves around values, and the foundations of a politics which takes those values into account. The great cultural debate, once we have crossed the Red Sea of relativism, might revolve around the study of values. At least this is a question whose answer can no longer be restricted to the confines of conventional relativism or conventional multiculturalism. How does a society survive after multiculturalism? Is it possible to make judgements after relativism? I do not have an answer to these questions but I think they are questions worth asking.

ACKNOWLEDGEMENTS

This English translation by Stephen Hart is based on the Spanish original which appeared in November 1997 under the title: 'Los estudios culturales y la crítica literaria en la encrucijada valorativa', *Revista de Crítica Cultural*, 15, 32–8. The editors take this opportunity to thank the editor of *RCC*, Dr Nelly Richard, for her kindness in allowing us to publish an English translation. The following notes and references are provided by the translator for those readers who would like some initial guidance on the work of the theorists Sarlo is alluding to in her article.

NOTES

1   Jean-François Lyotard (1924–88), a French philosopher renowned for his work *The Postmodern Condition* (1984).

2   Here Sarlo appears to be referring to the influence of Deconstruction within the field of literary criticism in the late 1970s and early 1980s particularly. Jacques Derrida (b. 1930), a French philosopher, has often been associated with this intellectual movement; see his works *Of Grammatology* (1974) and *Writing and Difference* (1978).
3   Richard Hoggart and Stuart Hall are both associated with the Centre for Contemporary Cultural Studies in Birmingham, which was founded in 1964, and which focused – in a way which was very novel for the time – on the analysis of the relationship between culture and society. Stuart Hall, in particular, was interested in the expression of youth culture as his work *Resistance Through Rituals* (Hall and Jefferson, 1975) suggests. Raymond Williams (1921–88), a major British Marxist literary critic was also highly influential during this period; see a selection of his essays in *The Politics of Modernism* (1989).
4   Walter Benjamin (1892–1940), a German philosopher and cultural critic, is best known for his far-reaching essay, 'The Work of Art in the Age of Mechanical Reproduction' (1936). For a selection of his work see *Illuminations* (1969). Massimo Cacciari is an urban theorist, renowned for his study on *Architecture and Nihilism* (1993). Pierre Bourdieu (b. 1930) is a French sociologist; a helpful selection of the latter thinker's essays is found in *The Field of Cultural Production* (1993).
5   Mikhail Bakhtin (1895–1975), a Russian philosopher of language and literary theorist, is famous for his study *The Dialogic Imagination* (1981).
6   Roland Barthes (1915–80), a French literary theorist and cultural critic, achieved fame with his study *Mythologies* (1972). Theodor Adorno (1903–69), a German philosopher and social theorist who was a key member of the Frankfurt School, evolved a complex theory of the relationship between culture, art and society; for a good sample of his work, see his *Aesthetic Theory* (1997). Georg Lukács (1885–1971), a German Marxist literary historian, was closely associated with the theory of Realism; his *The Historical Novel* (1962) was highly influential. Erich Auerbach (1892–1957) is best known for his seminal survey of the representation of realism in western literature, *Mimesis* (1953, German original 1946).
7   Jürgen Habermas (b. 1929), a German social theorist and philosopher who focuses on issues pertaining to perceptions of modernity; see his *The Philosophical Discourse of Modernity* (1987).
8   Michel Foucault (1926–84), a French philosopher who is arguably the most influential thinker of the postmodern age, produced a series of works on the operations of power within social constructs such as prisons and sexuality. For a good selection in English, see his *Power/Knowledge* (1980).
9   Michel de Certeau is a French sociologist known for his analysis of everyday life; see his *The Practice of Everyday Life* (1984).
10 Gayatri Chakravorty Spivak (b. 1941) is an Anglo-Indian feminist critic and cultural theorist who has worked specifically in the area of subaltern studies. For a good selection of her essays, see her *In Other Worlds* (1987).
11 Hannah Arendt (b. 1906) is a German political thinker who achieved notoriety with her study of *The Human Condition* (1958).
12 Julio Cortázar (1914–84) is one of the best known writers of the Boom, whose novel, *Hopscotch* (Spanish original, 1963, English translation, 1966), is considered

a classic of Argentine literature. For a selection of his short stories, see *All Fires the Fire and Other Stories* (1973).

13   Raúl Ruiz is a Chilean film director whose most important films are *Three Trapped Tigers* (1968) and *Socialist Realism* (1972). Caetano Veloso is one of the most important figures in contemporary Brazilian music. Silvina Ocampo (1903–93), an Argentine prose writer, poet and literary translator, is now chiefly remembered for her two collections of stories, *The Fury* (1959) and *The Guests* (1961). Laura Esquivel (b. 1950) is a Mexican author of best-sellers; her novel *Like Water for Chocolate* (1989) became a Hollywood blockbuster.

14   W. H. Auden (1907–73) is a British poet whose poetry is noted for its commitment to socialism and the use of urban and industrial imagery.

3

The place of literature in cultural studies
William Rowe

1

I will begin with some propositions about cultural studies in general and then go on to argue that the conjuncture which has brought us to ask 'What is Latin American Cultural Studies?' is best answered by considering how cultural studies in Latin America has been practised as distinct regional traditions. This will, in turn, make it possible to bring some focus into the question 'What is the place of literature?', and that will then give a context for further reflection upon the initial propositions.

Cultural studies is itself a cultural practice. This means that there cannot be any general model or theory of it, just ways of working in particular contexts, and their extension into other contexts. In other words, what we have at our disposal are examples of the practice of cultural studies and the possibilities they open up. How far the examples may be transferred beyond their initial context into new contexts is a question we will need to return to after discussing concrete instances of the practice of Latin American cultural studies. The internal logic of this situation, where the need for intellectual rigour, which I take as given, cannot be focussed through any single academic discipline, is shown in an essay by Eric Mottram:

> the main problem of cultural studies is easy to state and not at all easy to alleviate – it is to maintain some kind of focus, for the purposes of close consideration, when the materials themselves are without a fixed boundary... Since a culture is events in dynamic interaction, and ... every event intersects every other event, the problem is selection of events which give access to the pattern of interaction. (1978, p. 39)

He goes on to call this 'the art of selecting degrees of details so that the culture begins to reveal itself'.

It is always going to be the practitioner's responsibility to select 'degrees of detail' appropriate to the materials under study. The assumption of responsibility for the degree and mode of selection, for the type of 'cut' made through the unbounded events called culture, is particularly characteristic of the work of the Argentinian critic Josefina Ludmer; her work is enormously rigorous yet no single theory or methodology can be extracted from it (Ludmer, 1999, pp. 141–223). Selection is not simply a question of pragmatic convenience, it is the heart of the matter, since it is a question of the epistemic value of cultural studies and its political effectiveness. In broad terms of cultural history, the decision to give primacy to selection and to the ways it is carried out is part of a move away from Man as the Centre towards a post-humanist stance. As Charles Olson shows in his important essay, 'Human Universe' (1997, pp. 155–66), the trouble with the discursive habits inherited from Greek thought and transmitted to us via the Enlightenment, is that they tacitly use 'Man' as an instrument of definition, not particular human beings in particular places. Since Man is no longer available as subject, the burden falls upon the particular selection of materials as definition of the object of study. Unexamined selection falls into symbolism as a method – one of the bugbears of cultural studies – when events or objects are taken as symbolic without examination of how the socially symbolic is produced. Instead of the transferable 'universe of discourse', Olson argues for a multiple approach, in order to preserve the singularity of experience: 'for any of us, at any instant, are juxtaposed to any experience ... on several more planes than the arbitrary and discursive one which we inherit can declare' (1977, p. 157).[1]

Olson's 1950 essay is a crucial move towards cultural studies, not only in this refusal of universalities of thought, but also in the way it confronts modernity, which is where our current definitions of culture come from, with the cultural practices of a non-modern society, in this case Yucatán. Such is the blinding effect of a word like modern, placed by the currently hegemonic voices of Bush and Blair at the heart of Western morality and 'security', that non-modern immediately starts to mean 'archaic' and faulty, which of course it does for Mario Vargas Llosa (*El hablador*; The Speaker), when in fact it is simply a way of talking about cultural practices which were filtered out of 'The Western Canon' and other self-congratulatory ideas of our inheritance which disguise their degree of selectivity.

The fact that cultural studies does not belong to any given body of theory does not mean that it has no relationship with philosophy. Because the ideas in the best works of cultural studies are given not as ideas but as relations between the materials presented, such that – as I have argued elsewhere (Rowe, 1996, Part 1) – these works engage in a type of 'composition', the philosophy it relates to most closely would be radical empiricism (Deleuze, 1987, pp. 55–7) or radical constructivism (Maturana and Varela, 1996). Of course, to say 'the best works' is to make a value judgement. 'Cultural studies' in universities in the UK, the USA, and other English-speaking countries is used as a justificatory label in institutional power struggles, but as such it has no intellectual interest and little to offer the student who wants to explore critically the cultural environment. This type of cultural studies is conformist, even though it seems to be radical by dint of its inclusion of what used to be excluded from academic study, for example film, popular music, the behaviours of marginalised groups. It is conformist among other reasons because it goes along with the knowledge industry's merely accumulative approach to knowledge and because of what Peter Osborne has shown to be the unexamined pragmatism which underlies its way of working, which means that it cannot criticise cultural practices, only describe them (Osborne, 2000).

Discussions of cultural studies often cite the anthropological definition of culture as a sort of turning-point: 'The totality of socially transmitted behaviour patterns, arts, beliefs, institutions, and all other products of human work and thought' (Bové, 1997, p. 54). Yet, of itself, this type of definition is insufficient, because it does not say how or where the writer is producing this collection of objects of study. What is the relation between this creation of an object of study and, say, museums, newspapers, film, TV, oral narrative, rituals, different economies? It makes no distinction between different procedures for producing the object of study called culture.

This brings me to a further proposition: the way cultural studies produces its object of study (by what type of selection or 'cut') is regional. There may be an 'international canon of concepts' which students have to learn, but the actual object of study depends upon *relationships* among producers and receivers of signifying practices which are regional, even though globalised flows of information enter more and more into relation with those practices. For example, there is little advantage in theorising vernacular words like *mestizo* (miscegenated) and *hybrid* unless their particular local history and use is also taken into account (Rowe, 2000). Cultural studies is a regional practice in that the relationships between its materials are regional. Thus the object may have been invented elsewhere (the telegraph, railways, the radio, for example) but their particular relationships in an actual place generate regional forms of space (Canaparo, 1999). This does not mean that cultural studies is regionalist though, in the end and in its best examples, it is neither localist nor globalised, but refuses that binary in order to produce a critical sense of place (Casey, 1997; Canaparo, 1999), critical in the sense of opposing both globalisation and sentimental-nostalgic ideas of place. Region does not coincide with nation: it is an alternative term to the nation as that which gives meaning to literature. Region is in opposition to nation both geographically, in that types of cultural practice do not obey national boundaries, and politically, insofar as nation-building – to use a current term – has involved the suppression of differences within national boundaries. For example, the Andean region cuts across Venezuela, Colombia, Ecuador, Peru, Bolivia, Argentina, and Chile, and yet its literature has been disowned in differing degrees (to a high degree in Argentina) by the project of a national literature.

The subjectivities produced regionally are not subordinate to the nation, and in this sense overlap with Hardt and Negri's notion of the multitude as a multiplicity which opposes the concept of the people, which is produced by the nation-state and tends towards homogeneity (Hardt and Negri, 2000, pp. 102–3).

My final proposition is that there is not a single genealogy or line of transmission which we can label cultural studies, unless for the sake of institutional convenience. Attempts to anchor cultural studies in one set of influences diminish its rich and varied intellectual inheritance and universalise a particular regional practice.[2] That type of move becomes an obstacle to respecting the particulars of local practices while at the same time situating them within a larger field of cultural production. This is the dual thrust of cultural studies. Just as there are no simple languages, there are no simple cultures. Work which has been done in relation to one set of circumstances may or may not offer relevant interpretation of another; its relevance needs to be tested. What matters is to learn how to handle a multiplicity of articulations without imposing hasty schemata. In this sense, there has been a damaging tendency for discussions of cultural studies to leave out highly important figures who do not fit a certain Anglo-American orthodoxy. To give just three examples, William Empson is left out of accounts of Cultural Studies in Britain, Marshall McLuhan tends not to be mentioned in relation to US Cultural Studies, and those who speak for Latin American Cultural Studies have not read Alberto Flores Galindo. A prime characteristic of the work of all three is their invention of methods for moving between different levels and types of meaning. Given this, it may seem strange that they are not included in the 'canon'. But, once again, the internal logic of this situation is that as cultural studies becomes internationalised, so the emphasis on easily transferable knowledge increases. This is particularly acute with Latin America, where what are selected as interesting subjects for cultural studies have become more and more divorced from the real concerns of people on the ground. This is actually an abandonment of the first principles of cultural studies, which were developed out of the gap between what was being taught in universities and the types of cultural meaning that students were experiencing in their daily lives.

2

Although the practice of cultural studies cannot be traced to any single starting point, and it would be futile to try, one of the key experiences in Britain was that of Raymond Williams's university extension teaching after the Second World War. The need to include new materials in the English literature syllabus and find new ways of studying them arose out of the encounter between the university and social groups which had previously tended to have nothing to do with it. Control over the institution of Literature had previously belonged to the gentry, and media like newspapers, radio, and TV were not considered relevant to it. Literature was the real thing, and everything else was the 'background' – a rather dire situation given that background included science, religion, and philosophy, and that technology had not even got as far as the background. It was these initial conditions in England that also shaped the formation of the Birmingham CCCS, with the obvious difference that the social sciences played a stronger role there than in Williams's work. Nevertheless, there were other starting points, such as the work of Charles Olson, and Lewis Mumford (*Technics and Civilization*, 1934) in the USA, or Benjamin in Germany, and, in a different sense, Pierre Bourdieu in France.

By the 1990s, the single most important factor for cultural studies in English-speaking countries, was the loss of prestige of literature *vis-à-vis* film, TV, and other media. The story from that point is well enough known not to need repeating here (see Brantlinger, 1990). With regard to the formation of Latin American Cultural Studies, one of its pioneers, the Argentine critic Beatriz Sarlo, responded to the way literature had lost social prestige in an important essay published in 1997 (see English translation in this volume). She argues that whereas in the early decades of the twentieth century literary criticism had been 'a socially significant activity' (*socialmente significativa*) in Latin America,[3] in our time it has lost its influence in the construction of a modern public sphere. But her assertions are insufficiently focussed. Take the way she characterises the importance of literature in the early twentieth century: 'The debates about literature and national culture which occurred in the first two decades of the twentieth century galvanized the intellectual community of the time; they spilled out into the public sphere, magnetizing politicians and statesmen' (see above, pp. 24–5). The problem here, and it is one which extends through the whole of her article, is that the way literature affects socio-political reality is left vague; instead of indicating how the relationships work she relies upon scientific metaphors (*galvanized* and *magnetizing* refer to electro-magnetism), using what is in effect a neo-positivist language that gives an imaginary materiality to literature. She also confuses the two meanings of 'significant', having meaning and being important: all texts signify, the question is how and to whom. Here the problem is that having meaning depends upon context: we need to know the difference between early twentieth-century contexts and those of the past decade. If this is not done, the problems I have mentioned create a situation where the different ways in which meanings are produced and assembled together in what is called culture become difficult to grasp. When that is the case, one of the dangers is that university departments can produce a great many publications without having to confront what type of cultural practice they are engaged in. Interestingly, the difficulty applies not just to literature (i.e. literary studies) but also to cultural studies. This is not true of the best work in cultural studies, or to Sarlo's own best work, but it is symptomatic of what is happening both in Anglo-American

Cultural Studies and, increasingly, in Latin American Cultural Studies, which will be the subject of the rest of this chapter.

Latin American Cultural Studies can only be understood as the product of an encounter between Anglo-American and Latin American approaches. This is true of its two best-known practitioners, Beatriz Sarlo and Néstor García Canclini (even though the latter, in terms of methods, owes more to the French social scientist, Pierre Bourdieu, than to Raymond Williams). There are two possible responses to the implications of this fact. The first is to try to make a paradigm, i.e. a set of theoretical and methodological protocols and a canon of concepts. This is the case for example with subaltern studies, or with postcolonial studies applied to Latin America (see Beverley, 1999). I have already argued that the practice of cultural studies, in the best cases, is not a paradigm, in the strong sense of the word, but a regional practice; I will shortly give some particular examples.

The other option is to make the interest in Anglo-American Cultural Studies, which has now spread throughout virtually all of Latin America, into an occasion for re-reading Latin American traditions of cultural interpretation. Sarlo's study of Buenos Aires between 1920 and 1930 does this (Sarlo, 1988). It explores how different writers of the 1920s themselves composed (put together and interpreted) the culture of Buenos Aires, where culture is understood in Williams's sense of the signifying practices through which 'a social order is communicated, reproduced, experienced and explored' (Williams, 1981, p. 13); the result is a kaleidoscopic method, not the stable conceptualisation that is typical of ordinary literary studies. With García Canclini, it was the slightly different question of confronting the arts with the social science methods of the sociology of culture. Drawing on the strong development of the social sciences in Latin America in the 1970s and 1980s, this move was happening in various parts of the subcontinent. Nevertheless, literature, unlike say the visual arts, was a special case. There already existed in most places a strong interpretative tradition, even if it was not formalised as 'literary criticism', a term which was not consolidated institutionally until the 1980s in Peru, Bolivia, or Colombia for example. The existence of local ways of reading, and of relating literature to a sense of place, meant that sociologists were reluctant to encroach upon the territory of literature.

With anthropology, the situation was rather different: quite some time before Sarlo or García Canclini, Ángel Rama had already been using an anthropological approach in order to show how the novels of major writers of the latter half of the twentieth century, such as João Guimaraes Rosa or José María Arguedas, had taken their form from the local oral traditions of *mestizo* and native cultures. Here was a clear case of literature itself already changing so as to include cultural media and practices which previously had been excluded. Thus as Martín Lienhard, in a development of Rama's ideas, put it, Arguedas was writing for a reader yet to come, bilingual and literate in both the hispanic and the native traditions (Cornejo Polar *et al.*, 1984, pp. 12–20).

These readers, such was the logic of this position, would be creators of an alternative modernity. Rama, following Arguedas and Ortiz, used the term 'transculturation' to refer to this overall cultural process. If we take cultural studies as arising out of a need for an expanded definition of culture, not narrowly based on literature as a highly selective type of cultural practice, then it was already being practised by Rama in the 1980s, and perhaps before that by Arguedas in his anthropological work. Others, too, might be included in the list, such as Pedro Henríquez Ureña. Once we consider cultural studies not as an institutional paradigm but as itself a cultural formation, arising within particular histories, then the fact is that, as Jesús Martín-Barbero has said, Latin Americans were already doing it, which makes 'Latin American Cultural Studies' a problematic label. Given that it describes a response to developments in Anglo-American universities, it does not work as a particularly satisfactory term in Latin America except where universities run programmes in collaboration with US universities, something which is in fact becoming increasingly common.

3

What follows is a brief discussion of the meaning of cultural studies in Peru, which will give more substance to some of the above assertions about Latin American Cultural Studies and also afford an opportunity to present some detailed cases of the place of literature in cultural studies. Historically, José Carlos Mariátegui is the first Peruvian intellectual to develop a method for bringing about the multiple intersections that constitute a modern culture. His essays on the formation of Peruvian reality include economic, political, religious, and sociological perspectives; they recognise the regional nature of Peruvian history, as opposed to the inappropriate notion of Peru as a single nation; and they acknowledge the simultaneous existence of non-modern and modern forms of social organisation and imagination in Peru, making Peru a heterogeneous country. One of the ways he places the non-modern and the modern side by side, instead of subordinating the first to the second, is by giving prime importance to religion as a motivation in history (Mariátegui, 1964a, pp. 18–22).

Literature, for Mariátegui, produces meaning in all of these contexts and cannot be reduced to any one of them. There is also the fact that the different contexts are in some cases not easily reconcilable with each other; for example, the predominantly native population of the Andean region has produced different economic, social, religious, and political forms of life. This is, for Mariátegui, the major rift that runs through Peruvian reality, and he sees both its clearest manifestation and the possibility of overcoming it in the literature of *indigenismo*. Nevertheless, his famous essay on *indigenismo* cannot be taken as his whole view of literature (Mariátegui, 1964b, pp. 285–300). It needs to be read alongside his sense of the multiplicity of the aesthetic fact, and in particular his insistence that literature is capable of breaking with inherited contexts of meaning and creating 'el disparate puro' (pure nonsense). Thus the meaning and importance of literature is not for him confined to the issue of building a nation ('hacer nación'), of constructing a modern public space.

This latter aspect of Mariátegui's thought is part of its openness to the inventive capacity of the imagination, something which received little recognition until Flores Galindo's crucial book, *La agonía de Mariátegui* (1994), which locates him as a major creator of Peruvian cultural theory. Between Mariátegui's death in 1930 and the work of Flores Galindo, a different interpretation of his work predominated, in which he figures as a strict Marxist materialist, for whom everything, including the imagination, was subordinated to the class struggle. Interestingly, it is this version of Mariátegui which is shown to be incapable of understanding Andean Peru in Arguedas's first novel *Yawar Fiesta* (Blood Festival; 1941). *Yawar Fiesta* was written during the period of the Popular Front in Peru, when a rigid polarisation of politics had impoverished the available language for understanding Peruvian culture.

Arguedas himself is the next major practitioner (*avant la lettre*) of cultural studies in Peru. His novels can be read as a rejection of that impoverished language, and his anthopological work, which the novels and poetry overlap and interact with, displays a set of cultural practices which lay the basis for a tradition of cultural studies in Peru, in the sense both of ways of working and of the construction of institutions. In the late 1930s and early 1940s (the time of writing *Yawar Fiesta*) he went to work as a secondary schoolteacher in the Andean town of Sicuani, in the Department of Cusco. He taught his students to read Latin American (including Peruvian) *modernista* literature and European Modernist literature, while at the same time training them to use their local, bilingual knowledge to collect and assemble (*recopilar*) Andean narratives, songs, and rituals, and to publish these and write commentaries on them in the school journal. He was therefore teaching three types of reading, which required three different informational contexts; by placing them alongside each other he was giving equal value to different types of cultural competence, and placing his confidence in the possibility of constructing institutions that would embody a specifically Peruvian cultural synthesis. These institutions were only partially achieved in the post-war period; the main obstacle were those social groups who had a vested interest in building a westernised modernity in Peru, aligned above all with that of the USA.

The commitment to multiple cultural competencies (or interpretative practices) informs the writing of Arguedas's novels and also his anthropology; this made his practice as a social scientist heterodox and prevented it from falling into neo-positivist orthodoxy. In his novel *Los ríos profundos* (The Deep Rivers, 1958), the writing itself is shaped by heterogeneous cultural practices. These include Andean oral narratives (loosely called 'mythology'), as is the case with the *indigenista* novel. But they also include an avant-gardist way of reading language, where the play of letters and sounds is not subordinated to representational meaning. This is what Mariátegui had called 'el disparate puro' (pure nonsense), with reference to the Peruvian poet Martín Adán. Adán himself had written a novel, *La casa de cartón* (The Cardboard House, 1928), which invented a Peruvian cosmopolitanism, quite different from that of Borges, say, in Buenos Aires. In Adán's novel the screen on which the real projects itself is the back of a mule in Barranco, a suburb of Lima, in a deeply ironical and heterogeneous conjunction of modern media and non-modern society. Adán's work shows there is no general sequence of the development of modernity in Latin America and, by the same token, that it is problematic to speak of a general Latin American cultural studies.

Arguedas's *Los ríos profundos* offers a gallery of reading practices, which include that of Adán's cosmopolitanism. As with Mariátegui, literature is shown to be meaningful thanks to an irreducible variety of contexts of reading. In Arguedas's novel, these consist in avant-gardism, Modernismo, the Peruvian chronicles of the sixteenth and seventeenth centuries, and the native ability to read stones and water. These are the communicative forms which the novel assembles. In parallel with these there are three socio-historical contexts: the Andean haciendas and their feudal social relations; the Andean town (Abancay) with its violent intersections of commercial capital and native and *mestizo* populations; and the modern coastal society (the army officers). The complex relations between communicative forms and social contexts offer a way of understanding Peruvian culture which goes beyond the *indigenista* schema, and has the characteristics of cultural studies. In a similar way, Mario Vargas Llosa's novel *La casa verde* (The Green House, 1965) shows how the meaning of literature in Peru depends upon multiple contexts: the jungle and the coast; pre-modern and modern economies; mythical time-narrative and film-montage time. The differences are not necessarily lined up as parallel pairs, but interact in complex ways. Mario Montalbetti's long poem, *Fin desierto* (Desert End) may be taken as an example of a text which is marked by globalised flows. There space is both singular (the Peruvian desert with remains of native burials) and deterritorialised in such a way that the minimalist features of the desert become extensions of other places, other deserts. It is critical of the emptying out of place, and thus of the effects of globalisation: 'no hay lugar para el lugar' (there is no space for space; Montalbetti, 1997, p. 20).

That complexity may seem daunting to a student beginning to read Latin American literature. While this is true, it is so in the same sense that Peruvian culture is complex, and part of the difficulty has to do with learning ways of reading which fall outside the traditional discipline of Literature. The model of reading established by the traditional discipline of Literature is what produces obects of study like the 'Boom' and 'post-Boom' in Latin American literature, which have little to do with understanding literature as a cultural practice.

That model of reading, by divorcing reading from regional cultural practices, causes the major part of literature written in the case of Peru to be invisible, leaving only Mario Vargas Llosa and perhaps Alfredo Bryce and possibly Arguedas, but the Arguedas of *Los ríos profundos* and not the one of *Todas las sangres* (Every Blood). Methods which place reading within the context of regional cultural practices are exemplified, among others, by Lienhard (1981), Elmore (1993), and Ortega (1992). The latter includes essays on colonial Peruvian literature, a useful reminder that the study of colonial literature, pioneered among others by Rolena Adorno, has always tended to give careful attention to cultural contexts, given that the majority of the corpus of texts do not fall within the dominant Western definition of 'Literature'.

Cultural studies is a challenge to find the relations between literature and its many contexts. To value it – positively or negatively – merely because it studies film and other media instead of just Literature is to miss the point. Literature in Peru was already related to multiple and heterogeneous contexts, and required these for anything like a satisfactory understanding. Subsequent work to that of Arguedas continues to show this to be the case. Examples, necessarily incomplete, would include Antonio Cornejo Polar (1994), who developed the powerful concept of heterogeneity in literature; Mirko Lauer (1989), who has confronted literary history with social-scientific notions of cultural production; Alberto Flores Galindo (1986), whose fine historical work is always concerned with the production of subjectivity; and Nelson Manrique (1989), who has shown the way to link the analysis of economic forms with political consciousness and its manifestations in literature.

This brings me back to my initial propositions. It is precisely because cultural studies is a cultural action that major works of literature offer it ways of working out the key links between meaning and contexts. To say that is to suggest that both resemble each other as actions of cultural assemblage. The loss of prestige of literature can only be explained by investigating what has changed in terms of contexts and meanings, in other words by using a cultural studies method. Literature is neither subordinate nor superordinate to cultural assemblages, but exists alongside them on the same plane. Needless to say, though, to study literature in that way cannot be done without a thoroughgoing critique of literature as an institution belonging to a social minority or one used by selective intellectual programmes (as not just literary studies but cultural studies can be in Anglo-American universities).

Cultural studies is, at its best, a challenge to think the culture as a whole. The elements may appear to be the same from one region to another, but their *relations* are not. Radical empiricism holds that the relations are not given in the terms, in other words that it is not enough to apply a set of concepts to a given region since what needs discovering is how meanings are produced inside that region. Thus to investigage the culture as a whole is to be drawn more into the regional and what is not transferable about it. The practice of Latin American Cultural Studies often does the opposite. The aim should be to investigate all the ways in which meaning is produced in a given instance. The examples given in this chapter have been to do with how particular Peruvian novels relate to multiple contexts of meaning.

How far is the exercise of cultural studies in relation to literature extendable from one region to another? Key principles, which are in common between one region and another, would include the intersection of different cultural practices (popular and erudite; relating to groups with different ethnic histories; involving different mediations and media), the multiplicity of contexts, the modification of European genres by regional cultural practices. To say that these are common between different regions is to assert that there is a sense in which they are characteristics of Latin American literature as a whole. However, to think of the common characteristics that one finds as if they constituted a fixed set of classifications is to miss the point and to fall back into the attitude that isolates literature from cultural contexts. Theoretical frameworks need to be informed by an understanding of the processes of cultural production without which the materials which are assembled in literary texts would not exist. So the question becomes, what are the relationships which make a particular type of textual production possible? On the basis of this knowledge, comparison can be made across regional boundaries. Cultural studies is a potentiality of late modernity, but one that is constructed differently in each place. And since it challenges us to read literature in a post-humanist way, it is better taken as a necessary re-positioning of literature than an optional fashion.

NOTES

1 For the political importance of posthumanism, see Hardt and Negri (2000, pp. 214–18).
2 Answers to 'a call for comments on the actual or potential relations between cultural studies and the literary', published in *PMLA*, 112. 2, 257–87, can be compared with the ongoing 'Cultural Studies Questionnaire' published in the *Journal of Latin American Cultural Studies*. It seems clear that Anglo-American practitioners of cultural studies draw upon a considerably narrower corpus of theory and methods than do those who work in Latin American Cultural Studies.
3 But note the anachronism. Before around 1950 there was not, for example, any literary criticism in the sense in which it had become institutionally recognisable, which is the formation that Sarlo refers to.

4

Adiós
A national allegory (some reflections on Latin American Cultural Studies)

John Beverley

I want to start by noting what seems at first sight a paradoxical coincidence between the terms of David Stoll's much publicized attack on Rigoberta Menchú (Stoll, 1998) and the various critiques by Latin American intellectuals identified with the left of the pertinence of postcolonial and subaltern studies to the field of Latin American studies that have appeared in the last several years.[1] As those familiar with his book can attest, Stoll's argument is not only or perhaps even mainly with Menchú, or about whether several key details of her narrative are factually true, but rather is directed against what he perceives as the hegemony of the discourses of postmodernism and multiculturalism in the North American academy, which he feels consciously or unconsciously colluded to perpetuate international support for armed struggle in Guatemala by promoting *I, Rigoberta Menchú* and making Menchú into an icon of political correctness.[2]

The connection between multiculturalism and postmodernism that bothers Stoll is predicated on the fact that multiculturalism carries with it what, in a well-known essay, Canadian philosopher Charles Taylor calls a 'presumption of equal worth' (1994). That presumption implies a demand for epistemological relativism that coincides with the postmodernist critique of the Enlightenment paradigm of modernity – what Habermas would call communicative rationality. If there is no one universal standard for truth, then claims about truth are contextual: they have to do with how people construct different understandings of the world and historical memory from the same set of facts in situations of gender, ethnic, and class inequality, exploitation, and repression. The truth claims for a narrative like *I, Rigoberta Menchú* depend on conferring on testimonial writing a special kind of epistemological authority as embodying subaltern experience and 'voice'. But, for Stoll – who is arguing also against the emergence of what he calls a 'postmodernist anthropology' – this amounts to an idealization of the quotidian realities of peasant life to favor the prejudices of a metropolitan academic audience, in the interest of a solidarity politics that (in his view) did more harm than good. Against the authority of testimonial voice, Stoll wants to affirm the authority of the fact-gathering procedures of traditional anthropology or journalism, in which accounts like Menchú's will be treated simply as raw material that must be processed by more objective techniques of assessment.

The argument 'from Latin America' – to borrow a phrase from Nelly Richard – against what I will call in a kind of short-hand 'studies' (postcolonial, subaltern, cultural, women's, africana, gay, latino, and so on) as discourses 'on Latin America' seems to have three major components (I am aware that I am conflating distinct and perhaps incompatible positions here):

1 'Studies' represent a North American problematic about identity politics and multiculturalism, and/or a historically recent British Commonwealth problematic about decolonization, that have been displaced onto Latin America, at the expense of misrepresenting its diverse histories and social-cultural formations, which are not easily reducible to either multiculturalism or postcoloniality.[3]
2 The prestige of 'studies' as a discourse formation emanating from and sustained by the resources of the Euro-North American academy puts in shadow the prior engagement by Latin American intellectuals – 'on native grounds', so to speak – with the very questions of historical and cultural representation 'studies' is nominally focused on. That prestige portends an overt or tacit negation of the status and authority of Latin American intellectuals, a willful forgetting of what Hugo Achugar calls 'Latin-American thought'. The new hegemony of metropolitan theoretical models amounts in Latin America, therefore, to a kind of cultural neo-colonialism, concerned with the brokering by the North American academy of knowledge both from and about Latin America. In this transaction, the Latin American intellectual is relegated to the status of an *object* of theory (as subaltern, postcolonial, calibanesque, 'the other', etc.) rather than its *subject*. Antonio Cornejo Polar, in particular, was concerned in his valedictory essay with the fact that the very language of Latinamericanist theory had become English rather than Spanish.
3 By foregrounding the theme of the incommensurability of subaltern social subjects and the nation-state, and by displacing hermeneutic authority from high culture – and the canon of Latin American literature in particular – to mass consumer culture, 'studies' contributes to incapacitating Latin America's ability to implement its own projects of national or regional identity and development. Beyond an appeal to the agency of an abject, pre-capitalist or pre-modern Other that remains outside of (any possible) hegemonic representation, on the one hand, or urban mass cultural

reception, on the other, 'studies' lacks a sense of the political as grounded in the continuity of the nation, a more or less active, literate, and politically informed citizenry, a Habermasian public sphere, local memory, and projects that seek to affirm the interests of both individual Latin American nation-states and Latin America as a whole in a differential, even antagonistic, relation to globalization.[4] Beatriz Sarlo, notably, argues that the postmodernist celebration of Latin American mass or popular culture in the context of globalization and the 'soft authoritarianism' of neoliberal consumer societies undermines the authority of aesthetic culture and values, and it is only from the possibility of negation of the instrumental rationality of capitalist society that is contained in that culture that resistance and alternatives to the dominant reality principle are possible.[5]

Both Stoll and the Latin American critics of 'studies' coincide in seeing the discourse of US multiculturalism and postmodernist relativism as the culprit. They are also both, in some ways, attempting to police their respective disciplinary fields (anthropology and literary criticism) to prevent their destabilization by the intrusion into them of a subaltern subject which academic knowledge and aesthetics are in part implicated in constructing in the first place. As such, they both represent forms of what has come to be called in the United States 'Left conservatism', which I would define (inadequately) as a combination of social-democratic or 'Third Way' politics with positivist epistemology and/or modernist aesthetics.

What complicates the identification of Stoll and the Latin American critics of 'studies', however, is the fact that Stoll is a North American writing about a Latin American indigenous organic intellectual – Rigoberta Menchú – whereas the Latin American critics are responding to what they see as essentially a new North American intellectual fashion – 'the boom of the subaltern', as Mabel Moraña puts it. Whether he meant it to or not (and I take his claim that he did not at face value), Stoll's critique of Menchú has served the interests of the Right in both the United States and Guatemala by partially delegitimizing Menchú. But the Guatemalan writer and critic Arturo Arias has told me that there are also Guatemalan Right-wing journalists and intellectual figures who have attacked Stoll precisely as a North American 'dissing' a Guatemalan national figure.[6] Here a different kind of cutting edge comes into play, an edge that separates and places in antagonism what on the surface might seem like a shared critique of postmodernist relativism and multiculturalism. That cutting edge takes us back to the Ariel-Caliban question, except that now Rigoberta Menchú – that is, Caliban, 'the deformed slave', in Shakespeare's characterization – is in the place of Ariel, facing the power and vulgarity of the Colossus of the North, represented by Stoll.

This seems an appropriate moment to recall the famous passage in *The Philosophy of History* where Hegel envisions the future of the United States. Hegel writes:

> Had the woods of Germany been in existence, the French Revolution would not have occurred. North America will be comparable with Europe only after the immeasurable space which that country presents to its inhabitants shall have been occupied, and the members of its political body shall have begun to be pressed back on each other ... America is therefore the land of the future, where, in the ages that lie before us, the burden of the World's History shall reveal itself – perhaps in a conflict between North and South America. It is the land of desire for all those who are weary of the historical lumber-room of old Europe. (Hegel, 1956, pp. 86–7)

Hegel is intimating here what would be called the 'end of frontier' thesis in US historiography, which is quite far-sighted considering that in their original form the lectures which make up *The Philosophy of History* date from 1822–3. What is more interesting for our purposes here, however, is Hegel's passing remark that a conflict between North and South America may be necessary for the United States to attain world historical significance. Today perhaps the opposite could be said: that for Latin America to attain world historical significance in 'the ages that lie before us' will entail necessarily a conflict with the United States.

That prospect suggests Samuel Huntington's idea of 'the clash of civilizations': the notion that new forms of conflict in the post-cold war world will no longer be based on the bi-polar East/West model, but will crystallize along heterogenous 'fault lines' of ethnic–cultural–linguistic–religious differentiation: the Anglo–US axis, Europe (and then Europe divided into 'Western' and Orthodox Christian or 'Eastern' regions), 'Confucian' East Asia, 'Hindu' South Asia, the Islamic world, etc. (Huntington, 1993). What this vision portends for the coming period, Huntington suggests, is a new kind of bi-polarism which, borrowing a phrase from Kissghore Mahbubani, he calls 'the West versus the Rest'. In Huntington's taxonomy, Latin America states are 'torn countries', split between the West and the Rest.[7] Will they define their future in a symbiotic and dependent relationship with North American cultural and economic hegemony, or will they develop, singly or in a new kind of regionalism, their own projects in antagonism with that hegemony? On the whole, Latin America governments, including Fox's regime in Mexico, did not support the US war against Iraq in spite of enormous pressure to do so.

The nature of these questions provides the occasion for me to introduce my national allegory, which uncannily foreshadows aspects of both the Iraq war and the attempted coup – initially supported by the Bush regime – against Chavez's presidency in Venezuela in 2002. It is Richard Harding Davis's novel *Soldiers of Fortune*, which at the time of its publication in 1897 became something of a best-seller and fed the public enthusiasm for American intervention in Cuba. *Soldiers of Fortune* (which bears an obvious relation to Conrad's *Nostromo*), is set in the fictional Latin American republic of Olancho, recognizably Venezuela (where, as it happens, I was born). The hero,

Robert Clay, is a civil engineer who is hired by another North American, Langham, the owner of Valencia Mining Company to manage his iron mines in Olancho. Langham's concession depends on a contract negotiated with the president of Olancho, Señor Alvarez, which provides the Olanchan government with a 10 per cent share of the production. The nationalist opposition to Alvarez in the Olanchan senate, led by General Mendoza, objects to the concession, and introduces legislation to obtain a larger share of the mine's production. In a kind of Machiavellian double-cross, Clay meets secretly with Mendoza and offers him a huge bribe to block this legislation, which Mendoza accepts. Clay then reneges on the bribe, threatening at the same time to make public Mendoza's acquiescence in his plot. Mendoza responds by preparing a *coup d'état* to overthrow Alvarez and nationalize the mines. He puts into circulation the rumor that President Alvarez is a dupe of foreign interests, namely the Valencia Mining Company, Alvarez's wife (who is Spanish, and who Mendoza claims is plotting to restore the Spanish monarchy in Olancho), and Alvarez's chief of security, Stuart, who is a British subject. Mendoza also enlists in his plot a shadowy figure called Captain Burke, a gringo arms smuggler and filibustero (Burke anticipates in some ways the character of Mr. Danger in Rómulo Gallegos's *Doña Bárbara*).

Clay and Stuart get wind of Mendoza's plans and find out in particular that Burke has smuggled in a shipment of weapons for the plotters. Clay, who has won the loyalty of the Olanchan mine workers, organizes them into a kind of *contra* army *avant la lettre*. They locate the smuggled weapons and are able to capture them. This precipitates Mendoza's coup, which is initially successful: Mendoza's forces take over the presidential palace and imprison Alvarez. Sectors of the army, however, remain loyal to Alvarez's vice-president, Rojas. They put themselves under the command of Clay, whom they designate, in Bolivaran style, the Liberator of Olancho. Mendoza's coup collapses and he is eventually shot to death in combat. In due time, the United States Marines arrive. Clay directs them to preserve order until Rojas can be installed as the new president of Olancho. Rojas, it goes without saying, pledges to recognize the virtues of free trade and protect the security of the Valencia Mining Company.

At the beginning of the novel, Clay is engaged to Langham's older daughter Alice, who comes with her younger sister, Hope, to visit Olancho on the eve of Mendoza's coup. Alice is the archetypal North American upper-class woman: genteel, elegant, refined, ultra-feminine, educated according to European models. She seems an ideal match for Clay, who is clearly the man who will inherit the place of her father. In Olancho, however, the two come to regard each other differently. Escaping from an ambush by Mendoza's forces, Alice sees Clay working with his hands to repair a ship engine. The experience convinces her that he cannot be the man of her dreams, that he represents values and experiences at odds with her own. Like the nationalist opposition in the Olanchan senate, her values are anachronistic: they represent an older

North American bourgeois culture that is in the process of being displaced by the dynamic new forces of corporate imperialism – in Henry Adams's image, the 'virgin' as opposed to the 'dynamo'. By contrast, her younger sister Hope, epitomizes precisely these new forces. She is only 18, and has not come out into society. In a manner reminiscent of Henry James's Daisy Miller, her very youth and näiveté permit her to be open to the new, since she is as yet uncorrupted by the worldly wisdom of inherited privilege and arranged marriages, represented, on the one hand, by her sheltered upbringing in New York, on the other, by the oligarchy in Olancho, whose carefully coded distinctions of status she ignores. She is a more suitable match for Clay than Alice because her values are, like his, democratic, egalitarian, and pragmatic. She is a figure of modernity, the New Woman or Gibson Girl, energetic, self-motivated, physically active, and, unlike her sister, curiously androgenous or masculinized, in the novel's own words, 'like a boy'.

Hope, like Rojas and the Olanchan mine workers – and it is significant that it is the workers and not the elite who choose to side with Clay against Mendoza – symbolizes the advantages of an alliance with the emerging forms of American imperial power, involving a remapping of older national and regional loyalties and values, a remapping which is also Clay's *raison d'être*, and which requires the displacement of the traditional elites in both the United States and Latin America. To put this another way, the libidinal economy allegorized in the Clay–Alice–Hope relation serves as a 'foundational fiction' (in Doris Sommer's sense of this term; 1991), but here not so much for the nation as for the emerging supra-national territoriality of corporate imperialism that follows the close of the Western frontier in the United States. Although this territoriality is supra-national, coinciding in that sense with the idea of a post-national territoriality put forward in Antonio Negri and Michael Hardt's recent academic bestseller *Empire* (2000), the values that govern its identity remain in some significant sense North American: the triumph of those values, which the plot of the novel enacts, symbolizes the hegemonization of the Latin American imaginary by US culture and values.

I want to use *Soldiers of Fortune* to reflect on the resistance to 'studies' 'from Latin America'. Provisionally, I propose to read Clay-Hope, and their alliance with a new Latin American subject represented by Rojas and the miners, as a figure for 'studies'. 'Studies', like Clay–Hope (or Bush and Blair in defense of the Iraq war), speaks the language of democracy, anti-elitism, the popular, the subaltern, the new; but, in the eyes of many Latin American intellectuals, it appears to be at the service of US global and regional hegemony. By the same token, then, the resistance to 'studies' 'from Latin America', must be figured as Mendoza and the nationalist opposition, that is, as a reactionary, or, more generously, a reactive position.[8] Let me be clear here, because the possibilities for misinterpretation or willful misunderstanding are rife: there can be no question that the main enemy of democracy and economic progress in Latin America has been US hegemony over the region (time and again democratically elected regimes have been overthrown with US support or connivance). But the obstacles to democracy and social equality are also *internal* to Latin American nation-states; indeed, it is often those internal barriers – usually tied to forms of upper-class and middle-class privilege, and related forms of gender and racial inequality – that US policy has used historically to destabilize the Left and democratic regimes in Latin America.

I believe that the things that divide 'studies' from its Latin American critics may be less important in the long run than the concerns we share. I am sensitive in particular to the concern with the prestige and power of the North American academy in an era in which Latin American universities and intellectual life are being decimated by neoliberal policies connected in great measure to US hegemony at all levels of the global system, but particularly in Latin America. Nevertheless, if in fact globalization entails a displacement of the authority of Latin American intellectuals, then the resistance to 'studies' is itself symptomatic of the unequal or subaltern position of Latin American culture, states, economies, and intellectual work in the current world system.

Paul de Man memorably described the resistance to theory as itself a kind of theory (de Man, 1983). If I were to characterize the theory implicit in the resistance to 'studies', I would say that it amounts to a kind of neo-*Arielism*: a reassertion of the authority of literature, literary criticism, and literary intellectuals as the bearers of Latin America's cultural memory and possibility against forms of critical thought and theoretical practice identified with the imperialist hegemony of the United States. But 'studies' emerges precisely from the 'Left' of US culture: the civil rights movement, the New Left, feminism, the anti-war movement, the gay movement, etc. And *Arielism* by definition is an ideologeme of what José Joaquín Brunner usefully calls the '"cultured" vision of culture': that is, the vision that identifies culture essentially with high culture. For it is not only 'in theory' (subalternist, postcolonial, Marxist and post-Marxist, feminist, queer, or the like), or *from* the metropolitan academy that the authority of Latin America's 'lettered city' (to use Ángel Rama's term) is being challenged. This is also a consequence of the effects of globalization and the new social movements inside Latin America itself. Subaltern studies shares with cultural studies – that is the main point of convergence between the two projects – a sense that cultural democratization implies a shift of hermeneutic authority from the philological-critical activity of the 'lettered city' to popular reception, a shift which entails a corresponding displacement of the authority of what Gramsci called the traditional intellectual (and literary intellectuals are, along with priests or clergy, almost paradigmatically traditional intellectuals).

The problem, of course, is that the displacement of the Latin American intellectual occurs not only 'from below' but also 'from the Right', so to speak, as neoliberal policies restructure the Latin American university and secondary education system, and revalorize what counts as significant academic or professional credentials in a way that devalues literary or humanistic knowledge. One can understand neo-Arielism in these terms as a resentment of and reaction *vis-à-vis* the authority of US culture and the pernicious effects of US hegemony on Latin American intellectual and cultural life, just as Rodó's *Ariel* was a model of resistance to Anglo-American values at the turn of the century.[9] But by rejecting explicitly or implicitly the validity of forms of sociocultural difference and antagonism based on subaltern positions in Latin America, the argument against 'studies' may also entail a kind of unconscious *blanqueamiento à la Sarmiento*, which misrepresents both the history and demographic heterogeniety of even those countries its claims to speak for.

By asserting against 'studies' the authority of a prior Latin American literary-intellectual tradition, and by identifying that tradition with the affirmation of national or regional identity against a foreign other, the resistance to 'studies' undercuts its own argument in a way and misrepresents its own unequal situation of enunciation. In order to defend the unity and integrity of individual Latin American nations and of Latin America itself against their re-subordination in the emerging global system, the critics of 'studies' are forced to put to the side some of the relations of exclusion and inclusion, subordination and domination that operate *within* the frame of those nations and what counts as their 'national' culture. But the questions posed by those relations – beginning with the fact that the most important social groups that the concept of the subaltern designates in Latin America are women, peasants, the urban poor, and black and indigenous groups – are crucial in rethinking and reformulating the political project of the Latin American left in conditions of globalization.

We arrive in this fashion at the following impasse. The new forms of theory emanating in the main from the US and Commonwealth academy – that is, what I am calling 'studies' – may find allies in Latin America, but, as in the case of Clay in *Soldiers of Fortune*, only at the expense of destabilizing (or, perhaps more to the point, being accused of destabilizing) a prior progressive-nationalist Latin American tradition of critical thought. 'Studies' runs the risk in this sense of constituting, unwillingly perhaps but effectively, a new kind of pan-Americanism in which metropolitan knowledge centers work out *their* problem in 'knowing' and representing Latin America. But the point of 'studies' in the first place was not to contribute to expanding US hegemony over Latin America but rather to open up 'from the left' a new understanding and possibility of solidarity with forms of popular agency and resistance *in* Latin America.

The prior Latin American tradition displaced in the name of egalitarianism and the 'popular' or the subaltern by 'studies' may reassert or reinvent itself against the influence of 'studies', but it does so at the expense of reaffirming exclusions and hierarchies of value and privilege that are internal to Latin America and that represent 'survivals' into modernity of colonial and postcolonial forms of racial, caste and gender discrimination. In this sense, the resistance to 'studies', although it is undertaken in the name of the project of the Latin American Left, creates a barrier to fulfilling one of the key goals of that very project, which is the democratization of the Latin American subject and field of culture.[10] That is because what is at stake in this project, as Ángel Rama began to intimate in his last book (*The Lettered City*, 1984; English translation 1996), is inverting the hierarchical relation between a cultural-political elite, constituted as such in part by its possession of the power of writing and literature, and the 'people', constituted as such in part by illiteracy or partial literacy or otherwise limited access to the forms of bourgeois high culture.

US Latino critical thought might seem to point to a way beyond this impasse, since it is located 'in between' the Latin American and the North American. But, it comes as no surprise that it is currently dominated by a version of the same problematic: if it seeks a genealogy in a prior tradition of progressive Latin America cultural thought, as José David Saldívar tried to do in his *Dialectics of Our America* (1991) then, like the Latin American neo-Arielistas, it reinscribes the authority of the lettered city and its characteristic high culture ideologemes: *mundonovismo* (New Worldism), *mestizaje* (miscegenation), *transculturación narrativa* (narrative transculturation), *neo-barroco* (Neo-Baroque) and now, perhaps, hybridity. If it gestures too much at assimilating the values of popular and mass culture, as Saldívar attempted in his latest book, *Border Matters* (1997) or Gustavo Pérez Firmat in *Life on the Hyphen* (1994), it risks becoming an essentially affirmative discourse of US 'exceptionalism' with little relevance to Latin America (in fact, some of the critics of 'studies' – I am thinking of Hugo Achugar, in particular – argue that despite the fact that the United States may become by the middle of this century the second largest Spanish-speaking nation in the Americas after Mexico, US Latino cultures are not part of Latin American culture; they respond rather to the urgencies of US culture and to the needs of Latin American immigrants to naturalize themselves as US subjects).

What is at issue here is not the 'correctness' of arguments on one side or the other of this debate, but the fact itself of a new polarization between North America and Latin America and the charged affective fields that it sets up. Recalling a point made by Marx in his Preface to *A Contribution to the Critique of Political Economy*, this polarization is an objective force, 'independent of our wills'. It is not subject to argument or dialogue, in other words, and that is why the debate about 'studies' and Latin America has been signally unproductive. The most promising road out of the impasse would be the development of a subalternist and multiculturalist critical and political practice 'from Latin America', sometimes in resonance with US-based academic projects like the now defunct Latin American Subaltern Studies Group, sometimes from grass-roots local and regional situations. I would point out here as possible examples of such a practice Jesús Martín-Barbero's work on mass culture in Colombia as a mode of what Walter Benjamin called 'the experience of the poor', Víctor Gaviria's attempt to create a new kind of neo-realist testimonial film, the work of Silvia Rivera Cusicanqui and the 'performances' of Mujeres Creando in Bolivia, Marcos and the Zapatistas in Mexico, the new discourses of pan-Mayan identity politics in Guatemala that in part Rigoberta Menchú's prestige helped bring into the open, the ongoing genealogical studies by Beatriz González, Josefina Ludmer, Graziella Nouzeilles, and others of the formation of Latin American elite culture, Ricardo Salvatore's reconstruction of the formation of the Argentine working class in the mid-nineteenth century, the new forms of rap emanating from urban Afro-working class neighborhoods in Cuba today ... But for each project of this sort that is visible to someone like myself, there are a hundred, a thousand others, at all levels of Latin American society and knowledge production, that are not, and it is precisely on that invisibility to the 'lettered city' that their identity and agency depend.

I think these projects represent the most promising line of Latin American social thought and practice today. The question remains, however: Is it still possible to do cultural criticism from the US academy 'on Latin America' that is in solidarity with the cause of Latin America? In other words, is a progressive form of Latin American studies still possible? Like Latino criticism, progressive US Latin Americanism also seems to be caught in a bind: to the extent that it is something like an academic version of the preferential option for the poor of Liberation Theology, the political and epistemological implications of 'studies' are to destabilize the field of area studies, including Latin American studies, as such. 'Studies' are rather concerned with a postmodernist 'convergence of temporalities' (I borrow this term from Ranajit Guha) between, for example, the historical dynamics of South Asia, Latin America, and Sub-Saharan Africa that cannot be expressed adequately within the framework of area studies or by the signifier of regional or national identity. As in the case of Clay and the Olanchan mine workers, there is a possibility of solidarity between 'studies' and the Latin American subaltern, but it may be at the expense of solidarity with the resistance of Latin America nation-states to US domination. On the other hand, the possibility of solidarity with Latin American intellectuals and with the agendas of Latin American regional and national interests – which are, to a significant if not exclusive extent, of course, the agendas of the ruling classes of Latin America – precludes the possibility of solidarity with the Latin American subaltern: that is, the workers, peasants, women, Indians, blacks, subproletarians, street children, prostitutes, *descamisados* (the poor, literally 'shirtless'), *rotos* (destroyed, literally, 'broken') who are subaltern in part precisely because they are not adequately represented by the values and agendas of the 'lettered city' and intellectual. Does the identification with a Latin American subaltern or popular subject preclude then the possibility of solidarity with Latin America? We should not be in too much of a hurry to say no, of course, it doesn't. Because, as Ileana Rodríguez puts it, 'our choice as intellectuals is to make a declaration either in support of statism (the nation-state and party politics) or on behalf of the subaltern. We chose the subaltern.'[11]

Speaking for myself, that is, from the position of a 'gringo bueno' who saw his critical work as being linked to solidarity politics, what all this means is that the terrain of Latin American studies, as a discourse formation 'on Latin America', has become slippery and ambiguous. During the Cold War, one could say that the terrain of Latin American studies was *contested*, but it was – or at least seemed – solid. To the extent that it was more than an ethical impulse, the possibility of solidarity rested on the recognition of a synergy between the fortunes of the Euro-North American Left and the Latin American Left, a sense that the fates of both were, for better or worse, connected. To deny the possibility or the desirability of solidarity, which is the point of coincidence between Stoll and neo-Arielism, amounts to saying that this is no longer the case, if, indeed, it was anything more than an ideological illusion in the first place (what Nicaraguans call, referring to the taste for Birkenstock sandals among solidarity workers during the revolution, 'sandalismo' or 'sandalism').

I am beginning to think that the 'gringo bueno' is a bit of a fool, like Don Quijote, remembering as I write this Foucault's remark about the embarrassment of speaking for others. I am sometimes tempted to say that the time has come for me to take a certain distance from Latin American studies, a distance that would be marked, as my national allegory suggests, by a reinvestment in my always problematic and always deferred identification with the United States. This would be a taking leave of Latin America, the place where I was born and raised, an *adiós*: hence the title of this chapter. But I was persuaded by friends that things could not be as simple as that. And that is so in part because of the very logic of wanting to move into a US frame, for if one wants to speak of the political and cultural future of the United States, then it is clear that Latin America has become, in a sense, part of that future. What would it mean to pose the question of the United States 'from Latin America' – that is, from my own investment in Latin America and Latin American radical politics and criticism – instead of, as I have been doing for so many years, posing the question of Latin America from the United States?[12]

Perhaps, though, what I define here as an impasse in Latin American criticism and in my own work is peculiar to my own generation: the generation of the sixties in both Latin America and the United States and Europe. The experience of that generation, it goes without saying, was framed by the rise and then the defeat of a very ambitious revolutionary project – a project that, in one way or another, we were connected to; and it is the name of that project that we argue (as I do here) on one side or another of the current debate. The nature of the impasse, which our own work has paradoxically contributed to produce (just as Don Quijote's actions come to imprison him in their consequences), plus the clear signs of mid-life crisis in our discourse, produce a kind of melancholy or *desengaño* that is not necessarily shared by our younger colleagues, who bring new energies, new experiences, and new imaginaries to the field. Perhaps the time has come for them to take the banner from our hands and to find some way of changing the terms of the debate.

NOTES

1. See, for example: Antonio Cornejo Polar (1997), Hugo Achugar (1997), Rossana Barragán and Silvia Rivera Cusicanqui (1999), Nelly Richard (1991), Beatriz Sarlo (1997a), Mabel Moraña (1997b).
2. Thus, for example, '[i]t was in the name of multiculturalism that *I, Rigoberta Menchú* entered the university reading lists' (Stoll, 1998, p. 243). Or, 'with postmodern critiques of representation and authority, many scholars are tempted to abandon the task of verification, especially when they construe the narrator as a victim worthy of their support' (ibid., p. 274).
3. Expressing a similar concern, José Klor de Alva (1992) has argued that the conditions of coloniality were radically different in Latin America than in Asia or Africa – so much so as to challenge the viability of the very concepts of the colonial and postcolonialism for Latin America.
4. It is interesting to note in this respect that the aversion to US-derived forms of 'studies' is not matched by the Latin American critics with a parallel rejection of Western European – and particularly German and French – theory: witness, for example, the extraordinary – and to me inexplicable – prestige of Habermas in contemporary Latin American social thought. Beatriz Sarlo, for example (in her 2000 essay), is at pains to differentiate British Cultural Studies – Raymond Williams and Stuart Hall – from the 'bad' US kind.
5. Achugar writes, for example:

   > The image of Latin America which is constructed within the framework of so-called Postcolonial Studies, appears to suggest that the place from which discourse emerges is not, or should not be, the nation but rather the colonial past ... The place from which Latin America is interpreted seems, on the one hand, to be via the historical experience of the *Commonwealth*, and, on the other hand, the agenda appears to that of the North-American Academy which is focused on the history of civil society. (1997, p. 381)

   Achugar echoes, without apparently being aware of it, a previous critique of US-based Latin American studies as a kind of neo-Orientalism by G. Williams; see Williams (1996).
6. In remarks at the LASA panel on Rigoberta Menchú at the 1999 LASA meeting in Miami, Florida.
7. Huntington recounts the following anecdote in this regard:

   > In 1991 a top adviser to President Carlos Salinas de Gotari described at length to me all the changes the Salinas government was making. When he finished, I remarked: 'That's most impressive. It seems to me that basically you want to change Mexico from a Latin American country into a North American country.' He looked at me with surprise and exclaimed: 'Exactly! That's precisely what we are trying to do, but of course we could never say so publicly.' (1993, p. 51)

8. Moreover, what complicates the assumption that one can speak 'from Latin America' unproblematically is the fact that Latin America's knowledge about itself now passes through the North American and European academy, in part because of the massive diaspora provoked first by the military dictatorships of the 1960s

and 1970s, and then the effects of neoliberal economic policies on the professional middle class in Latin America in the 1980s. This mediation is not only a question of geographic location: even a nominally oppositional project like that of Nelly Richard and her colleagues at the Universidad Arcis in Santiago, for example, is funded partly by the Rockefeller Foundation, whose strategic connection to US corporate interests goes without saying. For some of the ideas on Davis's novel, I am in debt to Jay Andrews (1999).

9   Michael Aronna's argument that Rodó's anti-egalitarian construction of the Ariel/Caliban binary involves not only the opposition to the United States, but also class anxiety and 'homosexual panic' about emerging trends in Latin American societies, seems pertinent in this respect. Aronna writes:

> Rodó retained the sexually degenerate characterization of Caliban, which is inextricably tied into the gendered, biological denigration of the indigenous populations ... The suggestion of Caliban's ethnic and sexual enervation is also indicated by intimations of sexual deviancy within democracy .... Rodó refers to egalitarian democracy as a *zoocracia* (zoocracy) .... Rodó's vision of Caliban also borrows from Ernest Renan's reactionary and racist version of *The Tempest, Caliban, suite de La Tempête* (1878). In this work Renan condemns the Commune of 1870 as the product of a congenitally and sexually degenerate working class which Rodó calls the 'entronización de Calibán' (deification of Caliban) .... The concept of an uncontrollable and unjust national uprising led by supposedly 'inferior' elements of society, the Calibans and their 'barbarie vencedora' (triumphant barbarism), clearly reproduces the nineteenth-century Latin American discourse of civilization versus barbarism. Rodó links his proposal for pan-American regeneration to a sensually charged yet rigidly chaste masculine enclave of learning and introspection .... Yet the therapeutic program proposed in *Ariel* is plagued by anxiety concerning the potential for excessive self-absorption and homosexuality within Rodó's idealized and repressed vision of male bonding. (Aronna, 1999, pp. 117–18, 134)

10 The paradox is that in the very same journal – I refer to Nelly Richard's *Revista de Critica Cultural* – in which someone like Alberto Moreiras evokes the idea of 'critical regionalism' as a modality of Latin American cultural agency in globalization, subaltern studies and US-style Cultural Studies are faulted for reducing the Latin American subject to the status of the exotic or the marginal. But that criticism of subaltern studies and cultural studies is itself, of course, a symptom of the very critical regionalism Moreiras is talking about.

11 Rodríguez (2000). Quoted from manuscript.

12 It is the signal virtue of Eve Cherniavsky's suggestive 1996 article in *boundary* to transfer the problematic of the subaltern to US history, which Cherniavsky represents as essentially a postcolonial one.

PART 2
Cultural icons

5

Contesting the cleric
The intellectual as icon in modern Spanish America
Nicola Miller

Icons are for worship, but they are also for solace. As representations of the divine in a worldly context, they characteristically emanate warmth and radiance, giving the beholder a sense of personal contact with the revered being. Iconic images can vary, but only within certain limits, because of the need for widespread recognition. Hence, one tends to see the *same* portrait – in conventional pose – of an iconic individual. An icon is not a passive symbol, but one which in itself is deemed to be a touchstone of transformative power. During the twentieth century, the conventional associations of the term icon have shifted from the Orthodox Church's gold-leafed paintings on wood of holy figures, to the pop icons emblematic of modern life, such as the telephone (symbolizing the possibility of disembodied communication over distance) or the Coca-Cola bottle (evoking US capitalism, with all its attendant problems and possibilities). Recently, the word icon has been most commonly used to refer to a computing command. Thus icons have shifted from being artefacts of veneration to objects of consumerism to vehicles of facilitation, in turn symbolic of values, desires and options. When individuals, rather than objects, come to be regarded as icons, all three elements tend to be at work in the process. It follows that, as the Orthodox craftsmen knew, the material from which an icon is made requires certain specific qualities.

This chapter focuses on six intellectuals who acquired iconic status in twentieth-century Spanish America, and aims to identify the features that secured them such a status.[1] My starting point is that all of them were secular intellectuals, who sought to challenge the cleric and his dogmatism. To pursue the metaphor of the icon and its religious sub-text, I have characterised them as follows: *the apostle* – José Martí (1853–95), Cuban poet, journalist and leader of Cuba's Second War of Independence (1895–8); *the curé of souls* – José Enrique Rodó (1871–1917), Uruguayan essayist, journalist and Congressman; *the prophet* – José Carlos Mariátegui (1895–1930), Peruvian essayist, journalist and founder of the Peruvian Communist Party; *the prodigal son* – Diego Rivera (1886–1957), Mexican muralist and revolutionary militant; *the mystic* – Gabriela Mistral (1889–1957), Chilean poet, teacher and human rights campaigner; and *the scribe* – Gabriel García Márquez (b. 1928), Colombian novelist, journalist and human rights activist. What was it about these particular intellectuals that meant they became cultural icons rather than just admired creative figures? What does the process of making icons out of intellectuals tell us about the cultural history of Spanish America? I will discuss each intellectual in turn before drawing some general conclusions.

JOSÉ MARTÍ: THE APOSTLE (1853–95)

Martí was the first intellectual to be widely known throughout the Latin American region during his lifetime, which was indicative of the early impact of socio-economic modernisation upon conditions of cultural production. The syndication of newspaper articles, for example, was just beginning in the Americas during the 1880s. From his base in New York, Martí was a prolific journalist who wrote on every topic from the iniquities of Spanish colonialism to Oscar Wilde's poor taste in ties. He became best known for his analyses of the United States and the imperial threat it posed to Latin America. With hindsight, critics have tended to focus on Martí's political ideas, but at the time his stature as an intellectual rested mainly on his brilliant facility with the Spanish language, especially as demonstrated in his poetry. *Versos libres* (Free Verses) (1878–82) and, above all, *Versos sencillos* (Simple Verses) (1891) were acclaimed as landmarks in Spanish American verse, indicating – as their titles suggest – new possibilities of simplicity, authenticity and freedom from convention. His books of poems and short stories for children, *Ismaelillo* (1882), originally written for his own son, and *La edad de oro* (The Golden Age) (1889), inscribed 'for the children of America', won him a popular audience at the time and are still staple fare for Cuban children.

Martí's cause was Cuban independence, and he gave his life for it. He became politically active in his mid-teens, during the First War of Independence (1868–78). He continued his campaign through years of intermittent exile, founded the Cuban Revolutionary Party in 1891 and worked tirelessly to create the conditions that made possible the launching of a Second War of Independence in 1895. He famously rode a white horse and was baptized 'our apostle' by his followers. Although convinced of the need to fight for Cuba's independence, his image was always of a man of peace – an 'hombre flor' (man of flowers) amidst 'hombres mauser' (men with Mausers), as Gabriela Mistral put it. His martyrdom in battle in the very early stages of the war deprived Cuba of the man who would almost certainly have been the first president of any genuinely independent republic. However, as Martí had feared, although Cuba became nominally independent in 1902, Spanish colonial rule was rapidly replaced by the neo-colonial domination of the

United States. During the 1920s, when the disadvantages of Cuba's abject state of compromised sovereignty became all too manifest, nationalists across the political spectrum turned to Martí as an icon of the ideals that had been betrayed. From that point on, his life and work were plundered by any Cubans in public life who wanted to establish their nationalist credentials, and so extensive were his writings that most who cared to look could find a quotation that seemed to support their position. From 1940 onwards the Cuban state was active in promoting the study and dissemination of Martí's works. On the centenary of his birth, in 1953, it was evident that Martí was well established as *the* founding father of the nation. Other heroes and martyrs of the independence wars are ritually cited, notably Antonio Maceo and Máximo Gómez, but Martí's stature in the Cuban pantheon is unique and unrivalled to this day. Fidel Castro claimed Martí as the intellectual author of the Cuban Revolution, and anyone who has visited Cuba since the revolution of 1959 will have observed that most of the quotations emblazoned as slogans on billboards and buildings are not from Marx, Lenin, Castro or even Che Guevara, but from Martí. His image is also ubiquitous. A song circulating from about 1900, and still sung today (Cabrera Infante, 1997, p. 19), conveys how he is regarded by many Cubans:

> Martí should not have died
> If Martí had not died,
> A very different song would be sung,
> The country would be saved
> And Cuba would be happy.
> Martí should not have died,
> Alas, that he died!

Martí is identified above all with the ideal of independence, which he saw as going far beyond the basic political sovereignty of freedom from colonial rule to include economic and cultural autonomy. He is famous for the prescience of his critique of the consequences of rising US power. As early as 1889, when US Secretary of State James Blaine summoned the leaders of Latin America to a conference in Washington (the forerunner of the Pan-American Union), Martí insisted that the United States did not understand Latin America and could only do it harm. He argued for regional integration to counter the US threat, which he saw as both economic and cultural. A landmark essay, effectively a declaration of cultural independence, was 'Our America' (1891), in which he argued that Latin American countries must stop unthinkingly trying to imitate foreign models, start valuing their own people, and find their own path to development. Martí defied the prevalent ethos of racial pessimism to argue that if only Spanish Americans would ignore the 'sickly intellectuals' who insisted on dividing humankind into specious races, then the region could build a great future. He advocated what historians now call civic nationalism for

Cuba, namely a national identity built upon a shared sense of rights and duties, not one based on ethnicity. It is not difficult to see how he became the ultimate symbol of Cuban national unity and national potential.

JOSÉ ENRIQUE RODÓ: THE CURE OF SOULS (1871–1917)

Rodó is probably the most faded of our six icons. His name has less resonance today than the others, but it is hard to overestimate his influence during the first three decades of the twentieth century, when he was widely referred to as the *maestro* (teacher, mentor) of America. His house became the cultural centre of Uruguay, and his funeral – attended by the president – saw large public demonstrations of mourning. His public life was not heroic in the sense that Martí's was, but despite being temperamentally unsuited to the machinations of political life, he served for many years as a Congressional Deputy, dedicating himself to reformist causes, such as labour legislation, education, freedom of the press, university autonomy, and constitutional reform. His most sustained campaign, upon which his political career foundered, was to end the domination of Uruguay by a clique and to establish the basis for meritocracy. Rodó argued for direct election of the president and for proportional representation. Thus, although he was certainly no radical, nor was he the conservative that he is often claimed to be.

Rodó's fame was based on the instant success of his essay *Ariel* (1900), which reworked *The Tempest* to call for a cultural regeneration of Spanish America by educated youth through an emphasis on spirit (represented by the figure of Ariel). The essay did not, as is often alleged, advocate the subordination of reason to spirit, but argued instead for a broader conception of reason than is allowed by instrumentalism (the view that the success of an idea is more important than either its truth or its ethics). For Rodó, spirit included both reason and feeling; it referred to the life of the mind against irrationality and instinct. *Ariel* was primarily a protest against the spread into Spanish America of 'corrupting commercialism' (Rodó, 1957, p. 195), but it was received, despite Rodó's protestations to the contrary, as a critique of the United States as the materialistic, barbaric Caliban. Although it is true that the text did not explicitly link the United States with Caliban, it did so by implication, and Rodó certainly propagated stereotypes about both the United States and Spanish America. Whatever Rodó's intentions, *Ariel* undoubtedly became famous as a symbol of Spanish American humanistic resistance against the scientifically-oriented United States. Carlos Fuentes recalled student debates in which *Ariel* was ritually quoted (Rodó, 1988, p. 20). *Arielismo* was dominant among student communities for the next three decades, with even those who rejected its emphasis on spirituality being influenced by its call to take up metaphorical arms in the battle to defend Spanish America's distinctive culture. During the 1940s detractors emerged, accusing Rodó of intellectual dilettantism, aestheticism, sociological bankruptcy and elitism, but such arguments are over-simplifications and have not gone unchallenged. Carlos Fuentes captured the ambivalence of Rodó's legacy when he recently characterized him as: 'Irritating, insufferable, admirable, stimulating, disappointing Rodó: our Uruguayan uncle' (Rodó, 1988, p. 28). Significantly, Fuentes also saw in Rodó's work the basis of an argument for civil society that remained relevant in the 1990s.

There are two key ideas for which Rodó is remembered. First, he asserted the cultural distinctiveness of the region on the basis of its Latinity, arguing that it was the repository of the great humanist tradition, derived from Ancient Greek and Rome, that had become corrupted in Europe. Notoriously, he did not mention 'Latin' America's indigenous peoples, for which he has justly been criticised. Nor did he discuss key aspects of the Spanish tradition, such as the baroque, concentrating instead on the impact of liberalism and romanticism. Nevertheless, Rodó's elaboration of a cultural specificity based on a greater appreciation of all things spiritual was crucial to Latin American intellectuals' sense of increasing cultural independence. Second, his vision of young intellectuals as a regenerative force contributed to the development of the University Reform Movement, which arose initially in Argentina in 1918 in rebellion against outdated curricula and teaching methods. It spread to many other Latin American countries, eventually achieving autonomy and a degree of democratic accountability in universities, and making them important sites of political activism throughout the region.

JOSÉ CARLOS MARIÁTEGUI: THE PROPHET (1895–1930)

Mariátegui's existence has been described by a later Peruvian writer as 'an invitation to the heroic life' (Scorza, 1956, p. 11). Constantly plagued by poor health – he was crippled in an accident as a boy, and had his leg amputated in 1924 – he died aged only 34 in 1930. Mariátegui wrote prolifically on a wide range of political and cultural issues, but his reputation was based mainly upon his Marxist-informed and compellingly written analysis of Peruvian history and socio-economic conditions, *Seven Interpretive Essays on Peruvian Reality* (1928). He started work as a journalist aged 15, rapidly becoming involved in the worker and student struggles that arose in response to the disastrous economic impact of the First World War on Peru. To remove him from the scene, in 1919 the Peruvian government offered him a scholarship to Europe, where he met many of the leading left-wing thinkers. Returning to Peru in 1923, he became involved in the American Popular Revolutionary Alliance (APRA) founded by his fellow-Marxist Victor Raúl Haya de la Torre. After an acrimonious public debate with Haya de la Torre about how best to apply Marxist theory to Peruvian reality, Mariátegui broke away from APRA and founded the Peruvian Communist Party in 1928. He also put great energy into his periodical, *Amauta* (1926 to 1930), which was designed to be a beacon of regeneration for the youth of Latin America. Here we can see the influence of Rodó even on somebody whose political persuasions were far more radical. An 'amauta' was an Inca sage, and Mariátegui saw his cultural review – which ranged widely from literature to film, visual art and psychoanalysis – as the forum for a new ideological space in which to create a revolutionary consciousness informed by both local and universal thought. The magazine effectively displaced the University of San Marcos as the cultural centre of Peru in the late 1920s. As a result of these activities, he was imprisoned in 1927 and *Amauta* was twice closed by the state authorities. Unlike some other intellectuals who professed Marxism, Mariátegui had an extensive network of contacts among workers and peasants, who were regular visitors to his home. His writings were widely read and discussed within popular organizations; his death notices read as if he had died heroically in military combat; and his funeral was attended by thousands of workers.

Mariátegui's version of Marxism – challenging the revolutionary model promoted by the Moscow-based Communist International (Comintern) – had five main tenets, all of which remained influential in the thinking of the Latin American Left long after his death. First, he refuted the Comintern's view of Latin America as a feudalist economy. On the contrary, he argued, imperialism had brought capitalist development, albeit distorted. Whereas the Comintern advocated a democratic-bourgeois revolution to introduce the capitalist system that would ultimately, according to the Marxist laws of history, be overthrown by the proletariat, Mariátegui argued that the revolution in Latin America had to be immediately and fully socialist, attacking both the domestic elites and their imperialist backers. Second, he insisted that the indigenous peasantry of Peru should be regarded not as a separate race, as the Comintern was wont to do, but as the majority of the oppressed masses who would constitute the basis of a socialist Peru. His strategy for revolution entailed unity between workers and peasants, in contrast to the Comintern's emphasis on the proletariat alone. Third, he also rejected any alliance with the so-called national bourgeoisie, which had been identified as crucial to Latin American revolution by the Marxist-inspired but increasingly reformist APRA. Mariátegui maintained that the class interests of the Latin American bourgeoisie as property-owners would always prevail over any nationalist loyalties. He was ultimately proved correct, in that while the role of the national bourgeoisie was indeed a key factor in the removal of the existing dictatorships both in Cuba during the late 1950s and in Nicaragua two decades later, when it came to implementing revolutionary policies, most of them did retreat into opposition. Fourth, Mariátegui believed in the need for what he called a 'revolutionary myth' – a unifying idea (developed from the French anarchist thinker Georges Sorel) that would bring all sectors of the masses together in commitment to the process. He did not see revolution only or even primarily in material terms, stating that a revolution was religious in the sense that it involved the transformation of humankind. He argued that receptivity to revolutionary ideas was a matter of spiritual and emotional preparedness as much as intellectual conversion; the masses were entitled not only to bread but also to beauty. It followed that culture mattered, and that intellectuals had an important role to play in the revolution. Fifth, his preferred version of a revolutionary myth was nationalism, and Mariátegui went further than most Marxist thinkers anywhere in integrating nationalism into a Marxist framework, and thereby overcoming the perceived contradiction between national and class loyalties that proved so disastrous for many left-wing movements, both in Latin America and elsewhere. In keeping with the ideas outlined above, Mariátegui's version of Peruvian nationalism was based on the indigenous people – he challenged the view of the previous generation of intellectuals that the cultural unity of the nation had to be sought in its colonial past.

Mariátegui's immediate political impact was not great, particularly in the context of an authoritarian clampdown in Peru soon after his death. But his adaptation of Marxism to a Latin American context came to seem increasingly relevant by the 1950s, as the orthodox Communist Parties lost prestige and plausibility. He has been hailed as the intellectual precursor of what Cuban revolutionaries called Latin America's Second Revolution (for economic independence to complement political sovereignty) of the 1960s. In the wake of the failure of attempts to emulate the Cuban experience, his name was harnessed by one of the most successful guerrilla organisations that Latin America has ever seen, Peru's Shining Path, the full name of which was The Communist Party of Peru by the Shining Path of José Carlos Mariátegui. At its height, Shining Path was active in a majority of Peru's provinces, and was capable of bringing large areas of the country to a standstill. It is unlikely that Mariátegui would have approved either of their ideology (strongly Maoist-influenced) or their methods (authoritarian and intimidatory). What is significant for our purposes, however, is that they invoked his name as a crucial source of nationalist and revolutionary legitimacy.

DIEGO RIVERA: THE PRODIGAL SON (1886–1957)

Diego Rivera is the first of our examples whose reputation extended beyond Latin America to Europe and the United States. Rivera attracted international attention to Mexico with his magnificent, immense murals, depicting Mexican history as an epic in which the ordinary people became heroes alongside the leaders of the various liberation struggles. The extraordinary grandeur of conception and skill of execution behind these works still command a huge public for Rivera today. He was himself larger than life, and notorious for his tall tales. His propensity to exaggerate was called 'mythomania' by his third wife, the painter Frida Kahlo, but it became another prop to his inexhaustible creativity. In his autobiography, dictated during the decade before he died, we can see Rivera painting his life on a vast canvas – in effect, creating his own auto-icon. In the process, he revealed many of the cultural mores of his time and circumstances.

He represented himself first and foremost as a prodigy, who drew compulsively on any surface he came across from as young as he could remember. In order to stop the whole house being covered with his scribbles, claimed Rivera, his father set aside a room for him, with black canvas on the walls, where he made his first 'murals'. Thus he established art as his vocation. He was also prodigious – in energy, talent, ambition, romance and capacity to inspire devotion. Four wives, in statements at the end of the book, concurred that they did not regret their time with him, despite not only his continuous infidelity but also his at times cavalier, not to say callous, disregard for their feelings – for example, going out carousing while his first wife desperately tried to save their baby son from his eventual death. And Rivera was prodigal – both in the literal sense of being incapable of managing money effectively, and in the metaphorical sense of repeatedly squandering the cultural capital that he built up with the Mexican socio-political establishment, only to repent and make some conciliatory gesture designed to re-emphasise his commitment to the Mexican Revolution.

Rivera's identification with Mexico (despite long periods spent in Europe and the United States) was a crucial prop to his image. He dated his intimate connection with Mexico's indigenous people back to his relationship with an Indian nurse. He was sickly as an infant, and after the death of his twin brother he was sent to live with his nurse, Antonia, in the mountains of Sierra, with a goat to supply him with fresh milk and companionship. There he spent two apparently idyllic years, which made him feel closer to Antonia than to his mother. As he grew up, he maintained, he found indigenous Mexican culture far more sympathetic than European culture. Evoking his early excitement at discovering pre-conquest Mexican art, he claimed that the more he studied European art forms, the less he liked them. Later, after several years in Paris, he rejected Cubism for having 'little to do with real life' and being 'too technical, fixed, and restricted for what I wanted to say' (Rivera, 1960, pp. 58, 68). His return to Mexico in 1921 'produced an aesthetic exhilaration', he said, as if he were 'being born anew, born into a new world' (ibid., p. 72). The route to an authentically popular art – an art of the people – lay, he insisted, in rooting the universal in the local. At the end of his life, he left his possessions, including many of his works, to the Mexican people.

In terms of political commitments, Rivera was active from an early age. He told of his involvement in an abortive plot to assassinate the dictator Porfirio Díaz in November 1910; subsequently, he spent a short time with revolutionary peasant leader Emiliano Zapata and his soldiers. He depicted himself as repeatedly defying political authority, refusing to take orders from anybody, whether it was the Mexican Communist Party (from which he was expelled), Stalin, Trotsky, with whom he quarrelled over politics, or the Mexican state. In practice, he arrived at a somewhat tempestuous *modus vivendi* with the governing PRI (Institutionalized Party of the Revolution).

One aspect of Rivera's outlook that fitted well with the ideology of the Revolution, if not always its practice, was anti-clericalism. He told a fabulous anecdote to establish the strength of his feeling on that issue. On his first visit to a church at the age of six, having been smuggled there by a pious great-aunt without his Liberal father's knowledge, he experienced instant 'revulsion' (Rivera, 1991, p. 5). He told of being suddenly possessed by rage, running up the steps of the altar and denouncing the worshippers as idiots; they in turn began to scream that he was a child of Satan. The infant Rivera then defied the priest, challenging him to invoke the Virgin Mary to strike him down with lightning. That evening, a group of Liberal Party veterans came to invite the boy to join them, claiming that his defence of freedom of speech – within the very walls of the Church itself – outdid any of theirs. As an adult, Rivera repeatedly probed the boundaries of religious tolerance. Several of his murals were denounced as sacrilegious, most notably 'A Sunday in Alameda Park', in the Hotel del Prado, with its provocative quotation (from nineteenth-century Liberal reformer Ignacio Ramírez): 'God does not exist'. Rivera was not actually opposed to popular religiosity – in fact, he saw it as one of the great strengths of Latin American culture (see his San Francisco mural 'Marriage of the Artistic Expression of the North and South on This Continent'). Some years later, he changed the offending quotation, noting that 90 per cent of his fellow Mexicans were Catholic, but he could never resist the temptation to shock the bourgeoisie.

The most notorious instance of that kind of audacity was his introduction of an image of Lenin into a mural in Radio City, Detroit, commissioned by Nelson Rockefeller. Rivera's Lenin was depicted clasping the hands of a black American and a white Russian soldier/worker, which Rivera said represented what would be the necessary alliance of the USA and the USSR to defeat fascism. After Rivera had refused Rockefeller's request that Lenin's face be painted out, he was ordered to stop work and paid off. The mural was later destroyed, despite Rockefeller's assurances that it would not be, by smashing the wall, even though experts had suggested how to remove the mural without damaging either it or the wall. Rivera's version of this incident, which was recounted in his autobiography under the title, 'Holocaust in Rockefeller Center', gave ample substance to the claim that he always defended creative integrity against the forces of censorship, at home or abroad. Thus he cast himself as the irreverent revolutionary, challenging the imperialist bourgeois pieties, allowing a little of his glamour to rub off on the cautiously reformist Mexican state, and representing Mexico both to the Mexicans themselves and to a world audience (see Rivera, 1937).

GABRIELA MISTRAL: THE MYSTIC (1889–1957)

Mistral offers a fascinating case study of the creation of a female cultural icon in Latin America. Unlike the male figures discussed here, who are portrayed as inherently iconoclastic, her image is conservative – to the extent that the Pinochet dictatorship had no qualms about imprinting it on the highest-denomination Chilean banknote. Her haunting and distinctive poems were known throughout Latin America by the early 1920s, and she also acquired an international reputation through being the first Latin American writer to be awarded the Nobel Prize for Literature in 1945. Unlike Rivera's international fame, however, Mistral's has not endured: few people outside Spanish America, indeed probably outside Chile, would be aware of her work today, although there have been recent translations into English for the US market. Often compared to the sixteenth-century Spanish nun and mystic Saint Teresa of Avila, Mistral was conventionally invoked as a passive icon of virtue – 'the divine Gabriela' – rather than a symbol of social change. She was regarded as anti-intellectual, concerned not with ideas but with emotions, spirituality and the natural world. For nationalists, she was a mystical earth-mother who exuded the spirit of Chile and of Latin America. She was eulogised as the 'Mother of America'; on the presentation of an honorary doctorate to her at the University of Chile in 1954, it was declared: 'You always loved the earth and all its creatures, and you became a mother even to the frozen wastes of Patagonia' (Oyarzún, 1967, p. 75). The Mother of America tag was strengthened by her lullabies and poems for children, many of which Chilean children still learn by heart, and also by her public statements in support of motherhood – actual or metaphorical – as woman's true vocation. She was also known as the *Maestra* (teacher) of America, because of her work as a schoolteacher in Chile and post-revolutionary Mexico (1922–24). This combined figure of the mother/school-teacher served the Chilean state well in that it symbolized both conservative social values and the entrance of women into the workforce in service professions. Above all, Mistral has been officially deployed as a symbol of national and continental unity, of continuity in the face of change.

This conservative image was hegemonic until the 1980s, since when it has been challenged and Mistral reinterpreted – not least by a leading Chilean Communist – as an icon of anti-imperialism, Indo-Americanism and commitment to social reform (Teitelboim, 1991). Her biography has now become a site of highly charged cultural contestation. Some feminist critics have attacked her for being an anti-intellectual traditionalist; others have suggested that she employed a series of subtle strategies to carve out the maximum possible space in which to operate in the patriarchal cultural sphere of early twentieth-century Latin America. The relatively little that we know about her life tells a story that is far more divergent from her iconic image than is the case with the male examples analysed here. This woman who was supposed to be so provincial spent most of her life moving in international diplomatic and cultural circles, where she was highly respected for the range of her erudition, her poetic gifts and her political commitment. She was born and grew up in a small village in northern Chile, but her early assumption of the pseudonym Gabriela Mistral, an amalgam from the Italian poet Gabriele d'Annunzio and the Provençal poet Frédéric Mistral, suggests that the young Lucila Godoy de Alcayaga had relatively sophisticated reading tastes. The *Maestra* of America gave up school-teaching as soon as she could, and spent most of the rest of her life in Europe, Brazil or the United States as a roving Chilean consul. During these years, the supposedly apolitical Mistral was deeply involved in a broad variety of social and political causes apart from the educational reform with which she is conventionally associated. She campaigned on behalf of the Nicaraguan anti-imperialist guerrilla leader Augusto Sandino and in favour of Spanish Republicanism; she was active against Chilean neutrality in the Second World War and in the last months of her life drafted a petition against the Soviet invasion of Hungary. She championed social causes, especially agrarian reform and Indian rights, and was active on behalf of intellectual freedom, defending José Vasconcelos, Pablo Neruda, Thomas Mann and Victoria Ocampo, to name only the most famous, from political persecution.

Mistral is an elusive and contradictory figure. The great champion of motherhood had no children, and never married. Two youthful heterosexual love affairs have come to light, but some biographers claim that she was a lesbian for most of her life. She was ambivalent about the feminist movement, largely because of its middle-class character. It is safe to say that she was more interested in class issues than gender ones, but her mode of life demonstrates a refusal to conform to the gender role her society ascribed to her, notwithstanding her public reiteration of conventional pieties. Religiosity was one constant feature in her outlook, but it assumed a wide variety of forms apart from Catholicism, including theosophy, Buddhism, Judaism and Protestantism. Christian Democracy came closest to her political views, although she never joined the movement. The woman regarded as the essence of Chilean-ness spent as little time as possible in her own country once she had any choice in the matter, and had some bitter things to say about Chilean society. She did write about her country, but almost exclusively about the landscape not the people (compare Neruda's work). Her posthumously published *Poema de Chile* (Poem on Chile) (1967) was peopled only by a female narrator in the form of a spirit, who travels through the landscape with a small Indian boy. She was, however, immensely popular in Chile: when she eventually returned for a visit in 1954 after an absence of 16 years, she found a crowd of 100,000 people awaiting her at the central station in Santiago. We still have insufficient biographical information to resolve the tensions and contradictions identified above. All that can be concluded at present is that the recent debates about the connotations of her iconic status – was she a reactionary or a rebel? – are revealing about the still-troubled relationship between women and intellectuality in Chile and beyond.

GABRIEL GARCÍA MÁRQUEZ: THE SCRIBE (b. 1928)

Referred to familiarly and affectionately in Latin America as 'Gabo', García Márquez is the only one of the figures discussed here who has become a cultural icon not only in Latin America but also throughout much of the world. Starting with *One Hundred Years of Solitude* (1967), now widely thought of as the classic novel of the Latin American literary 'boom' of the 1960s, García Márquez has written a succession of novels that have achieved both critical and popular success: *The Autumn of the Patriarch* (1976), *Love in the Time of Cholera* (1988), and *The General in His Labyrinth* (1989). Not only are his books widely translated and sold, but he has evidently been influential on such famous novelists as Toni Morrison, Alice Walker and Salman Rushdie. One important point to bear in mind, however, is that the features that contribute to his iconic status internationally are not necessarily the same as those that maintain it in Latin America. Internationally, at least among intellectuals, he is known as the Latin American writer who revived the novel (a genre supposedly 'exhausted' by James Joyce), as the great master of magical realism, and as the exponent of the themes of Latin American identity such as fantasy, utopia and solitude. In other words, there is an element of exoticism in the way that he is regarded as a symbol of Latin American creativity.

Within Latin America, however, the perception is very different. García Márquez has often stated that he dislikes the term 'fantasy' being applied to his work; he sees himself as a realist, arguing that what he represents is the vividness of everyday experience in Latin America, with all its resilience, adventurousness, humour, irony, irreverence, exaggeration and delight in what is larger than life. It is indeed the case that García Márquez is loved in Latin America not for his descriptions of suffering, oppression or injustice, which, as he himself has noted, Latin Americans know more than enough about from their daily lives, but for his celebration of the social and family solidarities which constitute the opposite of solitude and which, for all their eccentricities, make life possible, bearable and often enjoyable. He is also appreciated for his sheer narrative drive – the capacity to tell a story around the perennial themes of love and loss, time and death. So while the literary critics acclaim him as Rabelaisian, seeing the village of Macondo (the setting for several of his novels) as a total metaphor for Colombia and, in turn, for Latin America, ordinary readers love him for having written a readable, accessible epic which captures the peculiarities of their own experience. As Carlos Fuentes put it, in *One Hundred Years of Solitude* there is 'a joyous rediscovery of identity ..., an instant reflex by which we are presented, in the genealogies of Macondo, to our grandmas, our sweethearts, our brothers and sisters, our nursemaids' (1988, p. 190).

García Márquez has often stated in interviews that he will never forget that he is only the son of a telegraph operator from Aracataca, near the Colombian coast. He has used his celebrity status to pursue a series of left-wing causes, including support for the Cuban and Nicaraguan Revolutions, activism against the human rights violations of the Southern Cone military dictatorships, and involvement in Panama's campaign in the mid-1970s to restore sovereignty over the Canal Zone. He has talked about his love of popular Latin American music, directed films and written soap operas. His literary fame notwithstanding, he has maintained his journalism as a way of being in touch with real life. When he won the Nobel Prize for Literature in 1982, the Colombian President declared that all of Colombia would go with him to receive the award, and a passer-by, seeing him struggling to start his car engine, cheerfully observed that the only thing he was good for was winning the Nobel Prize.

CONCLUSION

Each of these six cultural icons transcends history and national circumstance to symbolize a key Spanish American ideal: Martí – independence; Rodó – spirituality; Mariátegui – revolution; Rivera – epic artistry; Mistral – education; García Márquez – marvellous reality. What made this possible? All of them, on the basis of technical mastery, creative originality and cultural range, have developed reputations not only beyond their national borders, which is true of many Latin American intellectuals, but also beyond an educated elite. All in their lifetimes became objects of popular devotion, and all created works that came to be regarded as in some sense representative of the views or experiences of the majority of Latin Americans. It is no coincidence that these six intellectuals were from similar backgrounds, namely the socially precarious middle sectors; and they were further marginalized by choosing the profession of artist or writer. Furthermore, none of these figures had an institutional base for their intellectual activities in the academy. Their reputations derived from free exercise of the creative process; their products were unstained by the resin of convention – artistic or social. A lack of respect for established authority – religious, political or cultural – distinguishes all their works. All were effectively autodidacts, their formal academic training either abandoned (Martí, Rodó, Rivera and García Márquez) or never even begun (Mariátegui and Mistral). Their creative imaginations were thus free to range beyond the constraints of academicism, a term of opprobrium in virtually every Latin American country because of its association with Spanish scholasticism. Such a degree of experimental creativity was a necessary prerequisite to achieving the originality to transcend foreign models, and to create works with widespread appeal.

All six identified themselves strongly with Spanish America, and were optimistic about its cultural prospects. All argued that the region had distinctive qualities to offer the rest of the world, particularly in opposition to the positivism, materialism and pragmatism that had become dominant in the United States. In a variety of ways, all sought to challenge the US and European idea that Cartesian reason alone was sufficient to apprehend reality, arguing that reason needed to be complemented by other qualities, such as spirit, feeling or intuition. All sought to use language (visual language, in Rivera's case) in new ways. A final important factor is the character of the life beyond the work. Each of the six committed their lives to the furtherance of social justice and humanitarian causes. The degree and nature of their political commitments varied, but the key common factor is their concern to identify and sympathise with their fellow human beings, to be close to the masses. Although the intellectual's life is often represented as heroic in Spanish America, the emphasis is on dedication to a cause and self-sacrifice rather than on derring-do. That the life be lived nobly, however, is as important in the making of icons as creative achievements – one of the most frequently encountered claims in paeans of praise to these iconic figures is that their lives were as great as their art. In all these cases, then, the combination of exceptional creativity and committed authenticity enabled these intellectuals to reconcile the local and the universal, thereby becoming perceived as representatives of their people both at home and abroad. In the future, as the majority of people gain more opportunities to represent themselves, it is less likely that intellectuals, however defined, will be turned into cultural icons. This may not be a bad thing. There are, of course, problems that arise from making icons out of intellectuals, not least that their ideas tend to be reduced to one-dimensional form. Icons are touchstones of what Erwin Panofsky called 'intrinsic meaning': they are telling about the cultural concerns of any particular moment in history, but they do not allow for tension, conflict or debate about those concerns.

NOTE

1   Some would argue that Diego Rivera (a visual artist not a writer or political thinker) was not an intellectual, and many would not refer to Gabriela Mistral as one (arguably, gender precluded her). My view is that taking into account how intellectuals are defined in the Latin American context, both Rivera and Mistral do qualify. But the main purpose of this chapter is to identify what made a select few Spanish American writers/artists into cultural icons, not what made them intellectuals (for a discussion of that issue, see Miller, 1999).

6

Cultural myths and Chicana literature
A field in dispute
María Cristina Pons

> Culture is a field in dispute that in certain historical moments acknowledges, or recognizes, unifying axes, whether these are ethnic or social in nature, utopias or simply guiding ideas. In this way, culture generates identities, a sense of belonging, roots, origin and destiny, past and future. (Bernardo Subercaseaux)

Myth and literature have always been related, in some way. According to Borges, myth is in the beginning of literature, as well as in the end. Yet, the notion of myth cannot be considered as merely narrative. In a very real sense, mythology is a symbolic language. It is a way to comprehend ourselves and the world, or of ordering our experience. Our basic social faiths and verities, says Dardel, are grounded in myth: 'myth is the secret spring of our vision of the world, of our devotion, of our dearest notions' (1965, p. 50). Far from belonging to a given historical past, to archaic societies, or the world of religions, the world we understand, and deeply care about is re-mythicized every day (Labourdette, 1987, p. 71).

Myths belong to the symbolic universe of any given culture and, as such, still continue to appear to us as a highly complex reality with an unquestionable presence in the cultural dimension of any human group. Myths and myth-making reach into all aspects of life from the more quotidian to the most sacred; from politics and religion, to the arts and literature; in short, to all that constitutes the culture, memory and identity of a given social group. In this sense, and following perhaps more closely the line of thinking of Durkheim (for whom society rather than nature is the model for myths), the mythical universe of a culture could be seen as the symbolic representation of the social. As such, it is a great codifier of what is meaningful in the social and cultural life of a group.

In this study, then, I will consider myths as a privileged site reflecting the cultural dynamics, historical changes and struggles in identity construction of different social groups. I will focus on Chicana/o culture, giving particular attention to the relationship between myth and literature as two powerful vehicles in the constitution of identities, a central challenge at the turn of the century within the context of globalization and multiculturalism, which raises the question of the role of intellectuals and/or writers as critical public voices in the interpretation of history and reality, and in the production of meaning. Since colonial times, and particularly since independence, literature and intellectuals in Latin America have played a crucial role in creating and developing what could be considered the 'foundational myths' or 'guiding fictions', as Shumway (1991, pp. xi–xii) has called them: 'Nations need narrations', master narratives, he states, that remember (and also invent) an origin, a history, a pantheon of heroes, in order to create an identity and a sense of belonging. Furthermore, he suggests that the foundational myths and master narratives at the time of independence and frontier expansion were biblical, Apocalyptic narratives, where the sense of a redemptive mission was a strong guiding idea (ibid., pp. 1–2).

In what follows I propose to discuss: (a) the process of construction/deconstruction of foundational myths as a reflection of the dynamics of Chicana/o culture; and (b) how writings by Chicanas lead us to reconsider the relationship between myth and literature. More specifically, to what extent the broader cultural conditions of today authorize not apocalyptic narratives but new visions of chaos. In its positive connotation, chaos refers to the myth of creation, and takes the form of a challenge to the established security, certainties, hierarchies, limits and conformity of a given social or cultural order. At the heart of the transvaluation of chaos to its positive connotation is also the development of the theory of relativity, which enabled chaos to be conceived of as an inexhaustible ocean of possibilities rather than as a void signifying absence (Hayles, 1990, p. 8). With this in mind, I will concentrate my discussion around two key cultural tropes and myths that constitute part of the Chicana/o symbolic world: Aztlán and *la raza cósmica* (the cosmic race).

AZTLÁN AND *LA RAZA CÓSMICA*: TWO SIDES OF THE SAME COIN

The permanence and significance of the notion of Aztlán are without doubt a key cultural icon within the symbolic imaginary of Chicana/o experience. Equally undeniable are the role and influence the Mexican Revolution has had on Chicana/o experiences and culture. Since these issues have been broadly addressed by Chicana/o scholars, I will draw on some of their studies to offer a minimum frame of reference and a point of departure for my discussion, as well as to give an indication of the role Chicana/o intellectuals play in reflecting on their culture.

Aztlán, known as the mythical homeland of the Mexicas, was recuperated by Chicano nationalism as the symbolic place of the 'Chicano nation'. The legendary Aztlán was presumably located in what is today the US Southwest, part of the territory ceded by Mexico in 1848 after the Mexican-American war. Thus, the invocation of links to Pre-Columbian indigenous ancestry (specifically of Aztec origins), enhanced 'the relationship between Chicano cultural identity and the claim to a land that was home prior to the displacements and dispossession evinced by "1848"' (Pérez-Torres, 1995, p. 57). Introduced by 'El Plan Espiritual de Aztlán' in 1969, Aztlán was a notion that served during the political movements of the 1960s and 1970s both as a space of cohesiveness and to crystallize the history of colonization and dispossession that informs Chicano cultural identity. As Pérez-Torres states (ibid., p. 11), in the notion of Aztlán were 'inscribed issues of self-affirmation and self-determination, the claims for lands, a call to popular action, and the desire of cultural empowerment'. It became an icon that symbolized the spiritual union of the Chicanos (ibid., p. 58).

The Mexican Revolution also exercised a strong influence on the rhetoric of the leaders of the Chicano movements during the 1960s, and on the construction of their symbolic imaginary. In her study of Chicana history, feminist Chicana historian Emma Pérez proposes that the script written by the ideologues of the Mexican Revolution was appropriated in many ways by Chicano nationalists in the 1970s and again in the 1990s:

> 'They' wanted to cultivate a revolutionary motive and ideology, looking backward to leaders who had helped foment revolution. What appears is a cyclical tracking of the past's intellectuals to re-create the present. Many invoked Emilano Zapata, Pancho Villa, Ricardo Flores Magón, and las Adelitas as the heroes and heroines who could provide guidance for the Chicana/o movements. (1999, p. 9)

In fact, among the intellectuals who exercised a strong influence in the rhetoric of the leaders of the Chicano movements, and the symbolic imaginary of Chicanas/os, two are of particular interest. One is Ricardo Flores Magón, leader of the Partido Liberal Mexicano (PLM), analyzed by Emma Pérez. The other is José de Vaconcelos, Minister of Education under President Alvaro Obregón (1920–24), and author of *La raza cósmica* (1925).

The PLM, more than any other organization of the time of the Mexican Revolution was, according to Emma Pérez (1999, p. 72), imitated by the leadership of the Chicano movement of the 1960s and 1970s. Among other factors, the PLM 'platform demanded violent revolution, called for workers' rights, and professed equal regard for land and liberty', but their idea of land and liberty 'transcended a nationalism that demanded a Mexico for Mexicans' (ibid., p. 61). By the same token, the leadership of the Chicano movements of the 1960s and 1970s envisioned a transnational movement that would go beyond the borders of the Southwest and the US. In this context, as already anticipated by PLM, Aztlán became an imaginary 'land and liberty' (ibid., p. 72).

It should also be noted that, similar to what was proposed during the revolutionary movements in the 1960s and 1970s in Latin America, the link between political activism and an intellectual/literary production was considered a virtual imperative in the struggle for social change. The Chicano literature read today, says Cherrie Moraga, 'sprang from a grassroots social and political movement of the sixties and seventies that was definitively anti-assimilationist. It responded to a stated mandate: *art is political*' (1993, p. 57). In this regard, drawing on Pérez-Torres's work on Chicana/o poets of the Movement, Emma Pérez concludes that:

> the poetics of nationalism, then, refers to the poets who literally and symbolically chiseled the Chicano/a nation-Aztlán ... The Chicano nation has been framed linearly, but Aztlán, when taken out of the past, becomes a culturally constructed nation written into the present imaginary by poets, historians, and social scientists. (1999, pp. 59–60)

Central to Aztlán there was constructed another master narrative, namely that of *la Raza*, a concept that conveys the notion of *mestizaje*, or ethnic mix. The concept was memorably articulated by José Vasconcelos (1882–1959), in his famous essay *La raza cósmica*. To be sure, Vasconcelos was neither the first nor the only one to introduce the notion of *mestizaje* as an element of Latin American identity. From the very beginning that *cóctel* (as Cuban poet Nicolás Guillén would call Latin America) has always been defined in a very Borgean way: we are all of our ancestors, at the same time as we are none of them.

It was Vasconcelos, and his *La raza cósmica* that captured the imagination of the Chicano Movement's leaders in the 1960s, particularly those of the student branch, in their struggle for empowerment and in the process of cultural affirmation and identity formation. Vasconcelos became virtually the intellectual godfather of Chicanismo (John Reed, 1991). He is referred to, and quoted on several occasions in the 'Plan de Santa Barbara', a Chicano plan for higher education, where *La raza cósmica* in particular is invoked as 'a philosophical precedent' for Chicano cultural nationalism.[1] To a certain extent, it is not difficult to understand why. Not only had Vasconcelos lived on the Mexican–US borders and witnessed the racism of the US, but he was one of the few internationally recognized intellectuals (another was Octavio Paz) who made any reference to the people of Mexican descent in the US. He thus became a source of intellectual legitimation for their struggle. Furthermore, according to Paz, the Mexican Revolution 'was a search and an immersion of ourselves in our origins and being' (1985, p. 152). Who better embodied this than Vasconcelos, the founder of modern education in Mexico? The new education, Vasconcelos said, 'is going to be founded on our blood, our language, our people'. He not only spearheaded Mexico's post-revolutionary cultural renaissance in the 1920s and 1930s, but by doing so he also contributed importantly toward the re-valorization of tradition and popular culture, and the revival of indigenous cultures as one of the roots of Mexican national and cultural identity. Above all, Vasconcelos vindicated the *mestizo* race. For him, culture exists in relation to race, that same *mestizo* race that, according to him, put the spirit before matter, and emotion and aesthetics before *logos*, a concept summarized in his famous saying: '*Por mi raza hablará el espíritu*' (Through my race the spirit will speak).

Thus, within Chicana/o cultural nationalism, references to *la raza cósmica* multiplied to make it an institutionalized signifier of the affirmation, unity and glorification of the *mestizo* race. The presence of Vasconcelos is also evident in texts of authors such as Gloria Anzaldúa who, from a feminist/lesbian perspective, proposes a new Chicana consciousness, which challenges nationalist rhetoric and ideology. We will come back to this issue, but will just indicate that her path-breaking essay, 'La conciencia mestiza' (1999a, p. 102), opens with a reference to Vasconcelos's famous phrase: 'Por la mujer de mi raza hablará el espíritu' (Through the women of my race the spirit will speak). She sees in 'his theory one of inclusivity', and points out how Vascncelos's essay opposes the theory of the 'pure Arian' race, and 'the policy of racial purity that white America practices'.

Nevertheless, the persistent presence of Vasconcelos leaves us some questions. A close reading of his philosophy would show that it is not as good as its sounds. In fact, the underpinnings of *La raza cósmica* are, in many respects, at odds with the basic tenets of the struggles of Chicanas/os, both in the 1960s and today. For instance, the 'spirit' through which the Race will speak takes us back to *arielismo*, which informed Vasconcelos's thought and considered Greco-Latin culture to be the source of our moral and aesthetic spiritual values.[2] 'Greece', says Vasconcelos, 'laid the foundations of Western or European civilization; the white civilization that, upon expanding, reached the forgotten shores of the American continent in order to consummate the task of re-civilization and re-population' (1979, p. 7). In Vasconcelos's eyes, the indigenous civilizations not only are the diminished and poor heirs of a superior culture, but 'civilization' would develop on the other side of the Atlantic, only to come back to America 'thanks' to the 'portentous work started by iron-will conquerors and consummated by wise and selfless missionaries' (1979, p.12). 'A religion like Christianity', he states, 'advanced the American Indians, in a few centuries, from cannibalism to a relative civilization' (1979, p. 3).

Despite these 'philosophical precedents', neither Vasconcelos nor *La raza cósmica* were explicitly questioned and it is necessary to ask why. Unless we agree that Vasconcelos is probably one of those authors who, like Borges, are more talked about than read, the answer may lie elsewhere. Although I do not pretend to decipher the enigma, it has to do precisely, in my view, with the very nature of the hegemonic *mestizo* project of the post-revolutionary development of Mexican nationalism, and its paradoxical and contradictory relationship to Modernity. These paradoxes and contradictions are reflected (inherited?) in turn not only in the unquestioned vindication of *La raza cósmica*, but also in the notion of Aztlán and the dominance of Aztec mythology that pervades the Chicana/o cultural symbolic universe. In fact, I consider that these two Chicana/o foundational mythic symbols are part of the same master narrative that comes from post-revolutionary Mexican nationalism (including the *Indigenista* project). One goes with the other. I propose, then, to go back to the notion of Aztlán and *la raza cósmica* as the two sides of the same coin within the context of the project of Modernity.

MODERNIST FANTASIES, COLLECTIVE DREAMS

Myths are collective dreams, and dreams are private myths, said Freud. The term Aztlán is one of them. As Pérez-Torres states (1997, p. 37), Aztlán has been consistently used to refer to an absence: land, liberty, unity. But Aztlán was also 'a form of rejection of the most pernicious influences of the Enlightenment and capitalism, as a source of alternate and empowering forms of social organization, as a dream of contemporary Chicano life' (ibid., p. 173). That is, the idea of change and rejection of the immediate past, both essential components of Modernity, are also represented in the Chicana/o mythical Aztlán. In this sense, I believe that the Chicana/o myth of Aztlán is much closer to its ancient notion as 'point of departure' and to 'the painful labor in giving birth' than to the notion of homeland.[3] But it could be seen also as a rupture and rebirth, which take us back to the idea of chaos, and Modernity. Modernity, observes Pozas Horcasitas (2002, p. 12), is a succession of ruptures and rebirths. Hence its paradox: to be a tradition founded on the constant creation of the new (ibid., p. 10). Yet it is above all in crucial times of rupture or change, that the moderns required the leverage of history to open up their horizon. In order to be able to articulate, by differentiation, the new propositions, and provide them with meaning, continues Ricardo Pozas, the social agents that represent the emergent proposition establish a double relation with social time. One temporality (the immediately preceding one) that is denied, and the other that is identitarian. It is in the search for this second temporality that we leap into the remote past seeking an ideal that could encompass cultural diversity and differentiate ourselves from the traditional or immediate past (2002, p. 20). For Chicanas/os of the 1960s, who rejected Western thought entirely, it was Aztlán, along with the romanticization of the indigenous past, particularly the Aztecs (who were elevated to the category of the 'classic' culture), that provided the identitarian model that would encompass cultural diversity and mark the proposed change.

However, it seems that order and chaos always go hand to hand. The essentialist and universalizing nature of this model generated all kinds of contradictions, as we shall see in the course of this chapter. One of them has to do with the privilege given to Aztec iconography and symbology, which could be seen as yet another aspect that Chicano nationalism inherited from

Mexican post-revolutionary cultural nationalism. In fact, there were no Mayans, only Aztecs, of the kind associated with and reified by post-revolutionary Mexican national identity. Mexican muralism is an example of this, or statements like the following by Vasconcelos: 'We are the prodigal sons of a homeland which we cannot even define but which we are beginning at last to observe. She is Castillian and Moorish, with Aztec markings' (quoted in Paz, 1985, p. 153). This popularized Aztec iconography, in the equation Mexico = Aztecs = all (or the only) indigenous ancestors, would later constitute, incidentally, the image of 'Mexico for export'. It amounted to a kind of 'symbolic domination', to use a term from Karl Kraus (1976), whereby the Aztecs would function as equivalent to, and a substitute for any indigenous ancestry. And, of course, this symbolic domination comes dangerously close to that reductionist homogenization of indigenous cultures that characterized Eurocentric discourse. Furthermore, as Pérez-Torres notes:

> the culture of Chicanas/os does not derive directly or literally from this Nahua past. There were hundreds of tribes throughout North and Central America at the time of the conquest, and the cultural identity of Chicanas/os is as complex and diverse as the identity of any other people tracing their ancestry to the original inhabitants of the Americas. (1995, p. 181)

On the other hand, the romanticization of a distant and glorified past cannot be separated from the *indigenista* project and ideology of post-revolutionary Mexico, including that of Vasconcelos.

Post-revolutionary Mexican nationalism, as well as the *indigenismo* that sprang from it, as we know, were not indigenous but mestizo projects. Ángel Rama (1974, pp. 151–2) has suggested, in fact, that instead of *indigenismo* we should be talking of *mesticismo*. By its very nature, *indigenismo* always represented the *mestizo* point of view. The Indians themselves were the objects, not the authors, of *indigenismo*. In his article, 'Racism, Revolution and Indigenismo: Mexico 1910–1940', Alan Knight explores precisely this issue. According to his analysis, one of the impacts of the Revolution on *indigenismo* was to incorporate it, by the Constitution of 1917, into its official ideology. The *mesticismo* of *indigenismo* is clearly evident in this new revolutionary policy which stated, by decree, that the integration of the indigenous population would be 'planned, enlightened, and respectful of that culture' (Knight, 1990, p. 80). Such was the mainstream *indigenismo*, to which Vasconcelos subscribed, and its project was 'enlightened, planned', non-coercive integration. Education was to be the main instrument for achieving *indigenista* policies by inculcating through Indian and rural schools the 'new religion of post-revolutionary nationalism' and by acculturating Indian customs, music and dance, all woven into a new tapestry of folkloric nationalism. As noted above, the most celebrated representative of the new official philosophy was the revolutionary muralist movement.[4] We may also wonder who were to be included in Vasconcelos's project of a new education 'founded on our blood, our language, our people'. Not the indigenous cultures, for sure. The essential problem with regard to the ethnic question consisted in achieving homogeneity. Mestizo, looked upon as neither Indian nor European but 'quintessentially Mexican', was the 'national race', as Gamio affirmed (1960, pp. 5–6). In *La raza cósmica* (p. 14), Vasconcelos clearly states that 'Even the pure Indians are Hispanized, they are Latinized.' The red men went to sleep, never to awaken: 'There is no going back in History', 'No race returns …. The Indian has no other door to the future but the door of modern culture.' For this reason, the mix of all races, the *mestizo* race, would be the final race, fashioned out of the treasures of all the previous ones (ibid., p. 38), but at the cost of the extinction and/or assimilation of indigenous cultures. More than conveying inclusivity, as Anzaldúa sees it, underlying Vasconcelos's concept of *la raza cósmica* is the concept, so prevalent at the time, that indigenous peoples represented (at best) 'a problem', if not an obstacle to progress into Modernity, and should therefore be assimilated into the modern ways of *mestizo* culture and the new nation. At the same time, the official ideology has perpetuated a kind of instrumental Indianness, although it is at odds with social reality, for perceptions of Indian inferiority still permeate society. Hence the Indian dilemma imposed by official ideology and socio-political reality: Indians are discriminated against for being Indian, and at the same time vindicated as the soul of Mexican cultural roots. A leap into the remote past is again needed. For Vasconcelos this leap was represented by both the Aztec pre-Columbian past (more in its idealized and folkloric representation than anything else), and the Greco-Latin culture, that came from the Spain of the Renaissance that nourished, in colonial times, the cultural production of figures such as Sor Juana Inés de la Cruz.

In this context, the unquestioned vindication of Vasconcelos's philosophy and the dominance of Aztec iconography and mythology could be perceived as a gesture that endorses that hegemonic discourse that put indigenous populations in a position strikingly similar to that which Chicanas/os have to endure in the US. When set in the US, the parallels and differences between the two models stand out. In an effort to integrate the uniqueness of the particular to the universal, the homogenizing ideas express, in both cases, a longing for communion in the construction of a new nation, and the search in the tradition for ties that have universal validity. Tradition, we know, is one of the thorny issues in the ideology of Modernity. It is one of the main cultural constructions of identity and plays an ideological function (Pozas Horcasitas, 2002, p. 14). The *mestizo* race and a common past, represented by the legendary Aztecs, provided both Vasconcelos and Chicana/o nationalism later with the ideal that could encompass (or engulf) cultural diversity, and set the parameters for national identity. But while in Vasconcelos this represented the dominant ideology, for Chicanas/os it constituted a counter-hegemonic discourse. For the revolutionary nationalist rhetoric of the 1960s and 1970s, tradition was also seen as the patrimony in the construction of identity, and as a means to counter the alienating effects of Modernity. Of particular importance was the sacredness of the family, which in turn reinforced the idea of the unity of the grand Chicano family, the nation of Aztlán.

AN ALTERNATIVE SYMBOLIC WORLD: FROM MODERN TRADITION TO UTOPIAS IN THE TWENTY-FIRST CENTURY

The very concept of 'nation' of Aztlán became as problematic for Chicanas/os as it was for some Mexicans when conciliating Mexican reality with the national identity imposed and elaborated in post-revolutionary times. As Mexican writer Carlos Monsiváis has said: 'México is not only divided into 29 states, 2 territories, and 1 Federal District, but also into dozens of countries and historical times' (1970, p. 100). Similarly, as has been pointed out by many Chicana/o scholars, the foundational master narrative of Aztlán, as conceived by Chicana/o nationalist discourse, was far from representing the heterogeneous cultural realities of Chicanas/os, their discontinued histories and multiple subjectivities.[5] In his assessment of Chicano historiography, Alex Saragoza (1990) notes that from its beginnings the conceptualization of Chicano history, with its emphasis on a 'collective' Chicano experience, while romanticizing the past, failed to take class, gender, sexual, and regional differences into account.

Of course the works of Chicana intellectuals and writers, from their unique subject positions as women of color, feminists, lesbians, living in the US, were crucial in articulating a critical view that would provide the basis for redefining these foundational narratives in more comprehensive cultural, symbolic and ideological terms. Among other things, Chicana writers begin by pointing out that, as a symbolic language, the reality of myths is not only dynamic and social, but unquestionably gendered (if not sexist), in which tradition plays no small role. Historically determined in our modern world from a white, Western, heterosexual male point of view, it is clear that tradition not only plays an important role in the construction of identities (and their symbolic representations), but it is another form of pursuing and/or not renouncing the privileges one group has acquired at the expense of another.[6]

With the explosion of Chicana (lesbian) feminist consciousness, the dominant cultural figures, icons, and symbols of Chicano nationalist rhetoric began to be challenged. For Chicana feminists, the symbolic universe that dominated Chicana/o nationalism was a 'cultural tyranny', as Anzaldúa defines it, or a metonymy for patriarchy (Saldivar-Hull, 2000). It is not my aim here to analyze their work in detail, however, since many studies, particularly those by Chicanas themselves, have addressed these issues from different perspectives, particularly those related to the Virgin of Guadalupe, and La Malinche.[7] What I want to emphasize here is that Chicana writers are responding in part to an imposed or inherited, questionable masculinist cultural symbolic universe. Among other factors, the 'nurturing role of the revolutionaries' assigned to women, is a model that derives from the Mexican Revolution and is epitomized in the traditional image created around *Las adelitas*, or the myth of *las soldaderas*. 'Revolutionary women', says Monsiváis (1997b, p. 6), 'are mythified and the myth ... confirms and guarantees slavery, bitterly transforming natural virtues into a dead weight for their descendants'; that is, 'a fatal load of abnegation, silent suffering, stoicism and stubborn veneration for their men'. In symbolic terms, this was also represented by *la llorona*, the long-suffering mother, and the Virgin of Guadalupe, embodying purity, receptivity, and nurturing qualities, and the counter-figure of La Malinche, the legendary Malintzin Tenepal who has been perpetuated in the collective imaginary as *la chingada* by Paz in his famous essay, 'The Sons of the Malinche' (1985). *La Chingada* is the Mother forcibly 'opened, violated or deceived' (Paz, 1985, p. 79).[8] One of the main objectives of Chicanas was therefore to unteach this virgin/mother/whore paradigm that had kept women in check for centuries. Two main topics are always attached to these figures when Chicanas address and challenge them: the patriarchal notion of betrayal, based on gender roles and sexuality, and the negative sexual perception Chicanas have of themselves as sexual persons. Sexuality and gender roles are among the most important issues Chicanas address in their questioning of symbols and institutions rooted in Mexican and Chicana/o cultural traditions, and cherished by Chicano nationalist movements. In their writings Chicanas began to oppose and replace the masculinist symbolic universe with female deities, or they redefined the patriarchal construction (and use) of figures like Malinche or the Virgin of Guadalupe. For instance, they rejected *marianismo*, the veneration of the Virgin Mary, who as Anna Nieto Gomez notes (1997, p. 48), became the model of how to make oppression a religious obligation. By foregrounding an ancestral memory and/or the sexuality denied to women, they privileged the image of Tonantzin, the deity destroyed by the Spaniards and replaced by Our Lady of Guadalupe. Along with Tonantzin, a pantheon of other goddesses of fertility and sexuality are brought to light, all of them seen 'telescoped one into another', according to Sandra Cisneros (1996, p. 50), 'into who I am'. In this superimposition and identification with multiple female deities of Mesomerican mythology, Chicanas attempt, in Cherrie Moraga's words, 'to pick up the fragments of our dismembered womanhood and reconstitute ourselves' (1996, pp. 68–9). They also emphasize the validity of that other – unperceived or unwritten – history, namely that of those who refuse to conform. For many Chicanas, like Moraga, lesbian politics and sexuality are legitimate sites of theory: 'As a Chicana lesbian, asserting a sexuality that rejects the Chicano traditions of compulsory heterosexuality, Moraga risks being "outcast" from her culture, beyond salvation as she said' (Saldivar-Hull, 2000, p. 50). Similarly, Anzaldúa considers herself cultureless, alienated from her own culture, because of her lesbianism and feminism, although, at the same time, she perceives herself as cultured, because she is creating a new culture, a new consciousness (1999a, p. 103). However, theirs is a multiple feminist (lesbian) consciousness, whose gender politics are lived simultaneously with race, class, and sexual awareness. As women 'whose daily existence confronts institutionalized racism, class exploitation, sexism, and homophobia, US Third World Women do not enjoy the luxury of privileging one oppression over another' (Saldivar-Hull, 2000, p. 48).

In going back to the pre-Columbian past, Chicanas emphasize the search and the need to reestablish the wholeness of woman, a quest that goes beyond 'breaking down the bi-cultural mind', as the title of one of Moraga's writings eloquently indicates. It is a claim for a whole sense of belonging, and human rights: 'The one aspect of our identity which has been uniformly ignored by every existing political movement in this country is sexuality, as both a source of oppression and a means of liberation' (Moraga, 1983, p. 100). As much as women's sexuality, memory also holds the potential for both liberation and imprisonment. Thus, the de-colonization of memory, including collective memory, can be compared to the de-colonization of the indigenous body and the female body in general that is undertaken by Chicana feminists. And these, in turn, may make it necessary to redefine the idea of 'the' community and perhaps to restructure the family outside the patriarchal order.

One of the clearer and more challenging expressions in this regard is, without doubt, Cherrie Moraga's essay 'Queer Aztlán', in which she denounces the Chicano Movement for 'its institutionalized heterosexism and its inbred machismo' (1993, p. 151). For her, 'no progressive movement can succeed while any member of the population remains in submission' (ibid., p. 162). Thus, she proposes the idea of a 'Queer Aztlán', 'a Chicano homeland that could embrace all its people, including its *jotería* [homosexuals]' (ibid., p. 147). To the weaknesses of the isolated patriarchal, capitalist family structure, she proposes that the idea of *familia* could be extended by forming circles of support and survival (ibid., p. 166). Moraga is already well along the path of coalition building.[9]

'What would a movement bent on the freedom of women of color look like?' Moraga asks. 'In other words, what are the implications of looking not only *outside* of our culture, but *into* our culture and ourselves and from that place beginning to develop a strategy for a movement that could challenge the bedrock of oppressive systems of belief globally?' (1983, p. 100). In fact, this is the path many Chicana feminists seem to have followed: they started from inside themselves and their culture, and from there they open up the horizon to insert themselves in a broader canvas. The initial vision of a transnational movement that would go beyond the borders, absorbed by the movement's nationalist ideology, seems to have been picked up by Chicanas feminists, like Moraga and Anzaldúa, in their efforts to create a 'third space' without frontiers. This idea of a land without borders, or the borderlands as a valid site for identitarian construction of conflicting and multiple subjectivities, as much as for solidarity and agency in coalition building, constitutes the new metaphor in Chicana/o cultural symbolism. In her essay 'Art in América con Acento' Moraga proposes, in what she calls 'a vision', to redefine what an 'American' is, which in turn re-defines the concept of *la raza*:

> We must learn to see ourselves less as US citizens and more as members of a larger world community ... and no longer give credence to the geopolitical borders that have divided us ... Call it racial memory. Call it shared economic discrimination. Chicanos call it 'Raza' – be it Quichua, Cubano, or Colombiano – an identity that dissolves borders. (1993, p. 62)

It is true that here the concept of *raza* still works as an unproblematic identititarian label that could embrace a Quichua, Cubano or Colombiano, when from the other side they probably would not recognize it or be identified with it. However, it is also true that Moraga's concept of *raza* emphasizes more the idea of inclusivity than of homogeneity, and is not based so much on cultural traditions as on geopolitical alliances and transnational solidarity.

Without doubt, Gloria Anzaldúa is the Chicana writer who has worked most consistently with the idea of the 'borderlands'. In her landmark literary piece, *Borderlands/La frontera. The New Mestiza* (1999c), Anzaldúa portrays the Chicana/o border condition that exists within every aspect in dominant society. These borders serve as spaces of oppression, but Anzaldúa deconstructs them to infuse new meanings. Crucial in this regard is her essay 'La conciencia de la mestiza', included in this volume. Using Vasconcelos as a source for her writing could be misleading for an uniformed reader, but from Vasconcelos's (misread?) philosophy Anzaldúa develops her own theory of a new *mestiza* consciousness:

> By breaking down paradigms, and by creating new myths – that is, a change in the way we perceive reality, the way we see ourselves, and the ways we behave – la *mestiza* creates a new consciousness ... It is a consciousness of the Borderlands. (Anzaldúa, 1999c, p. 102)

Contrary to Vasconcelos, Anzaldúa not only conveys the idea of inclusivity in her theory, but also a sense of transition, of non-conclusive or fluid subjectivity, and from the point of view of one who is excluded, that is, from a sense of not belonging to the established order. Thus, as she says in 'The Homeland, Aztlán/El Otro México', a borderland 'is a vague and undetermined place created by the emotional residue of an unnatural boundary ... The prohibited and forbidden are its inhabitants' (1999b, p. 25). But if individuals who fail to subscribe to the social norm live in a border reality, in the margins, then to 'survive the Borderlands/you must live *sin fronteras*/be a crossroads' (1999c, pp. 216–17). In a way she articulates the two foundational narratives, Aztlán and *la raza cósmica*, into one narrative: the borderlands.

To conclude, then, the persistence of the notion of Aztlán should be noted.

It constitutes a clear example of myth as a symbolic expression of the world we comprehend and cherish that is 're-mythicized' every day to reflect the social dynamics of a group. As conceived by Chicano nationalism, Aztlán was initially a monolithic narrative. Today it would be considered a multilayered discursive construct or a palimpsest that allows for a more complex understanding of equally complex and fluid Chicana/o cultural identities and histories (Cooper Alarcón, 1988–90, p. 34). By the same token, I believe that the concept of *la raza* or *la raza cósmica* followed a similar path in the work of some Chicana feminists. In the writings of Moraga and Anzaldúa it becomes the metaphor of decentered, inconclusive and multiple subjectivities, as well as a site of collective global solidarity and agency in the struggle for social justice. In this sense, the political and ideological position, visions and dreams of Chicana feminists entail that notion of chaos, considered as the generating potential for a rebirth to a new order, in which multiple and different modalities co-exist. Chaos, the reservoir of everything: 'it is the site of all metamorphosis', 'plastic, fluid, inexhaustible' (Callois, 1996, p. 117). In some ways Cornejo Polar's affirmation with respect to a plural and heterogeneous Latin America could be applied to the work Chicanas are doing. Such a concept is not to deny either the common history of colonization or the uniqueness that results from our complex and varied heritage, but is to emphasize plurality. Such a concept 'would save us from being what we are not: solid and stable subjects, capable of configuring a self that is always the same, in order to explore ... a horizon in which we can recognize ourselves not in one but in several faces' (Cornejo Polar, 1993, p. 9).

NOTES

1. In April of 1969, the Chicano Coordinating Council of Higher Education held a conference at the University of California, Santa Barbara. Participants were interested in creating programs to help Chicana and Chicano students attending California's colleges and universities. The result was a master plan for the creation of curriculum and the related auxiliary services and structures essential to facilitate access to those institutions. This plan was called 'El Plan de Santa Barbara'.
2. *Arielismo* is the ethic and aesthetic thought that informed the *Ateneo de la Juventud* – an organization to which Vasconcelos belonged and was a founding member. It was born as a spiritualist reaction against positivist social determinism and the materialistic conception of humankind. The term *arielismo* derives from Enrique Rodó's essay, 'Ariel' (1900), and the influence it exercised on Latin American intellectuals of the time.
3. For the ancient cosmogonic mythical scheme by which Aztlán represented a 'point of departure', see López Austin (1998). For the relationship between Mesoamerican history and mythology, and the Chicana/o notion of Aztlán, see Cooper Alarcón (1988–90).
4. For the relationship between *indigenismo* and *muralismo*, see Shifra Goldman (2001).

5   See, among others, the works of Gilbert Gonzalez, Pérez-Torres (1997), Almaguer, Klor de Alva, Saragoza, Cooper Alarcón, Segura and Pesquera, and Moraga.
6   To be sure, at the same time as they were struggling against sexism and heterosexism within their culture, Chicanas had to deal with racism within the feminist movement. White-influenced, leftist feminists feared that a radicalized feminism could only mean indulgence in the concerns of a privatized self. That is, they dismiss 'identity politics' as a legitimate locus of struggle, while for US women of color identity politics was a tool of material and theoretical engagement; and for whom race and gender are interlinked (Salvidar-Hull, 2000, pp. 39–41).
7   See, for instance, Salvidar-Hull (2000), and Norma Alarcón (1990). For a re-envisioning of the figure of La Malinche, see Messinger Cypess (1997), Elizabeth Ordoñez (1984), Adelaida del Castillo (1977), Norma Alarcón (1983, 1989), among others. For a re-envisioning of the Virgin of Guadalupe, see in particular Castillo's *Goddess of the Americas*.
8   From this perspective, Paz claims that Mexican identity developed from a sense of being the bastard children of violence, rape, and betrayal, which has its origins in the Conquest and is symbolized in the figure of La Malinche. This interpretation serves Paz's analysis by foregrounding traditional sexual roles and what he considers two of the most characteristic trends of Mexican political and social behavior: *machismo* and *malinchismo*, a concept that encodes passivity, submission and betrayal.
9   Moraga co-edited with Gloria Anzaldúa an anthology titled *This Bridge Called My Back* (1981) to highlight the diverse experiences and voices of women of color who had been denied a space in mainstream culture and the Caucasian middle-class feminist movement. In *Loving in the War Years* (2000), Moraga also presents a comprehensive expression of Chicana/Third World feminism.

7

Recontextualizing violence as founding myth
La sangre derramada by José Pablo Feinmann

Rita De Grandis

> Facundo, spectre of terror, I summon you to arise and, shaking off the blood-stained dust that covers your ashes, explain to us the secret life and internal convulsions that disembowel a noble people! You have the secret. Reveal it to us!
> (Sarmiento, Introduction to *Facundo*)[1]

Violence and its relationship to literature in cultural studies are an overwhelming topic. One finds it everywhere.[2] Violence, in particular political violence, needs to be described and understood if we want to understand Latin America. Political violence is central to a nation's questioning its own being in its quest for self-knowledge and understanding. The assumption here is that self-knowledge, as Jopling (2000) defines it, could be viewed as an instrument of value in terms of promoting ethical action and a basis upon which other virtues can be cultivated. In order to recognize the truth of the statement that the theme of violence has proliferated in Latin American literature at different moments of its history, one has only to reflect on the number of novels about dictators, and on studies of the figure of the dictator and dictatorship that Latin America has produced since the first decades of the twentieth century (see González Echevarría, 1985). Since the 1980s in particular there has been a wealth of literature addressing the problem of political violence during the Pinochet and *junta* periods in Chile and Argentina (Vidal, 1985; Pratt, 1999), and in Central America (Lancaster, 1992; Green, 1994). Moreover, the topic has now extended beyond politics to include domestic conflicts, issues in gender, and other social manifestations of violence within the specific context of neoliberalism (Moraña, 2002b; Rotker, 2002).

As in the rest of Latin America, violence and authoritarianism have characterized Argentina's origins as a modern nation, giving rise to a literature founded on a mythology in which, not surprisingly, political violence is a characteristic feature of narratives of self-representation. The founders of Argentinian literature – Echeverría, Sarmiento, Mármol – contended with Juan Manuel de Rosas's regime of violence in the early republican period (1832–52) through a variety of genres (poetry, essay, the serial novel), within the aesthetics of both Romanticism and Realism. Violence was represented through a rich metaphorical tapestry of themes, myths, figures, styles, and techniques, which shaped the nation culturally. Sarmiento's *Facundo: Civilización y barbarie* (1845), chronicling the life of the *gaucho* Facundo Quiroga and his assassination, has become the foundational myth from which the debate on political violence and culture evolved, and it continues to resonate to this day. Since then, modern and contemporary Argentinian literature has never ceased to reinterpret this myth, particularly whenever periods of violence devastate the country, the last of these being the so-called Dirty War (1976–83).

Borrowing Edward Said's concept of the 'totemic' text, *Facundo* can be viewed as the paternal text *par excellence,* the one that laid the foundations for a collective image of self-representation based on violence, which successive generations of writers call on to strengthen the links between past and present. In discussing the Oedipal motif in relation to the concept of the text and the history of the text and its imitations, Said suggests that just as, to quote Freud, 'eating and drinking are attributed binding force among members of a community', gathered to commemorate a 'beginning deed', so, in the realm of the text, its 'users' – imitators, critics, parodists – establish a kinship defined by their common point of reference which is the text itself. The relationship between a previous text and a new one, Said notes, brings forth the idea of paternal authority as a major theme in literature, against which the writer of the new text must struggle (1975, pp. 108–10).

Whether invented, appropriated or implicit, even a 'beginning' text must often confront the authority of a previous, 'totemic' source. Ricardo Piglia's fundamental novel on the violence of the 1970s, *Artificial Respiration* (1980), written and published during the years of the *junta*, addresses the question of the totemic text in a very specific way: 'Sometimes (no joke), I think that we are the generation of 1837. Lost in the Diaspora. Who among us will write the *Facundo*?' (ibid., p. 76).[3]

A decade later, Feinmann has taken up the challenge. José Pablo Feinmann's *La sangre derramada: ensayo sobre la violencia política* (1998) (Spilt Blood: An Essay on Political Violence), is another take on *Facundo* and on the violence of the Dirty War, but now from an anti-modernist aesthetic. And the essay goes on to consider the continuity of violence in the 'democratic' period of the post-dictatorship, linking the post-*junta* hegemonic classes with the past. Feinmann's *La sangre derramada* employs, as did Sarmiento's writing, the rhetoric of the pamphleteer and the language of the press. In doing so, it seeks to escape from modernist aesthetics, establishing its radical difference from

Respiración artificial, by choosing to write in that ambiguous territory between journalism and literature.

In the 1990s, the intellectual scene in Argentina was flooded with an abundant debate in the press on the quality of democracy. Literary, cultural and political references to the nineteenth century form an interpretive framework to connect previous periods of dominance of Liberal ideology with the current one. From this connection a thesis on nation formation as a failed project of the Enlightenment is consolidated and developed in order to explain not only the continuous internal struggles that have marked the country's own history, but most importantly the endemic faults of Argentinian nationalism. The idea is that the last decades of democratic process, including the last crisis of 19–20 December, 2001, manifest themselves as resulting from some kind of internal dynamic that re-enacts past 'guiding fictions', as Nicholas Shumway describes this phenomenon. For the intellectuals engaged in this interpretive framework, from the very early days of the Republic the intelligentsia of the Revolution of May 1810 configured a model of political action and representation based on political divisiveness and on the inability to adapt successfully the ideas of the Enlightenment on Latin American soil. Shumway considers that this ideological legacy is somehow a mythology of exclusion more than a call for pluralist consensus, and has continued to manifest itself throughout the historical transformations that Argentina as a nation has undergone in the twentieth century. This connection between past and present produces a type of self-knowledge that in turn reveals itself in a certain irreducible Argentine style. This interpretive framework has been very productive in all types of discursive practices and genres, particularly in the novel (Andrés Rivera, Ricardo Piglia), chronicles and essays of the past two decades. *La sangre derramada* is the essay that best crystallizes this interpretive framework, and works on the assumption that the Argentinian and Latin American 'difference' is based on a false premise, that of failing to reproduce the original European model. As Julio Ramos affirms, Latin American representations portray this 'difference' by displacing the (European) origin through parody as 'a site forever traversed by contradictions'. Thus, literature in Latin America, from its very inception, has defied its institutional homogeneity and challenged 'truth and disciplinary formation'. This argument would imply that Latin American 'difference' is an effect of an originary purity derived from Europe or the West, which it dismantles 'even as it (voluntarily or involuntarily) represented, recited, or simulated the logic and function of First World codes' (Ramos, 2001, p. 78).

Returning to Feinmann's *La sangre derramada* and its connections with the past, strangely enough it is Piglia's essay, 'Sarmiento's Vision', which gives us the clue to describe the common denominators that link Sarmiento's aesthetics to Feinmann's essay style. For Piglia, *Facundo* has become 'a laboratory of forms and a thesaurus of styles and narrative solutions' (1993, p. 72). Sarmiento, contrary to 'the sad tradition of the liberal essayists' who claim to be Sarmiento's disciples (e.g., Eduardo Mallea and Ezequiel Martínez Estrada), 'is much closer, in language and style, to the great nationalist prose writers' (e.g., Ignacio B. Anzoátegui, Carlos Ibarguren and Julio Irazusta) (ibid., p. 71).[4] In Feinmann's prose we recognize the nationalist and populist tradition of Arturo Jauretche (1901–74),[5] as well as the acute observations of the daily life of Buenos Aires's impoverished middle class that Roberto Arlt bequeathed to the nation in his sketches. And Feinmann's interpretations also owe something to Rodolfo Walsh, with their strong claim to writing as social intervention and their choice of Peronism as a nodal point in the political and cultural life of Argentinian historical transformations. Sarmiento has become today a writer for writers, as a pamphleteer, a committed writer, who wrote with a practical and extra-literary purpose. Through a paradox established by Sarmiento, Piglia claims a piece that is written for political reasons and become a literary text. Thus, in *La sangre derramada,* as in *Facundo* and *Operación masacre,* by Rodolfo Walsh, how the essay is constructed is as important as its political contents and ideological declarations; it takes from the parent-text one of its main narrative strategies: analogy and its parallelisms.

La sangre derramada consists of three parts and a conclusion. The first part, entitled 'Criticism and Violence', is presented as a study of the causes and effects of the violence of the 1970s, whereas the second part, 'Narratives of a Violent Country', reveals how the violence of the twentieth century mirrors that of the nineteenth. The third part, 'Violence and the Sense of History', addresses issues around modernity, evil, dialectics, hatred, mass unemployment, the death penalty, war, utopia, and the intellectual. Finally, 'Conclusions: Violence and Democracy', is left inconclusive; the essayist addresses the topics in all their complexity but, as a post-modernist rejecting any claim to special authority, he declines to offer solutions. He condemns vengeance and advocates forgiveness as a necessary condition to overcome the horror of violence, but only at the end of the book. In spite of and, indeed, because of its repetitive and insistent style, *La sangre derramada*, like Sarmiento's *Facundo*, captures the urgency and brutality of an entire era.

CRITICISM AS UNDERSTANDING AND METHOD

The opening image of 'Criticism and Violence' ('The gun on the desk') prefigures the text: General Bussi,[6] Governor of the Province of Tucumán in the 1990s, is sitting at his desk playing with a gun while talking with two people. Against this concrete image of intimidation, the narrative describes a precise and eventful year both in the international and national scene: 1989, the year of the fall of the Berlin Wall, the crowning of a world-wide free market economy, and the beginning of the first Peronist administration of Carlos Saúl Menem. This 'foundational date', as Sommer might call it, would confirm for Feinmann the installation of the free market as the international and local ideology of democracy, as the ground zero of all ideologies, including fascism and even communism. Thus, General Bussi's gun is a metonym for a still violent state that now purports to embrace free market capitalism and democracy.

From that image, Feinmann leads us to reflect on the meaning and concept of critique in relation to violence. Basing himself on Kant's *Critique of Pure Reason*, Sartre's *Critique of Dialectical Reason*, and Marx's *Introduction to the Critique of Hegel's Philosophy of Law*, he defines critique as the 'understanding' of violence, not its condemnation, and he concludes that critique is the basis for any form of transformation. Within these parameters, he asserts that in the 1970s, all sectors on the political spectrum in Argentina engaged in violence, from Peronism of the extreme left – the *Montoneros* – to the extreme right – the military and Triple A (death) squads. All sectors were caught in a logic of death: the more they killed, the more they had to kill. History was repeating itself. In the early years of the Republic, Moreno ordered Liniers's death, Lavalle, Dorrego's, while Sarmiento celebrated Peñaloza's decapitation (p. 76). And there were so many more! Argentine national history is replete with violence and revenge. Yet the violence of the *Montoneros* occurred at a moment of unquestionable realities: dictatorships, repression, and death. None of these justify violence, but at least they allow us to comprehend its causes. Feinmann concludes that, although in the 1970s, the despotic, repressive, and militarized Argentinian society was very far from achieving institutional transparency and legal enforcement, in the 1990s, a democratic society demands a legal framework that allows the citizens to sue for justice for the sacrificial deaths of the Dirty War, just as they can demand reparations for the continuing and different forms of violence in the present.

Through analogy and equivalence, two aspects of Feinmann's critique are thus outlined: as method and as social intervention. Critique becomes a methodological principle of dialectical reasoning and a source of transformational power. In criticizing the history of his community, the essayist Feinmann, like Sarmiento before him, makes a public gesture that calls for social and intellectual renewal. The image of the critic emerges as a witness and *exemplum* of the public voice. In so doing, Feinmann vindicates the revolutionary critic of the 1960s and 1970s and distances himself from the uncommitted critic of his own, post-modern era.

VIOLENCE AS HISTORICAL FAILURE

In *La sangre derramada*, Feinmann claims that the violence of the nineteenth and twentieth centuries in Argentina is the result of mistakes made by the first Argentinian intelligentsia after the May Revolution of 1810. One was in following the more extreme, Jacobin trends of the French Revolution: Mariano Moreno's *Plan of Operations* is a manual for the use of terror. Thus, the first government of the new Republic, the *Junta de Mayo*, under the inspiration of Moreno, ordered the execution of Santiago de Liniers, the defender of Buenos Aires against the British occupation in 1806. Although he is considered the hero of the *Reconquista*, Liniers was a royalist based in Córdoba, who opposed the Junta and was executed in consequence. Liniers came to embody the violent eradication of all opposition. Another error on the part of the Junta, an elite body representing the interests of Buenos Aires, was to establish the predominance of that city over the entire country. Feinmann quotes Juan Bautista Alberdi, the brilliant nineteenth-century political thinker, who says that Buenos Aires assumed the role of Spain, subjecting the provinces to the power of the metropolis. From 1810 onwards, the Junta follows a process of internal colonization which leads to the polarization of Argentina: the Unitarians of Buenos Aires against the Federalists of the provinces, a regime of violent retaliation carried out by both sides, which includes the murders of a great number of the protagonists of nineteenth-century Argentinian history.[7]

TRAGEDY AND HISTORY, OR HISTORY AS TRAGEDY

In order to illustrate how the original violence of the Republic has shaped the subsequent violence that has characterized the modern Argentine nation, Feinmann considers the military coups of the twentieth century, thus establishing another line of historical, ideological and cultural continuity with the governments of the nineteenth century. Here the essayist distances himself from the interpretations that proliferated in the 1980s, particularly during the Alfonsín administration (1983–89), whereby Uriburu's *coup d'état* against Yrigoyen on 6 September, 1930 – the first military coup of the twentieth century – was considered to be the antecedent of the chain of military coups that have plagued the political landscape. These culminated in 1983, when Alfonsín appeared as the champion who restored the long-denied democracy to the people. Feinmann notes, however, that Uriburu's coup was not the first. The first was the one that Lavalle organized against Dorrego in 1828, which in turn made the destiny of both – Dorrego and Lavalle – inseparable from that of Rosas, who avenged Dorrego's death. Once again, through a series of equivalences, the essayist interprets the foundational texts of the nineteenth century – *Facundo*, *Amalia*, *El matadero* – in the light of tragedy understood as historical destiny. In so doing, the main protagonists of national history – Lavalle, Rosas, Quiroga – become tragic. The essayist develops his basic premise: the past is always present in our everyday life, and the tragedy of yesterday is also the tragedy of today. Feinmann, in *La sangre derramada*, recomposes the great totemic text – *Facundo* – by including not only the Peronist experience of the 1970s but also the violence of the democratic decades – the 1980s and 1990s – in the long-standing 'national' literary tradition, thus reinforcing the historical claim of failure through an entire political, literary and cultural style. In doing so, Feinmann's essay intersects with another line of the nationalist essay tradition best exemplified by Ezequiel Martínez Estrada's *Radiografía de la pampa* (1933) (X-Ray of the Pampas). In Feinmann's essay there resonates a Hegelian sense of the tragic in History, and the tragic becomes a form of emplotment used in the same way as Martínez Estrada to treat the historical material to reformulate Sarmiento's scheme of civilization and barbarism (González, 1999; Arias Saravia, 2000).[8]

STYLE

Like the totemic text *Facundo*, *La sangre derramada* is written on the basis of analogies and equivalences. Piglia reminds us that Sarmiento's vision has a magical function: it serves to establish the link between terms that at first sight have no relationship. Everything acquires meaning if it is possible to reconstruct the equivalences between what is to be explained and something else that is already agreed upon and written about (p. 73). In this chapter I have tried to illustrate the ways in which *La sangre derramada* is constructed, how it re-creates a certain cultural morphology, which narrations nurture it, which rhetorical figures the essayist uses to develop his argument, how he recycles and creates a new environment in his contact zone with the present, that is, with the historical, economic, ideological, social and cultural conditions of the late 1990s.

The argument Feinmann presents in *La sangre derramada* is based on a series of quotations from a highly crystallized body of texts and cultural references that the national community already identifies as its own. The essayist conceives of himself as a political and cultural philosopher who writes on behalf of the dead, to point out to his national community the trajectory leading to a historical destiny that has already been played out, and to warn them of the necessity for change in order to avoid repetition.

Within this general rhetorical framework, time is articulated as a constant oscillation between present and past, which is nevertheless open to projection into a future of transformative possibilities. The premise is that to understand the present requires a look back at the past, to discover its continuities, its ambiguities and its defeats. It implies renegotiations with the enforced and still enforceable silence that a long tradition of state terrorism has established through multiple punitive means (the 'Law of Due Obedience', the 'Law of Closure', torture, disappearance).[9] Contrary to the postulates of aesthetic realism (Barthes, 1986), in which the figure of the enunciator, as he emerges from the text, stands apart from and above the reality to be described and explained, the enunciator of *La sangre derramada* is formed by the experiences in which he participated, with the thoughts that preceded or even those with which he anticipated the images and concepts that these have produced, and which he wishes to record. The sacrificial deaths of the 1970s, those of the left-wing Peronists-*Montoneros*, just like those of the nineteenth-century heroes and founders of the nation, are thus connected in a network of analogies and equivalences. Each of them plays a specific role, at a precise moment, and in the na(rra)tion of a culture that outlines its own destiny and cultural style. *La sangre derramada* recovers the past not only to know it better, but to find in it the clues that make it possible to understand and transform the present, and above all, to reinforce the nature of violence as foundational myth for a nation that is forever attempting to (re)found itself. Feinmann's essay does not make any claim to originality; it is not written on a *tabula rasa,* but rather on a palimpsest of already created na(rra)tions, myths and legends that are the substance itself of resistance to historical 'truth'. One example is his reference to *El matadero* (The Slaughterhouse) by the nineteenth-century writer Esteban Echeverría, which confirms Sarmiento's theme of civilization and barbarity. A century later, in the 1950s, Borges and Bioy Casares would write 'La fiesta del monstruo' ('The Feast of the Monster'), a short story similar to Echeverría's. Both narratives are full of hatred and intolerance, but the hatred in the text by Borges and Bioy Casares is not the same as that expressed in the earlier text. The feast is in the square (the Plaza de Mayo where Peronists used to gather) and the monster is Perón. (Here we are reminded of Arturo Jauretche's essay of the 1950s, *Los profetas del odio* (Prophets of Hatred), another landmark in the nationalist essay tradition.) This overlapping and saturation of analogies and textual equivalences are the late twentieth century's response to violence: a desire to foster social understanding and civil responsibility through a culturally based memory. Hence the new role of the essayist, of the intellectual in democracy, advocates for the creation of a *res publica* able to challenge the establishment. Through self-reflection, the possibility of repairing past violent deeds allows the nation to break away from the tragic destiny of the forces of evil.

Analogy and equivalence are the key rhetorical devices in Feinmann's essay. The mass of quotations of other texts, which the new text declares explicitly to be its source, in fact constitutes a force that potentially opens a path to new interpretations and erases previous ones. The new text effectively accommodates, incorporates, and even forges, adds, defends, or conquers the previous texts. The quotations take on another sense by the simple fact of repetition, and this transforms and adds a new element to the essay.

CONCLUSION

Studying *La sangre derramada* at the dawn of the twenty-first century for its description of violence in the 1970s, particularly in relation to the new expressions of violence within democracy in the last two decades, has important consequences for the role of literature. In an era of the death of the subject, the end of history, ideologies and master narratives, and with literature in crisis through the predominance of the media, the publishing market, and the virtual world of the Internet, Feinmann's *La sangre derramada* reclaims the social function of literature and its will for self-definition. The essay, as a genre caught between the two institutions of modernity – literature and the media – maintains its ties with the search by nineteenth-century writers for a Latin American identity and for modes of representation that will transcend the mimetic impulse to imitate Western influences. As Cristina Kirklighter contends, how Latin American intellectual activists and revolutionaries used the essay still fosters a critique of the ills of elitism and promotes support for democratic ideals (Kirklighter, 2002). Just as in the nineteenth century the connection between politics and literature played a crucial role in the foundation of the nation, literature is again called upon to save the nation as a community, in contrast to claims concerning the end of nations in an era of so-called globalization. Once again, we return to Julio Ramos's insights in relation to the intersections and limits of autonomy between journalism and literature and the 'irreducible' particularity of Latin American literature, which entails the binarisms of parody and its tendency to ideologize the margin, as José Enrique Rodó's *Ariel* and Roberto Fernández Retamar's *Calibán* demonstrate. The heterogeneity of journalism in the nineteenth century was very important in producing an image of the nation, and in this process, as Anderson points out, writing became important for the regulation and delimitation of the 'national' space (Ramos, 2001, p. 88). In this context, the essay and its close links with journalism would not only destabilize the more institutionalized space of literature, but, later, with the impact of the critical moment of the avant-garde, would dismantle and continually erode the borders between art and life, history and experience. Moreover, the question of why violence is such a central topic of the Argentinian essay of recent decades makes us reflect on the public use of history in an attempt to narrate the experience of violence and come to terms with the sufferings and the truths of the past, something that was impossible to envision in times of repression. It also brings up the issue of violence in the bourgeois modern state, that is, the state as a site of concentration of the violence that the dominant classes exercise over the people. Violence appears as concealment and in this need to conceal the violent underpinnings of the modern state violence becomes a constitutive element of politics.

Finally, I must recognize that I chose *La sangre derramada*, or rather this text chose me, because, like Feinmann, I am a part of the experiences of the 1970s, faced with the loss of my sister and of many of my generation who were subjected to that era of violence. The relevance of such experiences for cultural studies and what they tell us about transformations in the realm of the intellectual field as a space of cultural and political struggle is that I am a survivor who, like Feinmann, must struggle to come to terms with the violence and the silence that accompanied it: the ostracism of those whose loved ones were 'disappeared'. One must remember in order to forget. That is why writers like Feinmann are so important.

Among other issues that arise are what cultural studies tell us about the relationship between author and intellectual critic, or the new relations established between literature and the media. Feinmann in *La sangre derramada* is both author and critic and, like Sarmiento's great work, his essay was first released in a series of articles and newspaper chronicles, which were aimed at a broad public, thereby establishing correlations or social, cultural, political, and literary networks. They create a language in which the passionate reader that Eco speaks of recognizes and identifies himself or herself with a way of feeling and naming things according to the principle of the recognition of belonging to a certain community as well as imagining the nation in a certain style.

Feinmann's style, based on analogy and equivalences, cannot avoid the risk of stereotyping, which carries the danger of reducing dialectical relations to polarization in black and white. The purpose of literature is to fulfil an ideological function, and the function of Feinmann's essay is to proselytize, that is, to put forward an ideological position. In the formation of that position, literary style is subordinated to all forms of other cultural considerations; the essay itself is submitted to a process of neutralization, and takes on the character of a cultural dough made up of archaic, contemporary and emergent elements that favour a concept of social discourse in which literature actively participates as one – but only one – of its practices. Above all, this concept points to the aesthetic of cultural appropriation and recycling that characterizes our post-modern condition. The essay as a genre, at the crossroads of literature and the media, aims to move public opinion in the direction of a democratic society in spite of and beyond its own tendency to polarize. If we could prove that after these two centuries of failed foundations, all the narrations that make up the national essay 'are repeated in the same disorder (which, repeated, would constitute an order: Order itself)', Feinmann and I, together with Borges, would rejoice 'in this elegant hope' (Borges, 1962, pp. 87–8).

DEDICATION

This chapter is dedicated in loving memory of my sister Tyna (1946–75).

NOTES

1 My translation. Although the opening lines of the Introduction to *Facundo* are known to every Argentinian, English translations of *Facundo* do not include the Introduction. Yet it is precisely the emotional force and tone of this exhortation that have fueled the myth of *Facundo*.

2   For example, at the seventh 'Encuentro de escritores' held in Monterrey, Mexico, in October 2002, which brought writers and scholars together from different countries in Latin America as well as from the United States and Europe to discuss violence from a variety of perspectives. This conference, titled 'Territorios de la violencia', addressed public and private violence, violence as witnessed through female eyes, as silence and censorship, as a particular phenomenon on borders and in other worlds, as literary inspiration, and as narrative.

3   The sense of bonding with a particular tradition of texts and writers has interesting consequences for the development of literature within our so-called era of globalization. Contrary to certain claims of transnational literatures that write against the grain of nationalism, Latin American literature of violence may be conceived as confined within the boundaries of its own national community. As has been amply demonstrated (Morello-Frosch, 1985; De Grandis, 1993; Colás, 1994; Pons, 1998; Maristany, 2000), Piglia's *Artificial Respiration* allegorizes the violence of the so-called Dirty War by telling the (hi)story of the violence of the 1970s with reference to Sarmiento's nationalist call, in order to interpret within a highly modernist aesthetic the terror and violence inflicted upon the nation.

4   No one has dealt better than Ricardo Piglia with the question of the totemic text in Argentine literature of the post-dictatorship period, both as a parricidal act and as a reinscription of the parent-text. And he does it through an aesthetic which owes more of its inventiveness to a Borgesian aesthetic than to the pamphleteering rhetoric of Sarmiento's essay. Nevertheless, Piglia's *Artificial Respiration* and Feinmann's *La sangre derramada*, no matter how different from each other aesthetically, are related in the sense that both are writing within the limits of what constitutes the nation.

5   Arturo Jauretche, along with Raúl Scalabrini Ortíz, played a leading role in the formation of FORJA, an anti-imperialist breakaway group of the Radical Party that advocated nationalization of foreign-owned companies. Later, Jauretche joined Peronism and participated in organizing the Peronist opposition after the 1955 coup and was opposed to the liberal economic policy lead by the Onganía military dictatorship in the late 1960s. His writings, although concerned with contemporary politico-economic issues, are imbued with a strong culturalist accent and language. This is seen particularly in the case of *Manual de zonceras argentinas, El medio pelo en la sociedad argentina*, and *Polémicas*. Interestingly, in December 2002 an exhibition on the works by Arturo Jauretche titled 'Basta de zonceras' was organized and sponsored by the Secretary of Culture and other private institutions in the city of Buenos Aires at the Sociedad Rural. The publication of his *Complete Works* was launched and important intellectuals gathered to discuss the importance and projections of Jauretche's ideas.

6   General Bussi was at the time Premier of the province of Tucumán, the same person who in the 1970s became deeply implicated in politically repressive campaigns against leftists in this province.

7   Incidentally Beatriz Sarlo, in a note for *Clarín*, also refers to Alberdi in relation to the political landscape of Argentina in May of 2001, which she characterizes as profoundly divided between Buenos Aires and the interior provinces. Alberdi was the first to claim that the May Revolution was responsible for this division, which has continued to shape the nation ever since.

8   Interestingly, Horacio González in *Fragmentos pampeanos* (1999) deals at length with this 'tragic' interpretation in the Argentinian essay tradition and Leonor Arias Saravia in *La Argentina en clave de metáfora: un itinerario a través del ensayo* (2000), following Hayden White's modes of emplotment as outlined in his *Metahistory* (1973), describes how Martínez Estrada reformulates Sarmiento's scheme of civilization and barbarism in light of the Argentinian crisis of the 1930s, the so-called the infamous decade (*la década infame*).

9   The Law of Due Obedience ('Ley de Obediencia Debida') and the Law of Closure ('Ley de Punto Final') were the laws enacted after the fall of the Junta, which pardoned the military for any crimes committed while in office. James W. McGuire asserts that 'the attempt to curb military power and to bring human rights violators to justice provoked armed rebellions by military in April 1987, January 1988, and December 1988'. These rebellions were not explicitly aimed at installing a new military regime; they were disruptive enough to cause Alfonsín to backtrack on the human rights trials. In December 1986, the government introduced a bill of closure that set a 60-day deadline for initiating further prosecutions, and in April 1987, it sent Congress a 'due obedience' bill that exempted all officers at or below the rank of lieutenant colonel from prosecution for human rights violations on the grounds that they had been 'just following orders. Congress quickly passed both bills into law' (McGuire, 1997, p. 186).

8

Eva Perón
One woman, several masks
Lidia Santos

> Y si no nos tomáramos tan a pecho su muerte, digo?
> ('What if we didn't take her death so much to heart?')
> (Néstor Perlonguer, *El cadáver*)

SCENE 1: THE SHORT STORY

In the first place, no one even knows what to call her: Eva Duarte, María Eva Duarte de Perón, Eva Perón, Evita Duarte, or simply Evita? All of these names along with many euphemisms such as 'that woman', the '*Señora*', the 'mother of the shirtless', 'the mare', among others, are indicators of the multiplicity of identities attributed to the woman who is the focus of this chapter.[1] Multiplied during the brief period of her life (1919–52), these various designations correspond to the different facets of the myth that transformed her into an icon whose reach extends beyond the borders of Argentina, the country of her birth.[2] With each rebirth Eva Perón seems to laugh at us yet again, masquerading and assuming a new identity. According to semiology, this is the nature of myth. A sign empty of all signified, pure signifier, a myth is characterized by a structural emptiness that allows it to be remade indefinitely (Barthes, 1957).

From the point of view of anthropology, the myth endures due to its symbolic nature. Considering Argentine society to be a complex society, the various sides of the Eva Perón myth seem to be the result of a manipulation of differing traditional symbols. In this manner, the objective of constructing the illusion of a continuous identity is achieved, something which is virtually impossible in complex societies (Taylor, 1979).

From this perspective, however, we would be opposing the myth to the historical figure, which cannot be denied. Eva Perón was part of an important chapter in Argentine history. Thus, the historians assert, one must seek the hidden truth in the myth's different trappings. In this area, the field is a slippery slope. Dates were erased, facts changed, frequently by the very historical figure in question (Fraser and Navarro, 1981; Navarro, 1981). Ultimately, her body, the only part of her life that seemed destined to maintain its essence, by means of the decision to embalm her, was stolen.

The myth, however, is at the same time a short story, if we focus on it from the perspective of literature. In the case of Eva Perón, César Aira reminds us: 'Eva Perón is a myth to the Argentines; a story that we all know and that we never tire of having retold again and again' (1991a, p. 106).[3] I show here how literature narrated this story, certain that literature and art will aid in understanding the transformation of the historical figure into an icon through which the past and the present, cultural memory, and the banalization of the everyday converge.

SCENE 2: LEGITIMATE OFFSPRING

Jorge Luis Borges narrated one of the first literary versions of the iconic coronation of Eva Perón (Borges, 1989 [1960]). The anticipation with which Borges perceived the multiplying capacity of the myth created during the populist rule of Juan Domingo Perón allowed him to extract from the tale one of the founding ideas of postmodern theory: the concept of simulacrum (Young, 1999, p. 231, and Cortés Rocca and Kohan, 1998, p. 113). Borges describes a funerary ritual that repeats Eva Perón's burial as farce. The false Perón who accepts the condolences of the population of the small outlying town, on the banks of the Paraná River (the narrator situates his history in Chaco province, one of the country's poorest, on the border with Brazil, thus as marginal literarily as in the Foulcauldian sense) is a *mestizo* of native Indian origin (*aindiado*) with 'the inexpressive face of a mask or a dullard' (Borges, 1964, p. 31) ('una cara inexpresiva de opa o de máscara') (Borges, 1989, p. 167). Eva Perón, on the other hand, is a blonde doll who lies in a cardboard box that looks like a casket. The last sentence of the brief story makes explicit the conception of a copy without an original (Baudrillard, 1981): 'The mourner was not Perón and the blonde doll was not the woman Eva Duarte, but neither was Perón Perón nor was Eva Eva' (Borges, 1964, p. 31) ('El enlutado no era Perón y la muñeca rubia no era la mujer Eva Duarte, pero tampoco Perón era Perón ni Eva era Eva') (Borges, 1989, p. 167).

Borges recreates one of the underpinnings of the Eva Perón myth: the impossibility of finding an *original* of her story. Her birth and death were placed into question. She made her own birth certificate disappear, and her embalmed body was mutilated, lost, and transported across two continents. Her acting career (1935–45) was erased from her official biography. Finally, the brief public part of her biography (1946–50) conferred on her euphemisms whose opposition annuls any definitive version of her historical role. Together, these facts transform her into a *fictional* character, that is, permanently reinvented.

It is no surprise, then, that such a character has generated countless narratives in many genres. In the case of the literature that takes her as its theme, the figure of the double, multiplicity of plots, and repetition of episodes are salient. Mainly, the tales recycle themselves in such a way that we can divide them into two kinds of family. As happened in Eva Perón's life, alongside a legitimate family of writers dedicated to the deconstruction of her public *persona*, there is also a bastard family of writers, occupied with reinventing her as an actress.

Her legitimate family situates the character in the intrigues of the Peronista State. The first story along this line, 'La señora muerta' ('The Dead Lady'), by David Viñas (1963), describes her funeral just as Borges did. The simulacrum of Eva, in this case, is her own apparition in line at the wake, transfigured into a 25-year-old woman, in other words, the same age that Eva would have been when she met Perón. Viñas recreates in the meeting between the narrator and the woman some oft-repeated episodes of the life of the then actress. The exchange of sex for food, or the ease with which the woman accepts the man with whom she has just crossed the street, recalls the stories of Eva Duarte's relationship with the singer and composer of tangos, Agustín Magaldi (in whose company she left the city where she was born), the writer Roberto Arlt (Ludmer, 1999, pp. 262, 390), and, finally, with Juan Domingo Perón. However, the euphemism used in the title – *señora* – refers the reader to Eva Duarte's life after she met Perón, in other words, to her official phase. The narrative's present tense is that of the wake of this *señora*, a title used under Peronismo to refer to the wife of the nation's President. But another tense – the past of the deceased first lady – is superimposed on the present by means of her resurrection in the form of 'that woman', a euphemism used by her enemies, with which they alluded to the *deviant conduct* of Eva Duarte pre-Perón.[4] The force of the Viñas short story is created by the battle between the dead Eva Perón and her young and healthy double, as seductive or even more so than the artificially made-up corpse. The epilogue of Viñas' 'La señora muerta' can be understood 'as the possibility that the other Evita may predominate' (Cortés Rocca and Kohan, 1998, p. 77). That is to say, in the battle between the historical figure and her anonymous double, the subject of Viñas' short story, the young healthy woman full of vitality would win.

This argument is confirmed in the 1970s. The Peronist Youth during those years, by choosing as a symbol the one whom they considered their 'mother', opt for an image saturated with vitality. Cortés Rocca and Kohan show how Evita, as she herself indicated that her 'shirtless' followers should call her, appeared in the photograph that circulated on the posters and pamphlets of the movement with her hair down wearing a masculine shirt, the preferred feminine attire in the 1970s. Creators of the revolutionary Evita myth – 'If Evita had lived, she would be a *montonera*' ('Si Evita viviera, sería *montonera*') was one of the *Montonero* Party slogans[5] – the young Peronistas respected her intention to bury her undesirable past. Calling themselves the 'children of Evita', they reinvented her as the heroic *Evita*, capable of giving her life for her shirtless ones. At the same time, they considered her a precursor to a violent program in the pursuit of social and political change. Affirming themselves as descendants of a lineage, they set out to rescue her lost body, interpreting her final political acts as a signal that pointed to a radicalization of the class struggle and therefore justified it. For them, their mother's legacy was action.

SCENE 3: THE BASTARD CHILDREN

Soon, however, Evita's bastard children appear. They are the writers who deny her ability to generate and unify a nation, underscoring, instead, her capacity to fragment it. In his 1975 short story titled, 'Evita vive (en cada hotel organizado)' ('Evita lives on [in every organized hotel]'), Néstor Perlongher reinterprets another slogan of the Peronista Youth – 'Evita lives' ('Evita vive!') (Perlongher, 1989). In Perlongher's tale, she appears as a ghost in heterotopical spaces, that is, physical spaces where social relationships are reconfigured according to new symbolic attributes (Foucault, 1986). Hotels of prostitution or flophouses for drug addicts were thus changed upon being called 'organized hotels', as the last refuge of Eva Perón's militancy. Although inverting and disputing Evita's political myth, these locations maintain its utopian outline. The profane rituals dedicated to her in these reclusive spaces fill the emptiness of her banishment from the public spaces where she reigned during her life.[6] The mixture of two complementary euphemisms – saint and prostitute – intersect in the characterization of her. Evita, as she presents herself to all who appear, refers to the fact of 'being in heaven' in the three episodes that constitute the short story, at the same time that she includes herself in scenes of group sex and drug use. Told as first person depositions – each narrator swears to having participated in the scene in which Evita appears – the stories have in common the irreverent treatment of her character. In the second episode, for example, Evita is a drug trafficker's companion. The narrator summarizes the commentaries following her disappearance in this way: 'Evita would return: she had gone to make a pick up and would be right back, she wanted to divide up the batch of marijuana with each poor person so that all of the humble would get high' ('Evita iba a volver: había ido a hacer un rescate y ya venía, ella quería repartir un lote de marijuana a cada pobre para que todos los humildes andaran superbien') (Perlongher, 1989, p. 42).

Besides the humor contained in the quote, there is a perceptible change in the concept of multitude that until then Peronism had attempted to embrace. On introducing the word *poor* into the imaginary about Eva Perón, Perlongher breaks with the concept of *people* that supported Peronism in its two versions. The poor of 'Evita vive (en cada hotel organizado)' are no longer those who, assisting the representation of the nation in the great political rallies of primordial Peronism, contributed to the development of the image of a national subject. Nor do they belong to the ideal and abstract representation of national identity, underlying the revolutionary ideal of the 1970s. On the contrary, where they live and what they do are known precisely: they are slum dwellers, prostitutes, drug addicts. In this way, Perlongher's poor are a first version of those excluded from the socially acceptable categories up to that time. The emphasis on their exclusion, in part covered by the old Marxist declassification of *lumpen*, in part including in them the embryo of the concept of *multitude* recently established by Paolo Virno, is evidence of the new critical understanding accompanying the work of the bastard sons of Eva Perón (Virno and Hardt, 1996, pp. 188–209).[7]

In the three episodes, Evita is, like Perón in the Borges short story, a mask. In the first, she is a funeral mask, described with the repeating images of the embalmed cadaver, as 'the patches of cancer underneath' ('las manchitas del cáncer por abajo') (Perlongher, 1989, p. 41) her shining skin. In the second episode, the mask recalls the prostitutes and drag queens, since she 'is a 38-year-old woman [the age at which Eva Perón died], blonde with a worn air about her, heavily made up, with a tight bun' ('es una mujer de 38 años, rubia, un poco con aires de estar muy reventada, recargada de maquillaje, con rodete ...') (ibid., p. 41). In the third scene, she is reduced to the 'husky sensual voice of a radio announcer' ('cascada, sensual, como de locutora') (ibid., p. 42); and to the smell of a dead woman. In all of these episodes, the character incarnates what several critics observed in Perlongher's work: his 'cultivation of the mask of dissimulation' (Masiello, 2001, p. 70). Nevertheless, unlike most of the previous authors, the mask is used in its meaning of performance artifice, transforming the passive corpse – stolen, hidden, lost – into a libidinal force that allows Evita to become a national icon. Once more, one perceives the rupture brought about by Perlongher. As opposed to the guerrilla movement, avenging Evita's young and healthy image, here the bets are on the victory of the artificially beautified cadaver.

The fact is most obvious in Perlongher's poetry, where Evita is a recurring theme. In 'El cadáver de la nación' ('The National Corpse') (Perlongher, 1997, pp. 177–83), poetic artifices are included in the author's 'politics of style': manipulation, make-up, decoration (Echevarren, 1997). The active nature of the 'corpse' is imitated in Perlongher's neo-baroque language. Even as a zombie, Evita is 'a flux of putrid power' ('un flujo de la potencia hedionda') (Perlongher, 1989, p. 177) that the poet reproduces in the poem's frenetic rhythm, emphasized by enjambments and enumerations. At the same time, prosaic and spurious details such as 'nylon Revlon', diminish the solemnity of her death. The influence of Latin American neo-baroque poets such as Lezama Lima and Severo Sarduy reveals itself not only in the poem's language but also in the conception of Evita as mother.[8] Precisely this theme – flight from the mother – feeds other poems, such as 'El cadáver' and 'Mme. S.' (Perlongher, 1997, pp. 42–5, 88–9). In all of them, the corpse, both still and active, of the goddess-prostitute Eva Perón, designated as mother, is treated as a political body, whose androgynous sensuality is shared with her husband.[9]

Perlongher is not the first-born of her bastard children. Copi, an Argentine-Uruguayan author who emigrated in his youth to France, premières his play *Eva Perón* in 1969 in Paris (Copi, 2000). The author stated that he portrayed Eva Perón as a Hollywood heroine because 'this was perhaps the only thing that she ever wanted to be and the only thing she was ever denied'. The fact that the theater where the play was performed was invaded by masked men who interrupted the performance and vandalized the set proves, in fact, that Copi was not far from being one of Eva Perón's legitimate offspring (Copi, 1990, pp. 5, 8, 13). However, the French critics proceeded to 'bastardize' the text and the performance, tarring it with all sorts of negative adjectives, arguing that 'Eva Perón did not deserve such treatment.'[10] And what was this offensive treatment? In the first place, that he had not respected the solemn aspect of her disease and her death. In the second, that he had made her character express herself in common language, even with swear-words. Finally, that he represented Eva Perón by means of unarticulated screams and all sorts of scenic exaggeration, played by a transvestite!

Copi is also not the first to portray Eva Perón from this perspective. *La traición de Rita Hayworth* (The Betrayal of Rita Hayworth), a novel by Manuel Puig, had already used the theme in a similar manner (Puig, 1982 [1968]). Although it does not refer specifically to Evita, Puig is the first to divide the literary field of the Argentine left by the way that it portrays Peronismo. The dresses and diamonds, an artifice that transforms her into the California heroine of Copi's play, meet in a semantic space similar to that of the films described by the protagonist in *La traición de Rita Hayworth*. Both parodies form part of the critical and political strategy practiced by homosexual groups, called *camp*. This definition of *camp* replaces its first reception as 'sensibility' (Sontag, 1966). In the 1990s *camp* comes to signify 'a parodic plan originating in the *gay* subculture, which offers the immediate possibility of a subtextual reading' (Kleinhans, 1994). Constructed as self-conscious *kitsch*, *camp* helps in this case to read the subtext of the Eva Perón myth, at the same time that it offers an alternative way of telling it as artifice.

SCENE 4: TRANSVESTITES

In Puig's case, *camp* is not as virulent, because his criticism of the predominance of critical reason among his contemporaries is steeped above all in melancholy (Contreras, 1998, p. 309). However, he is a master of the arts of artifice. In the play *Bajo un manto de estrellas*, first performed in Rio de Janeiro in 1982, he ends the stage directions for the first act with this sentence: 'Nothing is realistic; everything is stylized' (Puig, 1997, p. 13). His intention extends to the dialogues, characterized by a narrative syntax that sounds artificial in its orality. The clichéd adjectivization and the stereotyped literary tropes radicalize the stylization further, which extends even to the plot of the play. Although Evita is not mentioned, it is possible to recognize her as a subtext of the plot, where a bastard daughter and adulterous passions are not missing. The radio where her voice was first known is omnipresent in the dialogues. On the radio, the characters say, tragedies are broadcast 'with a musical background by the great maestros' ('con fondo musical de grandes maestros') (ibid., p. 16). By means of feminine consumption, men are reduced to 'radiolisteners' ('radioescuchas') (ibid., p. 19) and everyone – the men of the house and the maid – can always rely on the radio, whenever they want to hear 'other voices' ('otras voces') (ibid., p. 65). The presence of a nurse among the characters and the maid who finds a 'bundle full of jewelry' ('atado repleto de joyas') (ibid., p. 69) recall Copi's play. In it, Eva Perón kills the nurse – for most of the bastard authors Evita's nurses are a leitmotif – whose body is viewed at the wake in place of her, and she escapes with the jewels.[11]

It is here that Manuel Puig uses ellipses in order for other narrators to continue the story. By veiling the epic nature of her character, he exposes her disguises and masks, revealing in this way a secret that César Aira solves in his essay on Copi: Eva Perón is a transvestite! (Aira, 1991a). This assertion summarizes the point of view with which these authors approach Eva Perón. Considering her permanent capacity to construct and deconstruct herself, through performance, her gender identification is left open, like that of transvestites. Integrating this statement into his own poetics, Aira's narration of the short story about Evita is subtle. In a first version, he conceives of her as being responsible for the implantation of a matriarchal structure that marked the Argentina in which he grew up (Aira was born in 1949). In this way he reproduces the anthropological interpretation of the *black* myth of Eva Perón, in which she appears as the controller of a network that castrated, sometimes literally, the men of the Peronist regime.

As in the case of Manuel Puig, Evita is only a subtext in the autobiographical novels of César Aira. In *Cómo me hice monja* (How I became a nun) (1993), that takes place more directly during the Peronist period, Evita only appears as the name of a nurse, 'Nurse Perón on the Pediatric ward' ('la enfermera-Perón de la sala de Pediatría') (Aira, 1996a, p. 40). There is an evident reference to a rereading of Copi and Puig, in whose work, as we have seen, the Peronist nurse is a *leitmotiv*. But only in the stories by Aira does this character appear in the context she occupied during the Peronist regime. With the attribution of the surname, Aira transforms her into a simulacrum of Eva Perón, an interpretation compatible with the role that nurses occupied in the Perón regime. In the Eva Perón Foundation the women, 'beyond fulfilling their professional functions in the hospitals built by this institution, worked in the emergency services, prepared new works for inauguration, were social service assistants and even represented her [Eva Perón] in parades' (Navarro, 1981, p. 235). Even so, if the nurses multiplied the role of Evita, serving as her simulacra, in the novel they come to represent the process of multiplication that Aira attributes to fiction itself. In addition, removed from their temporal and historical context, they function in all of these works as Evita *clones*, transformed in this way more than ever into a postmodern simulacrum. In this sense, Aira departs from the treatment that Borges gives the same theme. In Borges' 'El simulacro' (The Sham), Eva Perón becomes incarnate in popular myth, in the many Evitas who multiply throughout Argentina after the death of the historical figure. In Aira's case, however, Evita herself is considered a simulacrum, in other words, a character capable of reproducing herself while still alive through other women, condemned by their subordination to blind obedience to the Peronist doctrine. The impregnable feminine network formed in this way confers a matriarchal tone on Peronismo that appears as a subtext in the narratives of Aira, which are peopled with phallic mothers, such as in *Cómo me hice monja*, or hysterical mothers, such as the protagonist of *La costurera y el viento* (The Seamstress and the Wind) (Aira, 1996b). Moreover, while parody of the surrealist tale predominates in *La costurera* – beginning with the syntagm of the title – one cannot deny that there is an allusion to the sewing machines that Evita presented to housewives.

Cómo me hice monja returns us to Perlongher. The accumulation of contradictory episodes and the characters' changing identities – note that the narrator's identity oscillates between masculine and feminine – align Aira with a group of writers I call the bastard children of Evita, whose commonality is to interpret her from a neo-baroque perspective.[12] The narrator finds the baroque in the personalities of the students who participated in his 'girlish' games, characterized by 'twisted, ludic, baroque personalities' ('personalidades retorcidas, lúdicas, barrocas'). Thus, baroque for the author is a synonym of a textual game.

Radio melodramas are brought into this baroque game. From them the narrator says he extracted the 'golden rule of fiction: it is too complicated not to be true' ('la regla de oro de la ficción: es demasiado complicado para no ser cierto') (Aira, 1993. p. 65). The narrator learned valuable lessons, above all from fictional melodramas – there were also historical and religious ones – because the radio dramas 'did not have a basic mechanism, they were a floating complication' ('no tenía mecanismo de base, era una complicación flotante') (ibid., p. 72). But what César Aira hides in this supposedly autobiographical tale is that the feminine voice that narrates *Cómo me hice monja* arose out of the radio melodrama serials.

It is clear that the radio is inscribed in the world Aira describes as 'the world of mothers' ('el mundo de las madres'), his 'new experience' ('nueva experiencia') following his father's imprisonment. Here also lies the root of the oscillation in the narrator's gender, in coming to share domestic experiences with his mother. Besides, his mother's profession after the family tragedy – laundry ironer – turns the home into a workspace. In this *shirtless* feminine universe, where the public and private are indistinguishable, the radio, according to the story, was omnipresent.

But how was the 'world of the mothers' not to be identified with the matriarchy led by Eva Perón? How not to relate 'the rock of solid love' ('roca de amor sólido') that according to the narrator characterized the radio dramas of love with the speeches that Eva Perón also disseminated on the radio? More importantly, how not to realize the importance of her voice, that subjugated all others, feminine or masculine, for so long in the minds of Argentine radio listeners? With all of this data, we can state that Aira's voice as a transvestite has its roots in Eva Perón, that matriarch who, like the transvestites, contained both sexes in a single body.

The enigma of the feminine narrative voice certainly also derives from Manuel Puig, who stated through the words of one of his characters that when he read a book he imagined that the words were reaching him in a woman's voice (Puig, 1980, p. 49). Aira interpreted the metaphor as the myth of Scheherezade, attributing the role of sultan to Puig (Aira, 1991b). This is a plausible interpretation, but I would like to add the importance of Eva Perón's voice in the fictional universe of these writers, whom I call her bastard children. All born during the period of the growth of radio, they declare a position in the political and literary debate of the period in which they lived or live by quoting its programs. By means of the 'voices of the ether' ('voces del éter') in Aira's words, these authors belong to a vanguardist group that recycles the voices from *below* integrating them critically into their novels. Among these voices, Eva Perón's is certainly one of the strongest.

FINAL SCENE: THE ARCHIVE

The end of the twentieth century returned Evita to her origins, that is, to mass culture. If Copi was correct, she would have liked to see herself portrayed in films produced in such distant and diverse countries. On the other hand, her Dior dresses are exhibited in the Metropolitan Museum of New York and we, academic researchers from the most varied disciplines, dedicate our time to investigating her myth. As the protagonist of a conservative modernization, she knew unlike anyone else how to prepare her appearance for global postmodernism.

According to Marysa Navarro, Evita's theatrical experience facilitated her success. To a large degree, she invented her public *persona* from the radio dramas that she had read, which appeared to have been her only cultural repertoire. The sentimental culture of the radio dramas spread easily to her speeches (her first editor, in fact, was the author of the radiodramas) and her life, ultimately, was the full realization of their melodramatic plots (Navarro, 1981, pp. 336–51).

Delving further, we can find the reason for her transformation into an icon. The authors whom I term her bastard children give us additional clues. Lamborghini names the parturient in his story, 'El Fiord', Carla Greta Terón

(Lamborghini, 1988). In addition to the androgynous nature of the name, the opposite poles that make up the Evita myth coexist within it. Carlos Gardel and Greta Garbo, themselves androgynous figures, are joined in this name, annulling not only the opposition of masculine and feminine but also the juxtaposition of local and outsider. The last name (Terón) is a *porte-manteau* that joins Perón and *tesón*, a word that denotes inflexibility, masculinity, and also libidinal energy (erection). In this way, the transvestites of Perlongher and Copi simply make the same idea explicit.

Aira, alternatively, explains Eva Perón's embodiment as a transvestite in this way: 'Just take the elements (of the myth of Eva Perón) one by one (the phallic female, the humiliation of being a woman, the Dior dresses, the Revolution ...) and shuffle them as if to interpret them.' Puig's work, whose range of mass culture is broader, perhaps best helps us comprehend the permanent inclusion that characterizes the myth of Eva Perón. From his books we can extract almost all the stereotypes found in the fiction of mass culture. Román Gubern points out the difference between a dark woman and a blonde in American movies. The former is always a Latin, valued for her sensuality, while socially disdained. The blonde, at the dawn of film in Griffith, was the stereotype of innocence, although later she would come to be identified with the femme fatale, also representing freedom from cultural norms (Gubern, 1988, pp. 201–4). The two types, opposed in most of Puig's novels, appear mixed in Eva Perón's case. She went from being dark-haired to blonde; from sultry to innocent, thus she is powerful and free to return symbolically to the dark-haired woman of her origins.

If we apply the formula of Latin American melodramas to her, we will find striking similarities. Eva Perón was the illegitimate daughter who populated many plots of Mexican films from the 1930s and 1940s. She follows the destiny of many young women in these melodramas; in other words, she abandons her family in the countryside to try her luck in the big city. She ends up married to a wealthy rich man and is punished with the illness reserved for the rich, cancer (Oroz, 1992).[13] The young sinner returns to religion and becomes a saint. The list would be interminable, because what characterizes the Eva Perón myth is her complete return to the range that makes up the feminine pantheon of mass culture. Her myth is an archive, in the computer sense of the term, of the mass culture models that upon becoming the rhetoric of our time allows itself to be used in a neo-baroque esthetic.[14] In dominating the codes of this rhetoric, because she used them for so long, Eva Perón guaranteed her survival as an icon when she erased the Manicheistic oppositions of those codes.

Once again, César Aira helps us to read the myth in this way, which proves that literature also offers analytic instruments to the Humanities. The concept of the transvestite supposes, in this case, a kind of accumulation of feminine attributes. The proof is in the definition of the Peronist nurse in Copi's play, characterized by Aira as a product of the 'complete return to transsexuality' and from the outset 'on the other hand ... simply as a woman' (Aira, 1991a, p. 106). On the other hand, the performative identity contained there reveals what intuition these authors had about the failure of the one, continuous subject constructed by the first Peronism. It is not by chance that Lamborghini and Perlongher confine the Eva Perón myth to closed spaces. Their stories denote the confinement of a myth that was no longer identified with the unified nation constructed by populism. The failure of the guerrilla movement, so the two writers seem to say, was based on their ignorance of this factor. If Evita triumphs now, it is because her identity, since the birth of the myth about her, was multiple and performative. Such multiplicity allows for the glory of her past as a historical figure to be fused with the daily rituals dedicated to a popular and miraculous saint, producing with this mixture an enduring icon.

The literary treatment that her bastard sons gave her highlighted the process. While not portraying her seriously, they perceived the wiles of that woman who knew so well how to exploit the 'social artifacts' from which Latin American women are constructed (Ludmer, 1984). Her ability to hold at the same time the qualities of good and bad, feminine and masculine, magnanimous and authoritarian permitted these authors to include in her character all the levels present in the spectrum of the rhetoric of mass culture, even the absolutely complementary ones. The resulting staging was so efficient that it became a subtext for one of the vanguardist currents of her country's literature. The one that privileges the imaginary to the detriment of the documentary, perhaps for having learned with Eva Perón that even documents can be invented in order to compose some fictions of poor quality that the official histories would have us believe.

ACKNOWLEDGEMENTS

An earlier version of this article was published as 'Los hijos bastardos de Evita, o la literatura bajo el manto de estrellas de la cultura de masas', in *Canadian Journal of Latin American and Caribbean Studies* 24 (1999), 195–213.

NOTES

1. The plurality of names demonstrates the multiplicity of signifiers contained in her identity, that is, it indicates the plural materiality of the feminine construct of Eva Perón (Butler, 1993).
2. I believe that the transformation of Eva Perón into an icon, that is, the identificatory appeal that her figure acquired, began with the myth created while Peronism was still active.
3. Except for the translation of Borges, all others are mine.
4. The euphemism nourished a cycle of literary narratives. Rodolfo Walsh begins the cycle in 1965, with the short story 'Esa mujer' a title designating her embalmed

corpse (Walsh, 1981). That is how the Colonel, instructed by the post-Peronist state to make her disappear, refers to her. The officer's morbid passion for the corpse, which impedes him from fulfilling his task, moves Tomás Eloy Martínez to write the novel *Santa Evita* (Martínez, 1995), a kind of development of the Rodolfo Walsh short story. The figure of the Colonel, only an outline in 'Esa mujer', is transformed into a mad character in Martínez's conception, whose work alternates between his predecessor's two genres: the deposition and the detective novel. In Martínez's novel the simulacrum is the corpse that reproduces itself in a postmodern manner (in other words, quoting Borges) as fake dolls. Closing the cycle, the screenplay 'Eva Perón' by José Pablo Feinmann (Feinmann, 1999), sets out to answer the Hollywood version of the character in Alan Parker's film *Evita* (1996), starring Madonna. Feinmann bases his story on the historical character, narrating the political intrigues underlying the candidacy of Perón-Perón (Evita as a possible vice-president in 1951) in a realist manner.

5   The name *montonero* alluded to the informal army, made up of mounted brigades – *los montoneros* – that formed spontaneously during the Argentine wars of independence, during the nineteenth century. The radicalization of the struggle against the military dictatorship during the 1970s takes the Montonero Party underground, literally transforming it into an armed brigade. Its tactic now becomes revolutionary war, characterized by guerrilla actions against the state.

6   Oswaldo Lamborghini adopts a similar procedure in his treatment of Peronism during the 1970s. His stories are characterized by a succession of caves where the clandestine figures hid, where the closed hierarchies generated perverted relationships and sadomasochistic rituals (Lamborghini, 1988).

7   I refer, above all, to the opposition to the concept of people with which Virno characterizes the multitude. Elsewhere, I set out the first bases of this new critical understanding in the work of Manuel Puig, where I also analyze the presence of Eva Perón in *La traición de Rita Hayworth* and *La tajada* (Santos, 2001).

8   Roberto Echevarren calls attention to the epigraph of one of Perlongher's poems: 'Am I fleeing from Lezama Lima's mother?', recalling the reference to the following verse by the Cuban poet: 'desirous is he who flees from his mother'.

9   Juan José Salinas refers to the fact that the 'multidirectional and exuberant' sensuality used to mythify Juan Domingo Perón is extended at times to the point of making him bisexual (Salinas, 1989).

10 Maurice Rapin, *Le Figaro*, 7 March 1970 (quoted in Copi, 1990, p. 17).

11 That story is rewritten in Perlongher's short story 'Evita vive (en cada hotel organizado)'. Its third episode is narrated by the thief of one of Evita's necklaces, stolen after a sexual scene with her.

12 It is interesting to note how the authors who include mass culture in their fiction are concerned with attributing to themselves a genealogy that almost always has its roots in the baroque. In a previous study, I noted how the baroque can be considered the first vanguardist gesture, because it is based on groups that differentiated themselves by the use of encoded language, making difficulty itself the principal stimulus for attracting new followers and readers (Santos, 1998). In postmodern authors, this becomes transformed into a kind of differential rhetoric, a point of view that places them in a privileged group because they share, above all, technical stylization and artificial narratives.

13 According to Oroz, in Latin American melodramas, cancer is always an illness of the rich, while the poor are left with tuberculosis.
14 I conceive of mass culture as a rhetoric that substitutes learned rules with easily accessible generic media models, organized like the files of a computer.

PART 3
Culture as spectacle/commodity

9

The spectacle of identities
Football in Latin America
Eduardo P. Archetti

As industrialization started to transform many major cities in Latin America around 1900, new urban elites, both landlords and industrialists, emerged and became part of the international trade and financial system. In many ways, they adopted the lifestyle of businessmen and officials from the dominant countries of the world system. While in cultural life the influence was French, in sport the ideal was British. At private clubs the members of the elite participated in cricket, tennis, rowing, fencing, golf, polo, track and field, even boxing, and football. While most sports remained limited to upper and middle classes, football was rapidly popularized, and the same happened later with boxing. British sailors and especially railway workers, who were present in important numbers, played a crucial role in this process. It was not by accident that the oldest football clubs were founded in the main ports visited by sailors and traders: Rosario and Buenos Aires in Argentina, São Paulo/Santos and Rio de Janeiro in Brazil, Montevideo in Uruguay, Lima/Callao in Peru and Valparaiso in Chile (see Deusta Carvallo et al., 1984; Arbena, 1988; Mason, 1995; Archetti, 1996; Van Bottenburg, 2001). By the 1920s football was the most important sport practiced in most Latin American countries with some important exceptions that have remained until today. In Cuba, Puerto Rico, Nicaragua, the Dominican Republic, Panama and Venezuela that were, in different degrees, under the economic and political/military influence of the United States, baseball and boxing became the 'national sports'. Mexico is quite an interesting hybrid with football and baseball, predominantly in the Yucatán Peninsula, as the most popular sports.

The history of football in Latin America is, without any doubt, a successful one. Football was gradually professionalized in the 1930s and, since then, European hegemony has been under constant threat from the great Latin American teams. The first World Cup was held in Montevideo in 1930 and the host country, Uruguay, won. The Cup has been played 17 times and Latin American teams have been in the finals on 11 occasions: Brazil has won the Cup five times, Argentina and Uruguay two each, a great historical achievement. Moreover, since the 1920s until today, brilliant Latin American players have been bought by the wealthy clubs of Southern Europe and, more recently, by clubs in England, Holland, Turkey, Greece and Switzerland. The world is the 'home' of Latin American football players. Globalization started before it became an important subject of analysis in social sciences. Latin America's teams have had an enormous impact on the development and consolidation of world football.

In this chapter I will focus on the search for identities, or more exactly, the ways identities are displayed in the practice and spectacle of football. The search for identity in football is tied to style, both in the sense of individual and collective style. This implies the achievement of a difficult balance between individual characteristics and communal belonging in a game that is basically collective. The great player can transcend the style of given teams, but, nevertheless, in the quest for identity the great heroes are always associated with the success of teams – they need each other. In the first section, I will concentrate my analysis on the question of national identities. Football is a powerful masculine expression of national capabilities and potentialities and, in this sense, constitutes a symbolic and practical male arena for national pride and shame, joy and sorrow. The role of sport heroes in this respect is of crucial importance. A sports hero is an idol and icon who exists within a separate dimension of time, the time of heroes. The second section will deal with this cultural spectacle, exemplified in the archetypal lives of Garrincha and Maradona. In the final section, I will elaborate on the way identities are constructed and performances enacted by engaged supporters and audiences.

THINKING AND PRACTICING THE NATIONAL IN FOOTBALL

It has often been argued that a nation is an 'imagined political community' in the sense that its members share a sovereign boundary and have a strong feeling of communion. Hence, the ideology of nationalism should be integrated in social practices that can, over time, create an image of 'the people' having 'something' in common. For that purpose, it is crucial to identify social practices which appear to reflect ideas of nationalism and investigate the 'content' of these practices with respect to the actors involved and the meaning of the values conveyed. Presenting different cases will permit us to examine how certain bodily practices are involved in the formation of national imaginaries.

According to Leite Lopes (1999), a typical Brazilian way of playing football began to be recognized during the 1938 World Cup in France. Brazil had a strong team with two black stars, Leônidas da Silva and Domingos da Guia. European journalists admired a style of playing which led to improvisation, an ability demonstrated in specific acrobatic moves like the 'bicycle-kick'. This international recognition helped to strengthen the local perception of the originality of national players. Football acrobats were seen as the best image of the country. The transition from amateur to professional football in 1933 had, then, important consequences: 'it created a diversified labour market for players, coaches and related professionals; it resulted in football's enormous popularization and in the formation of a national identity with this sport at its centre; it also consolidated a characteristic style of play' (Leite Lopes, 1999, p. 94). However, this transformation was not without conflicts. Leite Lopes also points out that for decades there was a struggle between the coaches, formed in the physical education schools, and the players, molded by popular football, with its spontaneous body techniques. Thus, the Brazilian style of play can be seen as the working classes' appropriation of football.

DaMatta (1982) has argued that an emphasis on the role of football in the construction of the national in Brazil implies adopting a 'positive' perspective toward society and history. Brazil, according to DaMatta, is a society articulated by the sharp division between the 'home' and the 'street', and between the family – a system of hierarchical social relations and persons – and the market and free individuals. For DaMatta these divisions are less geographical or physical places than symbols of moral and ideological universes. The role of football is privileged because the personalized social world of the home and the impersonal universe of the street are combined in a public ritual (1982, p. 17). Impersonal rules regulating the game make possible the expression of individual qualities: 'football, in the Brazilian society, is a source of individualization ... much more than an instrument of collectivization at the personal level' (ibid., p. 27). The players escape from fate – the fate of class and race – and construct their own successful biographies in an open arena, as actors performing in the stadiums. Football makes it possible to experience equality and freedom of creativity in hierarchical contexts. In order to triumph, a football player (like a samba dancer) must have *jogo de cintura*, the capacity to use the body to provoke confusion and fascination in the public and in their adversaries (ibid., p. 28). A disciplined, athletic but boring player has no place in Brazilian football (ibid., p. 39).

This vision, however, is historically much more complex (see Rodrigues Filho, 1964; Vogel, 1982; Caldas, 1989; Rosenfeld, 1993; Leite Lopes, 1997; Guedes 1998; and Helal, Soares and Lovisolo, 2001). Leite Lopes (1997, p. 69) has shown that, while white Brazilian players were exported to Europe in the 1930s, especially to Italy, black players became virtually non-exportable. Black players appeared to be condemned to local success, to be Brazil's greatest players. If Vasco da Gama was the first Brazilian club to recruit working-class and black players in 1923, then Flamengo, the popular Rio de Janeiro club, in 1935 became the 'example of a universally "mixed-race" Brazilian club' (ibid., p. 69).

Football has been seen as a field in which miscegenation and racial co-existence modeled the new Brazil. The intellectual and political elites imagined Brazil, above all, as an example of *democracia racial* (racial democracy). It was an explicit nationalist ideology, a cultural myth, and, in many ways, a dream of how things ought to be. Football made possible social and economic mobility for mulattos and black players but this achievement has not brought racial equality in society at large. At the same time, and in spite of racial democratization in football, stereotypes and prejudices were prevalent in sports in the 1950s. The Brazilian defeat by Uruguay in the final game of the 1950 World Cup, held in Brazil, focused on the color of several black defenders who were accused of lacking courage and stamina. They were targeted as the scapegoats for the nation's tragedy because, as Vogel (1982, pp. 95–100) and Leite Lopes (1997, pp. 70–5) argue, the Brazilian sense of inferiority was related to racial stereotypes. The victory in the 1958 World Cup, later consolidated in 1962 and 1970, with a 'multi-racial' team, confirmed the excellence of the Brazilian style and the qualities of many black players, including defenders like Nilton Santos and Djalma Santos. Leite Lopes maintains that the Brazilian style of football resembles physical activities which have ethnic Afro-Brazilian origins, like *samba* or *capoeira* (a martial sport of African origin) (see also Roberts, 1972, pp. 26–9). The European identification of a Brazilian style of playing relating football and *samba* (or eventually *capoeira*), manifested in the current expression of '*samba*-football', is therefore not an arbitrary creation; it is rooted in Brazilian self-imagery and identity. This identification establishes important cultural differences, because the existence and development of European styles of playing football are not linked to music and dance.

The case of Argentina confirms with variations the Brazilian historical and sociological trend (see Archetti, 1994, 1996, 1999). In the nineteenth century, British immigrants not only brought to the new country industrial capital, new technology in agriculture, and financial institutions, but their modern sports. The first 'official' football match was played in 1867, only four years after the creation of the Football Association of London. This first national league and, until 1911, the dominating clubs emerged from British schools. Not only was the game a British export but so were the standards and the quality of the play too. Argentinian football grew under the influence of the excellent British professional teams that came to play in Buenos Aires since 1905 and until the First World War – among them Southampton, Nottingham Forest, Everton and Tottenham Hotspur.

In the accepted national narrative, the first basis of football was British and the second was *criollo* (creole/national) (see Archetti, 1996). One of the arguments used refers to the ethnic origins of the players in the most famous teams and also those playing for the national team. In the era of the British founding – from 1887 until 1911, the year when the hegemony of the Alumni, the 'glorious British team', was broken – players of British origin predominated. The *criollo* basis began in 1913 when Racing Club, without a single player of British origin, won the championship for the first time. From that moment the 'British' clubs declined in importance, and their players slowly disappeared from the national teams. In Argentina, a country of immigrants from Europe, the *criollo* was related to the predominance of players with Spanish and Italian surnames. The *criollo* was founded through the sons of Latin immigrants. The sons of 'British' immigrants were never conceived of, in football, as *criollos*, and could not become *criollo* by playing football. 'Britishness' was identified with being phlegmatic, with discipline, method, with the collective, force and physical power. These virtues helped to create a repetitive style like a 'machine'. The *criollo*, thanks to the Latin influence, is exactly the opposite: restless, individualistic, less disciplined, with personal effort, agility and skill. The notions of opposing British and *criollo* would remain. The metaphor of the 'machine' as opposed to individual creativity is a constant in the Argentinian football imagery. 'Britishness' is associated with the industrial, the *criollo* with the pre-industrial social system. Faced with the machine, or the repetitive, the typical *criollo* response would be the dribble. Dribbling, which would later be called the *gambeta* (a word derived from gauchesque literature which describes the running motion of an ostrich), is eminently individual and cannot be programmed; it is the opposite of the industrial, collective game of the machine.

In contrast to the values of technocracy, expressed in the importance of 'work', the 'machine', 'science', and the 'collective game', the dominant narrative proposed 'indolence', 'art', 'intuition' and 'individualism' (Archetti, 1996, p. 51). These values were those that would define a national style and a *criollo* tradition. The image of masculinity and masculine virtues are related to an exaltation of skill, cunning, individual creativity, artistic feeling and improvisation. Similarities to the Brazilian way of playing are striking. One could say that in these two cases the imaginary world of football reflects the power of freedom and creativity in the face of discipline, order and hierarchy. The masculine ideal of football represents improvisation and play, and constitutes an opposition to the strong and responsible man in other areas of society. Moreover, football in Brazil was a tool of racial democracy and the affirmation of the black population, while in Argentina it was a strategy to integrate new immigrants.

Argentina and Brazil are successful countries in the world of football and positive images are expected, but what about other countries with a different history? Sánchez León (1993) argues that for Peruvians in general, and Peruvian football in particular, success is a wish difficult to achieve and is generally associated with the use of tricks and moral misery. He affirms that in the Peruvian football supporter a predisposition to defeat is a state of mind (1993, p. 76). It is quite interesting, however, that the imagined qualities of the Peruvian style – an elegant and technical way of playing – are closer to Argentina and Brazil. The lack of international victories is related to the absence of tactical sense, speed when it is needed, and modern organization. The Peruvians play a 'slow-motion football' (ibid., p. 79) and direct attacks are unthinkable. Sánchez León concludes that the indirect and baroque way of playing must be seen in relation to the way the Peruvian people reacts against power, avoiding, if possible, confrontation.

Villena Fiengo (2000) has shown that in Costa Rica, a relatively successful nation in Middle American regional competitions, the expansion of the practice of football was connected to rural feasts and religious festivals held in rural areas. Moreover, Costa Rican political nationalism of the first three decades of the twentieth century was ideologically based on the exaltation of the virtues of peasant life. Villena Fiengo writes that 'the articulation of football with the early growth of nationalism has been so profound that football can be considered as an important dimension in the peasant national tradition' (ibid., p. 148). The apotheosis of the national team was the participation in the World Cup of 1990 in Italy. To support the team was defined as a civic duty (ibid., p. 149), as a patriotic mission. The players were key participants in what Villena Fiengo calls 'the moral economy of sacrifice' (ibid., p. 153). Nationalist ideas and feelings were mobilized along the lines of rural qualities: the player was defined as a typical Costa Rican peasant: humble and unsophisticated. It was important to present the participation of Costa Rica in Italy as a way of recuperating the tradition and values of peasant rural life. In this narrative the emphasis was on sacrifice and moral integrity more than on the technical or esthetic qualities of the players. In this way, the sport idols reproduced the dominant nationalist mythology (ibid., p. 156).

The different cases show that football is an important social and cultural arena for creativity and performance, and that 'high' and 'low', 'elite' and 'popular', 'global' and 'local' were at work in the process of creating national imaginaries. Identity is thus highly dependent upon multiplicity. Over time, sport has created blocks of identity that are undeniable, a kind of 'national and international space' in which different social classes, races and nationalities enter into a dialogue because the social, economic and cultural interconnections are so very strong.

ADORING THE HEROES

A nation needs heroes even in times of peace, and sports provide them. The cult of sport heroes unites the admiration for their performances with the moral and social impact of their lives on followers. The history of real individuals provides a social model to perceive paradoxes and dramas in society, and to recognize and question key values. The meaning that the lives of two archetypical football players can have for millions of people will elucidate some of these postulates.

Manuel Francisco dos Santos (1934–83), better known as Garrincha, the extraordinary right winger of the fantastic Brazilian team which won the World Cup of 1958 and 1962, died as an alcoholic and in extreme poverty in 1983. The nation was shocked. In life he had been called 'the joy of the people' and his death produced profound sorrow. His body was displayed at the mythic Maracaná stadium in Rio de Janeiro, and thousands upon thousands of Brazilian football lovers paid him a last tribute. His casket was followed by the multitudes, and his funeral became a part of national history.

Leite Lopes and Maresca (1989; Leite Lopes, 1992) have tried to interpret the meaning of this dramatic spectacle for Brazilian society. As a player, Garrincha represented perhaps even better than Pelé, his contemporary, the quality and essence of the Brazilian style of playing football: a disconcerting dribbling based on improvisation and intuition, which transformed the way wingers played. Before him, the technique had been primarily based on speed. His slow dribbling style and maniacal possession of the ball were seen as a typical product of the *peladas* – the kind of football played in the streets. Before he joined Botafogo, a great club in Rio de Janeiro, he played in the Sporte Club Pau Grande. It had been founded in 1919 by the textile factory where Garrincha was working (see Castro, 1995).

Leite Lopes and Maresca maintain that in Brazil the introduction and practice of football among industrial workers were an important mechanism helping to discipline and 'civilize' the body. Garrincha represented the final, paramount product of this tradition, because from the 1930s it became possible for talented young players to be directly recruited by professional clubs. Garrincha remained, in many ways, an 'amateur' in a highly competitive and cynical world of professionalism. His life can be seen as antipodal to the life of Pelé, the other great Brazilian football icon. Garrincha never abandoned his working-class roots nor adapted to the requirements of a successful public social life outside the football field. He did not learn business management or master public relations, and he continued to play even when his body was exhausted and deformed by alcoholism and injuries. He was not sufficiently educated to become a coach, the normal job after a long career as professional player. In 1962 at the top of his career he, and he 'alone' as the myth tells it, won the World Cup in Chile. In contrast, his private life was marked by constant failures and scandals.

According to Leite Lopes and Maresca (1989; Leite Lopes, 1992), the crowds following his casket in silence in the streets of Rio de Janeiro were participants in a social drama, showing the most profound respect to a son of the working class who had suffered from injustice, maladjustment, and prejudice. The nation wondered how it had been possible for them to abandon so heartlessly the player defined as 'the joy of the people'. His death was interpreted as marking the end of the romantic epoch in football now being transformed by business, capitalism, and a growing international market of players. Garrincha was seen as the last great 'amateur', a product of the street and the factory. Today, Garrincha remains a powerful symbol of the consolidation of the Brazilian style of playing.

Diego Armando Maradona is the modern answer in Argentina to Garrincha, and like Garrincha, the myth relates – and reality confirms – that he 'alone' won the World Cup of 1986 for his country. He was born in 1960 into a working-class family, and his childhood in the slums of Villa Fiorito in Buenos Aires, was marked by poverty and football. Maradona has been a 'winner' since the start of his career. As a very young player with Argentinos Juniors, a club from Buenos Aires, he won everything in local competitions. He then began his journey to the first division with the same club shortly before his sixteenth birthday. His precocity and talent made possible his debut in the senior national team before he was 17 years old. In 1979, in Tokyo, at the age of 18 he won, as a captain of the team and indisputable leader, the title of the World Junior Cup with the Argentinian national team. Later he went to Boca Juniors in Argentina, won the league in 1981, moved to Barcelona FC in 1982, where he won the Copa del Rey in 1983. Two years later he moved to Naples where he became an idol, helping the hometown team to win the Italian league in 1987, the first time a southern team had done so. His nomadic life as a player did not hinder his image as a national hero. For almost two decades, until his retirement in 1994, the Argentinian national team 'depended' on him, and he never refused to play, becoming the symbol of Argentinian football in the 1980s.

His life was also marked by scandal. It was well known in Naples in 1990 that Maradona had taken drugs and participated in dubious parties. Tests taken on March 1991 proved positive. Maradona's urine was found to contain cocaine. He was immediately suspended by the Italian football authorities. His life since has been marked by cocaine and other drugs. He left football temporarily and made a return in October 1993 in Argentina. Football experts and above all supporters clamored for the return of Maradona to the national team for the World Cup of 1994. Maradona surrendered to this irrational demand and he committed himself to a physical effort that an addict could not normally afford. Maradona joined the national team and traveled to the United States. He played as well as ever in the first two victorious games. After his second match he was chosen for the dope test. The test was positive. Maradona summed up what he felt when he was dropped: 'They have cut my legs off.' The game against Nigeria was his last one: he left football forever.

He was called *el pibe de oro* (the golden boy), and is, indisputably, the historical synthesis of the Argentinian construction of a national style based on the playing qualities of the *pibes* (young boys; Archetti, 1996). Maradona belongs to the special world of *pibes*-players which adult players cannot enter. The ideological emphasis is on the border between childhood and adulthood, not on the transition from one condition to the other. In the ideal construction of an Argentinian football style, a harmonic universe is created by *pibes* in which freedom of creativity and irresponsibility in inventing the unexpected dominate. Maradona, like Garrincha in street football, learned to play football in the *potreros* – open fields, and nobody taught him the art of dribbling. In this social and moral context, Maradona is thought of as the most archetypical player. His chaotic life is explained by his condition of being a *pibe*. Disorder is expected from a *pibe*. A *pibe* is creative, guilt-free, self-destructive and, ultimately, a poor moral example to other players. However, in the global moral evaluation of these kind of players, the ultimate criterion is the creative use of their bodies. Explicitly, the great joy given by the *pibes* is more important than any consistent moral evaluation (see Archetti, 2001). Adoring spectators have a kind of emotional contract of joy with their heroes that transcends bourgeois morality and the logic of order and hierarchies of nation-states. Football can, therefore, produce transgression and rebellion when freedom of creativity is valued the most.

ENGAGED SUPPORTERS AND AUDIENCES

Sport, as enacting modernity, is imagined as an active practice producing healthy bodies, and as a democratic activity open and recommended to women and men of all ages. Professionalism in sport has also produced 'marginal' participants: they are the supporters following athletes and sports spectacles as spectators, the passive television viewers and radio listeners. The most important narratives of sport have been historically produced by journalists, and have centred on the history of playing styles, clubs, national teams, and players (see Leite Lopes and Faguer, 1994; Archetti, 1996; Villena Fiengo; 2000; Helal *et al.*, 2001; and Gastaldo, 2002). In the past two decades, coaches and retired players have joined journalists in the ideological construction and interpretation of the meaning of football. However, in spite of this process the voices of the audiences and supporters have not been silenced.

Neves Flores (1982) has demonstrated that in the arena of football the supporters 'narrate' and 'perform' social stories and even produce what he calls 'ideologies of transformation'. The popular clubs, like Flamengo in Rio de Janeiro and Corinthias in São Paulo, are seen as courageous, with lots of stamina and a will to win. The 'elite' clubs, like Fluminense in Rio de Janeiro, show discipline and fair play. The clubs where sons of immigrants are most represented because their origins was 'ethnic', as with the Portuguese in Vasco da Gama or the Italians in Palmeiras, are usually perceived as less national than the others. In addition to the clubs that are 'national', minor clubs always represent moral and social qualities of a given neighbourhood and, in this sense, are very local in the manifestation of their identities (see also Lever, 1983). Neves Flores shows how the symbols of identification that the supporters create reproduce many of these ideological representations. Neves Flores argues that the organized activity of the supporters displays the class and the ethnic divisions in society, stresses masculinity, and, finally, exhibits violence. In this view, the supporters in the football arena act against the dominant values of Brazilian society of national equality, populist integration, and political paternalism (1982, p. 57). Sander Damo (2002) has recently shown the importance of regional identities in the construction of the Brazilian national space of football. His ethnography is based on the study of Gremio, a large and successful team from Porto Alegre, the capital of the state of Rio Grande do Sul. Gremio has been conceptualized by journalists and supporters of teams from Rio de Janeiro and São Paulo as representing a kind of 'anti-Brazilian' style of playing based on tactical sense, discipline and, even, violence.

Magazine's (2001) study of the supporters of the Pumas of the National University of Mexico, one of the four 'national teams' with supporters in most regions of Mexico, demonstrates the importance of a common identity. Pumas fans are attracted by the team's philosophy of *puros jóvenes* (pure youths). He writes that 'unlike other clubs, Pumas "give young players a chance" by using players from its *fuerzas básicas* (basic forces) – a youth league – rather than signing proven players from other teams' (2001, p. 191). At the same time, among other fans of other teams, the philosophy of the Pumas is important because the team is known as the breeding ground for the country's best players. An extreme case of Mexicanism is the team Las Chivas, from the city of Guadalajara, and also a national team with a large base of supporters. Fábregas Puig (2001) has shown the importance of a tradition of just using and signing Mexican players, against the constant flux of Argentinians, Brazilians, Colombians and Uruguayans to other teams. Las Chivas is then seen as a tangible symbol of a national fraternity, and the continuity of the Mexican roots in the field of football (ibid., p. 70). This is, moreover, related to the importance of the state of Jalisco as the source of some of the most important markers of Mexican identity: the cultural origin of the *charros* and the land of tequila. One city, Guadalajara, capital of Jalisco, is the site of a local team representing the region and the nation.

In the study of the chants of football supporters in Argentina the importance of sexuality and masculinity – real against dubious men – has been stressed (Archetti, 1992). However, alongside the dramatization of sexuality there is a set of chants that refer to the elusiveness of the 'world', to a sort of disenchantment and loss of hope. Professionalism and football as a spectacle have brought a set of new problems, of which two are apparently central: the overweening ambition of the managers and the disloyalty of the players. The spectators chant that loyalty, although continuity cannot be guaranteed by the players or by the managers of the clubs. The themes of disillusionment and loneliness implicit in loyalty to a club appear in many classic chants. They often stress the pain that the supporter of a great club must endure when its managers, coaches and players perform badly. What remains as something 'pure' in this complex world is a love of the club's colors, passion for the club's jersey, nostalgia for the glorious past and pride in what was and is to come (Archetti, 1992, pp. 230–2).

In other words, football allows the perception of a world as socially constructed by its various actors, especially by the supporters and their militant vanguard. Supporters appear as 'moral actors' in the sense that they assign values to particular objects, players and particular actions. It is, accordingly, a varied and complex world full of explicit and implicit meanings exemplified by the cases presented. The spectacle of football without active and engaged supporters, reduced to the virtual reality of television, is unthinkable in Latin America.

10

Modernity, modernization and melodrama
The bolero in Mexico in the 1930s and 1940s

Vanessa Knights

The 1930s and 1940s were crucial decades for the formation of Mexico as a modern nation-state. This was a transitional period characterized by rapid urbanization, industrialization, incorporation into the international economy and the institutionalization of the revolution. The accelerated growth of the capital, in particular through rural migration, led to the emergence of a new social underclass characterized by a sense of uprootedness or dislocation as previous community bonds and social continuities came under threat. This was a crucial moment of power for the mass media as the development of popular urban mass culture supplied a means of mediating the fragmentation of modern social structures through the creation of an imagined community.[1] While this process was taking place in various Latin American metropolises, in Mexico it was compounded through the project of post-revolutionary national reconstruction which deliberately attempted to create unity from diversity and complexity through the invention of a national cultural tradition. 'Lo mexicano' is closely identified with the development of the city in contrast to an idealized vision of the countryside, and particularly sanctioned regional representations centring above all on the western region of the Bajío from which many of the cultural elite originated (Pérez Montfort, 1998). For Mark Pedelty (1999) the Mexican bolero song genre is crucial to the consolidation of national identity because it paradoxically appeals simultaneously to a nostalgic discourse of loss and longing while being orientated to the future as a product of the modern imagination through its urbane and cosmopolitan sound. It is pivotal to the evolution of an urban sensibility tied in to modernity and modernization through the development of the mass media of the time: radio, the recording industry and film. For the composer and music historian Juan S. Garrido this is the Golden Age of the 'era romántica del cancionero mexicano' (romantic era of Mexican songs) (1981, pp. 68–9).[2] The focus on interpersonal relationships formed a counterpoint to the urban anomie caused by modern social structures and the individualism of modernity to connect with the shared cultural space of collective memory. Radio and cinema, as the main means of dissemination of the bolero, were key mediators of modernity expressing new social and political demands through the constitution of hybrid cultural forms in which tradition was not rejected or denied but reworked to create a new national image. Jesús Martín-Barbero cites the well-known phrase by the Mexican cultural critic Carlos Monsiváis to explain the popularity of Mexican cinema, as opposed to Hollywood productions, during this period. Nationalism and nation are consumed as spectacle by audiences not only searching for escapism but to 'aprender a ser mexicano' (learn to be Mexican) (Martín-Barbero, 2000, p. 65). The popular song collection compiled in 1987 for the Dirección General de Cultura Popular explicitly identifies the romantic urban song complex of the bolero with the 'sentimiento del pueblo mexicano' (emotions of the Mexican people) (Kuri-Aldana and Mendoza Martínez, 1992, vol. 2, p. 184). Why was this originally Cuban genre so popular amongst Mexican composers, record producers and the public that many have come to erroneously identify it as Mexican?

Over the course of more than one hundred years the bolero has developed into a truly transnational phenomenon. Its origins lie in the late nineteenth century in the traditional Cuban *trova*, the singer-songwriters of Santiago de Cuba. Cuban musicologist Helio Orovio describes it as the first great Afro-Hispanic vocal synthesis (1981, p. 52).[3] The early Cuban bolero had a strict rhythmic base, primarily in the melody, known as the *cinquillo cubano* comprised of a group of syncopated notes forming five beats of note value long-short-long-short-long usually followed by non-syncopated notes. This alternation, which can be traced back to Yoruba batá drumming patterns, was originally played on the clave (a pair of hard wooden sticks struck together).[4] It has been suggested that the term bolero was adopted to describe the genre because of the agile guitar-playing of intuitive musicians such as José 'Pepe' Sánchez which might be described as playing 'bolereadamente' (in a bolero-like fashion).[5] This narrative of origins and authenticity is troubled by the Cuban musicologist Argeliers León who postulates that this style of guitar playing originates in the Mexican Yucatán region (1984, pp. 210–11). As many compositions of the time were not transcribed or officially registered it is impossible to fix a date or determine who invented the genre. However, it is commonly accepted that the composer who consolidated the genre's structures was Pepe Sánchez who was the first to register a Cuban bolero in 1883 with his composition 'Tristezas' (Sadness). While love in its multiple variations, both positive and negative, is the predominant theme of the bolero, it was also linked to constructions of nation from its inception. Sánchez and other members of the early *trova* such as Nicolás Camacho and Sindo Garay were activists linked to leading members of the independence movement against

Spain such as Antonio and José Maceo, Guillermón Moncada and Quintín Banderas who attended musical soirées in Santiago which combined culture and politics. The songs they composed were not only about love between individuals but also collective love for one's country as well as homages to particular political figures (Betancourt, 1995).[6] Despite this cultural politics of location in many early Cuban boleros, it has become part of a transnational music culture which is not easily delimited in terms of social or cultural demographics. The Cuban composer Rosendo Ruiz Quevedo describes it as transcending frontiers to constitute 'más que un patrimonio nacional, un patrimonio cultural hemisférico de los pueblos hermanos del Caribe y de Latinoamérica' (more than a national heritage, a cultural heritage of all the neighbouring nations of the Caribbean and Latin America) (1988, p. 5). Studies of the bolero throughout Latin America by researchers such as the Cuban musicologist Helio Orovio (1995) or the Colombians Hernán Restrepo Duque (1992) and Jaime Rico Salazar (2000) have amply demonstrated the rich variety of national developments and international successes of this simultaneously localized and globalized form. There are a number of reasons for the extraordinary mobility of the bolero, including the ease with which its duple metre can fuse musically with a wide range of vocal and instrumental formats (Loyola Fernández, 1997, pp. 21–2). Furthermore, the looseness of reference of romantic lyrics makes them widely accessible to all sectors of society. Unlike ballads, boleros tend not to have a narrative format, preferring to focus on a particular emotion. On the whole, lyrics are impersonal and difficult to localize. The majority are sung dialogues between an indeterminate 'yo' (I) and 'tú' (you) which shift in meaning according to the context in which they are performed or listened to. Mechanisms of recognition are set into play which invite the emotional involvement and participation of the listener. The listener may identify with the singing subject or the 'tú' (you) who is addressed. In the second case the listener is made to feel both special as the unique addressee of the song but also part of an implicit community being addressed who share the same desires, dreams and also disillusions. Boleros act as a polysemic 'collective palimpsest' upon which individual desires are articulated through the dynamic experience of listening (Leal, 1992, p. 41).

The growth of the bolero also coincides with the emergence of the new mass media and cultural industries. In 1925 the first recording company in Mexico was set up by the Venezuelan impresario Eduardo C. Baptista. He had previously been importing records from the US but these could not meet the demands of the Mexican public. The company was registered in 1931 under the brand name of Peerless and, along with the international record companies Columbia, Edison and RCA Victor, was instrumental in the success of Mexican artists at home and abroad. These companies required products that could easily cross national borders in order to consolidate their market position throughout Latin America. The bolero, as well as the advantages cited above, was already relatively well known by the close of the nineteenth century in

Puerto Rico, Dominican Republic and Mexico through Cuban variety shows and circuses which toured the Caribbean. Helio Orovio cites the *trovador* (singer-songwriter) Emiliano Blez as remembering a trip made to Puerto Rico and the Dominican Republic in 1894 alongside another great *trovador* Sindo Garay as part of the circus troupe Los Caballitos de Griñán (1995, pp. 31, 33). The bolero also arrived relatively early in Mexico due to the close relations between Cuba and the Yucatán region. According to Pablo Dueñas Herrero, the first documented tour of a variety company which may have included performances of boleros occurred between 1902 and 1904 when Raúl de Monte brought the *trovadores* Adolfo Colombo, Alberto Villalón and Miguel Zaballa to Mexico with his troupe (1990, p. 17). In 1909 Cuban boleros such as 'Tristezas' by Pepe Sánchez appeared in the song collection *Ruiseñor yucateco* (The Nightingale from the Yucatan) compiled by the Yucatecan *trovador* Cirilo Baqueiro, although they were often catalogued as other more familiar genres such as *guarachas* (Dueñas Herrero, 1990, p. 17). The first identifiable Mexican bolero was 'Morenita mía' (My Beautiful Dark-Skinned Woman), composed by Armando Villareal Lozano in 1921. Although boleros were perhaps being composed earlier in Mexico, it is not until after the violent disruption of the Revolution that the genre develops and takes off.

The bolero cultivated in the Yucatán, although generally slower and less rhythmic than its Cuban counterpart, nonetheless shared many similarities with that of the *trova* from Santiago such as the musicalization of existing romantic poetry by well-known authors such as Luis Rosado Vega, simple guitar accompaniment and the tradition of serenades. However, while both regional traditions have been maintained in Mexico and Cuba, the bolero went on to develop in both countries into a rather different urban genre linked to the capitals Havana and Mexico City.[7] In Mexico two key figures proved the link between region and national metropolis: Guty Cárdenas and Agustín Lara. The Yucatecan *trovadores* had enjoyed official support through the radio station La Voz del Gran Partido Socialista and several made their way to Mexico City following the execution of the Governor of Yucatán, Felipe Carrillo Puerto, by firing squad in 1924. Cárdenas arrived in 1927 to compete in La Feria de la Canción in the Teatro Lírico. There he premiered the bolero 'Nunca' (Never) in the fashionable rhythm of a *canción clave*. In 1928 he secured a recording contract in New York with Columbia and subsequently toured the USA. Encouraged by the success of 'Nunca' in the clubs and salons where he played the piano, Agustín Lara composed the bolero 'Impossible', which was recorded in 1928 by various groups including the Trío Garnica-Ascencio. His aim was to compose a bolero which would be easy to dance to and have accessible lyrics (Dueñas and Flores y Escalante, 1995, p. 12).[8] With Cárdenas's premature death in 1932 in a bar shootout, Lara was to become the star of the Mexican bolero pantheon. According to Adela Pineda (1990), Lara's iconic status is only partly due to his innovative compositions and performance style; more important is his emergence during this key time of social transformation and cultural development. Lara became an early product of the cultural industry's star system, whereby music was a saleable commodity produced by a recognizable individual who could be successfully marketed. His initial success was through personal contact with his audience through his performances as an accompanist for Juan Arvizu in theatres and also in the cinema where music was not only played as a background for silent movies but also featured as part of the entertainment during the interval. In the 1920s and 1930s theatrical revues were important means of showcasing new music and Lara's first big success, 'Mujer' (Woman) was composed in 1930 for the revue *Cachitos de México* at the Teatro Lírico.[9] The show played for more than one hundred performances and the press began to pay attention to Lara. This was a crucial year for the development of the Mexican bolero, with the inauguration of the highly influential radio station XEW in which Lara was the only popular lyrical composer to feature in the first show. In 1931 the first Mexican 'talkie' *Santa* (The Saint) included a bolero by Lara as its theme tune and featured another entitled 'Amor de ciego' (A Blindman's Love) by Juan Alberto Villegas. (Although there had been experiments with sound in 1929, *Santa* was the first Mexican film to use the system of direct synchronized sound recording.) Lara's revues at the Politeama theatre, recordings with RCA Victor, radio shows for XEW, and contributions to the nascent Mexican film industry both as composer and actor elevated him to the status of international legend as well as confirming his position as national icon.

It was radio rather than records which initially facilitated the immediate spread of popular songs throughout the continent as artists would copy down the lyrics and melodies of songs that they heard. For example, in 1937 the singer Pedro Vargas and pianist Pepe Agüeros heard Gonzalo Curiel's 'Vereda Tropical' (Tropical Avenue) on the radio while on tour in Caracas and the next day they premiered the song in Venezuela. Crooners as far afield as Argentina and Chile copied the style of Mexican tenors such as Juan Arvizu, Alfonso Ortiz Tirado and Pedro Vargas. The first radio transmission of a musical nature took place on 21 September 1921 from the Cine-Teatro Ideal, although initially popular music programming was limited with preference accorded to operatic voices performing traditional songs and classical music due to the edict of the Secretary of Education that 'seriousness' be promoted on the radio (Dueñas and Flores Escalante, 2000, p. 10). CYL was the first commercial radio in Mexico City founded by Raúl Azcárraga Vidauretta and *El Universal* newspaper in 1923. Also founded in 1923 by the Compañía Cigarrera del Buen Tono was CYB which later became the popular XEB. As a promotional offer they gave away self-assembly radios in exchange for cigarette boxes. Between 1924 and 1926 CYX (*Excelsior* newspaper), CYH (*High Life* magazine) and CYJ (General Electric) were also founded. The development of radio is thus clearly tied in to other media and the expansion of a capitalist economy and the rapid growth of the industry led to state legislation in April 1926 through the Ley de Comunicaciones Eléctricas (Electric Communications

Law). Commercial jingles appeared featuring the most popular artists in arrangers' adaptations of popular music successes and a number of shows were subsidised by brands such as Colgate, Palmolive and Picot, prefiguring the later creation of national advertising agencies during the 1940s. Picot also famously continued the nineteenth-century tradition of the *cancionero* (anthology), a means of transmitting songs prior to recording techniques, through the free distribution of a compilation of the year's greatest hits, the *Cancionero Picot*, via drugstores throughout Mexico. This was done initially in collaboration with XEB in 1928, then XEW from 1932, facilitating the spread of popular songs while simultaneously providing excellent publicity for Picot's effervescent salts.

On 18 September 1930 the most important station in the history of Mexican radio was inaugurated, XEW founded by Emilio Azcárraga Vidauretta as part of the México Music Co., which was the Mexican distributor for Victor. It began broadcasting with the aim of disseminating Mexican compositions at both a national and international level. In his inaugural speech Azcárraga Vidauretta explicitly allied the station with the nationalist project of creating a Mexican national culture and 40 per cent of programming at XEW was 'national' music. However, he also highlighted the importance of Mexico as 'abanderado en el desenvolvimiento cultural del continente' (the flagship in the cultural development of the Continent) (Moreno Rivas, 1979, p. 85). Indeed, XEW was so successful that it became commonly known as 'La voz de América Latina desde México' (The Voice of Latin America from Mexico). In a canny piece of subliminal marketing it was commonly referred to as 'la W' pronounced 'doble-u' rather than 'uve-doble' to phonetically suggest a link with the modern culture of the USA whose radio station signals started with a 'W'. Music was predominant in the programming of XEW until the late 1950s and in the 1930s and 1940s romantic music was extremely important. In particular, the bolero was heavily promoted in shows such as *La hora azul* (The Blue Hour) directed by 'El príncipe de la radio' (The Prince of Radio) Pedro de Lille, *La hora de los aficionados* (The Fans' Hour), the morning show *El club de la escoba y el plumero* (The Broom and the Feather-duster Club), *Una guitarra en la noche* (A Guitar at Night) directed by Manuel Álvarez Renterías aka 'Maciste' (composer of the famous bolero 'Angelitos negros' [Little Black Angels]), and perhaps most successfully in *La hora íntima con Agustín Lara* (The Intimate Hour with Agustín Lara) which ran from 1931 to 1955. These shows played throughout the day with earlier shows performed before a live studio audience and the late shows after 11 p.m. broadcast live from dance halls and hotel ballrooms. Radio provided a constant soundtrack to everyday life with the popular boleros providing a verbal and melodic space for the expression of intimacy, hopes and desires. The sense of intimacy was heightened by the common practice of telephone requests and the fact that these performers were playing live on the radio until well into the 1950s when the use of recordings took over.

In the dance halls recent arrivals to the city mixed with the urban workforce as 'los primeros espectadores de una modernización que los modifica sin incluirlos' (the first people to witness a process of modernization which changes them without including them) (Monsiváis, 1988, p. 52). These were transgressive spaces providing an outlet for the anxieties, frustrations and dissatisfactions of the masses simultaneously fundamental to the radical transformations of modernity but marginalized by uneven development. To some extent mass urban culture developed in response to the need for representation and expression of a new way of life, hence its anchoring in the everyday. It represented new ways of being and acting; an urban sensibility in contrast to the violence of the revolution. While the formulaic, repetitive nature of many bolero lyrics and melodies may respond to the market driven needs of the mass media for rapid production of recognizable and easily marketable products, its reiterative quality and focus on the quotidian or everyday emotions also allow for close audience identification with the genre. Intimacy acts to mediate the depersonalized relationships but lyrics, as well as providing an idealized escape, focus on the flipside of romantic love or deception and disillusionment, jealousy, abandonment and betrayal. Rafael Castillo Zapata, in his phenomenology of the bolero, describes it as a 'práctica estética comunitaria' (community aesthetic practice) which responds to a collective need for catharsis in order to alleviate the alienation produced by urban reality in the context of uneven development and the fragmentary processes of modernization (1991, pp. 33, 37). It could be decribed as one of Monsiváis's 'rituales del caos' (rituals of chaos) which are coping mechanisms for the chaotic urban milieu (2001b). However, despite the identification of the bolero with the popular classes, it is a cultural product which has transcended divisions to become popular with all social classes. The three rooms in the famous Salón México became popularly known as 'mantequilla' (butter), 'manteca' (lard) and 'sebo' (fat) according to the different social classes which frequented them.[10] Each space had its own dance and dress codes although these of course could be imitated allowing for social climbing through consumption. In the rapidly expanding urban metropolis of Mexico City, previously marginal spaces such as the cabarets where Lara began his career became tolerated hedonistic spaces, fashionable with the middle classes in the 1940s as a sign of their cosmopolitan nature, modernity and Mexico's economic development. As Monsiváis states in his discussion of the commercialization of nightlife, 'ser moderno [fue] oponerse al horario de las buenas costumbres' (being modern meant rejecting the timetable of civilized custom) (2001a, p. 81). Broadly speaking, cabarets could be divided into de luxe black tie venues such as the Patio and El Retiro and more risqué clubs such as the Waikiki worked by 'muchachas de lujo' (high-class call girls). In these clubs it was common to parody popular boleros with more openly erotic versions. These zones of permissiveness were indicative of a shift in moral attitudes reflecting secularization and changing social conditions after the Revolution.

Many of Lara's innovations in composition seem to relate to this eroticization of culture. His velvet melodies are freed from the rhythmic constraints of tropical syncopation to follow the prosody of the lyrics and Lara's improvisory piano swoons to a slower tempo over a background of sensual and romantic violins (Pineda, 1990, pp. 11–15). Singers associated with Lara such as Pedro Vargas also had a particular style, sensual through its breathy tone, almost spoken with drawn-out cadences. Lara's texts were highly polemical, crossing the division between high and low culture. He was a self-identified bohemian who hung out in the cafés which sprung up around the XEW where writers and composers would meet (Gelpí, 1998, p. 204). His lyrics drew on common metaphors from *modernista* imagery such as the swan, thereby earning him the nickname of the 'músico poeta' (poet-musician). However, Lara began his career playing in brothels and he famously glorified the marginalized figure of the prostitute in the nineteenth-century romantic tradition. In 1936 Lara was prohibited in schools by the Secretaria de Educación Pública because of his lyrics about *femmes fatales* with soubriquets such as 'vencida' (vanquished), 'pervertida' (perverted), 'aventurera' (adventuress). The woman was commonly portrayed as a 'pecadora divina' (divine sinner) redeemed of her sin through love, and passionate adoration of his sensual muse simultaneously redeemed the composer. Unsurprisingly, Lara also became the target of the League of Decency, guardians of Catholic morality, who banned songs and insisted on changes to lyrics they considered indecent or blasphemous such as 'aunque no quiera Dios, ni quieras tú, ni quiero yo …' (although neither God, nor you, nor I want it to happen …) from 'Palabras de mujer' (A Woman's Words) (1945) which was transformed into 'aunque no quieras tú, ni quiera yo, lo quiere Dios' (although neither you or I want it to happen, God does).[11] However, in the late 1940s the League's influence declined and songs linked to the *cabaretera* cinema genre proliferated. Lara's 'Lágrimas de sangre' (Tears of Blood) (1947) is a clear example of openly erotic lyrics: 'yo que tuve tus besos, y tus manos y tu pelo / y la blanca tibieza que derramaste en mí …' (I had your kisses, and your hands and your hair / and the white warmth you poured into me …). Lara came to symbolize bohemia, limitless love and passion (without hope). He was ridiculed for his sentimental backwardness by Carlos Chávez, director of the national symphony orchestra in the 1940s and 1950s, yet romantic songs, along with other melodramatic genres, were to come to be seen as consolidating the home and family (Monsiváis, 1997a, pp. 174, 179).[12] In Doris Sommer's analysis of romantic novels as foundational fictions in Latin America in the late nineteenth and early twentieth centuries (1991), Eros and Polis come together in the project of national consolidation. Monsiváis makes a similar argument for the function of romantic song following the Mexican Revolution. The language of rapture provides a language of community which crosses social classes and regional divides (1997a, pp. 170–3). Romantic passion provides a possible scenario for bringing together heterogeneous communities under the unified banner of the seemingly homogenous nation-state through cultural products which hold together the tensions inherent between progressive modernity and regressive tradition.

Melodrama was one of the staple genres of Mexican cinema in the 1930s and 1940s. The first successful Mexican sound feature *Santa* (The Saint) (1931), was adapted from a well-known melodramatic novel by Federico Gamboa about a prostitute with a heart of gold. During the presidential term of Manuel Avila Camacho (1941–45) sound cinema was consolidated. This period of increased political stability and economic development came to be termed the 'Mexican miracle' as the wartime pact between the USA and Mexico favoured capitalist development and the acceleration of the industrialization process. It also favoured the development of the Mexican national film industry which, with the aid of US backers such as RKO, became the fifth largest sector of the national economy and took over from Argentina as the most important Spanish language producer of film (Vega Alfaro, 1995, p. 86). The immediate post-war period was one of crisis for the Mexican film industry but this critical phase prompted the production of low-budget films focusing on urban/suburban themes. In the late 1940s directors such as Alejandro Galindo and Ismael Rodríguez had box-office successes with films chronicling the lives and struggles of the urban poor. The 'arrabal' or marginalized neighbourhood location is a liminal space bridging the transition between the old and the new. In Rodríguez's 1948 smash *Nosotros los pobres* (We Poor People) Pedro Infante, as the humble carpenter Pepe el Toro, comes to represent the multiple crossings involved in the '(fragmentary) assimilation' into city life (Monsiváis, 1995a, p. 125). When asked what kind of cinema he preferred, Lara stated: 'El que mueve mi corazón. El que me sitúa en la cumbre de mis emociones. Un cine también que habla de los míos y de mi tiempo' (One that moves me. That takes me to an emotional climax. Also a cinema that talks about the people I know and the times I know) (Taibo I, 1984, p.65). His views are echoed in the productions of late 1940s which saw the re-establishment of a generic cinema for popular consumption in which melodrama and comedy mediated urban poverty. Echoing the success of scandalous dancers such as Ivonne Móntes Farrington, better known as the exotic Tongolele, in revue theatres such as the Tivolí and Folies Bergères, the *cabaretera* or brothel-cabaret melodrama flourished during the presidential period of Miguel Alemán (1946–52). In these films the popular urban locale of the cabaret has been distorted to construct morality tales of family virtue which reinforce a long list of ideals as cited by Paco Taibo I, 'el honor, la castidad, el recato, el decoro, la decencia, el civismo y en último extremo la devoción por la Virgen de Guadalupe' (honour, chastity, reserve, decorum, decency, civility, and, lastly, devotion for the Virgin of Guadalupe) (1984, p. 21). Old values and modernizing tendencies clash in the key female figures of the self-abnegating, suffering mother usually identified with the rural morality of utopian provinces and the sexually independent cabaret singers or *rumberas* identified with the evils of the city through explicit links to the worlds of crime and prostitution. However, while the plots outwardly tend to exhort morality through exaltation of the family and honour, the audience is drawn to attractive images of adultery and lingering shots of 'fallen women' who are empathized with through pathos. A number of melodramas do feature bad or wicked mothers for example in *Aventurera* (Adventuress) (1949) the supposedly respectable provincial mother is actually shown to be a brothel and cabaret owner in the city, and the 'cabaretera' is admired and eventually rewarded for her street-smart strength. Prostitution and working in cabarets are presented as the only alternatives for women otherwise facing destitution and the plight of these women might be seen as symbolic of the difficulties faced by many who migrated to the city in search of opportunity. It is important to remember that Mexican nationalism is a highly gendered discourse which interpellates women as mothers of the nation, both biological and symbolic, through the figures of the self-sacrificing Virgin of Guadalupe and the treacherous Malinche/Malintzin.[13] Women are thus paradoxically positioned as both guardians of the nation's morals and a threat to the body politic (Wade, 2000, p.16).

In the *cabaretera* films there is an ambiguous appeal to both moral decency and profane sexuality with the latter explicitly identified with the modern look of Cuban actresses such as Amalia Aguilar María Antonieta Pons, Rosa Carmina, the atypically blonde Ninón Sevilla, and the Mexican star Meche Barba. Provocative images of sensual dance scenes operate under the double sign of cosmopolitanism and forbidden decadence to suggestively challenge morals; 'each choreographed shake of Ninón Sevilla's *rumbera* hips ... stands in for all the couplings prohibited by the censors' (Monsiváis, 1995a, p. 121). Melodrama provides a cathartic scenario in which these contradictory attitudes can be addressed through a discourse of emotional excess which cannot be contained. This ambivalent combination is also a key feature of Lara's output which combines spirituality in boleros which divinize the object of his affections and carnality in boleros which elevated the figure of the prostitute to iconic status. Identification with the *cabareteras* is encouraged as audiences could sing along with well-known songs providing a participatory cinema experience. Many films were named after boleros, they featured as theme tunes and leitmotifs, they were sung within films and even, albeit often rather tangentially, provided the basis for film plots (Calderón González, 1996). Popular singers featured physically as well as verbally in films including Pedro Vargas, Toña la Negra and Elvira Ríos, and the aura of artists such as Lara could be used to ensure box-office success. Films provided a suitable marketing arena for hits, for example, Gonzalo Curiel's smash 'Vereda tropical' (Tropical Avenue) from *Hombres del mar* (Men of the Sea) (1936) in which the actress Esther Fernández was dubbed over with the voice of Lupita Palomera.

The bolero in Mexico in the 1930s and 1940s 137

Paradoxically, through a process of transculturation the Cuban bolero genre was appropriated by composers such as Lara to symbolize a popular, urban, musical nationalism representative of a modern Mexico that was to find one of its maximum expressions in the bolero *ranchero* as promoted by the radio station XEQ.[14] The first example of this hybrid genre was 'Amorcito corazón' (Little Loveheart) by Pedro Urdimales and Manuel Esperón, and recorded by the film idol Pedro Infante for Peerless in 1949. ('Amorcito corazón' sung as an orchestrated bolero was featured in the 1948 box-office successes *Nosotros los pobres* and *Ustedes los ricos*.) This style, in which singers are accompanied by mariachi instrumentation and orchestration, was popularized by the composers Rubén Fuentes and Alberto Cervantes whose works were immortalized by singers such as Lola Beltrán, María Elena Sandoval and Lucha Villa, and film stars identified with the figure of the Mexican singing cowboy, the 'charro cantor', such as Pedro Infante, and Javier Solís. It combined the romantic urban bolero with the traditional instrumentation of the Mexican 'conjunto' including violins, *jarana*, vihuela, guitar, *guitarrón* and the modern innovation of the trumpet. The new cultural industries and electronic mass media thus continued to adapt existing traditions to consolidate post-revolutionary Mexican national identity (Monsiváis, 1994, 2000).[15] Simultaneously they favoured the development of internationally marketable cultural forms as Mexico sought to position itself as a cultural exporter within the global market. An interesting multidirectional flow of influences can be traced with the USA in particular. New technologies speeded up the evolution of the genre with the sonic requirements of the radio and cinema favouring a more orchestral approach to the arrangements of boleros, as strings alone did not carry well on early audio equipment, and influential stations like XEW hired exclusive orchestras such as Gonzalo Curiel's Escuadrón del Ritmo. Prominent arrangers such as Juan García Esquivel and Ernesto Riestra looked to the New York big-band and jazz orchestra style to bring the bolero into the more upmarket dance salons such as the Retiro or Grillón from the mid-1930s. In a further transnational cross-fertilization, Cole Porter travelled to Cuba in 1933. Influenced by the bolero and other Caribbean genres he created the beguine rhythm which in turn was taken up by Mexican composers such as Alberto Domínguez Borras to great international success with boleros such as 'Perfidia' (Betrayal) and 'Frenesí' (Frenzy) (1939) which were subsequently recorded by popular US artists such as Benny Goodman, Artie Shaw, Jimmy Dorsey and Glenn Miller.[16] The bolero also crossed over into Hollywood cinema, featuring in films such as *Tropical Holiday* (1938) directed by Theodore Reed for Paramount and Disney's *Los tres caballeros* (The Three Caballeros) (1944). In the 1940s and 1950s New York was to become an even more important nexus for the development of the Mexican bolero with the popularization of the return to the string-based Yucatecan tradition through the trio format as exemplified by the hugely successful Los Panchos formed in 1944. The bolero is a highly hybrid genre in which the local, national and transnational interact. Through the possibilities afforded by the new mass media, in particular, Mexican radio and cinema, it spread throughout Latin America and indeed beyond to the USA and Europe, adapting in response to the needs and demands of each locale. Within Mexico itself, the regional style of the Yucatecan bolero was transformed into the national bolero *ranchero* and internationalized in the urban bolero. Despite its transnational nature, the bolero is not necessarily deterritorialized or homogenized into a single global product. It remains a heterogenous product of the processes of transculturation in constant flux and development appealing to past nostalgia while continually being transformed in response to present circumstances.

In *La jaula de la melancolía* (The Cage of Melancholy) published in 1987, Mexican intellectual Roger Bartra critiques the institutionalization by the political elite of a stereotyped sentimentality and aggressive emotivity as national culture. Suffering is legitimated and the stoicism of the proletariat promoted as a means of surviving the 'inhospitable world of modernity' created by modern capitalism (1987, p. 127). The cracks of uneven development, marginalization and alienation are papered over by escapist cultural products promoting a cathartic subjectivity. Arguably these are all accusations which could be levelled at the bolero and other melodramatic cultural products. However, Bartra's view is a rather apocalyptic view of popular culture as the unidirectional means of imposition of a particular ideological viewpoint on the passive masses. In numerous essays Carlos Monsiváis provides a more nuanced view of cultural practices as constructed through historical processes and consumption of popular culture as a dynamic activity through which identities are articulated, disarticulated and rearticulated. A complex set of negotiations is involved in the process of producing meaning which is affected by the desires and needs of particular individuals or groups who may have competing social interests. Meaning thus becomes a site of ideological struggle and negotiation in the constitution of subjectivities for different social groups. If popular cultural products such as the bolero are a mediation, rather than a reflection, of lived experience, they can be reappropriated as a means of negotiating the relationships between state ideology, the difficult processes of modernization and urbanization and people's direct experiences of them.

ACKNOWLEDGEMENTS

This chapter was partially researched with the help of the University of Newcastle Small Grant Fund. Various people contributed their time and materials including José Antonio Robles of CENIDIM, Julia Palacios of TV Azteca, and the foremost collectors and historians of the Mexican bolero, Pablo Dueñas, and Jesús Flores y Escalante.

NOTES

1. The term 'imagined community' is taken from Anderson (1991).
2. For a history of 'cancioneros' (collections of popular songs in the public domain), see the prologue to Kuri-Aldana and Mendoza Martínez (1992) by Juan Garrido.
3. The historical information about the bolero and melodramatic cinema in this chapter comes from a variety of sources including Dueñas Herrero (1990), Dueñas and Flores y Escalante (1995 and 2000), Garrido (1981), Paranaguá (1995), Orovio (1995), Rico Salazar (2000), Zavala (1990, 1991).
4. There is some debate as to whether this rhythmic figure originates in Cuba or was brought over from Haiti by slaves brought to the island with their French masters fleeing the revolution of 1791–1804.
5. The Cuban bolero shares its name only with its Spanish hononym and the two should not be confused as they are very different in rhythm and structure.
6. This nationalistic strain of bolero was later developed by Puerto Rican communities on the US mainland.
7. See Pineda (1989, 1990) for a detailed analysis of the structural changes between the 'bolero yucateco' and 'bolero urbano', within Lara's production and between early and later performances of the same bolero.
8. In Cuba the bolero was also becoming increasingly danceable over the course of the 1920s due to the influence of the popularity of 'son'.
9. In poorer neighbourhoods shows were put on in mobile performance spaces known as 'carpas'.
10. Salón México was immortalized in the film of the same name directed by Emilio 'el Indio' Fernández in 1948.
11. Lara was not the first, however, to scandalize polite society. In 1901 'Perjura' (Swear) by Miguel Lerdo de Tejada was considered highly provocative because of its allusions to physical desire (Monsiváis, 1997, pp. 167–9).
12. A shorter version of the following discussion of melodrama in relation to the novel *Arráncame la vida* by Ángeles Mastretta appeared in Knights (2001).
13. See Franco (1989) and Melhuus (1996) for detailed analyses of these figures.
14. Transculturation is a term coined by the Cuban anthropologist Fernando Ortiz to describe a dynamic, syncretic process of contact between cultures resulting in new cultural practices. See Davies (2000) for a lucid account of the development of the concept and its usefulness for postcolonial theory.
15. In the North of Mexico, in Chihuaha, Tamaulipas, Monterrey, Coahuila and Sonora, traditional instrumentation and singing style was similarly combined with the bolero format in the late 1950s and 1960s to produce the 'bolero norteño' (Northern bolero) popularized by artists such as Chelo Silva.
16. Another great international hit in the 1930s and 1940s was 'Cuando vuelva a tu lado' (When I Come Back to You) (1932) by the Mexican composer María Grever based in New York. This song was also recorded in English as 'What a Difference a Day Makes'. 'Bésame mucho' (Kiss Me a Lot) (1941) by Consuelo Velázquez spent 11 weeks in the number one spot of the US hit parade and was also performed by artists of the stature of The Beatles and Frank Sinatra.

11

Stars
Mapping the firmament
John King

> The actor has gone beyond what her craft demands: she has invented herself, she has become her own persona. An invention that is also a transfiguration: the new persona is and is not the actor. It is a creature that whilst sharing the same face and body, emanates all the strange and magnetic attributes that belong to fable and to myth. She has become a *star* as the popular expression has it. The expression is exact: stars are celestial bodies that we can see and even photograph, but which we cannot touch. They are here and they are there. Cinema, more than theatre, has offered us this mysterious transformation of an actor into a being that possesses the properties of the demigods and heroes of mythology: they are creatures of flesh and blood like us and, at the same time, they are made up of the weightless matter of images. Creatures of the air and of dreams … The Mexican actress that most embodies this transfiguration is María Félix. (Paz, 1992, pp. 9–10)

The Mexican poet and essayist Octavio Paz's definition of stars and stardom is very similar to that offered by Ginette Vincendeau in a recent study of stars in French cinema. Vincendeau writes:

> By *stars,* I mean celebrated film performers who develop a 'persona' or 'myth', composed of an amalgam of their screen image and private identities, which the audience recognises and expects from film to film and which in turn determines the parts they play. The star's persona is a commodity, positioning the performer and his/her work in the market-place and attracting finance: the name in huge letters on the posters and the marquee. (2000, p. viii)

This chapter seeks to review the critical literature on stars and on stars in Latin America and to indicate areas of future research. It offers its own sociocultural approach to the history of film-making in the region.

ARE ALL STARS MADE IN HOLLYWOOD?

Most histories of early film see the concept of the star emerging about 1910, when the film industry's publicity and promotion drive began to concentrate less on the technical aspects of the medium itself, how film created its illusions, and more on individual stories about actors and directors (see DeCordova, 1990). In this year, a story was put out that Florence Lawrence, the 'Biograph Girl' had been killed by a tram in St Louis. The news of the death was followed by an angry rebuttal the next day, denouncing the story as a lie. This naked publicity stunt has been seen to illustrate both the deliberate creation of a star image as well as an early response to the public's demand for 'star' features (Dyer, 1998, pp. 9–10).

Coincidentally, this was the year when, with the advent of the Mexican Revolution, a larger than life 'social bandit' would come to the attention of the American public: Pancho Villa. US cameramen would follow journalists such as John Reed south of the border to catch up with this charismatic revolutionary. Political charisma would be turned into star charisma as Villa signed an exclusive contract with Mutual Film Corporation for $25,000. In the terms of the contract, he agreed to keep other film companies far from his battle scenes, to fight in daylight wherever possible, to move his executions to dawn, when the light was better, and to reconstruct scenes from battles if satisfactory pictures had not been obtained in the heat and the dust of the conflict (see de Orellana, 2003). Arguably, Pancho Villa was Latin America's first film star, but he owed the star status to the American publicity machine, the trade papers and photo journals that kept him as front-page news for a time, especially between 1913 and 1914. His image changed from colourful revolutionary to bloodthirsty bandit in March 1916, when he led a raid on the US frontier town of Columbus, the first and only incursion of foreign troops onto American soil.

Some 90 years later, in November 2002, Hollywood began shooting on location in northern Mexico a TV movie of Pancho Villa's film stardom – *And Starring Pancho Villa as Himself* – with the Spaniard Antonio Banderas playing Pancho Villa. The same month saw the release in the United States of *Frida*, starring and in part produced by Salma Hayek, a Mexican actress who had, by the late 1990s, become Hollywood's leading *latina* actress. In this film there was a perfect 'fit' between the character of Frida Kahlo and what Richard Dyer calls the 'powerfully, inescapably present, always-already-signifying nature of star images' (1998, p. 129), in this case, Hayek's amalgamated image of the sensual *latina* and the committed Mexican actress. The publicity for the film revealed some of the central aspects of stardom, in particular the link between the personal and the professional, the private identities that blend with the screen persona. The published screenplay, *Frida: Bringing Frida Kahlo's Life and Art to Film*, is packed with material for the fans: colour stills from the film, interviews with the main protagonists and, in particular, a statement by Salma Hayek about her commitment to the work of Frida Kahlo – that had fascinated her from the age of 14 – and her personal and professional commitment to the actor Edward Norton. It was Norton, she argued, who had stepped in when the script had lost direction, 'delivering a brilliant screenplay ... He wrote at night since he was acting in another movie during the day. He hardly ever slept' (2002, p. 18). The production company Miramax's publicity machine, through interviews, advertisements in trade papers such as *Variety*, and a wealth of publicity photographs constantly spoke to Hayek's star persona as a 'committed' Mexican beauty in a relationship – a meeting of minds as well as beauty – with a committed Anglo film star. This couple could embody not just what Helen Delpar has called – referring in the main to the 1920s and 1930s – *The Enormous Vogue of Things Mexican* in the United States, but also a myth of ethnic fusion and harmony at a time when the US Bureau of Census was predicting that by 2050, the *latino* population would be half that of the 'white' inhabitants and double that of African-Americans. If onscreen Norton would play Nelson Rockefeller, the patron but also the censor of Mexican artists, off-screen the meeting of cultures was proving to be more felicitous. Approaching the theatre where the Oscar ceremony was taking place on 23 March 2003, Hayek, on the arm of Norton, remarked to an interviewer that she was the only Mexican actress ever to be nominated by the Academy for an Oscar award, a recognition, she felt, for her mother country.

From Pancho Villa to *Frida* Hollywood has always produced different representations of Latin America in its movies and has cultivated a number of stars to embody these representations. Critics of these films can draw on a great deal of academic literature because, in the view of most critics, the word star is synonymous with Hollywood stars. To quote just a few titles, Richard Dyer's *Stars* (1979) and *Heavenly Bodies* (1987), Jackie Stacey's *Star Gazing: Hollywood Cinema and Female Spectatorship* (1994), along with the edited collections by Christine Gledhill, *Stardom: Industry of Desire* (1991) and Jeremy Butler, *Star Texts* (1991) all refer almost exclusively to Hollywood cinema. Ginette Vincendeau, as we have seen, has recently offered a model analysis of how a national cinema outside Hollywood constructs its own star system. Yet where do the national cinemas of Latin America fit into this discussion? Can we talk of a star system in Latin America and where are the academic works to support these claims?

STARS ECLIPSED: THE REIGNING ORTHODOXY OF THIRD CINEMA

At the time when Richard Dyer was publishing his seminal work on stars in the late 1970s, the critical discourse on cinema in Latin America was still dominated by the revolutionary theoretical statements of the late 1960s, which can be summed up in Fernando Solanas and Octavio Getino's famous essay 'Towards a Third Cinema'. Dyer's concluding statement to *Stars* is that, 'while I accept that beauty and pleasure are culturally and historically specific, and in no way escape ideology, none the less they are beauty and pleasure and I want to hang on to them in some form or another' (1979, p. 162). Beauty and pleasure were not seen to be the dominant concerns of 'new' Latin American cinema. For Getino and Solanas, by contrast:

> Imperialism and capitalism, whether in the consumer society or in the neocolonised country, veil everything behind a screen of images and appearances. *The image of reality* is more important than reality itself. It is a world peopled with fantasies and phantoms in which what is hideous is clothed in beauty, while beauty is disguised as the hideous. On the one hand, fantasy, the imaginary bourgeois universe replete with comfort, equilibrium, sweet reason, order, efficiency ... and on the other, we the phantoms, we the lazy, we the indolent and underdeveloped, we who cause disorder. (1997, p. 45)

In this analysis, the star system is an integral part of the Hollywood capitalist, imperialist system, which is referred to as 'first cinema'. Films in Latin America that attempted to incorporate stars – say the classic Mexican or Argentine melodramas of the 1930s and 1940s – were dismissed as reactionary and fatalistic (see, for example, Colina and Díaz Torres, 1978, pp. 50–3).

In the trenchant view of Solanas and Getino, even the European 'new wave' or *auteur* cinema of the post-war era, what they called 'second cinema', was too compromised within the capitalist market system, to constitute a radical break. And it should be remembered for the purposes of our argument that 'new wave' actors were themselves the antithesis of mainstream stars; with the new wave, the director/*auteur* became the centre of attention. New wave cinema, like Solanas and Getino, was opposed to the triumphant individualism of studio film stars and developed what Vincendeau has called 'collective' stardom (2000, p. ix). Yet Solanas and Getino wanted to take the break to its ultimate expression: to work outside studios, to incorporate non-professional actors, to embrace popular/revolutionary struggle, to work, in the words of the Brazilian film-maker, Glauber Rocha, with a camera in hand and an idea in one's head, to find the appropriate film language for particular situations. In Bolivia, for example, the director Jorge Sanjinés replaced the close-up – the preferred framing for the star – with the sequence shot, that offered a more 'collective' framing, in keeping, he argued, with the belief structures and social organisation of the Quechua-Aymara peoples.

Stars thus became elided in theory and practice for two reasons. First, because the 'new' cinema movements the world over from the 1950s proposed modes of film-making that were 'atheistic' with regard to the screen gods and goddesses of previous times. Second, because criticism, especially Anglo-American criticism, tended to share the critical assumptions of the 'third cinema' thesis, albeit in less strident terms. This in turn had certain effects. Third cinema was taken from its historical moment, the revolutionary optimism of the late 1960s and early 1970s, and began to act as a template against which other films would be judged, and also serve as a definition of what Latin American cinema should be. The fact that 99 per cent of cinema production in Latin America did not adhere to the strict tenets of third cinema did not seem to be of great critical concern. When Channel 4 in the United Kingdom offered an important season of Latin American films in the early 1980s, accompanied by a two-part framing documentary by Michael Chanan and a pamphlet also edited by Michael Chanan, *Twenty-five Years of the New Latin American Cinema*, the selection of films shown were almost exclusively the classic 'revolutionary' films of the 1960s and early 1970s (Birri, Sanjinés, Guzmán, Gutiérrez Alea, Leduc, Littín, Alvarez), with a smattering of documentaries from Nicaragua, the revolutionary 'hope' of the early 1980s. While it was invaluable to have such a selection broadcast, the presentation and selection did imply that this was the present and also the future of Latin American cinema, which was a misconception based on a very partial, 'third cinema' reading of cinema and society. By 1983, when most of these screenings took place, societies and cultural practices in Latin America were moving in very different directions to the situations outlined in the selected films, and had been doing so for a number of years.

In the same way, most Anglo-American criticism of the 1970s and 1980s took cinema in Latin America to mean 'new' or 'revolutionary' cinema and produced a number of sophisticated analyses of key texts, creating a radical canon that became a touchstone for other work in the region. Some of the book titles from this period reveal the dominant interest: Julianne Burton (ed.), *Cinema and Social Change in Latin America*, 1986; Michael Chanan, *The Cuban Image*, 1985; Teshome Gabriel, *Third Cinema in the Third World*, 1982, Ana López, PhD dissertation, 'Towards a "Third" and "Imperfect" Cinema: A Theoretical and Historical Study of Film-making in Latin America', University of Iowa, 1986; Armand Mattelart, *Multinational Corporations and the Control of Culture*, 1982; Zuzana M. Pick (ed.), *Latin American Filmmakers and the Third Cinema*; Jim Pines and Paul Willemen (eds), *Questions of Third Cinema*. It would take, perhaps, the major ideological and political shifts of the late 1980s, to create an intellectual climate that was more accommodating to different approaches in film studies, pioneered inside and outside the continent.

PIONEERING APPROACHES TO STAR STUDIES: CARLOS MONSIVÁIS AND MEXICAN STARS; THE FICTIONAL WORLD OF MANUEL PUIG

We had faces then.
(Gloria Swanson in *Sunset Boulevard*)

It is in the work of the Mexican Carlos Monsiváis above all others that critics could find, and can still find, ways out of the critical impasse offered by third cinema. It was Monsiváis who offered a more subtle reading of the nature of cultural imperialism and cultural dependency that, in the 1970s, was seen in the Manichean terms expressed in such influential works as Ariel Dorfman and Armand Mattelart's *How to Read Donald Duck*. In a series of engaging and always entertaining essays dealing with cinema and culture in Mexico, Monsiváis offered new ways of approaching both Hollywood and also Mexican cinema.[1] His readings were new to the Latin American context in at least two important respects. He affirmed, like Dyer, that beauty and pleasure were important factors in the experience of movie watching, which led him to the analysis of the Mexican stars of the 1930s and 1940s. He also argued that Hollywood, and certain Latin American films, were key mediators and teachers in the transition to modernity in Latin America (see Schelling, 2000). Through cinema, spectators would learn not just to dream, but how to behave and think, in modern ways, in a secular world:

> With hindsight, we can see the basic function of the electronic media at their first important moment of power: they mediate between the shock of industrialisation and the rural and urban experience which has not been prepared in any way for this giant change, a process that from the forties modifies the idea of the nation. (Monsiváis, 1995b, p. 151)

If the main models for 'modern' behaviour were the Hollywood stars, Mexican and Latin American cinema could not and would not offer merely local copies of the Hollywood model. Monsiváis again:

> However, for a long period, despite their admiration and amazement at the landscape of shadows sent by the US, Latin Americans did not entrust and could not entrust to Hollywood their own representation and sentimental formation. For that they relied on Mexican, Argentine and Brazilian cinema. 'This is how we speak, this is how we look, this is how we move, this is how we treat our fellows.' (1995b, p. 57)

Local audiences listened to and watched their own stars. Carlos Gardel, Pedro Armendáriz, Jorge Negrete, Cantinflas, Dolores del Río, María Félix, were all models to be emulated, alongside a host of minor stars who caught the inflections of humour, the phrasing of a song, and offered the models of female beauty and male good looks. Monsiváis, therefore, opened up the field for star studies in Latin America, by giving weight to the positive as well as just the negative effects of the Hollywood system and by recognising and exploring the complex issues of audience reception and identification. He has also published perhaps the most influential essays to date on the Mexican stars Cantinflas, Dolores del Río and Tin Tan and on the crooner whose songs put the *melos* into the drama of many Mexican films of the 1930s and 1940s, Agustín Lara.

Monsiváis work is echoed in the fictional universes presented by the Argentine writer Manuel Puig, especially in his novels *Betrayed by Rita Hayworth* (1968), *Heartbreak Tango* (1969) and *Kiss of the Spider Woman* (1976). Among their many merits, Puig's novels address some of the dominant concerns of film studies, in particular the ways in which ordinary moviegoers express their pleasures. The most widely cited and influential academic study of this field is Jackie Stacey's *Star Gazing*, a book based on an extensive survey of British women who were asked to talk about film stars of the 1940s and 1950s. Paul McDonald offers a useful brief *précis* of the work: 'Inside the cinema some [of Stacey's] respondents described how they admired and worshipped the star as someone whose life was different and unattainable' (1998, pp. 138–45). Others, while recognising the difference of stars, determined to overcome it, either by aspiring to the ideals of feminine 'attractiveness' which the star represented, or taking inspiration from the confident way in which stars appeared to handle situations (ibid., pp. 151–8). Stacey calls these relationships 'cinematic identificatory fantasies' as they are formed by the moviegoer in the cinema imagining the star as an ideal other' (McDonald, 1998, p. 191). Stacey also explores the identification with stars that is carried on in the 'real' world outside the movie house, what she terms 'extra-cinematic identificatory practices'. These include the imitation of gestures, copying clothes or hairstyles, buying the products displayed in the movies, the lipsticks, the powder puffs: 'poaching' or borrowing mass-culture images and reworking them into individual lifestyles (see Jenkins, 1992).

The influence of the Hollywood star on consumers/spectators is noted by an American diplomat in the 1930s:

> A group of well-dressed Argentine businessmen called on the head of a United States film company some years ago with a request. 'It may seem ridiculous', they explained, 'and you may turn us down. But we are in the men's furnishing business and the new Clark Gable film *It Happened One Night* is ruining our trade.' 'How?' asked the movie man. 'Well, in one scene Gable takes off his shirt to go to bed and he wears no undershirt. Now our young Argentines are refusing to buy undershirts and our business is being seriously affected.' The movie man was first amused, then astonished. If one Made-In-Hollywood film could set such a trend, what might a whole series of pictures do? (Bruce, 1953, p. 332)

1930s' Argentina, Hollywood glamour, the attempts to emulate the star and 'act out' identificatory fantasies: this is the world of Manuel Puig's fictions. Himself an ardent movie and star fan from the time his mother first took him to the cinema aged four, Puig – like Monsiváis – is responsive to the beauty and the pleasure of the entertainment industry and is also aware of its perils. If the young character Toto is 'betrayed by Rita Hayworth' in the novel of the same name, it is not just because this is a integral part of Hayworth's star persona, the role she played in many movies, but because there is also an impossible gap between the pleasures and perils betrayed on the screen and the realities of a small Argentine town in the middle of the pampas. If the two characters locked in a cell in *Kiss of the Spider Woman* – who have 'fallen in love' through the seduction of movies – think that they can escape political and gender restrictions, they remain caught acting out the roles and behaviour ascribed to them, in the last instance, by the Hollywood and Mexican melodrama. Puig who, with eminent good taste, liked to be called Julie, after his favourite star Julie Christie, has expressed perhaps better than any critic, the moviegoer's fascination with the star system.

TOWARDS A DEFINITION OF STARS AND STARDOM IN LATIN AMERICA: WORK IN PROGRESS

In keeping with the overall orientation of this chapter, this section addresses in the main the work of Anglo-American scholars who are beginning to map in some of the contours of the field. There is not the space to survey the work carried out in this area, especially in Brazil and Mexico, but details of these studies are given in two anthologies edited by Paulo Antonio Paranaguá: *Le Cinéma Brésilien* (1987) and *Mexican Cinema* (1996).

Perhaps the first question to be asked is whether we can talk of a star system. It is clear that there is nothing in Latin America that duplicates the studio system of the 1930s and 1940s in Hollywood where the major studios such as Warner Bros or Paramount would contract stars for a specific length of time – usually a seven-year contract – and be responsible, through the 'vertical integration' of Hollywood cinema, for every stage of the star's image, from production through to distribution and exhibition. It was only from the 1950s in Hollywood that stars tended to be hired on a single film basis. The pattern in Latin America, as say in France, tended to be that of a 'cottage industry': small production companies that remained in being for short periods of time, perhaps the duration of one or two movies. With regard to film financing, there have been a number of studies of the importance of state funding in Latin America, but more work needs to be done on private producers and production companies and on the important work of film technicians such as cinematographers rather than just emphasising the importance of leading directors.[2] The economics and management of stardom are therefore areas for further research.

But if we cannot talk of stars as a *managed* system, we can certainly chart the importance of stars to film production in the 1930s and 1940s, especially in the 'big three' Latin American industries, Argentina, Brazil and Mexico, with the Mexican stars in particular achieving a pan-Latin American success. Stardom in Latin American cinema refers essentially to home markets within the region. There are next to no examples of the French pattern of stars like Bardot, Delon or Départdieu achieving worldwide success through their work in *national* cinemas, simply because Latin American cinema has always found it very difficult to break into world markets. It is interesting in this respect to see that in *The New York Times* review of the Mexican film *El crimen del Padre Amaro*, 'A Priest Who Makes the Women Swoon' (15 November 2002), the reviewer refers to the leading actor Gael García Bernal as someone 'who has become an international star with *Amores perros* and *Y tu Mamá también*'. It is likely that García Bernal is on the threshold of international stardom – Almodóvar is reported to be wanting to use him in future projects – but his notable appearance in three Mexican films that have achieved international distribution and success in the space of only two years – between 2000 and 2002 – is an almost unique phenomenon in Latin American film history.

Currently there is a critical consensus that we can speak of stars in the 1930s and 1940s. The case is not clearly made for actors or actresses after, say, the mid-1950s, *pace The New York Times* and Gael García Bernal. While, as we have seen, there has been great critical attention paid to 'third' cinema and its active dethronement of stars in favour of representations of the *pueblo* in its many forms, there has been little attention paid to the trajectory of individual actors in box-office or cinephile cinema from the 1970s to the 1990s. Salma Hayek is a star in Hollywood's *Frida*. Can we say the same of Ofelia Medina who gave an extraordinary performance as Frida Kahlo in Mexican director Paul Leduc's *Frida: naturaleza viva* (1984)? The Mexican María Rojo appeared in many of the most important films in Mexico between the 1970 and 2000, though these films – apart from *Danzón* (1990) – usually appealed to an educated middle-class audience and were not sold as 'star' vehicles. The same could be said of the work in Mexico of Ernesto Gómez Cruz or Daniel Giménez Cacho: these are not the 'monstruos sagrados' of earlier years, representing male images of virility or embodying the nation, but fine character actors appearing in a 'secular' film world.

Certain contemporary directors have often worked with particular actors: Luisina Brando, for example, appeared in a number of María Luisa Bemberg's films. However, when Bemberg and other directors looked to include 'international' stars in their movies as a way of attracting co-production money and facilitating access to world-wide markets, it was clear, at least to the home audience, who the star was in these films. Julie Christie went out to Argentina in 1985 in the immediate aftermath of the Falklands/Malvinas war to film *Miss Mary*, taking on the 'problematic fit' – in Dyer's terms – of a star role as a repressed English governess in Bemberg's autobiographical tale of aristocratic life in the 1930s. Analysis of press cuttings from Argentine newspapers and magazines reveals that all the press attention before and after the release of the film focused on Christie, rather than on the leading Argentine actresses Luisina Brando and the famous *café-concert* singer Nacha Guevara, her co-'stars'. The question of how 'foreign' stars are incorporated into contemporary cinema is an interesting one, which is beginning to receive critical attention (see King *et al.*, 2000). There still remains, however, the issue of whether the term 'star' is the right one to use of the many prominent actors working in national cinemas throughout the region in the past fifty years.

Returning to the 'agreed' critical terrain of stars in the 1930s and 1940s, so eloquently mapped by Carlos Monsiváis in Mexico, there have been important developments in Anglo-American criticism throughout the 1990s. Ginette Vincendeau talks of three broad types of material that make up film stardom: 'the stars' performance in the films themselves, trade promotion and publicity and commentaries/criticism' (2000, p. x). Of these, she stresses the centrality of the films themselves, a point taken up by critics in the Latin American field. While there has been some work on publicity, in particular the book of vivid and illustrative film posters of the Agrasánchez archive in Mexico brought together by Charles Ramírez Berg in the bilingual edition *Carteles de la Epoca de Oro 1936–1956. Cine Mexicano. Posters from the Golden Age 1936–1956* (1997), most critics now concentrate on film performance. Close film analysis is, in itself, is a welcome break from the largely contextual and historical accounts of cinema in the region. Let us refer briefly to several books on Mexican film that can offer a model for future work. Jeffrey Picher's *Cantinflas and the Chaos of Mexican Modernity* (2002) offers a carefully documented portrait of perhaps Latin America's greatest and most enduring star. Although Picher makes no reference at all to the theoretical work on stars, his analysis chimes with many of the interests of star theory. He shows the importance of stage and vaudeville performers to the early development of film. He analyses the film industry and how it created local stardom. He explores the articulation of the professional with the private in Cantinflas's screen image and shows the way in which Cantinflas embodied and authenticated a specific type at a particular historical moment: the *pelado* or scruffy street-wise neighbourhood wide-boy who lived on his wits and managed to subvert, through verbal dexterity, the hierarchical structures of society. The analysis of Cantinflas's performance includes attention to both his extraordinary physical elasticity and mobile face and also his use of language, in which words, delivered at breakneck speed, go desperately in search of meanings, knocking over sense and polite society in an exhilarating rush. Joanne Hershfield has begun to explore a similar terrain in her analysis of representative films and stars of the Mexican Golden Age. In *Mexican Cinema/Mexican Woman, 1940–1950* (1996) and her analysis of Dolores del Río, *The Invention of Dolores del Río* (2000), she focuses in part on female stardom, the star personae of Dolores del Río and María Félix, the ways in which they embody different myths of a woman and different aspects of the nation.

Future work should include analysis of the different ways of being 'a man' in Mexican cinema, from the singing *charro* Jorge Negrete to the somewhat softer machismo of Pedro Infante. And, of course, as Octavio Paz reminds us, there is María Félix, whose recent death in 2002 will doubtless lead to a reappraisal of her work. Félix is a quintessential star. She was, in the words of the Mexican writer Carlos Fuentes, 'an independent woman in a country where women over the centuries were destined to be nuns or whores. She presented herself as an independent woman, who owned her own body.'[3] She came to play in a number of films whose titles reveal her screen persona: *Doña*

Bárbara, La mujer de todos, La devoradora, La bandida, La generala. Her well-publicised *amours* with Jorge Negrete and the singer Agustín Lara (who wrote the best-selling 'María Bonita' in her honour and sang it on a white piano which contained the inscription 'on this piano I will play only my most beautiful melodies for the most beautiful woman in the world'), not to mention the Mexican President Miguel Alemán, added weight, and countless newspaper column inches, to her legendary status on and off the screen. Her career in Mexico and also in France (playing alongside France's legendary star Jean Gabin in Renoir's *French Cancan*, 1955) offers rich material for incipient stargazers and star critics. We will leave the last words of this brief survey to Octavio Paz who looks at Félix with the eye of a utopian poet, in whose gaze this star would never be merely an object of consumption and manipulation, but rather the active producer of her own special magic:

> Despite the fact that Mexico is a country where masculine values – the father, the patriarch, the grandfather, the chief, the macho – have held sway, many feminine images have illuminated the Mexican mind and imagination. Some are sweet like the Virgen of Guadalupe, maternal hill, refuge for orphans; others are unfathomable like La Malinche; others are an inconsolable scream, a black river in the night, like La Llorona; others are sunny and free like Adelita for the revolutionaries. The myth of María Félix is different. It is a modern myth and it is not entirely imaginary, like almost all of those from the past, but rather the projection of a real woman … María Félix is a very strong woman who has had the bravery not to conform to the macho ideals of women. She is free as the wind; she disperses or brings together clouds, she cleaves them or illuminates them with a spark, with a look. Her magnetism is concentrated in her eyes, by turn serene and tempestuous: they attract and they strike with lightning. Like Armida – the comparison is inevitable – one moment she is ice, the next moment fire. Ice that the sun melts into streams, fire that is transformed into clarity. (1992, p. 13)

NOTES

1. Monsiváis is a most prolific essayist. Students of film culture could start with the selection of his writings translated into English contained in *Mexican Postcards* (1977a). Some key texts in Spanish are the essays in *Amor perdido* (1977), *Escenas de pudor y liviandad* (1988), *Rostros del cine mexicano* (1993), *Aires de familia: cultura y sociedad en América Latina* (2000).
2. On state funding, see in particular, Randal Johnson, *The Film Industry in Brazil: Culture and the State* (1987), and Randal Johnson and Robert Stam (eds), *Brazilian Cinema* (1995). See also Jorge Schnitman, *Film Industries in Latin America: Dependency and Development* (1984), and Seth Fine, 'From Collaboration to Containment' (1999).
3. Carlos Fuentes, an interview with John King (King, 1987, p. 147).

12

Los globalizados también lloran
Mexican telenovelas and the geographical imagination
Laura Podalsky

A poor, young woman with ties to the countryside falls in love with a rich young man from the city. While the heroine struggles to adapt to her new urban environment, the hero must battle the corrupting influence of his sophisticated peers who plot to separate the two lovers. Such plots have been typical of Mexican *telenovelas* from the classic Mexican serial *Los ricos también lloran* (The Rich Also Cry) in the 1970s to the more recent *Esmeralda* (Emerald) (1997–98).[1] In highlighting geographical and class divisions, *telenovelas* traditionally have addressed conflicts that are central to modernization and nation-building. The dilemma of the young hero and heroine – their inevitable separation and eventual reunion – has symbolized the types of social tensions arising from urbanization and the ensuing conflicts between traditional and modern values.

At the same time, *telenovelas* have promoted a sense of national identity uniting diverse peoples (living within the territorial boundaries of the nation-state) by incorporating art forms, iconography, and discursive traditions that are unique to or characteristic of that national space. Mexican *novelas*, for example, frequently feature *mariachi* and *ranchera* music and include specific locations and character-types drawn from early Mexican film melodramas.[2] Even the dominant narrative structure of Mexican *telenovelas*, in which the poor characters' unerring moral goodness allows them to triumph over the perfidy of the rich, recalls local discursive traditions that emerged in the aftermath of the Revolution in *corridos* and in films to legitimize the downfall of the Porfirian elite and anoint the humble as the privileged subjects of the 'new', post-revolutionary nation. In sum, *telenovelas* have contributed to the consolidation of modern national and *urban* sensibilities, particularly in moments of social transition, as their convoluted plots give voice to social tensions between older and newer values and, in the end, offer parables of familial and societal reconciliation. In the final archetypical episode, when the poor young girl marries the rich young man, the Mexican *novelas* suggest that differences between classes and regions can be overcome in the modern nation by retaining the humility and honesty of the countryside in the context of the modern city.[3]

The way in which *telenovelas* contribute to the cognitive re-mapping of society has encountered a new challenge in the contemporary context of globalization, a tension-filled process wherein neo-liberal economic policies and technological innovations have accelerated continuous exchanges of products and information across national borders and, in so doing, have placed pressure on the sovereignty of nation-states and the viability of nationalist discourses. This chapter takes a closer look at the way in which contemporary *telenovelas* register the complex processes of globalization by examining recent changes in their narrative structure and setting in relation to the contemporary challenges faced by media companies. The chapter will place particular emphasis on the ideological work performed by contemporary *telenovelas* and, more particularly, on the ways in which they reformulate notions of citizenship in the context of globalization. We will examine how their stories about globe-trotting characters promote globalization while attenuating fears about the loss of local values and traditions. In other words, we will look at how the *novelas* serve the needs of transnational corporations by opening up new markets and, more generally, by generating desire for new types of products. We will then suggest why these programs attract viewers, arguing that *telenovelas* provide sites through which their viewers can negotiate the new consumer imperatives.

These issues will be addressed through a circumscribed analysis of Televisa-produced *novelas* shown on Univisión, the leading Spanish-language station in the US.[4] Given the context of NAFTA[5] and the rapid growth of the Latino/a population in the US, this case study can provide a privileged perspective on the complex ways in which globalization affects cultural production and consumption. We will explore not only how contemporary *telenovelas* register industrial imperatives as Televisa reaches out to audiences on both sides of the border, but also some of the reasons for the genre's continuing success in the US (and Mexico) despite the growing heterogeneity of the Latino/a population and the criticism expressed by community members and activists.

VYING FOR VIEWERSHIP: THE CHALLENGES OF GLOBALIZING MEDIA

Although Mexico's Televisa has easily dominated the Mexican television industry for decades, a number of recent events have begun to destabilize the company's hold over domestic audiences. These events include the ups and downs of the Mexican economy in the 1980s and 1990s, the company's top-heavy management structure, the relative saturation of the television market within Mexico, and competition from the upstart TV Azteca.[6] Even as it has begun to change its programming to retain its hold over Mexican audiences, Televisa has placed special emphasis on expanding its exports to foreign markets (where it has successfully sold its *telenovelas* for many years).[7] Because of its large Spanish-speaking population, the US has long functioned as a seemingly 'natural' market for Televisa and it has become even more appealing in the 1990s as Latino/as have become the largest and fastest growing ethnic group in the nation and wield the type of immense purchasing power (over $450 billion dollars in 2001) that attracts advertising dollars.[8]

Up until recently, Televisa's interest in marketing its shows to US audiences had been welcomed by Univisión, the dominant Spanish-language network in the US. Indeed, Televisa-produced *novelas* have long been a staple of Univision's prime-time programming.[9] Nonetheless, Univisión itself has been facing a number of challenges that threaten to undermine its preferential relationship with the Mexican media conglomerate. In the first place, the composition of the US Latino/a population is changing. Although people of Mexican descent continue to constitute the largest sub-group, there has been a 97 per cent growth of non-Mexican Hispanics over the last decades (Chang, 2001b). These demographic changes as well as the increasingly vocal dissatisfaction of some Latino/as (particularly younger viewers with the type of disposable income most sought after by advertisers) have made the continued success of programming privileging Mexican cultural traditions, as do the Televisa-produced *telenovelas*, increasingly questionable (Aguilar, 2002; Dávila, 2002, pp. 25, 33). At the same time, Univisión has faced increasing (if still marginal) competition from Telemundo, the other major Spanish-language network purchased by Sony in 1988 and then by NBC in 2002. With the backing of such media giants, Telemundo has tried to gain a stronger foothold in the market through a variety of strategies intended to speak to the diversity of the Latino/a community, including producing other programs based on old US dramas like *Charlie's Angels* and *Starsky and Hutch* and importing *novelas* like Colombia's *Betty la Fea* (Ugly Betty) and Brazil's *Xica da Silva*. Some of these programming strategies have been more successful than others. And, although none has allowed Telemundo to knock Univisión off its top position, some have chipped away at its ratings (Freeman 2000, Chang, 2001b).

In this context, Televisa's *telenovelas* have had to devise new strategies to appeal to highly diverse audiences in the US (and elsewhere) without losing their hold over their primary, domestic market where they recover their production costs (Mato, 1999, pp. 252–3, 258; Hernandez and McAnany, 2001, p. 392). As detailed below, many of the new *novelas* have done this by highlighting the issue of border-crossing in their narrative structure and *mise-en-scène*. Incorporating sequences set in Madrid hotels, Texas ranches, and on Miami beaches, the *novelas* also feature numerous scenes in the local *cantina* where the *cuates* exchange insults in dialogues heavily inflected with the traditions of the *teatro bufo* (popular theater). Often cross-cutting between scenes set in a foreign city (identified by stock establishing shots with graphic titles) and those set in Mexico, they encourage spectators to travel along with protagonists who journey between Miami Beach and the local *barrio*. Through these and other strategies, the serials celebrate Mexico's participation in globalization even as they valorize local traditions.

GLOBAL TRIUMPHS, LOCAL PLEASURES

While a large number of contemporary Mexican *telenovelas* like *Esmeralda* and *María José* (c. 1995) still address the division between the rich and the poor as a conflict between the purity of country and the corruption of the city, others like *Volver a empezar* (Starting Over Again) (c. 1994), *Acapulco, cuerpo y alma* (Acapulco, Body and Soul) (1995–6), and *Amigas y rivales* (Girfriends and Rivals) (2001–2) emphasize the relationship between the nation and the world.[10] These 'transnational' *novelas* frequently develop conflicts between a poor heroine associated with the national and a rich hero associated with the global, and frequently take place both in Mexico and abroad. In so doing, they contribute to the reformulation of their viewers' understanding of their place in the world.

Many recent Televisa *telenovelas* have made the movement of people and goods across national borders central to their plot structure. More often than not, they constitute this border crossing primarily as a function of economic imperatives as one or more of the central protagonists travel abroad to earn money or pursue careers. Most often the protagonists are middle- and upper-class entrepreneurs or professionals. In *Mi destino eres tú*, a Mexican-based textile company tries to break into the US market and the two main protagonists are lawyers who fly to Las Vegas for a professional conference. Less frequently *telenovelas* feature the travel of working-class characters as did *Amigas y rivales* in which Nayeli and Abelardo cross into the US illegally to work in low-paying jobs in Los Angeles and Waco while Johnny, another working-class character, gains international renown as a championship boxer. Such narratives portray their Mexican characters either as cosmopolitan subjects who triumph abroad or as hard-working emigrants who use the difficulties they encounter outside the nation to triumph at home. In *Mi destino eres tú* (You're my Destiny), the heroine's recognition by her US colleagues at the Las Vegas conference served as a sign of Mexico's new, post-NAFTA stature as an equal trading partner with the US and Canada. In *Amigas y rivales*, in a somewhat different scenario, Nayeli's experience as an illegal immigrant in LA becomes the springboard to social mobility. Upon returning to Mexico, she begins working at Televisa and eventually becomes the star of her own *telenovela*, *La Frontera del Amor* (The Border of Love). By characterizing the cross-border flow of even blue-collar workers as professionally enriching experiences, such narratives implicitly counter the criticisms voiced by opponents of NAFTA who argued that the treaty would make Mexico merely a supplier of cheap manual labor for companies based elsewhere.

The *novelas*' promotion of economic globalization depends upon reworking traditional formulations of national identity – as became visible in *Acapulco, cuerpo y alma*. Premiering in 1995, the *novela* repackaged the standard conflicts of Mexican *novelas* in a new glossy format. Featuring numerous on-location shots of Acapulco's stunning scenery, the *novela* used the struggles of David and Lorena, its main protagonists, to symbolize the conflicts between global and national interests. In *Acapulco*, the rich characters are international 'players' who are able to compete successfully as businessmen in the global marketplace and reap the benefits of being international consumers. The hero David is a successful entrepreneur who builds hotels and resorts in Acapulco, the internationally popular tourist center. His business ventures take him to Mexico City (the location of some of the key sequences in the plot) and allow him to vacation in New York and in Spain. David's best friend Humberto, who also falls in love with Lorena, is a successful Miami-based entrepreneur who frequently travels back and forth between his US home and the Mexican resort town for both business and pleasure (often several times during one hour-long episode).

In contrast, the poor characters are most closely associated with national pleasures. Don Aurelio, Lorena's father, runs a supposedly modest *cevichería* (a restaurant serving typical dishes made from fish) on the beaches of the nearby Zihuatanejo (a smaller resort town 130 miles north of Acapulco). Numerous scenes foreground the playful interchanges between don Aurelio and his friends, highlighting Mexicanisms and the broad humor seen in *bufo* or popular theater. Unlike David and Humberto, don Aurelio and his *cuates* refuse to leave Acapulco even after an unexpected inheritance enables them to do so and even when certain danger awaits them in the local area. Thus, the program highlights their love of and loyalty to the national space.

While allowing its viewers their own imaginary frequent flyer points by shifting between Acapulco and Miami many times within one episode, the *novela* does not give these two locations the same treatment. Rather, even as it spotlights the rewards of transnational mobility, *Acapulco* critiques the untethered pursuit of a jet-setting lifestyle as rich characters exploit and abuse those around them. Unadulterated greed motivates the evil schemes of the two main villains: Marcelo, David's half-brother, and Aidé, David's ex-fiancée. Early on, Marcelo plots to kill David in a helicopter crash. Later, with the help of Aidé, he pretends to sleep with a drugged Lorena and succeeds in separating her from David, who sees them in bed together. Marcelo then kills Humberto by placing a bomb in his Mercedes, again attempts to kill David, and subsequently kills himself and his mother after they struggle over a gun and plunge to their deaths from the balcony of his cliffside dwelling. While the poorer characters do not have the same access to consumer luxuries, the *novela* suggests that they are much happier with their simpler pleasures. Even David, the hapless hero, must suffer great remorse (episode after episode after episode) for having lost Lorena to his own blind jealousy. In *Acapulco, cuerpo y alma*, while the poor may suffer, 'los globalizados también lloran' (jet-setters also cry). Through such plot twists, the *novela* suggests that Mexicans can benefit from globalizing trends, but warns against the excessive greed of the 'jet set' (who, 'in the end', die like Marcelo or go to jail like Aidé). In other words, *telenovelas* like *Acapulco, cuerpo y alma* encourage Mexican viewers to 'buy into' NAFTA without abandoning their loyalty to their homeland.

The way in which this promotion of the nation fits within the commodifying logic of globalization is evident in the *novelas*' *mise-en-scène* – particularly in the frequent sequences shot on location in Mexico that function as display windows showcasing the nation as a marketable product. *Acapulco, cuerpo y alma* featured numerous location shots on the beach and in cliffside mansions at a time when Acapulco itself was being rediscovered by locals and foreigners alike. In less spectacular fashion, *Amigas y rivales* included a sequence in Xochilmilco, the popular tourist site of the 'floating gardens' outside of Mexico City, where Johnny, the Mexican boxing champ, is reunited with family members who had been living in New York. These sequences are not limited to the 'transnational' *novelas*. Even *telenovelas* like *Alguna vez tendremos alas* (One Day We'll Have Wings) (1997) and *Esmeralda* (Emerald), in which the characters stay within Mexico, featured abundant location shooting and frequently included scenes in which their characters travel to cities famous for their stunning colonial architecture and indigenous cultural legacies like Zacatecas and Oaxaca.[11] Such scenes appeal to local viewers and promote domestic (and, at times, foreign) travel,[12] but they also allow companies like Televisa to offer a unique product to the foreign market by providing those audiences elsewhere a privileged view of some of Mexico's 'national treasures'.

Business imperatives also influenced Televisa's inclusion of Mexican singing stars as lead characters in its *telenovelas*. Like other entertainment corporations, the Mexican conglomerate emphasizes synergy between its media products. In the 1990s, that meant, among other things, using the musical score of its *novelas* to promote the CDs produced by its musical division under the Melody/Fonovisa label. For example, *Acapulco*'s Lorena was played by Patty Manterola, a singer who had broken away from the group Garibaldi to launch a solo career on Melody.[13] In 1995 when *Acapulco* premiered, Manterola carried its theme song 'high onto the Mexican chart'. There are numerous other examples of similar phenomena – most notable among them, the use of Thalía, another Melody/Fonovisa artist, in three Televisa *novelas*: *María Mercedes* (1992), *Marimar* (1994) and *Maria, la del barrio* (Maria, the Girl on the Block) (1995).[14] In fact, the mixing of *novelas* and music was part of a corporate strategy initiated in the early 1990s when Luis de Llano, the vice-president of Televisa's musical programming division, altered the standard *novela* format to include more music and video clips – thus creating a subgenre, the musical *novela* (Paxman, 1996b). The 1994 *Volver a empezar* centered around a transnational romance between Reni, a popular Mexican singer (played by Yuri, a popular Mexican singer) and Chayanne, a famous Puerto Rican singer (played by Chayanne, a famous Puerto Rican singer who was previously part of Menudo). The *novela* featured their rehearsals (where Reni and Chayanne sang out their love and frustrations) as well as the big show (where Reni suffered a near-fatal accident). With such tactics, Televisa hoped to hook into the MTV/MTV Latino phenomena and appeal to teen audiences within Mexico who hear the music on Televisa-owned radio stations or on its televized variety and talk shows.[15]

Recently, those type of synergies have given way to others as some of Televisa's top music stars like Thalía and Lucero have signed record deals with other labels. Although the fluctuations of the music industry led the Mexican conglomerate to sell its Fonovisa label to none other than Univisión in late 2001, Televisa continues to feature its former stars on its *novelas* and on its recently revamped live entertainment subsidy *En Vivo*.[16] As Univisión itself has expanded its radio holdings and launched a music division,[17] the promotion of music through *novelas* (and vice versa) has become a profitable venture for both companies as it promises to appeal to a wide range of consumers. Indeed, in *Mi destino eres tú,* the professional triumph of Andrea (played by singing star Lucero) at the conference in the US, would have been perfectly legible for audiences, allegorizing as it did the success of the singer herself whose CDs have sold immensely well on both sides of the border and who now has a contract with Sony's Columbia Records.[18]

SEEING THROUGH THE GLOBAL VILLAGE

Although the business imperatives influencing the structure of recent *telenovelas* are readily understandable, their immense success with audiences – particularly US-based audiences – is more puzzling. As noted by numerous community members, activists and scholars, Mexican *telenovelas* (and many other Univisión programs) fail to address the complex lives and experiences of the amazingly diverse Latino/a community. Featuring Mexican characters, locations, cultural traditions and speech patterns, the *novelas* do not reflect the ethnic and linguistic diversity of the Latino/a population (a third of which speak English exclusively) or the specificity of life within the US.[19] Why then do such Spanish-language programs continue to appeal to Latino/a viewers? The reasons may be as diverse as *novela* audiences themselves. On the one hand, there are few alternatives. English-language channels on both network and cable television offer few 'Latino/a-centered' programs. Although several programs include important Latino/a characters like *NYPD Blue*, few offer substantial storylines revolving around Latino/as as do PBS's *American Family* and Showtime's *Resurrection Boulevard*. Some critics argue that the only programs that have increasingly featured Latino/as in significant ways are daytime soap operas which are trying to attract Latino/a viewers (Cottle, 2001).[20]

However, Latino/a audiences have also demonstrated a preference for *telenovelas* over other types of programs on Univisión and Telemundo and (with the exception of the immensely popular talk show *Cristina*) even over those that feature Latino/a characters or people. When Telemundo replaced its *telenovelas* with other types of programming like *Angeles*, a remake of *Charlie's Angels* set in a fictional coastal town in the US featuring a Mexican, a Cuban, and an Argentine character, during the 1998–9 season, its ratings dropped precipitously. The company quickly returned to a night-time schedule dominated by *telenovelas* – this time importing *novelas* like the Colombian serial *Betty la Fea* as well as the highly celebrated Brazilian *Xica da Silva* – and the strategy quickly turned around the network's ratings (Whitefield, 2001). The fate of Telemundo's more recent attempt to address Latino/a experience with sit-coms like *Los Beltranes* (The Beltran Family), about a LA-based Cuban-American bodega owner with a Chicano son-in-law, and *Sólo in America* (Only in America), about a Venezuelan, Spanish-speaking Latina mother and her two bilingual and bicultural daughters living in Brooklyn, also failed. As argued by scholar Arlene Dávila, the shows did little to register Latino/as' linguistic diversity (as inconsequential English words were peppered into the Spanish dialogue) or the specific place of Latino/as within US cities (Dávila, 2001, p. 175). If the failure of *Angeles* and the two sit-coms can be attributed to some degree to their unconvincing portrayal of Latino/as, the continuing popularity of *telenovelas* may depend, ironically enough, on the way they entirely ignore the 'reality' of Latino/as in favor of a melodramatic aesthetic that allows for allegorical readings.[21]

For recent arrivals, border-crossing *novelas* may help mediate the shock of adapting to US culture by providing access to familiar programming. Mexican *novelas* are shown in many Latin American countries and may not appear foreign to the recent immigrants targeted by Univisión regardless of national origin (Dávila, 2001, pp. 158, 160). Such *novelas* may also resonate with recent arrivals because the struggles of their protagonists, like those of *Acapulco, cuerpo y alma*'s Lorena, allegorically address and attenuate the difficulties of border-crossing experienced by immigrant-viewers. From a modest family in Zihuatenejo, Lorena reaches new heights in the elaborate mansions of Acapulco's wealthiest citizens through her love affair with David. Her hardships and triumphs lead her eventually to Miami (first to marry Humberto), then back to Acapulco (after her broken engagement), then back again to Miami (after Humberto dies and she inherits his money). While

Lorena enters the realm of the jet-set, *Acapulco, cuerpo y alma* suggests that, unlike the others in this sphere, she retains a sense of humility and honesty, and ultimately represents the incorruptibly national. As her sister reminds Lorena when they are in Miami, 'Your body is here, but your soul will always be in Acapulco.' By fostering the spectator's identification with Lorena, *Acapulco* mediates the tensions between globalizing and nationalistic projects by simultaneously imagining a happy future in a transnational utopia while expressing nostalgia or longing for an 'authentic' national place.

At the same time, by featuring light-skinned protagonists, *novelas* help sublimate racial tensions. Unlike many immigrants and long-standing Latino/a citizens who confront racism in a variety of contexts, the struggles of the *novelas*' protagonists are always clearly characterized as based on class differences. By ignoring questions of race, *novelas* foster the belief in social mobility that lies at the heart of the 'American Dream'.[22] The promise of class ascension unmarked by racial difference is also held out by commercials shown alongside the *novelas* on Univisión. An AT&T ad that aired during an episode of *Acapulco, cuerpo y alma* featured a well-dressed, light-skinned couple coming out of their two-story house carrying a garment bag (presumably on the way to the airport) who praise AT&T's True-Reach International savings program before getting into their car. Investing the couple with all of the accoutrements of suburban life, the ad portrayed Latino/a families as part of the upwardly-mobile, middle class – happy where they are but with strong ties to someplace else. Although in somewhat different terms, these commercials along with Mexican *telenovelas* like *Acapulco* encourage their spectators' ties to their 'home' cultures of origin and, at the same time, their hunger for worldly consumer pleasures. They project the promise of economic mobility while deflecting the threat of acculturation by coding difference as a linguistic (rather than racial) issue.[23]

But what of viewers who are long-standing US citizens and who may have less direct ties to Latin America? How do recent *telenovelas* appeal to their concerns and interests? There is some ethnographic evidence that, for some Latino/as, *novelas* offer the possibility of reconnecting with 'lost' cultural and linguistic traditions (Barrera and Bielby, 2001). For others, the attraction may lie in the way in which the genre's central conflicts (namely, one's place in the world and the problem of communication) register what some critics have characterized as the dominant sensibility of contemporary life in the US – specifically, the feeling of growing disconnectedness and isolation on the part of individuals as increasingly demanding jobs cut down on leisure time, as domestic technologies (cable TV, the Internet) allow the home to function as a refuge from supposedly dangerous public places, and as networks of intimacy fracture as families and friends are separated in literal and metaphoric ways. In other words, *telenovelas* engage contemporary social crises allegorically by staging and then resolving problems of identity and community breakdown.

This occurs in a number of different ways. As in older melodramas, recent

Televisa productions feature characters whose 'true identity' is at first hidden and only acknowledged later on as the plot develops. These characters often go away (frequently traveling to the US) and then return, near the end of the *novela*, to be recognized for 'who they really are' by the wider community. In *Amigas y rivales*, Nayeli's journey to the US becomes the central means by which she realizes her dreams at home (by becoming a successful *telenovela* star) and gains the recognition of the upper-class Mexican characters who had previously spurned her. In the highly successful *Salomé* (2001–2), the rich, married hero (Julián Montesinos) falls in love with a seductive cabaret singer (Salomé) with whom he has a child. As a result of the plotting of Julián's mother and his wife, Salomé flees to 'the north' (in this case, to the border city of Ciudad Juárez) with her son and two other young boys whom she courageously adopts. Years later, she returns to Mexico City as Fernanda de la Valle, a businesswoman running an immensely successful spa, with her three sons who are now young men, and gains the type of social acceptance that had eluded her as a cabaret performer. Such plot lines assure viewers that hard work and perseverance allow individuals to control their own destinies and ensure their recognition by the larger community.

Yet, even as they celebrate the power of the individual to shape her future, they also reassert the coherence of the community, the sense that 'society' is a comprehensible totality, by resituating traditional serial melodrama's 'closed community' within a global context.[24] By revealing, in the end, the familial connections that tie together all of the main characters, the *novelas*' convoluted plots suggest, in Dickensian fashion, that the social order is coherent and know-able even when it transcends national boundaries. They tease viewers with the promises of the 'global village' (bringing the world together) while deflecting the threats associated with globalization (e.g. growing inequalities).

In this context, one of melodrama's key characteristics (what Peter Brooks calls the crisis of speech or the inability to talk) and one of serial melodrama's key plot devices (the incessant retelling of a single event) take on new functions. If, as argued by Colombian critic Jesús Martín-Barbero, serial melodramas initially gained popularity and mediated the trauma of urbanization in the mid-twentieth century by mimicking older traditions of oral storytelling characteristic of rural communities, the dramatization of speech acts in recent *telenovelas* addresses a new problematic: the question of 'connectivity'. In an era when cell phones and the Internet guarantee instant communication, some sectors are left out of the loop. Such technologies have also tended to exacerbate, rather than overcome, communicational gaps. The Mexican *novelas* address these issues both directly and indirectly. Through a couple of different plot devices, *Amigas y rivales* foregrounded the communicational difficulties that arise when families, lovers, and friends are separated by long distances. When Laura's sister was severely injured by a gas leak set by the villainous Roxana, the *novela* dedicated several episodes to spotlighting the agony experienced by her boyfriend Abelardo, who had been working illegally in Waco, Texas, and was unable to reach his comatose girlfriend in Mexico City in a timely fashion. If such moments might be particularly appealing to viewers who are or were im/migrants, the incessant staging of 'excessive' dialogue works to counteract or redress the more generalized feelings of isolation characteristic of contemporary society at large. For example, when Roxana's horrific misdeeds, once revealed, become the fodder of endless discussions and retellings among other groups of characters in a variety of settings, these repetitive dialogues become the means by which to sew together the diegetic community and, by extension, the viewers themselves, either by stimulating dialogue among spectators[25] or merely by projecting a model of society as integrated and unified.

In sum, the *novelas* contribute to and, at the same time, mediate what urban geographer and social theorist David Harvey has called the time-space compression of the contemporary era in which advances in communication, transportation, and information technologies promote a sense of instantaneous connectedness that bridges geographical distance. Despite the democratizing promise of such innovations, the transformation of contemporary life also threatens to exacerbate existing inequalities as people and communities have differential access to such technologies. Clearly, this unease is not in any way isolated to the Latino/a population or, indeed, shared by all members of that community. Yet, for some, the appeal of *novelas* may relate to the way they mediate societal transformations being experienced by Latino/as and non-Latino/as alike while spotlighting linguistic and cultural traditions that are almost entirely ignored by English-language television.

THOSE ARE THE BREAKS OF GLOBALIZATION

Although these new globe-trotting *telenovelas* mediate the trauma of globalization for their viewers and serve the interests of business conglomerates on both sides of the border, they also reveal the difficulty of bridging national and global imperatives. As I have argued elsewhere regarding classic Mexican films, the formal awkwardness of melodrama (e.g. its abrupt narrative shifts, excessive sentimentality, and improbable resolutions of narrative conflict) ultimately disrupts the genre's otherwise conservative ideological project. These narrative ruptures often occur with greater frequency and intensity as the *novelas* wind to a conclusion and attempt to 'tie up' multiple storylines and resolve the seemingly insurmountable tensions that had been driving the plot for months. The forced and implausible nature of such conclusions can be seen in the final episodes of *Acapulco, cuerpo y alma* about the troubled love affair of David (the jet-setting hotel impresario) and Lorena, the humble young woman from the nearby Zihuantanejo. Having spent months chronicling Lorena's ascension into the globalized elite (through her relationship to David and then through her inheritance of Humberto's fortune), the *novela* must, in the end, reassert her allegiance to the national. Although Lorena decides to return to Miami after Humberto's death, she vows to return to Mexico to give birth to the child she conceived with David before their separation. The *novela* expresses the intensity of her desire to return home (and, thus, in symbolic terms, the overwhelming pull of the national) by compressing the story time drastically. Immediately after articulating her desire to return to Acapulco, the *novela* cuts to a new scene several months later in which Lorena is lying in an Acapulco hospital bed experiencing contractions. Through this startling elision of the difficulties of both pregnancy and border-crossing, *Acapulco, cuerpo y alma* characterizes the 'return home' as a utopic moment unmarred by the pain of re-adaptation. At the same time, even as the *novela* eliminates the contentious 'in-between' of migration, the temporal jump in the narrative also creates an unavoidable interruption – one which the spectator must acknowledge and then disavow. A similar narrative break occurs in the reconciliation of David and Lorena on the balcony of his magnificent home overlooking the ocean in the last two minutes of the very last episode. After highlighting the tensions between the local and the global for four and a half months, this abrupt ending fails to assuage the tensions painstakingly built up over that period. The awkwardness of the *novela*'s conclusion suggests that global and national imperatives cannot be as easily brokered as *Acapulco*'s final tableau suggests: David (the global), Lorena (the local), and their baby (the hybrid) against the spectacular backdrop of Acapulco (the site where national and international forces meet).[26] As suggested by Tania Modleski, the unconvincing endings of melodramatic texts may, in fact, account for their continuing popularity as their strained conclusions are only momentarily satisfying and viewers must return to see another *telenovela* to be 'reconvinced' (1982). Thus, although these new *telenovelas* aim to suture global and national interests, they also register the implausibility of doing so.

THE YOUNG AND THE RESTLESS: THE FUTURE OF THE *TELENOVELA*

In sum, the *telenovela* is a remarkably resilient genre whose continuing popularity can be attributed to the ways in which it mediates – assuaging and yet never resolving – contemporaneous social tensions. As such, it must constantly address emerging social issues of interest to diverse audiences and, at the same time, respond to new business imperatives of media conglomerates looking to expand their markets. In the coming years, the fate of *novelas* shown on Spanish-language television in the US will depend on their ability to engage younger viewers – specifically, the 18–34-year-old demographic sector most sought after by advertisers. This will not be easy as it has been members of that very group who have been most vocal in their criticisms of the genre (Dávila, 2002, pp. 25, 33–5). Yet, the effort is already underway. While Televisa has long produced *novelas* revolving around young adults, recently the company has begun to include substantive stories about young adults in other *novelas* and to produce *novelas* that address 'grittier' social problems like alcoholism, drug abuse and HIV/AIDS, often through the trials and tribulations of characters who are in their teens and twenties. If these changes respond in part to the success of TVAzteca's *novelas* about political corruption and drug-trafficking (Hernández and McAnany, 2001, pp. 401–3; Quiñones, 1997), they also are clearly directed at younger viewers in the US. During episodes of *Amigas y rivales* in which one of the main characters has HIV, Univisión featured public service ads in which several young adults spoke about the importance of safe sex practices. The attempt to appear 'up-to-date' in ways that might appeal to younger viewers on both sides of the border was also evident in the references to the 11 September 2001 attack on the World Trade Center towers in *Amigas y rivales* as Abelardo had to contend with the xenophobic attitude of the Anglo owner of the ranch where he was working. Yet the inclusion of realist touches is not the only tactic being employed to capture younger viewers. There has also been a contrary shift toward parody in other *telenovelas* like *Betty la Fea*, the Colombian serial that was a huge success when its debuted on Telemundo in 2000. Encouraging audiences to laugh at the genre's excesses (and to identify with the trials of their heroines), such self-parodies may appeal to younger, more educated viewers who glory in the pleasures of ironic spectatorship. Both Telemundo and Univisión are betting on that possibility. After the success of *Betty la Fea*, Univisión quickly 'snatched both sequel and syndication rights' to the serial as part of a new five-year programming alliance with RCN, *Betty*'s Colombian producer. Their sequel, *Eco Moda*, premiered on Univisión in the fall of 2001 (Chang, 2001b). Telemundo fought back with other serials that mixed humor with melodrama like the Colombian serial *Pedro el escamoso* and Brazil's *Uga Uga* (Chunovie, 2001). To find out what happens, tune into the next episode of …

ACKNOWLEGEMENTS

I want to thank Mark Hernández, Lisa Opper and Tamara Falicov, for their generous help in obtaining copies of recent *telenovelas*.

NOTES

1   *Telenovelas* are serial melodramas often compared to US soap operas with several important distinctions. *Novelas* run for months, rather than years; they have definitive endings; and they are shown during prime-time hours. Unlike soap

operas, *novelas* form the base of local television industries in Latin America pushing out imported programming (López, 1991b, p. 600).

2   *Novelas* include 'typical' Mexican locations like the *rancho*, the cabaret, and the *vecindad* (neighborhood) familiar from films like *Distinto amanecer* and *Nosotros los pobres*. Their polarization of female characters into good, sexually pure women and bad, promiscuous women can be seen, respectively, as embodiments of the Virgin of Guadalupe and La Malinche, two local archetypes considered fundamental to the construction of Mexican national identity (Estill, 2001, p. 185). This polarization was also characteristic of earlier filmic melodramas (López, 2000, p. 508).

3   For a provocative discussion of how *telenovelas* offer a 'repository of models of modernity' for audiences in rural Yucatán, see Greene (2001).

4   As *telenovelas* are an unwieldy topic (produced in several Latin American countries with daily, hour-long episodes lasting for months), it would be impossible to provide a comprehensive overview of the contemporary workings of the genre in the context of globalization. See Daniel Mato (1999, pp. 246–50, 406–7) for a discussion of the methodological difficulties of studying the *telenovela*.

5   NAFTA is the acronym for the North American Free Trade Agreement, initiated in 1994 to promote increased trade between Mexico, the US, and Canada. For a wider perspective on how NAFTA has affected the cultural industries, see McAnany and Wilkinson (1996).

6   For a discussion of the intricacies of the recent challenges facing Televisa and its new business strategies, see Hernández and McAnany (2001, pp. 392–6) and Sutter (2002, pp. A11–12, 20).

7   Televisa began to export its *novelas* starting in the 1970s (López, 1995, p. 260). In 1997, Televisa's *telenovelas* exports brought in $100 million dollars (Mato, 1999, p. 257).

8   According to the 2000 census, there are approximately 35.5 million Latino/as in the US (vs. 30 million African-Americans). The Latino/a population is expected to grow by more than 2 per cent annually for the next 10 years (Chang, 2001a, 2001b). Advertising expenditures aimed at the Hispanic market reached $1.9 billion in 1999 (Terry-Azios, 2002).

9   Indeed, Televisa was one of the founders of Univisión (originally known as SIN) in 1961. Today Univisión is owned in conjunction by several conglomerates including Mexico's Televisa and Grupo Cisneros' Venevisión. Univisión is the fifth ranked network in the US behind ABC, CBS, NBC, and Fox (Terry Azios, 2002) and, although it lost some of its market share to its main rival Telemundo in the late 1990s, it remains the dominant player in Spanish-language television in the US (Chang, 2001b).

10 López was one of the first scholars to discuss in a substantive way the appearance of 'telenovela stories set in multinational contexts and featuring, most often Miami resort sites, and the experiences of world-travelers whose home is always the national capital' (1995, pp. 265–70).

11 *Alguna vez tendremos alas* featured a montage sequence of its protagonists (Ana and Guillermo) enjoying a romantic interlude in Zacatecas where they meandered through stores selling 'typical' Zacatecan crafts. In an episode of *Esmeralda*, two of its secondary characters traveled to Oaxaca; after they discussed the beauty of

Mexican telenovelas 165

12 Few *novelas* include on-location scenes shot outside Mexico. When they do, as in *Mi destino eres tú*, such sequences are given special prominence and offer viewers a travelogue account of the city as the protagonists visit important tourist sites.

13 Manterola went on to star in Telemundo's series *Angeles* and has released several CDs with Universal Latino and RCA.

14 *Novelas* also have included singing stars like Celia Cruz in secondary roles and featured the music of groups like Los Broncos on their soundtrack (López, 1995, pp. 268–9).

15 Both Yuri and Chayanne appeared on Univisión's music programs, although neither had a record deal with Televisa.

16 For example, although Thalía left Fonovisa for EMI in the mid-1990s, she later starred in Televisa's *Rosalinda* (1999).

17 In mid-2002, Univisión bought the Hispanic Broadcasting Corporation, the 'largest holder of Spanish-language radio stations' in the US (the purchase was pending FCC approval as this chapter went to press). The purchase of Televisa's Fonovisa label tightened the relationship between the two companies. Televisa's stake in Univisión has increased from 5.8 per cent to 15 per cent. Univisión also acquired a stake in Disa Records of Mexico (Rutenberg, 2002; Sutter, 2002, p. A12).

18 For more on the integration of the US and Latin American music industry, see Yúdice (1999).

19 The Latino/a population includes people of European, Native American, African and Asian heritage as well as people of ethnically-mixed heritage. While some Latino/as are English-dominant, approximately 68 per cent speak some Spanish at home (Terry-Azios, 2002). While some of that group are monolingual, others code-switch between English and Spanish. The linguistic practices of Spanish-speaking Latino/as also can be differentiated in terms of lexicon and accent – differences often attributable to national origin – and allow one to distinguish, for example, between 'Cuban Spanish' and 'Dominican Spanish'.

20 As soaps have lost viewers, they have begun to mine *telenovelas*' narrative strategies. ABC's *Port Charles* recently began to incorporate '*telenovelar*-like story arcs' to draw younger viewers (Freeman 2002). Meanwhile, NBC added 'closed-caption, Spanish-language translations to broadcasts of *Days of Our Lives* and *Passions* in July 2001, several months before the network purchased Telemundo (Chang, 2001b).

21 In fact, the only successful Latino/a-centered or Latino/a-engaged programs shown on US Spanish-language stations have been *telenovelas* like Telemundo's *MaríElena* (that also became a smash hit in Mexico where it was shown on Televisa's competitor, TVAzteca) and Televisa's *Dos mujeres, un camino* starring Erik Estrada as 'an LA-based truck driver on a route that takes him regularly across the border' (López, 1995, p. 268).

22 Dávila argues that the media products shown on Univisión as well as those produced by US-based companies favoring the English language ultimately are defined by the 'dominant notions of US citizenship' (2001, pp. 157–8, 166–7, 178).

23 There have been a number of fine studies of how US-based media targeting

Latino/a consumers construct 'Latinidad' or Latino/a identity. In addition to Dávila (2001) and Levine (2001), see Harmony Wu's analysis, 'Negotiating Place on Latin TV Programming in the US: Performing and Pathologizing Culture on the *Cristina* Talk Show', unpublished paper, Console-ing Passions Conference, Madison, Wisconsin, April 1996.

24 For a discussion of how this 'closed community' functions in *novelas* set entirely within Mexico, see Adriana Estill's analysis of *Vivo por Elena* (2001, pp. 177–81).

25 Feminist scholars like Tania Modelski have argued that soap operas' repetitive dialogues offer their traditionally female viewers the ability to build communities as they discuss and debate the plots among themselves.

26 There are plenty of examples of other 'transnational' *telenovelas* whose ideological tensions strain the seams of their narrative in even more extreme ways and exceed all attempts to resolve them. The transnational romance in *Valentina* functioned so poorly that its producers killed off the protagonists and completely rewrote the plot after relocating the narrative within more traditional geographic markers (López, 1995, pp. 268–9). The serial *Volver a empezar* also had to be reworked. While featuring an intertwined Yuri and Chayanne in its commercial spots throughout its broadcast, the *novela* eventually dropped Chayanne into a secondary role and introduced a new hero: Tony, a Mexican impresario living in New York. The final episodes of this highly convoluted plot featured a Mexico City cabaret where Reni, disguised as the red-haired Cuban singer Chaquira, cha-cha-cha'd the night away.

13

Local(izing) images
Montevideo's televisual praxis
Victoria Ruétalo

Remote controls synchronously attune around the globe to exotic spectacles of unrequited love, melodramatic plots and Latin bombshells. Nonetheless, television production in Latin America has not always been defined by its globally accepted *telenovelas*. The landscape of television, the dominant source of entertainment and information in the region, has changed from its predominantly live and local programming in the 1950s to one cloaked in US exports in the 1960s as it began to rely on video technology. The 1970s brought the development of a few key networks (TV Globo in Brazil, Televisa in Mexico and Venevisión in Venezuela), which would later control not only local but also regional markets. In this period the same *telenovelas*, contests, variety and comedy shows bombarded the airwaves from one end of the continent to the other. Ironically, despite globalization effects, local productions have increased during the 1980s and 1990s in most Latin American countries. This chapter aims to question recent televisual praxis in Uruguay. By historicizing the development of television in Montevideo and acknowledging the efforts by the municipal government to localize images and produce a healthy amount of national programming I will suggest that the agenda behind recent State initiatives collides with those in the private televisual sectors, a group which has historically been protected by the State.

In Uruguay, where the State's presence hovers over all segments of society with its hefty interventionist policies, the mass media in general and television in particular relish in 'absolute freedom'. For some this deregulation of audiovisual markets, accompanied by diminished government participation in the development of the media, raises suspicions, questions intentions and alludes to corruption (Martín Posadas, 1992, p. 34). As one scholar argues: after the recent dictatorships 'privatization, liberalization and deregulation have been the mantra of media policies' in the Southern cone region (Waisbord, 2002b, p. 5). Nonetheless, in the case of Uruguay, retracing television's history in Montevideo and its connection to the audiovisual expansion in the rest of the country contextualizes the complex nexus between public and private sectors.

In Montevideo, three private channels (4, 10, 12) whose motto is to produce little and at low cost, and a fourth, a state-owned channel (5) (SODRE [Servicio Oficial de Difusión, Radiofusión y Espectáculos] based on the BBC model), dominate the airwaves (Rama and Delgado, 1992, p. 50). The private channels in the hands of three family-owned companies enjoy hegemony over the weaker state-run SODRE. Despite the launching of SODRE in 1963 during a period of fervent nationalism at a time when videotape technology flooded the local screens with US imports, the government did not limit the growth of commercial broadcasting, a private sector that arose a few years earlier and would later become powerful enough to block the growth of Channel 5. As early as 1956 the De Feo-Fontaina group (Channel 10) was the first to shift popular variety shows and comedies from radio to the new and modern visual media known as television. In 1961 two other companies, Romay Salvo and Sociedad Televisora Larragaña or group Scheck (with strong links to *El País*, the most widely read newspaper in the nation), appeared on the local small-screen scene to provide a broader choice for the urban consumer: thus were born Channels 4 and 12 respectively. From that moment, the three companies controlled the panorama of national television in the southern zone of the country, where half of the population resides (García Rubio, 1994, p. 81), leaving the inadequately funded SODRE behind in both quality of production and ratings.

In retrospect, communication policies during the implementation of new pay TV channels in Montevideo disconcertingly exposed the State's agenda and *laissez-faire* politics regarding the future of media development in the country. The process towards monopolization by the three open channels based in the capital city began previously, in 1990, during negotiations for a new pay TV service in the interior, where the option for diverse programming was already limited. That same year, all three channels formed a united front under Equital SA, a separate corporation which designated itself the delegate body that provided counseling on technical, judicial and financial issues for all those interested in delivering the paid service to regions outside the capital (García Rubio, 1994, p. 143). The president, vice-president and secretary, positions solely occupied by representatives from the three channels, who periodically rotated roles among one other, operated Equital SA with no objections from government or other private providers. A few years later, the same corporation was to partake in a similar bid in Montevideo. On July 6, 1993, the government issued a public call for the operation of pay TV services for the capital region. Of the 11 companies that submitted a proposal for participation, five belonged to Equital SA and the other six were independents. Despite the fact that all 11 met the requirements stipulated by the State, the Executive Power, through resolution 117/994, sanctioned only five of the 11 companies to deliver the service with the justification that the state must 'defend the economic reasonableness of the authorized companies and "allow healthy competition"' (García Rubio, 1984, pp. 156–7). Four of the five chosen belonged to Equital SA. In other words, the three open channels based in the urban metropolis were going to dominate yet again all levels of television for most of the nation.

Critics denounced the bidding for signals in Montevideo on the grounds that a 'cartel-like' system dominated the industry, shattering competition while limiting the terrain to already local participants (Waisbord, 2002a, p. 14). One of the bidders, a company affiliated with the newspaper *La República*, accused the three channels of 'paying lip-service to nationalism' as a justification against foreign intruders into the market (Waisbord, 2002a, p. 14). Ironically, the only channel that does provide more locally produced programming is the public SODRE. Statistics from 1989 reveal that 60 per cent of its programming is based on national and independent productions; meanwhile the private channels offer a trivial 28 per cent of such local programming (Rama and Delgado, 1992, p. 52). Considered by UNESCO to be one of the countries with the poorest percentage of national programming (Alvárez, 1992, p. 46), Uruguay's low numbers in national production include news, journalistic, children's and entertainment shows, and undermine any and all claims made by the big three privately owned channels.

Historically, public policies and practices have favored the evolution of private providers rather than public producers. Even though the State has not directly supported the expansion of the private sector, the three most influential broadcasters have always benefited from privileges such as tax breaks for equipment. Yet another concrete example of partiality towards a monopolization of the media occurs during regular election campaigns. The electoral court compensates the channels with a sum of $3.50 per vote, taken from tax pesos, in exchange for running election propaganda (García Rubio, 1994, p. 84). Conscious of the role of the media, politicians are clearly apprehensive about reforming policy that would democratize television, and would rather preserve close and amicable ties with the most powerful private broadcasters. This questionable tactic on the part of the politicians is certainly politically motivated since the same media will be directly responsible for constructing or destroying the bureaucrats' image on small screens across the nation.

Simultaneously, the outright political neglect of the situation by the State and the continued pressure from the private sector have certainly had an impact in the dwindling of Channel 5. At odds, the public and private divides climaxed during two key incidents when Carlos Maggi and Juan Martín Posadas, both station managers for SODRE resigned in 1985 and 1991, respectively, because of pressures from private broadcasters (Waisbord, 2002a, pp. 11–12). Despite SODRE's constant struggle to sustain itself, the eventual end to this public space would also bring a halt to most of the local production. Walter 'Cacho' Bagnasco, a more recent director of the local Montevidean public channel, sees a clear danger in the current programming trend of the country: 'If we were to see someone dressed in *faja* and *bombacha* we would advise him or her to look for a new drug dealer, but we don't find it strange if television were to imagine our ancestors as cowboys' (Israel, 1997, p. 4). In this statement Bagnasco laments how foreign images infiltrate the Uruguayan shared unconscious by replacing local histories with a standard global History. The challenge of the world imaginary is particularly acute for small countries like Uruguay, which have never sustained an audiovisual industry.

Given the current globalization crisis clearly expressed by Bagnasco, and to respond both to local criticism and the renewed fervor of recent years in the film industry, where such productions as *La historia casi verdadera de Pepita la pistolera* (directed by Beatriz Flores Silva) and *El dirigible* (directed by Pablo Dotta) attained national popularity, the municipal government in Montevideo was going to be the first to provide an obstacle to the private sector's continued manipulation of the State. This audacious government deemed it necessary to actively encourage domestic audiovisual production and would shift politics nationwide. The thought of laying the foundation of an industry seemed too overwhelming and redundant given that this framework was already in place. What better vehicle for funding and promoting national production than the teams of private television channels already in play who had modern facilities, better qualified technicians, and more available funds than the neglected public channel? The negotiations between the providers of the pay TV service in Montevideo and the various layers of government were not going to be as flawless as expected. The original decree that granted the private providers the legal right to offer the new service was accompanied by a high tax, which was meant to supply between $2–3 million in revenue for the purpose of advancing national audiovisual production (Israel, 1997, p. 2). The three channels frowned upon the decrease in profits that this decree would signify, and thus decided to begin an anti-government campaign by accusing bureaucrats of denying the television population the option of subscribing to a new service.

Finally, in June of 1995, after a long, hard-fought battle of negotiations, an agreement was reached between IMM (Intendencia Municipal de Montevideo), the Ministry of Education and Culture, and the private channels. In exchange for the waiver of the high tax, the private channels donated some of the profits produced by this new venture directly to FONA (Fondo para el Fomento y Desarrollo de la Producción Audiovisual Nacional), a municipal body, founded primarily to foster the creation of local images. The final contract allowed the channels to market and institute the new pay TV service without having to pay the high tax. In return, they donated $70,000 per year (28 minutes of air-time publicity) per channel, in order to finance and secure the continuity and production of nationally based images (Israel, 1997, p. 2). The following year FONA awarded its first prize. In theory, this was a victory for those struggling to produce fictional films/television series in a country better known for its documentary, newscasts and animation productions.

Subterráneos (Underground) was one of the FONA's first recipients, whose winning script was rewarded with the sum of $50,000 to commence production. Considering the high cost of production in Uruguay, $50,000 was not a large sum of money. The average commercial cost $25,000, and each year there were close to a dozen that exceeded the $60,000 mark. One example of such lavish spending on publicity is a Peugeot ad (made by the agency Viceversa and produced by Metrópolis) that was just over one minute in length and cost $500,000 (Israel, 1997, p. 3). Despite the small amount of financial support, the FONA prize brought with it other fringe benefits, such as use of equipment and technological assistance from the sponsoring entity.

Before the trend towards privatization of film industries sweeping Latin America, as in the case of Embrafilme in Brazil, this sudden concern on the part of the government to protect and promote local efforts was a positive move for a small nation like Uruguay, which in the past had been unsuccessful in sustaining a constant production of local images, let alone an industry. This government initiative gave birth to a project like *Subterráneos*, and has sparked other ongoing struggles to keep the images alive. As a result of this renewed zeal for local audiovisual production, the Asociación de Directores Uruguayos de Cine (ADUC, a support organization for directors) was created in 1996, and has thus worked towards protecting and encouraging local audiovisual projects. What became of those projects that won the highly coveted monetary and technical prize first awarded in 1996? The rest of this chapter will trace the trajectory of one of the early winners (*Subterráneos*) to show that despite governmental and private support, these projects were hindered by long established political-economic barriers linked directly to the development of television in the capital city. Unable to shed the lurking history and power dynamics of television, *Subterráneos* remained a one-episode pilot, putting on hold the long awaited dream of locally produced fictional shows bombarding the Uruguayan small screen.

TO BOLDLY GO WHERE NO TELEVISION SHOW HAS GONE: THE CASE OF *SUBTERRÁNEOS*

Set in a non-specified future, the 1996 TV show entitled *Subterráneos* and subtitled *La imagen* ('The Image'), in neo-*noir* fashion, tells the story of a private eye, Gutiérrez (Osvaldo Laport), who is hired to unravel a web of economic power, beauty, and political corruption within the higher echelons of Uruguayan society. Gutiérrez's search for a missing model, Andrea Zunino (Natalia Méndez), the third victim of a supposed cult conspiracy, leads him to the underground where he uncovers a resistance group refusing to partake in the above ground superficial culture of the image. However, the subterranean dwellers are not the ones responsible for the disappearances. Instead, a crooked Minister and his political team are behind the two deaths that caused Andrea Zunino to flee to the underground where Gutiérrez finally finds her.

Unfortunately, despite its intriguing plot, a deadly combination of politics and image production, this promising story line was not developed beyond the first episode. Perhaps its content may have been one of the determining factors in the eventual death of *Subterráneos* itself. The lack of funding within Uruguay combined with its inability to sell in the Mercosur market destined the show to gather dust on the shelves of the Instituto Nacional del Audiovisual, where I was lucky to come across a copy on videotape. Its $67,000 budget could have been too excessive for the potential Montevidean television audience of 1.5 million. Ironically, the show found itself entangled in the historical intricacies of political and economic obstacles, becoming as a consequence a victim of its own criticism, and has remained a one-episode pilot. Insufficient funds impeded the director, Alejandro Bazzano, from filming the projected 13 episodes that were to follow (Langleib, 1997, p. 21). In part, the problem lay in the inimical relationship between Bazzano and the Uruguayan Channel 4, the sponsoring entity for the venture. The director of the show, Bazzano himself, claims that from the beginning Channel 4 showed little interest in the project. On the other hand, the program director for the channel justifies the position of the channel because of the show's lack of profitability: it was too costly for a weekly run. Despite the positive response and relatively high rating of 15.6 points that the show received (Langleib, 1997, p. 21), excellent for local programming standards, Channel 4 refused to participate in the remaining episodes. The star cast and their professional level of acting – rare in Uruguayan television where actors are bound by theatrical norms – along with the high production values that the show achieved, were not enough to ensure its run. Why then was *Subterráneos* unable to sustain itself locally? In spite of recent institutionalized efforts to advance local media production and facilitate distribution, the case of *Subterráneos* exposes the still existing hurdles created by the profit-based private channels that make it difficult for an innovative national product to succeed. *Subterráneos* in content and as product becomes a lesson in the dangers and risks involved in image production.

According to the director, the contract signed between the FONA and the sponsoring channel did not stipulate that the latter was obliged to air the show 'but they [Channel 4] never showed too much interest in continuing the program or in participating in its production' (Langleib, 1997, p. 21). Channel 4 provided Bazzano with access to the editing studio from 11:00 p.m. to 6:00 a.m. When Bazzano requested help with transportation and a few minutes worth of advertising on the show to offset some of his own costs, the channel denied these. Despite the admission by Carlos Navarro, program director of Channel 4, that he had never seen such a product like it for TV, the risk seemed too high. Yet, unlike other local shows *Subterráneos* was not a cult film or even experimental, it had a commercial appeal. Its use of important actors such as Osvaldo Laport (a local celebrity in *telenovelas* who became a star in the region and abroad) and its dramatic tension made it quite unlike the more artistic or *auteur* cinema common in Uruguay. Therefore, the risk, mentioned above, refers solely to money. As the words of Carlos Navarro attest: 'In prime time the maximum advertising that an hour show sells is 15 minutes, which translates into $22,500. It is easy to argue that if the channel invests, he [Bazzano] could do a series: if the channel makes the funds available, anybody could' (Langleib, 1997, p. 21). Unveiling yet a greater problem, Navarro's words confirm that it all boils down to funding. There is very little interest in local productions if these do not bring in the hard money.

In this chapter I will continue to argue that State initiatives do not necessarily coincide with the objectives of the corporate television sector in Montevideo. The case in point is the experience and outcome of the show *Subterráneos*. The lack of support on many fronts and the low priority that it received in the studios of Channel 4 expose the private channel's unwillingness to produce local shows despite what governmental rhetoric deems a priority for sustaining a national identity in the face of globalization. By returning to a Hollywood genre of the 1940s and 1950s *Subterráneos*, as a product of global influences, paradoxically overcomes the simplistic dichotomy between local and global as it bears in mind the local within the constraints of a foreign form such as *film noir*. As I will demonstrate, the show's adaptation of this *film noir* form and aesthetic goes well beyond the questioning of nation and its place in the global village. Like the original, it comments on the relationship between the surface and what lies beneath, thereby leaving an air of suspicion about institutions in the nation-state. Television, particularly Channel 4, the State and the corrupt parasitic relationship between the two become suspect and highly criticized throughout the show. In other words, the concrete political and economic connection between the media and the Uruguayan State, as explored in the first half of this article, is the subject of criticism in *Subterráneos*, as it unveils another reality, contradictory to the rhetoric of both government and private media. Consequently, in content and aesthetic, *Subterráneos* challenges the mediocrity of television in Montevideo. It achieves too high a standard for television and leaves its viewer expecting more: what the private channels are not ready to provide for their customers. A closer look at the content of the show and an in-depth analysis of particular scenes further reveal these problematic dynamics between State and television in Montevideo, and is perhaps yet another reason to cut funding of the series.

Noir expression was a means towards hidden or subtle significance at a time when to express certain views was impossible. Because of censorship bodies, control of the image portrayed in 1940s' Hollywood was obtained only through *film noir*'s staging of innuendo and subtleties (Naremore, 1998, p. 104). In post-dictatorship Uruguay, where no such barriers supposedly exist, those implied insinuations appear to be rather excessive. *Subterráneos*, however, is an example of how the excess continues to point to the very space that is being protected, that which remains on the surface: the image. Everyone, including the protagonist Gutiérrez, is thereby included in the scheme not only to safeguard the image, but become a mere spectacle within its layers. And yet, despite the seeming transparency of the surface, *Subterráneos* employs *film noir* aesthetics to expose other issues relevant to the overall construction of image creation in Montevideo, nuances that are not necessarily hidden too deeply beneath, and relate directly to the implication of the media in political corruption.

Like *film noir*, the narrative of the TV show pairs superficial confusion with outright answers right from its opening scene. In the first shot of Gutiérrez's apartment the overexposed lighting, an aesthetic reminiscent of German expressionistic films akin to *The Cabinet of Dr. Caligari*, later appropriated by *film noir* style, produces a hazy, unclear picture of the room. As the camera zooms to the door, the unevenly leveled frame exposes the conscious manipulation of the shot through its canted angle. Behind the door, Gutiérrez's landlord knocks with the electric bill, 'el recibo de la luz', in hand. Suddenly there is a cut and the camera is on the other side of the door as the audience puts a face to the voice demanding Gutiérrez's presence. Although the scene begins in Gutiérrez's empty private room, the camera travels to the door and immediately and anti-climatically unveils what lies behind it. Indicative of the aesthetic that the whole program adopts, this scene emphasizes the surface. The camera and the dialogue no longer taunt the spectator with its subtlety. Desire, thus, is not fostered through what is missing but instead through its excess, through its exposure. Technical maneuvers such as the haziness and the canted angle artificially replicate a sense of illusive depth and allude to the (in)effectual system of communication in place. By clearly obstructing or deceiving vision to show what lies beneath, *Subterráneos*, right from its opening scene, sets itself apart from other TV shows, ones that claim to provide a *clear* picture of the world, and will explicitly become the focus of a severe critique in Bazzano's version of *film noir*.

The parodying of television is more explicit during the second sequence of the show. Once *Subterráneos* returns from its first commercial break, the first shot, a male facing the camera addressing the spectator about the desperate situation of today's youth, is framed by a television-like iris (square with rounded corners), an unmistakable reference to the fact that the male in the picture is behind yet another camera. This self-referential framed shot, of a much lesser quality than the one the spectator has thus watched, alludes to the poor quality image of antique televisions due to the faded colors and blue tinge. But it may also be referring to the literally poor quality of talk shows that reach Uruguayan audiences from abroad. This particular talk show resembles *Hola Susana*, starring Susana Giménez, one of the most popular contest shows on television when *Subterráneos* first aired. As the camera reverses in this scene, it cuts to a shot of a seductive, alluring woman, the talk show host, Viviana, listening attentively until her guest's speech acquires a political twist. This sudden shift annoys Viviana, who abruptly cuts to a commercial break. Now 'behind' the camera, surrounded by equipment, lights, and staging, the spectator witnesses the machinery in support of the construction of the image. In this shot, the color returns and the image is fuller, vivid and life-like in nature. The back stage divulges Viviana's discontent with her guest for tainting the show with dystopic, fatalistic, and political views, what can no longer be tolerated as a part of the disseminated image. The dialogue develops in the following way:

> Viviana: The program has an image. I have an image.
> Her guest: We all have an image.
> Viviana: Yes, but you've smeared it!

By providing an inside look into the production of images, this scene displays the inevitable clash between the machinery's insistence to sustain the façade of objectivity and a personal effort to tarnish such picture perfect ideals. All in all, this scene helps to question the *clarity* of vision that television constructs. In particular, Bazzano and his show are critiquing imported talk shows like *Hola Susana,* but more importantly, this scene makes evident the many hidden agendas that lurk behind the seemingly simple construction of certain images. There is no consolation in the guest's violation of the show's image. His discourse too hides behind the image that he so consciously wishes to construct.

In the final scene, Gutiérrez meets the Minister for a pay-off in exchange for his silence, a trap set up specifically for the Minister to confess his crimes. An abandoned warehouse serves as a background for the meeting between the two characters, where the spectacle will play out its own conclusion. Gutiérrez is backed by the protection of the police chief and the Minister has his assistant awaiting in the corner. However, the spectator quickly discovers that the police chief and the Minister's assistant are both implicated in the intrigue. They were aware of the Minister's involvement in the disappearances of the models. As 'custodians of the image' they were responsible for protecting the Minister. Once the image escaped their grasp, once it was uncontrollable, they had to take matters into their own hands, finally assassinating the politician. Unfortunately, Gutiérrez is unable to resolve the crime fully, for although the Minister was punished by death, the others implicated in the conspiracy will continue to guard the image, regardless of the crimes they may commit on behalf of this or other politicians. Unveiling the truth is no longer the end goal. As Gutiérrez quickly discovers, on the one hand, he won the personal battle against the Minister, but the war was a useless one. Society has moved on and now erases its history by hiding behind its surface. Institutional corruption is everywhere, disguised behind different masks, and Gutiérrez is but a mere player who will be forced to continue the useless battle of unveiling the different images.

Like Gutiérrez, *Subterráneos* ends in the same predicament. As a project in local image production, Bazzano successfully completed the first episode that aired on the private channel 4 in 1996. *Subterráneos* won the battle, but the war was far from over. In the end the monopoly and control of the media would keep innovative local projects from access to funding, as the series would experience first hand. The unwillingness of the private channels to contribute to the production of fictional TV shows continues to block national attempts to change the fate of how the Uruguay shared unconscious imagines itself.

The parallel between Gutiérrez's frustration and the show's eventual fate continues in the final shots as Gutiérrez confronts his own image in a narcissistic moment. The image of himself that he perceives in the water is not the image constructed in the quest for perfection and beauty, that same image which led to the death of the two models, but the image of a rebellious, disheveled and neglected man. Overcome by frustration Gutiérrez throws into the pond the useless document that implicates Ministro Sarto in the crime, causing ripples in the water, and thereby undoing his image. Unlike Narcissus who falls in love with himself and in so doing falls into the water, Gutiérrez needs to turn away, as he is disgusted with his image, or the image *per se*. The final panoramic shot of the abandoned factory and of Gutiérrez from behind prevents the spectator from seeing him again. The background suddenly blurs, and Gutiérrez appears once more in a final black and white caricatured version of himself, yet again on the surface. The private eye learns the hard way that his resistance is futile. Perhaps this very same point marks the hubris of *Subterráneos* itself. For a television show it was too critical, too well done, and had too many obstacles to surpass. By suspecting the images it sees, *Subterráneos* implicitly questions all those behind its own creation, including its sponsoring products and particularly the television channel that sponsored it. The show most certainly leaves its spectator with many unanswered questions, not about whodunit, but about why its funding was really discontinued.

14

The young and the damned
Street visions in Latin American cinema

Geoffrey Kantaris

> 'Space' is created out of the vast intricacies, the incredible complexities, of the interlocking and the non-interlocking, and the networks of relations at every scale from local to global. ... Space is by its very nature full of power and symbolism, a complex web of relations of domination and subordination, of solidarity and co-operation. (Doreen Massey, 1994, p. 265)

INTRODUCTION

In the last of his three-volume state-of-the-world report entitled *The Information Age*, the Catalan urban theorist Manuel Castells examines the rise of what he calls the 'Fourth World' within the new world order of information-based global capitalism:

> The Fourth World comprises large areas of the globe .... But it is also present in literally every country and every city, in this new geography of social exclusion. ... And it is populated by millions of homeless, incarcerated, prostituted, criminalized, brutalized, stigmatized, sick, and illiterate persons. ... Everywhere, they are growing in number ... as the selective triage of informational capitalism, and the political breakdown of the welfare state, intensify social exclusion. In the current historical context, the rise of the Fourth World is inseparable from the rise of informational, global capitalism. (1998, pp. 164–5)

I shall examine here some examples of recent Latin American cinema which are responding, in different ways, to the violence inherent within, indeed generated by the structural transformations of global capitalism. I shall be comparing these recent examples to the historical tradition of films dealing with social exclusion in Latin America, with a focus (although not exclusively) on the particular phenomena of street children and urban youth culture. The social exclusion of juveniles poses a particular nexus of representational problems within cinema, mostly deriving from the fact that in many Latin American societies street children occupy an unacknowledged or disavowed representational space within the social imaginary itself. Film makers have been drawn, historically, to this disavowed social representation because it seems to offer the chance for cinema to intervene in an issue that transgresses the historically constructed boundary between the imaginary and the social. The film maker can use the representational power of cinema to 'make visible' the invisible lives of the socially excluded, although always at the risk of implicating the medium itself with the very structures of power (and representational systems) that produce social exclusion in the first place.

I shall examine two 'classic' films within this tradition, Luis Buñuel's Mexican film *Los olvidados* of 1950, and the Brazilian film of 1981, *Pixote*, by Héctor Babenco. These will be compared with three contemporary films from Argentina, Colombia, and Mexico: *Pizza, birra, faso* (Caetano and Stagnaro, 1997); *La vendedora de rosas* (Gaviria, 1998a); and *Amores perros* (González Iñárritu, 2000). In broad terms, all these films can be said to belong to the tradition of social realism in cinema, ultimately stemming from Italian neo-realism, although each also problematizes clear-cut categorization. The differences between them will, however, provide us with a conduit between the polarized analytical horizons of the national and the global, for these films, while responding to specific national-historical frameworks, progressively and increasingly suggest the ways in which local crises lie at the intersection points of wider, *systemic* crises.

VIOLENCE AND VISION

It is unsurprising that all of these films should be caught up with representations of violence, since social exclusion is produced – and its spatial grid is policed – through extraordinary levels of discipline and control, latent forms of systemic violence. One of the films, *Pizza, birra, faso*, makes this abundantly clear not only through the shots of night-time police activity in its opening sequences, but through the overlaying on the audio track at several key moments of the sound of police radio transmissions, infiltrating and infusing their way invisibly throughout the entire spatial grid of Buenos Aires. However, the violence represented in these films is abruptly discontinuous with the violence registered in mainstream (US) popular culture of the type beamed to television screens virtually the world over. In mass-cultural globally marketed forms, the violence of social exclusion is almost always rendered monstrous or else eroticized/fetishized. Even in, say, the more subtle classic noir genre, the gritty criminal underworld is subsumed into the libidinal disorder provoked by the *femme fatale*, and the possible resolution of this disorder is linked firmly to the re-establishment of the patriarchal social order. The violence registered in Latin American urban cinema is somehow more symptomatic.

I am working here with the assumption that the symptomatic is the antithesis of the fetishistic, since fetishistic modes of representation depend very precisely on a more or less perfect process of veiling or disavowal of the symptom. A symptomatic reading of violence – and these films *are* a reading in this sense – much like the allegorical, insists on displacement and dislocation, violence not as the screen (of phallic, masculine identity, for example) but as the cut in the screen, the present form of some *other* scene.[1] The films I am looking at here refuse any fetishization of violence, indeed actively work against, or complicate, the well-nigh Pavlovian association between violence and spectacle programmed into US popular culture.

If the films attempt to engage with an *other*, invisible scene, it is logical that they can only do so through a questioning of their own mode of representation (as forms of visual culture) and through their engagement with unconventional forms of filmic expression. On one level, this makes vision itself into a major theme of all of the films in their different ways, from Buñuel's *Los olvidados*, where it is staged through the character of the blind old man, Don Carmelo, and through the insistent thematizing of eyes (one of the characters is nicknamed 'Ojitos' [Li'l Eyes]), through to *Amores perros*, where the television screen and the publicity awning become synecdoches for the function of spectacle-as-fetish within the globalized cityscape. On another level, this engagement is manifest in a conspicuously anti-illusionist visual style to the films, their challenge to the conventions which structure and contain the spectator's gaze within classical cinema.

NEO-REALISM

Any account of the intense turn to urban realism in the cinema of the late 1990s needs to start with the influence of Italian neo-realism in Latin America from the 1950s to the 1970s. The pioneering cinematic work on street children is, after all, Vittorio de Sica's 1946 film *Sciuscià* ('Shoeshine'), and the making of *Los olvidados* ('The Young and the Damned') four years later was clearly influenced by the Italian film, as Buñuel himself wrote in his memoirs: 'I'd loved Vittorio de Sica's *Shoeshine*, and Oscar [Danciger]'s idea for *Los olvidados* seemed very exciting' (1994, p. 199). The precise relationship of *Los olvidados* to neo-realism is in fact rather more complicated, as is suggested by Buñuel's more disparaging comments in a lecture of 1953:

> Neo-realism has given cinematography some elements which enrich its language, but nothing more. Neo-realist reality is incomplete, conventional; above all, it is rational; but the poetry, the mystery, that which completes and expands tangential reality, is completely missing in its productions. (quoted in Evans, 1995, p. 77; author's translation)

These comments go a long way towards explaining the presence of oneiric elements within *Los olvidados* – sequences which are edited 'in the worst tradition of Hollywood Freudian surrealism', as André Bazin put it, but so intense in their imagery that they 'leav[e] us palpitating with horror and pity' (1951, p. 211). The slow-motion nightmare of neglected rape-child Pedro, a textbook Freudian condensation of imagery of food (raw meat) and sexual desire/revulsion on the part of his mother, together with the use of Eisensteinian montage to intimate the subjective death-delirium of the anti-hero Jaibo, are the two most obvious examples of a network of surreal images and symbols which pull against the straight characterization of this film as neorealist. The oneiric elements will have strong repercussions in two of the later films examined here, but it would be wrong to deny the influence in *Los olvidados* of those aspects of neo-realist film-making which were to galvanize independent film production in Latin America over the next few years and which would lay the foundations of the New Latin American Cinema. These aspects are: the use of (some) non-professional or 'real-life' actors, the preference for location shooting, long takes with constant foreground, background, and out-of-field activity (giving a sense of a filmic reality which exceeds the immediately visible), the use of direct sound without balancing, the 'documentary' focus on the experiences, actions, and language of the powerless and the underprivileged, and, not least, the possibility of making feature-length films on shoestring budgets.

Neo-realism found fertile ground, through the 1960s and early 1970s, in the work of Latin American filmmakers who, imbued with revolutionary or strongly ethical sensibilities at times of crisis or profound social change throughout the region, found in this style of filmmaking the possibility of a national-revolutionary cinema 'of the humble and the offended' (Birri, quoted in Hess, 1993, p. 110). John Hess argues convincingly that the key difference between Italian neo-realism and the New Latin American Cinema lies in the latter's emphasis on history and memory (the urgent need to recover these), while the former is marked by a kind of wilful historical *amnesia* (towards the question of popular complicity with fascism). These urban films, however, are driven by a fundamentally different episteme to that of the nationalist revolutionary moment, responding as they do to unprecedented restructurings of space and time, and to their material effects on the minds and bodies of a forgotten generation of young men and women.

DEFETISHIZING THE SPECTACLE

Los olvidados and *Pixote* retain much of their emblematic power through their radical insistence on defetishizing their representations of poverty and social violence. Their focus on orphans and street children carries with it the danger of reducing complex social problems by simplifying the spectator's response to one of attachment to and pity for one or other adorable/adoptable orphan. Yet both avoid any such reduction by complicating our moral responses, by questioning the (voyeuristic) status of our own gaze, and by deploying shock images designed to desublimate our potential attachment to particular icons. The slab of quivering meat offered by Pedro's mother during his nightmare in *Los olvidados* has, in *Pixote*, its direct counterpart in the aborted foetus of the prostitute Sueli lying in a rubbish bin next to her toilet in her filthy bathroom, with the knitting needle she used to extract it still stuck into its bloodied mass.

We are first introduced to Sueli in the glittering surroundings of a nightclub, dressed up as a sexual spectacle for consumption, the camera voyeuristically lingering over her body, as her former pimp comments in voiceover on her sexual prowess and negotiates her sale to the runaway boys with the proceeds from their drug deals and street robberies. Next morning, a haggard Sueli stumbles into her bathroom to find the ten-year-old orphan Pixote (one of the runaway group) looking intently at the rubbish bin. She sits down to pee while Pixote stands staring at her tired, feverish face. Glaring back at him, she asks:

> Sueli: What are you staring at? ... Should I have kept the baby?
> Pixote: What baby?
> Sueli [*POV shot from Pixote*]:[2] That one there. Or what do you think it is? [*Strangling a sob*] A steak? ... Didn't your mother tell you the facts of life? It even looks like you ... [*Embarrassed pause*] Stop staring at me! [*Sueli picks up needle and points it at Pixote*] Get out or I'll stick you with the same needle!

That Pixote later attempts to turn Sueli into a substitute mother figure (at the end of the film he suckles her breast in a scene that meshes sexuality and maternal desire in a highly confusing and destabilizing way) makes this toilet sequence particularly unsettling as a defetishization of Sueli as pornospectacle. The direct allusion here to *Los olvidados* not only functions through the shared imagery of meat as a matrix of desire, nurture, and death, but also through the film's insistent, lingering focus on Pixote's gaze, often directly framing his wide eyes (like the character Ojitos in the earlier film), and at other times adopting his point of view.

The insistence on vision, eyes, and the gaze in *Pixote* is only matched in intensity by the imagery concerning vision which suffuses the entirety of *Los olvidados*, but with a crucial difference which brings *Pixote* closer to the films of the 1990s: vision in the later film is mediatized, self-consciously played out over the screens of television and cinema. *Los olvidados* assaults the viewer's gaze with as much force as the razor-blade opening of *Un chien andalou*: not only through its themes of vision and blindness, but through its systematic deconstruction and defetishization of the icons of Mexican cinema, from Ojitos' rural sombrero and poncho – out of place on the mean streets of Mexico City – through the icon of the self-sacrificing asexual mother (subverted in Estela Inda's performance of Pedro's mother), to the substitution of Gabriel Figueroa's postcard landscapes for the gritty slums and half-constructed tower blocks of Buñuel's film.[3] *Pixote* does so through its literal and metaphorical framing of the screen, from the opening close-ups of the transfixed eyes of an audience of young boys rounded up in a police detention centre, all staring motionlessly at the violent thriller being screened on an overhead television, through the home-cine projection of a porno film in the house of a drug dealer where the boys end up after running away from the corrupt orphanage, to their first purchase with the proceeds from pimping Sueli: a colour television. Violence, too, can be a claim to visibility: the literal transubstantiation of street crime into a television set becomes, somehow, emblematic of the boys' invisibility, of their desire for the gaze, and of their final, violent, consumption as images on our own virtual screens.

PERIPHERIES OF VIOLENCE

Castells argues strongly that:

> there is a systemic relationship between the structural transformations ... of the network society and the growing dereliction of the ghetto; the constitution of an informational/global economy, under the conditions of capitalist restructuring; the crisis of the nation state ... the demise of the patriarchal family ... the emergence of a global, yet decentralized, criminal economy ... and the process of political alienation, and communal retrenchment, among the ... poor and disfranchised. (1998, p. 138)

The frameworks of *Los olvidados* and *Pixote* are, ultimately, psychoanalytical and national: psychoanalytical because they invoke a Freudian framework of disturbed family structures (substitute paternal and maternal relationships); and national because, although each director virulently questions the dominant discourses and images of the nation (and, at least in the case of Buñuel, decries any kind of nationalism), the critique of dominant national images still posits the nation as its ultimate framework.[4] What differentiates them from the films of the 1990s is that the latter insist on the *systemic* relationships at work in their representation of interstitial violence, the lacerations and gashes in the screen of globalization. They hint at the linkages – but also the particularity of the linkages – between crime-violence-poverty in one place and global flows of wealth in another; they engage in 'a global sense of place' and expose 'the *power geometry* of time-space compression' (Massey, 1994, p. 149).[5]

Pizza, birra, faso ('Pizza, beer, fags') was made in Argentina in 1997 by a couple of young, virtually unknown directors – Bruno Stagnaro and Adrián Caetano – on the shoestring budget (for a feature film) of US $400,000, and has been credited by the influential film review *El amante cine* with having substantially changed the course of recent Argentine cinema (Noriega, 2001). The film's new visual style and challenging themes are evident from the credit sequence: instead of the immobile establishing shots of traditional filmic discourse (such as those in the documentary prologue to *Los olvidados*), we are presented with a frenetically speeding camera, a rush of movement in a fragmented cityscape where the *durée* of place has been replaced by velocity, smeared into a blur along lines of transportation and displacement. The credit sequence sets the scene for the violent mugging of a businessman in a Buenos Aires taxi by two of the youths who are the subject of the film, working in league with a corrupt taxi driver. The camera is hyper-mobile to the point of disorientation, showing frantically edited snippets of city bustle, either filmed from some fast-moving mode of transport or jerkily hand-held, twisting this way and that as if time itself had gone into overdrive, while the audio track is overlain with radio transmissions by the police and radio news reports about city violence, unemployment, and crime. The audio and visual representation of transport and (electronic) communications systems, key components of time-space compression, creates an overwhelming effect: not only is the camera almost always travelling in the opening sequences, but at least five types of rapidly moving transport are signalled: cars, taxis, buses, trains, and the businessman's missed aeroplane (implying global space). That such transport signifies velocity and time-space compression, is obvious, but that velocity and rate substitute for temporal depth in the global megalopolis is carefully signalled by a close-up of the driver's digital taximeter in the roof of his car at the beginning of the taxi-mugging sequence.

TEMPORAL DYSPHASIA

Jameson indeed argues that time can no longer be perceived as a depth formation in what he terms the era of postmodernity. Time is now 'a function of speed, and evidently perceptible only in terms of its rate, or velocity as such: as though the old ... opposition between measurement and life, clock time and lived time, had dropped out' (1994, p. 8). If time has now become velocity, the rate of change of fashion designs on the store front or its web page, or the rate of change of the locales in the shopping-mall, of the built environment itself, time thereby in a sense fizzles out in an instant, since velocity is a measure of a displacement *over* time. Jameson also claims that this new, absolute temporality, 'has everything to do with the urban ..., its postnaturality to technologies of communication as well as of production and ... the decentered, well-nigh global, scale on which what used to be the city is deployed' (ibid., p.11).

Pizza, birra, faso, is a film about the rebellious, youthful, criminal underworld of Buenos Aires; it follows the violent lives of a group of adolescent boys and a pregnant girl, who resort to crime in order to supply their basic necessities, the pizza, beer, and fags of the title. They live the lives of the teenage youths analysed in Mario Margulis' fascinating study of the Buenos Aires nightlife, for whom

> In the refuge offered by the night, the city is resignified and power appears to recede. It is an illusion of independence which encourages a playing with time; uncolonized time in which they are released from control; time not used up in economic production, industry or banking. If all the spaces are colonized, there remains the shelter of time, time as a refuge. (1994, p. 12; author's translation)

Although not the first urban film of the post-dictatorship period in Argentina, and certainly not the first to portray violence, *Pizza, birra, faso* is the first such film to return to the use of largely non-professional actors, to engage uncompromisingly with the idiolect of the street, and the first to avoid any kind of moralizing metacommentary. In this sense, it is not that far removed from *Los olvidados*, to which it pays explicit homage by restaging the infamous attack by the boys on a legless beggar. My main conjecture, however, is that the film links the temporal dysphasia of these adolescents, their sense of no past and no tomorrow, to the culture of violence which pervades their lives, a theme which resounds also in the Colombian film, *La vendedora de rosas*.

Released in 1998, *La vendedora de rosas* ('The Rose Seller') is the second feature-length film directed by the Colombian poet and film-maker, Víctor Gaviria. His earlier film of 1988, *Rodrigo D. No futuro*, whose title is an explicit homage to Vittorio de Sica's neo-realist classic *Umberto D.*, explored the truncated lives of the teenage boys in Medellín's working-class suburbs. Like *Rodrigo D.*, *La vendedora* was made in the only manner conceivable for it to maintain ethical integrity *vis-à-vis* its subjects: in full collaboration with its natural actors, adopting both their vision and their language, in a painstaking two-year period of investigation, 12 months of pre-production work, and a long 16-week shoot. Set mostly over the two nights before Christmas, the story follows the violent lives of a group of girls in their early teens, all separated from their families and making a living for themselves in the rough, selling roses in late-night clubs, sometimes selling themselves, going out with the drug-vending teenage boys, stealing money to buy new clothes, and sniffing glue to fill the desperate emptiness with passing visions of lost family and friends.

The film is largely shot in the twilight of Medellín's night-time streets, lit up here and there with garish Christmas illuminations, the flare of celebratory fireworks, and the lights of passing traffic. Gaviria himself, using a poetic paradox, talks of the displaced light that bathed the production of this film: a nocturnal light that made visible, for a few fleeting weeks, 'los días de la noche' – the night-time days or the day-time nights – of Medellín's street children and homeless youths. During the nocturnal shoots, he writes, with the streets bathed in the unaccustomed clarity of the set lights,

> the street children, I mean the actors and their friends, were thrilled to see their regular street corners lit up with the show lights as if it were the middle of the day, or rather lit with the true light of their night-time days, because people don't realize that these street children live out just a handful of highly compressed days, of singular, eclipsed days, during their long nights on the streets. These are night-time days, whose secret light only they can see. (1998b, p. 40; author's translation)

The attempt to screen the invisible – 'los días de la noche' – is a project common to all of these films in one form or another, and Gaviria makes more-or-less explicit homage to Buñuel's use of dreams and deliria by cinematically reconstructing the children's solvent-induced visions at several points, a technique also deployed in a single sequence from *Pixote*. These sometimes desperate visions add an intense imaginary dimension to the otherwise stark portrayal of poverty and social exclusion, and also provide us with a symbolic matrix (but without the psychoanalytic framework of the earlier films) for interpreting the film's projection of the apparent (postmodern) antinomies of time and space (Jameson, 1994, pp. 1–71).

The first such sequence begins with an extreme close-up of the protagonist Mónica's face as she is breathing in the solvent vapours from her pot of glue (*sacol*). The camera then cuts to a subjective shot of some fireworks over a distant building, then tilts and pans down from the sky-line to reveal the backs of an old woman (her dead grandmother) and young boy and girl walking hand in hand along a semi-flooded street. In frame over the top of a wall to the back of the street, a torch flare is blazing, while the camera slowly tracks their movement through the water to the amplified sound of splashing. At a couple of points the camera cuts back to a close-up of Mónica's face, sniffing the glue, her eyes wide and staring. The whole sequence lasts no more than thirty seconds, but it gives the impression of having been slowed just slightly, at least in comparison to the hustle and bustle of the surrounding sequences.[6] Against the frame of the bursting fireworks and the burning torch (linked throughout the film to the flammable vapours of the *sacol*), the water, like the river to which the film returns again and again, seems to evoke temporal density, the persistence of memory, genealogy, but also another kind of permanence: death. This sequence is particularly significant because it seems to set up a spatial metaphor for temporal consciousness: the imagery of genealogical time (water, the grandmother) is evoked precisely through the frame of temporal burn-out (fire, *sacol*), as movement through an imaginary cityscape. This creates a structural link which is more than simply that of opposition (water–fire/space–time), and acts as a blueprint for all our subsequent readings of temporal and spatial paradoxes in the film.

Crucially, Gaviria, like Jameson, links the flattening of temporal depth to the empty time of the commodity, a trait common to all three of these later films, and foreseen by Buñuel in the dumping of Pedro's body on a rubbish tip at the end of *Los olvidados*. In his article entitled 'Un ojo de nadie' ('The Eye of Nobody'), Gaviria explains:

> Time has been paralysed in a consumable present, in the imminence of consumption. The present in which the product lives sealed in its empty packaging, which at any moment will be eaten, consumed, and then will become a piece of junk in the rubbish tip. The past and the future have been abolished. … In Medellín, No Future is strewn about everywhere.… (1989, p.4; author's translation)

A perfect example of the kind of retroparadoxes that emerge from this new global deployment of time dissolved into speed, and strewn about the streets of Medellín as Gaviria suggests, is the sequence from *La vendedora* which deals most explicitly with prostitution. Judy, who is slightly older than the other girls, has taken to charging her boyfriends for sexual petting, and in this sequence we see her in a kind of speed-rush. The camera is mounted on a fast-moving car, framing Judy standing through its front passenger window, whistling and shouting to other cars as she and a boy (who is driving the car) speed along the course of the river through the night-time city, past the dazzling lights of traffic and Christmas decorations. Then, slumped in the front seat against the windscreen, staring up at the garish but beautiful lights that pass overhead, she negotiates sex with the boy for 15,000 pesos: 'But you won't put it in, will you?', she says; 'What will we do then?' asks the boy; 'Just touch each other and suck my tits.' Emptied of all emotion, reduced to a commodity, she tries to fend off the inevitable, losing herself in the rush of speed and light.

JUMP CUT

Amores perros ('Love's a Bitch'), released in 2000, has had wide international distribution, and has received almost universal critical acclaim for its intense urban vision. It does not use natural actors, and is not focused exclusively on children or adolescents in the same way as the other films examined here, instead casting its net somewhat wider in its examination of the interlocking power grids of modern urban society. The film uses dog-fighting as a displaced metaphor, an allegory even, for human violence, and indeed dog-fetishism generally in the film takes the form of a displaced and dislocated cipher and substitute for impeded human relationships. The functioning of this allegory could not be clearer: if human relationships are mapped onto canine ones, then the business of dog-fighting becomes in itself a powerful allegory for the systemic violence inherent within globalized capitalism. The owner of the dog-fighting business runs his firm according to strict and sound neo-liberal, market-oriented practice: 'Esta es mi empresa', he explains to the two new lads, 'no pago impuestos, no hay huelgas ni sindicatos, puro billete limpio' ('This is my firm ... I don't pay taxes, there are no strikes or unions. Pure, clean cash'). As an example of no-barriers private enterprise, of 'flexible' accumulation operating with a labour force battered into passive submission, the IMF would no doubt approve.

At an even more fundamental level, the dog metaphor functions to *defetishize* social relations for the spectator. Because the dog-fetishism of all the characters, rich or poor, is ironized, it makes visible in a most uncomfortable manner the very libidinalizing processes by which this systemic violence is disavowed or masked behind the screen of glossy images, beautified poses, and image status-symbols. One particular sequence, which marks the transition between the major focus of Part I ('Octavio y Susana') and Part II ('Daniel y Valeria'), serves to illustrate the way in which the film makes these systemic links. The sequence begins in an illegal dog-fight and ends in a television studio. Indeed, it is precisely in the *juxtaposition of these two scenes*, in the cinematic gaze which dares to think them together and to relate them, that the radical nature of *Amores perros* lies.

The mean, tough, streetwise bully Jarocho has challenged Octavio, one of the young protagonists, to a private dog-fight, after having lost several previous fights to him. Determined not to lose again, El Jarocho shoots Octavio's dog and then taunts him. Octavio knifes El Jarocho in the stomach, and he and his friend drive off at high speed through the traffic chased by El Jarocho's henchmen. Signalling pure velocity through a close-up of the white road-marks whizzing past into a blur, there begins, over a filtered audio track, an edited replay (from a bewildering variety of camera angles) of the high-speed car chase with which the film had begun, and through which all the dispersed urban stories of the film are interconnected. Moments before the devastating crash, the camera is switched to a POV shot from within Octavio's car. At the moment of impact itself, the screen blacks out, the musical theme of the television programme *Gente de hoy* forms a dramatic audio bridge (replacing the expected crash), and the screen is suddenly filled with the monitor of a television camera, showing the presenter of the programme (part of which was shown immediately prior to this sequence) telling viewers not to switch off during the commercial break. On the studio stage is the international super-model Valeria Amaya, the subject of Part II of the film, who has just told a pack of fibs about her supposed relationship with star Andrés Salgado.

The film could almost be a case-study example for Jameson's dictum that:

all thinking today is also, whatever else it is, an attempt to think the world system as such. ... On the global scale, allegory allows the most random, minute, or isolated landscapes to function as a figurative machinery in which questions about the system and its control over the local ceaselessly rise and fall. (1992, pp. 3–5)

Apart from the dog allegory, the film achieves this through the constant theme of mediatization, from (mobile) telephones to the mass-media, particularly in the story of Valeria. This helps to explain the startling juxtaposition in the above sequence between street violence and television screen, the screen representing very precisely – and in a self-reflexive fashion for cinema – the disavowal and dissimulation of the systemic violence underlying global image capitalism.

CONCLUSION

Like all of these films, *Amores perros* poses questions about visibility and invisibility, and in particular about (in)visibility as simulation and dissimulation. In *Los olvidados*, as Evans points out (1995, p. 86), the blind Don Carmelo, referring to the street children he has been abusing, cites the Spanish proverb 'cría cuervos ...', leaving implicit the corollary 'y te sacarán los ojos' ('bring up crows, and they'll peck out your eyes'). In one of the closing scenes of *Pixote*, the young boy vomits while staring transfixed at the *television screen* he and his now dead friends had bought with the proceeds of their crimes: what remains of their lives is now a flat televisual surface, and his vomit is the accumulation of all that somehow does not fit within the sanitized screens of Brazilian society. In *Pizza, birra, faso*, the protagonists attempt to get into a glitzy nightclub from which they are barred by virtue of their social status: their bodies must remain invisible, slinking in the dark and dangerous corners of the city, and violence is the only way for them to transgress the spatial lines of power which govern the right of access to public visibility. In *La vendedora de rosas*, the orphan Mónica stares through a plate-glass shop window, a kind of virtual screen, at an absurd commodified Santa Clause with its synthesized Christmas jingle; she hears a scraping noise, jarring against the jingle, and looks round to see a woman dragging her entire impoverished family along the street on a go-cart. Finally, in *Amores perros*, the old tramp and ex-guerrilla El Chivo makes strategic use of his social invisibility to transgress the power-lines of the city, violently shattering the plate-glass screen of a Japanese restaurant with his assassin's bullet, or playing, literally, with his image as he sticks a photograph of himself into his estranged daughter's graduation photograph. As such, he is the perfect corollary for the image-conscious Valeria, who, with her carefully simulated TV-relationships fabricated for global televisual consumption, is forced to confront the lack which those images disavow, as the car crash leaves her beautiful body mutilated and amputated. Her image on the advertising hoarding for global beauty product manufacturer *Enchant* is thus revealed as pure façade and simulation. It is the screen of a violence whose very terms cannot be understood without thinking its linkages to the power-geometry of informational global capitalism.

NOTES

1. These terms relate to psychoanalytical film theory, for example, Metz (1982).
2. POV = shot taken from a character's supposed point of view, but not directly through his/her eyes.
3. Figueroa was one of the great film directors of the Golden Age of Mexican cinema. For more on Buñuel's implicit subversion of the visual rhetoric of his films, see Acevedo Muñoz, (1997, pp. 4–5, 7). Note, however, that Figueroa appears in the credits for *Los olvidados*.
4. The documentary-style prologue to *Los olvidados*, with its mention of the global problem of poverty in the great cities of the world, is very much an afterthought, either ironic in its paternalistic tones, or an (unsuccessful) attempt to anaesthetize knee-jerk reactions against the film's 'unacceptable' images of Mexico.
5. Time-space compression is a term used by David Harvey (e.g. 1989b) and others to signify the speed-up of communications experienced as the annihilation of space within the regimes of deregulated, 'flexible', global capitalist accumulation.
6. Later visionary sequences, particularly at the end of the film, use discernible filmic slow-motion, as does Buñuel in his analogous sequences.

PART 4
Culture, hegemony and opposition

15

Identity, politics and *mestizaje*

Amaryll Chanady

In an article published in 1996, Martín Lienhard criticized the Latin American discourse on *mestizaje* (racial as well as cultural mingling), which he described as an ideology destined to maintain the power of the creole elite on the eve of independence. Although this discourse affirmed equality between ethno-racial groups, it actually served to cover up the exclusions of certain sectors of society (1996, pp. 66–7). Klor de Alva makes a similar argument when he claims that the myth of *mestizaje* was used 'to promote national amnesia about or to salve the national conscience in what concerns the dismal past and still *colonized* condition of most indigenous peoples of Latin America' (1995, p. 257). Although this view of the discourse of *mestizaje* is undoubtedly correct in many cases, contemporary cultural and postcolonial theory allows us to reread it in a new light. Going beyond its deconstruction as false consciousness, we can examine the complex links established by Latin American intellectuals between identity, politics and *mestizaje* from the perspective of the poststructuralist emphasis on the symbolic construction of reality and the emergence of new subjectivities. Instead of considering the paradigm exclusively as an instrument of hegemony of the predominantly white and Europeanized ruling classes, we can examine the various ways in which it has been constructed in different ideological contexts and from different positionalities. *Mestizaje* can function just as much as an oppositional discourse as a national ideology, or both at the same time.

After a brief discussion of official discourses of *mestizaje* that stress assimilation, Europeanization and whitening, as well as of the influential concept of 'our *mestizo* America' developed by the Cuban essayist, poet and revolutionary José Martí in the last decades of the nineteenth century (for a more detailed study of Martí's work in this context, see Chanady, 2000), I will concentrate on the ways in which some major Latin American intellectuals of the twentieth century worked within or reconstructed the paradigm. Finally, I will consider some academic works that examine concrete cases of cultural *mestizaje* as strategies of empowerment and at times opposition and resistance within marginalized sectors of society. It is interesting to see in which ways the issue of *mestizaje* (cultural as well as racial) is associated with questions of power, hegemony and the construction of new identities.

The transformation of theoretical paradigms in various disciplines during the twentieth century has profoundly changed the way in which we think about society. Instead of seeing it as relatively homogeneous, we now emphasize the differences within by studying minorities and emergent social groups, as well as hybrid cultural practices in what is sometimes called Border theory. At the same time, numerous sociological and political studies influenced by postmodern theory, as well as gender and feminist studies, have drawn our attention to the constructed nature of society and of concepts which we have always considered as natural or given. Nation, race and gender, for example, are now seen as symbolic constructions. Although these are frequently criticized for maintaining dominant ideologies and unequal power structures, they are just as often seen as ubiquitous and positive cultural practices that provide a sense of identity and purpose to groups and individuals, and foment social cohesion and nation-building.

In Latin America, discourses on *mestizaje* emerged partly to rally the diverse ethno-racial groups in a common struggle against the Spanish colonial power at the time of independence and during the period of national consolidation in the nineteenth century (for a detailed discussion of this issue, see Villoro, 1996). José Martí, for example, used the concept of 'our *mestizo* America' to exhort all Latin Americans, regardless of race, to resist the expansionist designs of the United States (for a selection of his most influential essays, see Martí, 1999). At the same time, he emphasized the importance of racial tolerance and solidarity in Cuba's independence movement against Spain. While racial harmony was an ideal rather than a reality, it became a powerful symbol of Latin American identity in contradistinction to Europe and especially the United States, which Martí criticized not only for its materialism, but also for its exclusion of Blacks and natives. Although the discourse of *mestizaje* throughout Latin America was often racist and Eurocentric, since it advocated 'improving' the population by racial mingling in which Europeans (mainly northerners) would eventually whiten society and assimilate the more 'primitive' indigenes, it also served as an important national myth that created a sense of specificity and a positive self-image in the face of external threats and internal strife.

In a recent book on the 'mestizophily' of certain Mexican intellectuals, especially of the politician and scholar Andrés Molina Enríquez (1868–1940), Agustín Basave Benítez (1992) defines it as the belief that racial and cultural miscegenation is desirable. He explains that the main premise of Molina's thought is that the *mestizos* are 'Mexicans by antonomasia, the authentic depositaries of Mexicanness' ('son los mexicanos por antonomasia, los auténticos depositarios de la mexicanidad') and that Mexico 'cannot become a developed and prosperous nation until it completes the process of miscegenation and succeeds in the ethnic homogenization of the population through the racial fusion of the Indian and Creole minorities in the *mestizo* masses' ('Mexico no puede convertirse en una nación desarrollada y próspera mientras no culmine su proceso de mestizaje y logre homogeneizar en lo étnico la población mediante la fusión racial de las minorías de indios y criollos en la masa mestiza,' 1992, p. 13). While the second statement illustrates the drive to homogenize the diverse sectors of society in a project of nation-building, the first statement about Mexicanness confirms the symbolic value of the idea of *mestizaje* for representing the nation. Basave Benítez situates the discourse of *mestizaje* in the context of a search for national identity and criticizes the adoption of European theories of nation, developed in an entirely different context. But he also condemns Molina's (and other mestizophiles') conception of racial mixing and acculturation for its asymmetrical view of *mestizaje* (1992, p. 144) in which Western acculturation and even assimilation are the desired goal. He argues that a genuine two-way cultural hybridization and synthesis of cultures are vastly preferable (ibid., p. 142). The notion of national unity is here paramount, and he explicitly rejects any notion of a 'pluricultural' nation in which ethnic groups maintain their separate identities, associating this with divisiveness, marginalization and social conflict.

Basave Benítez's ideas are diametrically opposed to more recent Latin American paradigms of cultural heterogeneity and pluralism, since he insists on the importance of 'a single, new nation different from the sum of its predecessors' ('una nación única, nueva, distinta a la suma de sus predecesoras'; ibid., p. 144). His distinction between a divisive nation in the past and present and a future harmonious one echoes Martí's plea for unity almost exactly one hundred years earlier. But he goes beyond Martí's call to tolerance and solidarity in the face of a threatening neighbour and a still-present colonial power by insisting explicitly on amalgamation and the elimination of internal differences (ibid., p. 145). Is he simply echoing the nineteenth-century intellectuals and politicians examined in his study, or is he responding to the problems of internal divisions and Mexico's peripheral status in the global market by explicitly rejecting newer paradigms of difference advocated largely by postmodern, postcolonial and cultural theory within hegemonic societies? His conclusion suggests that his explicit rejection of multiculturalism or pluriculturalism must be situated in the context of the postmodern global system in which the successes of modernity have eluded Latin America. In his final comments, he argues that the constitution of a strong, homogeneous nation is the only way of fighting against what he calls 'the present international subordination of those who are unequal' (ibid., p. 145).

The Mexican educator and essayist José Vasconcelos, who was Minister of Education between 1920 and 1924, shared this concern with Mexico's vulnerability in the first half of the twentieth century, when the nation was in the throes of post-revolutionary unrest and conflicting projects of nation-building. His essays are also an interesting example of the contradictory nature of discourses of *mestizaje* in the context of prevalent attitudes toward race, in which the appeal to tolerance and racial solidarity clashed with negative portrayals of non-Europeans. Vasconcelos explicitly erected *mestizaje* as a symbol of the future nation in his essay *La raza cósmica* (The Cosmic Race, 1925). Criticizing what he considered as the cultural and spiritual poverty, as well as the materialism, of the United States in a gesture reminiscent of earlier essayists such as José Enrique Rodó, he argues that superior Hispanic taste will eventually lead to the emergence in Latin America of a fifth race, which will amalgamate and supersede the four others. Like Martí, Vasconcelos was profoundly concerned about US intervention in Latin American affairs. In his autobiography, *A Mexican Ulysses* (1935), he claims that the main danger faced by his country is northern imperialism which could bring about a 'Texan Mexico with the Anglo-Saxon acting as owner and builder, and the Indian as roadmender, peasant, and fellah, in "Mexican towns" such as you see from Chicago to New Mexico, more miserable than the medieval Ghetto' (ibid., p. 125).

Vasconcelos's anti-imperialism and intense nationalism, as well as his antipositivism which he shared with other members of the *Ateneo de la juventud*, thus provide the context for the development of his ideas on *mestizaje*. Constructing a positive image of Mexico in opposition to the United States, Vasconcelos insists on Latin America's greater sympathy for foreigners and thus ability to assimilate and convert all men to a new type (1925, p. 32). He believes that it was this 'universal human sentiment' (ibid., p. 33) that had inspired illustrious leaders such as Bolívar to declare social and civil equality for whites, Blacks and Indians (ibid., p. 34). In spite of his praise of racial tolerance and condemnation of US racial oppression, however, Vasconcelos has a very problematic attitude toward race, as is obvious in his comments on Asian immigrants. He claims that they 'breed like mice' and will inevitably 'degrade the human condition' at a time when 'base zoological instincts' are being repressed by the intellectual faculties (ibid., pp. 34–5). It is ironic that he then argues that Latin Americans have less repulsion for 'foreign blood' and practice 'sincere and cordial racial mingling' (ibid., p. 35). Miscegenation, which he describes in this passage as a source of strength and rejuvenation, will come about not by coercion, but by the 'free choice of taste' (ibid., p. 43), which will lead to the eventual predominance of European characteristics. He exhorts his fellow Latin Americans to participate in the 'collective redemption' of humanity, since they possess the necessary 'biological material', the 'predisposition' and the 'genes' (ibid., p. 60). While other societies are exhausted, the 'Hispanic race' has the energy to initiate the genuinely universal epoch of humanity (ibid., p. 62).

Vasconcelos, like many of his predecessors, also sees *mestizaje* in the cultural sense as part of a civilizing mission, in which education leads to the integration of indigenous sectors of society and in which he took an active part as Minister of Education. He condemns several leaders of the Mexican Revolution for wanting to return to the 'primitivism of Montezuma' (1935, p. 105). His problematic attitude toward race in *La raza cósmica* becomes even more explicit in his autobiography, in which he echoes racialist beliefs in the debilitating effects not only of climate, but also of racial mingling. He claims that the climate in certain parts of Mexico has weakened the race, that the *mestizo* population of Mexico does not possess the 'vigor necessary to create ballet' (ibid., p. 180), and that the *mestizos* of Puebla are 'characterized by weakness and trickery' (ibid., p. 184). In Europe, he considers the white immigrant superior to the Latin American *mestizo* (ibid., p. 265). He points out that São Paulo was built by Italians and Portuguese and that the most backward provinces of Brazil are those in which extensive miscegenation has taken place (ibid., p. 267).

This attitude contrasts markedly with his desire to create 'a new race and a new culture, on the solid basis of our Spanish tradition, which was itself a magnificent synthesis of the most fertile antiquity' (ibid., p. 215), and with his explanation that whereas Europeans look down on miscegenation, his essay on the cosmic race was 'defensive and hopeful about race mixture' (ibid., pp. 266–7). However, he apparently resolves the contradictions in his conception of miscegenation when he explains that 'racial mixture, which is indispensable and can be our salvation, has not had time to bear fruit' (ibid., p. 191).

The cosmic race is thus the culmination of a lengthy process of amalgamation and homogenization, in which all traces of alterity are eventually erased. This immediately brings to mind the ideologeme of the melting-pot, in which diversity is distilled in a new purity. The main difference between the two concepts seems to be that the US melting-pot image generally included predominantly European immigrants, while the native peoples and Black Americans were symbolically excluded, whereas the concept of the cosmic race includes all races. However, Vasconcelos's theory of 'taste', according to which aesthetic considerations will eventually determine the characteristics of the cosmic race in what is quite obviously a process of whitening and eugenics, implies a 'purification' rather than a genuine hybridization, and thus bears striking parallels to melting-pot theories. Moreover, Vasconcelos's remarks in his autobiography on various cultures, religions and races leave no doubt as to his attitude toward the non-European Other in general.[1] In spite of the highly problematic nature of Vasconcelos's racial theory and esthetic idealism, however, his essay illustrates the importance of *mestizaje* as a symbol of cultural value, specificity and self-affirmation.

While Martí and Vasconcelos are closely associated with concrete projects of nation-building and resistance to threatening external powers from the perspective of the creole intelligentsia, the Peruvian novelist, poet and ethnographer José María Arguedas, who committed suicide in 1969, constructed his discourse of *mestizaje* from an entirely different position. As an ethnographer who grew up speaking Quechua and Spanish, wrote poetry in Quechua and identified closely with the *mestizos* and indigenous Peruvians, he had a deep personal interest not only in studying the indigenous cultures, but also in preserving them. In the context of ethnographers' perceived mission as the protagonists of an 'emergency' operation to salvage, as an object of knowledge, native cultures before they are assimilated in the relentless progress of modernization, Arguedas provides two important redefinitions of the ethnographic project. The first is the emphasis on social, political and economic justice, in the wake of indigenist movements inspired by the socialist intellectual Mariátegui and the journal *Amauta* (1926–30). The second involves the very conceptualization of native culture in general and Peruvian identity in particular.

Arguing against the 'folklorization' of indigenous cultures, in which they are considered as the depositors of timeless identities, Arguedas insists on the inevitable transformation undergone by these groups as they come in contact with the forces of modernization. Although he uses the term transculturation in his ethnographic essays (Arguedas, 1975, p. 3), he generally prefers *mestizaje*, which he defines in terms of culture rather than race, pointing out that there are white Indians as well as dark Westernized Peruvians (ibid., p. 2). His observation of numerous Peruvian towns leads him to conclude that the process of cultural *mestizaje* is extremely widespread, including among the elite, who sing songs containing Quechua expressions, adopt native-inspired dance forms such as the *huayno* and drink chicha. Since he sees cultural purity as an exception in a largely transculturated society, both in rural and urban areas (ibid., p. 4), he argues that the study of the *mestizo* should be one of the major tasks of contemporary anthropologists, who had always been more interested in native traditions. These traditions, he argues, are in no way 'pure'. They frequently involve the creative appropriation of European elements, as in the case of the native 'danza de las tijeras' (scissors dance) which is 'exclusively an Indian dance for an Indian public' (ibid., p. 24). His argument that native cultures are not destroyed by change but retain their specificity in spite of important transformations will be echoed by major ethnographers many years later in other contexts.

His plea in favour of *mestizo* studies is not simply that of a disinterested ethnographer redefining his object of study in accordance with changed social realities. Following in the tradition of Latin American intellectuals, he is passionately interested in the question of national identity and the future of his society. In contrast to the indigenists, who equate 'authentic' Peruvian identity with the native culture, Arguedas considers the *mestizos*, in their infinite stages of hybridization, as the basis of the nation. Furthermore, Arguedas considers *mestizaje* as positive, in marked contrast to anthropologists and nostalgic Indianists (those who celebrate the past glories of the native population before the Spanish Conquest) who see change as degradation and contamination of supposedly pure identities. Comparing Peru, in which many native communities have remained in poverty and isolation, with Mexico, where *mestizaje* has made more progress, he praises the 'splendour' of Mexican culture which he considers as proof of the limitless future of the Indo-Spanish, Indo-Latin and Mestizo nation in the north (ibid., p. 6). Whereas Mexico takes great pride in its indigenous past, Peru harbours widespread prejudice in favour of all things European, thus leading to the imitation and exclusive valorization of European culture (ibid., p. 7).

In his fieldwork in several rural communities in Peru, Arguedas observed that those that were more developed economically, and had thus been better integrated within modern market forces through selective acculturation, had also developed more varied and successful cultural practices in music, art and dance inspired by indigenous traditions, which they increasingly exported to other areas. *Mestizaje* therefore enabled the communitiy to keep alive native traditions, which the poorer and economically marginalized native communities could not. According to Arguedas, these changes did not affect the identity of the communities in any significant manner. Since the communities of the Mantaro valley modernized and incorporated contemporary models of production and economic organization through an 'organic process', they did not have to reject their indigenous customs and suffer cultural upheaval (ibid., p. 124). He praises the cultural vitality of Huancayo, in which the numerous native and mestizo migrants merge harmoniously. While they are still profoundly indigenous, they are also stimulated by the 'impulse of activity, trade, and the modern spirit' (ibid., p. 129).

But Arguedas did not see the economic development of native groups as merely a precondition for maintaining their cultural traditions (limited acculturation in the service of identity preservation). He considered *mestizaje* in general as a source of cultural renewal. Not only were transcultured communities better off economically, and less subject to the loss of group identity; their in-between position allowed them to develop innovative cultural practices in music, dance and the visual arts that acquired great success in other communities, including those of the rapidly expanding capital, Lima. Arguedas attributes these innovations to the 'harmonious amalgamation of cultures' (ibid., p. 12) in certain regions such as the Mantaro valley.

Arguedas' interest in the emergence of hybridized art forms was not merely due to their esthetic qualities, but also involved political dimensions. Critical of the exclusive emphasis on European culture, and the concomitant marginalization of other cultural traditions, as well as of those sectors of society not identified with the creole elite, Arguedas argued for a reconceptualization of the nation as *mestizo* and the valorization of traditions inspired by native culture. Politics, identity and the discourse of *mestizaje* are thus closely linked in his intellectual project of redefining the nation, advocating social justice and emphasizing the innovative cultural developments that lend the nation a specificity situated between Western and autochthonous culture.

It is interesting that Arguedas rejected *mestizaje* as homogenization and explicitly insisted on the importance of maintaining internal differences. When he evokes the 'new unity' of a future Peru, he insists that it should be as diverse as the present nation (ibid., p. 27). In his description of the migrant communities in Huancayo, he praises the democratization that allows natives and *mestizos* to participate in the economic activities of the city and share restaurants with wealthy officials and public servants, without losing their regional identities (ibid., p. 129). Every migrant is free to associate with those of similar background and express his particular identity in cultural practices that distinguish him from other migrants, while being fully integrated in the larger urban community in a model of integration without assimilation. In Arguedas' ethnographic writings, *mestizaje* thus in no way implies a merging of all cultural forms and practices. Nor does it necessarily imply oppositionality to dominant market forces, even if it can be seen as a strategy of resistance to Western cultural homogenization and the erosion of subaltern identities.

As several critics have argued, difference is very much part of the postmodern transnational capitalist culture, which requires constant innovation and infinite variety in order to expand. Alternative cultural practices are thus not always transgressive, but contribute to the maintenance of transnational capitalism, since they are either appropriated by the 'Empire', to use Hardt and Negri's term (2000), or simply illustrate local ways of becoming integrated in the global economy. In no way do they challenge the 'system' that offers an ever-growing smorgasboard of cultural commodities in which, as the French philosopher Alain Finkielkraut has lamented, products of lofty thought are on an equal footing with the chewing of betel nuts and the art of knitting (1987, p. 11).

In a recent discussion of García Canclini's influential monograph on 'hybrid cultures' in Mexico (1990), John Kraniauskas argues that his study

> is not a critique of the logic of development but rather an example of cultural development in which, from the subalternist perspective of Charkrabarty, the chronological and abstract 'time of capital' not only remains intact but may even be strengthened. (2000, p. 250)

He makes a similar argument with respect to Ángel Rama's frequently cited study of transculturation in the Latin American novel (1982): 'Narrative transculturation thus possibly figures a process of contradictory cultural democratisation and integration, the widening of hegemony's cultural parameters under the impact of the expanded reproduction of capital and the ideology of development' (2000, p. 238). He concludes that 'Rama is not analysing a process of transculturation "from below"' (ibid., p. 238).

Several recent studies of emerging hybrid cultural forms in Latin America, however, have stressed their emergence in popular and marginalized sectors of society (in contrast to the canonical novels studied by Rama). Arguedas' studies of popular art forms in Peruvian *mestizo* communities is an obvious early example. Toward the end of the twentieth century, Latin American cultural studies started producing a steadily increasing volume of research in this area. While many cultural practices analyzed are not oppositional, some do express a position that challenges dominant values. Even Arguedas pointed out certain strategies of resistance on the part of popular artists who refused to mass-produce their work. Although this may not prevent them from becoming integrated within the transnational market economy (on the contrary, many seek precisely that), they often provide a discourse that may be explicitly linked to their status as modern hybridized and marginalized individuals in an all-powerful global system in which they struggle for survival and a positive sense of identity. In his study of Peruvian chicha music, which is a mixture of Afro-Hispanic cumbia, salsa, rock and roll and *huayno*, George Lipsitz argues that this new hybrid art form, produced by *mestizo* immigrants in the shantytowns of Peruvian cities, 'challenged racial hierarchies by celebrating *mestizaje* and claiming prestige from below' (1998, p. 308). Not only did it provide a positive sense of identity, but it broke down racial divisions, created new alliances among people and gave rise to a new community of artists and spectators in which the 'highland past and the urban present blended together in aggressive festivity that imagined and instantiated new identities among Andean migrants' (ibid., p. 309). Rather than seeing these new art forms as a contamination of traditional 'pure' ones, one should see them as an illustration of the 'dynamic nature of national and ethnic identity in an age of fast capital' (ibid., p. 309).

Although there has been an obvious shift from discourses of *mestizaje* that stress nation-building and the unification of conflictual societies to the contemporary interest in popular hybridized cultural practices, the earlier paradigm has not disappeared in the face of continuing conflicts and inequalities or, in some cases, in the face of emergent social movements considered as a threat to national harmony. While some critics may argue that contemporary celebrations of *mestizaje* (not from a subaltern position but as a strategy of national solidarity) are not very different from older ones in which members of the elite attempted to counteract contestatory movements, emergent minority discourses also raise legitimate concerns about social fragmentation.

In Guatemala, for example, the emergence of Mayan social movements and the accompanying identity politics in the last decade of the twentieth century has led to a criticism of binary constructions originating within indigenous groups. Mario Roberto Morales argues that the essentialist opposition between Mayans and non-Mayans (*mestizos*) deforms complex social phenomena, since globalization, tourism and the increasing importance of mass media have generated hybrid identities that do not allow us to establish clear distinctions between these groups. Furthermore, these binary constructions are discriminatory toward those not considered Mayan because of their essentialism, culturalism, ethnicism, and insistence on a pure, uncontaminated Mayan identity that has supposedly remained alive for five centuries in spite of colonization (1998, p. 303). The category of *mestizos* or *ladinos* is constructed in an equally essentialist and simplistic manner (ibid., p. 304). Morales argues that in spite of their emphasis on the pre-colonial past, the Mayan ethnic movements do not reject modernization and the global market economy, or provide a utopian alternative, but simply desire 'a slice of the cake of domination and hegemony' and thus constitute a postmodern subalternity that wishes to continue the modern project (ibid., p. 317). Morales sees the new Mayan identity as a strategic essentialist construction in the service of counterhegemonic politics (ibid., p. 318), but criticizes it for its 'exclusivist fundamentalism' and self-affirmation based on the negation of the 'other' (ibid., p. 323).

It is in this context of emerging ethnic movements in the Guatemala of the 1990s that Morales resuscitates the notion of *mestizaje*. Rejecting previous ideologies of *mestizaje* as whitening, assimilation and national homogenization by Latin American oligarchies during the Mexican Revolution of the first half of the century and the Guatemalan Revolution in 1944–54, he points out that the valorization of *mestizaje* may also bring about the deconstruction of essentialist identities and the harmonious and democratic coexistence of different national cultures. He insists on the fluid boundaries between these cultures, which are hybridized in a continuous process of cultural mixing. In spite of his use of the term 'multicultural' for this new reality, a term that often suggests the rigid boundaries of the mosaic, Morales distinguishes between difference, which implies the maintenance of boundaries, and cultural *mestizaje*, which entails myriad forms of mutual transculturation. At the same time, he sees cultural *mestizaje* as a common denominator for a new national identity in which the various specificities are not negated. He concludes that 'intercultural and interethnic democratization' is only possible if the dichotomous identity constructions are abandoned in favour of an emphasis on hybridization, transculturation and cultural *mestizaje* (ibid., p. 324).

Contemporary discourses of *mestizaje* can often be situated within the tradition of national self-definition, self-affirmation, racial justice, and the development of autonomous cultural paradigms represented by Martí. Sonia Montecinos (1993), for example, criticizes the negative attitudes towards miscegenation in Chile and the concomitant denial of what she considers an essential part of the country's history and cultural traditions. She thus stresses the necessity to recognize the specific '*mestizo* imaginary' (1993, p. 25) that still characterizes the country today, in spite of the hegemony of Western paradigms. Furthermore, she rejects the transnationalization of (Western) knowledge and the imitation of universal paradigms that impedes the development of particular (*mestizo* and Chilean) forms of knowledge. The analysis of family structures in Chile, for example, may make an original contribution to areas such as gender studies. In her analysis of the figure of the mother, the orphan, and the *mestizo* in Chilean literature, Montecinos redefines traditional (Western) gender roles in the context of single-parent families in which women (indigenous or *mestiza*) were left to care for their *mestizo* children in the absence of the (white or *mestizo*) father. In her essay, *mestizaje* is thus linked not only to social justice, identity and national politics, but also to the politics of knowledge production in a global context, in which abstract theory emanates from cultural centres of power and is applied to entirely different social contexts on the periphery of the cultural market.

In conclusion, the discourse of *mestizaje* has an ambiguous status. While it has often been associated with nation-building, it has also more recently been applied to emerging cultural forms and minority subjectivities. But even if other paradigms are frequently considered preferable, because of the racist and homogenizing connotation of the term, its reemergence among contemporary scholars such as Basave Benítez, Morales and Montecinos may point to the continuing consternation of intellectuals in many Latin American countries in the face of the incompletion of the modern project in the periphery. Whereas the terms transculturation, creolization, hybridity, nomadism and migrancy stress a postmodern interest in difference, deconstruction of traditional conceptions of identity, local histories, resistance and emerging identities, *mestizaje* has frequently implied an emphasis on the viability of the national community as a whole in societies riven by conflict and social injustice and lagging increasingly behind in the global economy. As Martín Hopenhaym's study on Latin American modernity indicates (1996), *mestizaje* remains a powerful concept in that it provides us with a necessary utopia for the future in a particularly heterogeneous society (ibid., p. 280).

NOTES

1   He describes the Alhambra in Granada, for example, as 'typically Muslim' and concludes that it 'does not deserve to come to life', since the 'civilization that erected it left us nothing. Some translations, perhaps, translations of Aristotle and science that the Arabs had imported, but had not created themselves' (1925, p. 201). He also refers to the 'pity' and 'childish repugnance' he used to feel for the 'colored race', which he considers afflicted with the 'physical curse of a subhuman face', adding that this feeling prevented him from appreciating the 'dances and shouts of the vaudeville Negro' (1925, p. 60).

16

Brazilian cinema
Reflections on race and representation

Robert Stam

As a vast continent-size New World country, similar to the US in both historical formation and ethnic diversity, Brazil constitutes a kind of southern twin whose strong affinities with the US have been obscured by ethnocentric assumptions and media stereotypes. While in no way identical, the two countries are eminently comparable. After millennia of indigenous habitation and culture, both Brazil and the US were discovered as part of Europe's search for a trade route to India. Indeed, the histories of Brazil and the US run on parallel tracks. Both countries began their official histories as European colonies, one of Portugal, the other of Great Britain. In both countries, colonization led to the occupation of vast territories and the dispossession of indigenous peoples. In the US, the occupiers were called pioneers; in Brazil they were called *bandeirantes* (bandits) and *mamelucos* (mamelukes). Subsequently, both countries massively imported Africans to form the two largest slave societies of modern times, up until slavery was abolished, with the Emancipation Proclamation of 1863 in the US and the 'Golden Law' of 1888 in Brazil. Both countries received parallel waves of immigration from all over the world, ultimately forming multicultural societies with substantial indigenous, African, Italian, German, Japanese, Slavic, Arab and Jewish (Ashkenazi and Sephardi) populations and influences.

The complex national culture of Brazil is richly expressed in what was recently commemorated, in 1998, as the century of Brazilian Cinema. This rich history takes us from the earliest cinematic views, in the 1890s, through the 'belle époque' that lasted from 1908–11, during which Brazilian cinema dominated its own market, through the *chanchadas* (studio musical comedies) of the 1930s and 1940s, through the just-like-Hollywood ambitions of Vera Cruz (1949–54), to the various phases of *Cinema Novo* beginning in the late 1950s, and on to the stylistic pluralism of the present-day, a period which has seen Brazilian Cinema honored by Oscar nominations for films like O *Qautrilho* and *Central Station*, and by a resurgence of cinema within Brazil itself.

What interests us here is how Brazilian cinema stages and represents a multicultural society. To what extent have Afro-Brazilians and indigenous Brazilians, for example, been able to represent themselves? How does Brazilian cinema stage its racial representations? How useful are such notions as stereotypes, positive images, realism? What is the role of cultural difference within the spectatorship of reading films? What voices have *not* been heard in Brazilian cinema?

Brazilian films inevitably reflect, or better reflect on (since the reflection is never a question of direct correspondence) the ambient realities as filtered through the competing ideologies and discourses circulating within the social atmosphere. The lack of rigid racial segregation, the fact of a *mestiço* (mixed-race) population, the ubiquity of Afro-Brazilian cultural expression, combined with the equally undeniable reality of the social powerlessness of people of color, all leave traces in the films. The challenge is to discern the structuring patterns within these traces, for films do not merely reflect social reality in an unmediated way; they inflect, stylize, caricature, allegorize. Although poststructuralist theory reminds us that we live and dwell within language and representation, that we have no direct access to the real, nevertheless the constructed, coded nature of artistic discourse hardly precludes all reference to a common social life. Human consciousness, and artistic practice, Bakhtin argues, do not come into contact with the real directly, but rather through the medium of the surrounding ideological world. Literature and, by extension, cinema do not so much refer to or call up the world as represent its languages and discourses. Rather than directly reflecting the real, or even refracting the real, artistic discourse constitutes a refraction of a refraction, i.e., a mediated version of an already textualized and discursivized socio-ideological world (for more on Bakhtinian theories and their relevance to the novel, see Stam, 1989). The issue is less one of fidelity to a pre-existing truth or reality, then, than one of a specific orchestration of ideological discourses and communitarian perspectives.

As Ella Shohat and I have argued elsewhere (Shohat and Stam, 1994), the positive/negative image approach entails more general methodological/theoretical problems, which could be summed up as essentialism (a complex diversity of portrayals is reduced to a limited set of reified stereotypes); verism (characters are discussed as if they were real); ahistoricism (a static analysis ignores mutations, metamorphoses, altered contexts, changes of valence); moralism (social and political issues are treated as if they were matters of individual ethics); and individualism (the individual character, rather than larger social categories, is the point of reference). As a portrait of a gay black mafioso transvestite, *Rainha Diaba*, for example, completely scrambles any notion of positive and negative image. Is it positive that a talented black actor gets to play title roles? Milton Gonçalves' acting is an artistic *tour de force*, and that is important for other black performers. Moreover, his character is portrayed as a powerful leader, in a country where blacks are treated affectionately even as they are shorn of power. *Rainha Diaba* poses the question of power indirectly by positing a black leader of indisputable energy and charisma, playing provocatively with a whole series of spectatorial stereotypes. With a drag queen black mafioso as hero, one can hardly accuse the film of being either merely positive or of being merely stereotypical. Although the *Rainha Diaba* character was based on a real-life historical prototype, a literal-minded sociological approach would point out the demographic improbability of such a character; only a tiny percentage of black Brazilians are actually transvestite mafiosos. But in fact the film's truth transcends demographics. Anyone who thinks that blacks cannot be homosexual, or that homosexuals cannot be macho, or that blacks cannot be mafia godfathers, is being prodded to think again. By mixing gayness with tongue-in-cheek machismo, the film suggests that the macho world might have unconfessed and subterranean feminine and homoerotic tendencies (expressed, for example, in the homosociality of the biracial male buddy films). In this sense, the film elaborates an insight into the repressed gay underside of exaggeratedly masculine behavior.

That films on some level reflect ambient social life and ideologies should not lead us to a naive mimeticism. For example, Brazilian films, taken as a whole, do not reflect the majority status of its black, mulatto, and *mestiço* citizens. Although the majority population of Rio de Janeiro, the chief center of film production in the silent era, was black and *mestiço*, similarly, this demographic fact is not reflected in the films of the period; Afro-Brazilians thus constituted a structuring absence. On another level, this very absence really reflected, if not the demographic reality, at least the real power situation in Brazil. As Abdias de Nascimento puts it in relation to Brazilian theatre: 'the white monopoly on the Brazilian stage reflects the white monopoly on land, on the means of production, on political and economic power, on cultural institutions' (quoted in Sussekind, 1982). In demographic terms, *Dona Flor and Her Two Husbands* portrays a Bahia considerably less black than the real one; Disney's *The Three Caballeros* portrays a Bahia without any blacks at all. Antunes Filho's *Compasso de Espera*, to take a different example, reflects on racial repression in Brazil, yet the film's protagonist, a black poet and advertising agent closely allied with the São Paulo élite, is, sociologically, a highly atypical figure. But the point is not to demand point-for-point demographic equivalence, only to be aware of the social stratifications informing representation.

The most striking absence within Brazilian cinema, though, is that of the black woman. The *chanchadas* feature Afro-Brazilian male performers, but very few black women. The romantic involvements of black men in Brazilian films (for example, Jorge in *Compasso de Espera*) tend to be with white women, a portrayal consistent with a tendency in real life for upwardly mobile blacks to link up with lighter-skinned partners. *Cinema Novo* features a number of black women's roles (Cota in *Barravento*, the mistress in *A Grande*

Feira [The Grand Fair]), but they are rarely the political or social equal of the male characters. Adaptations of novels often cast white actresses for what in the source novels were mulatta roles: Bete Faria as Rita Bahiana in O Cortiço (The Hive), Sônia Braga as Gabriela in *Gabriela*. A few rare films feature prestigious white men in love with black women, notably Diegues' *Xica da Silva* and Senna's *Diamante Bruto* (Rough Diamond, 1977), a film about a TV star who returns to his native Mínas to find his long-lost love. Even the films by (male) Afro-Brazilian directors tend to neglect the black woman. The black poet Saul, in Onofre's *Aventuras Amorosas de um Padeiro* (The Amorous Adventures of a Baker), falls in love with white Rita, not with a black woman. The posited alliance between black men and white women ends up leaving black women without male allies, while ignoring solidarity among black women themselves. Documentaries such as *Mulheres Negras do Brasil* (Black Women of Brazil), not surprisingly, try to take up the slack in representation. The other major striking absence is of black gays and lesbians, one of the few exceptions being the transvestite mafioso protagonist of *Rainha Diaba*. Black gays appear briefly in a number of films (e.g., *Toda Nudez Sera Punida* [All Nudity Will Be Punished, 1978]) but usually in caricatural or ephemeral roles. Moreover, gay characters die off with suspicious rapidity and regularity. Here too, the documentary and fiction shorts by such directors as Eunice Guttman and Karim Ainouz take up the representational slack.

A privileging of social portrayal, plot, and character often leads to a slighting of the specifically cinematic mediations of the films: narrative structure, genre conventions, cinematic style. Eurocentric discourse in film may be relayed not by characters or plot but by lighting, framing, *mise-en-scène*, music. Some basic issues of mediation have to do with the *rapports de force*, the balance of power as it were, between foreground and background. In the visual arts, space has traditionally been deployed to express the dynamics of authority and prestige. The cinema translates such correlations of social power into registers of foreground and background, on-screen and off-screen, silence and speech. To speak of the image of a social group, we have to ask precise questions about images and sounds. How much space do the diverse characters occupy in the shot? Which of the characters are active and dynamic, which are merely decorative props? Do the eyeline matches identify us with one gaze rather than another? Whose looks are reciprocated, whose ignored? How do body language, posture, and facial expression communicate attitudes rooted in social hierarchies, attitudes of arrogance, servility, resentment, pride? Whose music dictates the emotional response? What homologies inform artistic and ethnic/political representation?

Many Brazilian films, in this sense, can be seen as staging the protocols of racial democracy. In the *chanchadas*, for example, white performers are foregrounded, along with an ocasional black major or minor actor (Grande Otelo, Cole, Blecaute), with other people of color relegated to the barely observable background. Although African-inflected music and performance are a key presence in the *chanchadas*, that presence goes largely unacknowledged. They convey an epidermic simulacrum of racial democracy, but ultimately fix blacks in a subaltern place. Moacyr Fenelon's musical *Tudo Azul* (Everything is Fine, 1951) illustrates this process quite clearly. The film is focalized around the dreams and frustrations of white characters, especially a songwriter romantically torn between his wife and a popular radio singer (Marlene). In a nightclub sequence, the two women encounter the singer, Blecaute, already familiar to us from *Carnaval Atlântida*, who is placed, barman-like, behind a counter. At the songwriter's request, he sings a popular carnival song, 'Maria Candelária' (also the title of a famous Mexican film), while the white clubgoers dance enthusiastically. The white singer Marlene, meanwhile, sings another 1950s' hit ('Lata d'água na Cabeça' [Carrying a bucket of water on her head]) which tells of poor *favelada* women who lack running water. As José Gatti points out, the staging of the sequence realizes the racial conventions of the period. Blecaute socializes with the whites but also serves them. Marlene is shown in close-up in her middle-class apartment, while illustrative shots of black women in the *favelas* (slums) accompany her singing. The white woman singer speaks for the black women, much as the white male film-maker speaks for and places blacks in general. The representation is of blacks and whites living in apparent harmony, but with the subaltern status (barman, entertainer, *favelado*) of the blacks taken for granted.

In the classical musicals, then, Afro-Brazilians constituted not only a suppressed historical voice but also a literally suppressed ethnic voice, authorizing a Euro-Brazilian signature on what were basically African-American cultural products. In a power-inflected form of ambivalence, the same dominant society that loves ornamental snippets of black culture excludes the black performers who might best incarnate it. Like Hollywood musicals, many Brazilian musicals thematize the struggle between high culture (opera, legitimate theatre, ballet) and low culture (vaudeville, popular music), a struggle that is also racial. A sequence from *De Pernas para o Ar* (Upside Down, 1957) makes this racialized hierarchy explicit. The sequence begins with blacks in African costume dancing Afro-style to a polyrhythmic *batucada*, and then segues to big band music and sophisticated dance, in which tuxedoed whites literally expel the black performers. In this choreographed version of Social Darwinism, black artists seem to shrink in fright at the vision of a seemingly more powerful form of music.

In terms of the cinema, blacks and indigenous people have had only a minimal role in scripting, directing, and producing Brazilian films. There is no equivalent in Brazil to 1930s' black independent directors like Oscar Micheaux and Spencer Williams, or to Native American directors like Bob Hicks or Loretta Todd. Although the 1970s witnessed the emergence of a handful of black directors in Brazil (Haroldo Costa, Antônio Pitanga, Waldyr Onofre, Odilon Lopes, Zózimo Bulbul), few of them have managed to make second features. Their films, furthermore, have not enjoyed the degree of success generated by the films of African-American directors like Spike Lee, Charles Burnett, Mario van Peebles, Julie Dash, Robert Townsend, Bill Duke, and the Hughes Brothers in the US, although this lack of success doubtless has more to do with the general crisis of the Brazilian film industry than with any special hostility toward black directors.[1] Nor do the films by black directors necessarily foreground racial issues. The question therefore becomes: in what way do these black directors foreground, or elide, black experience and concerns? How does their self-representation differ from the representations proffered by their white colleagues? The answer has to be that their representations, while slightly more sympathetic to blacks, do not differ greatly from the films of sympathetic white directors such as Nelson Pereira dos Santos. And then the question becomes: are black Brazilian directors less angry or race-conscious? Or is their anger simply repressed from within or rendered taboo from without?

In both the US and Brazil, the situation within the film industry mirrors that of the country as a whole. Blacks are visible, especially as performers, but they are seldom in control of their own image. The major area in which blacks have worked is not as directors but as actors. We have discussed the work of Sebastiao Prata ('Grande Otelo'), Antônio Pitanga, Milton Gonçalves, Zózimo Bulbul, Eliezer Gomes, and Zezé Motta. We have not mentioned Jorge Coutinho, Marcílio Faria, Aurea Campos, Francisca Lopes, Samuel dos Santos, and many others. While Grande Otelo became 'king of the chanchadas' in the 1940s and 1950s, Ruth de Souza played the maid in the films of Vera Cruz, and black performers like Antônio Pitanga (*Barravento*, *Ganga Zumba*, and *The Big City*), Marcos Vinícius (*Xica da Silva, J. S. Brown: O Último Heroi*), Milton Gonçalves (*Macunaíma, They Don't Wear Black Tie*), Zózimo Bulbul (*Terra em Transe, Compasso de Espera*) and Zezé Motta (*Xica da Silva, A Força do Xangô*) developed distinguished careers within *Cinema Novo*. Performance too, it is important to remember, has subversive potential. At times a black actor can undermine the intentions of a white-dominated film. In a Hollywood context, Donald Bogle focusses on the ways African-American performers have signified and subverted the roles forced on them, battling against confining types and categories, a battle homologous to the quotidian struggle of three-dimensional blacks against the imprisoning conventions of an apartheid-style system. At their best, black performances undercut stereotypes by individualizing the type or slyly standing above it, playing against script and studio intentions, turning demeaning roles into resistant performance (Bogle, 1989, p. 36). Grande Otelo, in this same spirit, claimed in interviews that he always tried to put 'a little resistance' even into demeaning roles. In the Brazilian version of *The Adventures of Robinson Crusoe*, where Grande Otelo plays 'Friday', for example, Otelo subverts Defoe's colonialist classic by playing a Friday who refuses to accept the colonizer's power to name; 'Me Crusoe', he repeatedly tells the Englishman: 'You Friday!'

The choice of actors is central to the issue of racial self-representation. Third World and minoritarian peoples in Hollywood have with great regularity been represented not by themselves but rather by white actors in blackface (Jeanne Crain in *Pinky*), in redface (Jeff Chandler in *Broken Arrow*), in yellowface (Paul Muni in *The Good Earth*), and brownface (Charlton Heston in *Touch of Evil*). The choice of white actors to play people of color thus inevitably raises the question of racial discrimination. In the US, furthermore, black actors and actresses have tended to be invited to perform only those roles previously designated as black, under the tacit assumption that roles such as astronaut, doctor, lawyer are not to be played by blacks unless so designated; the implicit norm is whiteness. The Brazilian situation is both similar and distinct in this respect. As we saw in the case of *Gimba*, there have been occasional complaints about the bypassing of black actors for certain roles. When Brazilian playwright Nelson Rodrigues, in the 1940s, presented O *Anjo Negro* (The Black Angel), a play with a black protagonist, he was shocked to be told by the Municipal Theatre that he would have to cast a white in blackface. Zezé Motta, similarly, recalls the intense pressure put on Carlos Diegues to cast a light-skinned mulatta for *Xica da Silva*.[2] But usually, for good or for ill, Brazilian casting seems less race-conscious than casting in North America. Black actors are not usually thought of as somehow incarnating the black race; nor are they read by the audience in such a light. The black actor Marcos Vinícius in *J. S. Brown: O Último Heroi* (J. S. Brown, The Last Hero, 1979) plays a Brazilian who adores American detective films and therefore changes his name João da Silva to J. S. Brown. Victim of an imported aesthetic, he wears detective-style trench coats even in the tropics. But the actor's blackness is irrelevant to the film's allegory of alienation; the protagonist could have been portrayed by a white actor without significantly altering the film. In this sense, certain negative roles played by Afro-Brazilians in Brazilian cinema can paradoxically be a positive sign; the very lack of self-consciousness about whether an image is positive or negative signifies the assumption that the choice of actors is not always allegorical, i.e. that actors do not always encapsulate their race.

A purely epidermic, chromatic, physiognomist approach simply does not work in the case of Brazilian cinema, and not only because of the practical problem of defining who is black. In Brazil, the corporeal and the cultural are often delinked, a process that began already with the de-culturation and Europeanization of the Indians. But the reverse process, i.e., the Africanization of the Europeans, has also taken place. Thus some Brazilians with European features can be deeply involved in African or indigenous culture, and, conversely, people with African or indigenous features can feel little affinity for indigenous or Afro-Brazilian culture. An ethnocentric vision based on American cultural patterns often leads to the racializing of filmic situations that Brazilians would not see as racially connoted. The differing racial spectrum at times leads to cultural misunderstandings. For Brazilian audiences, some American films which treat racial discrimination, for example, *A Soldier's Story*, are confusing because for them some of the characters portrayed as victimized by racial discrimination are played by actors that for Brazilians are not black. The converse also applies; American and European viewers can misperceive the racial implications of Brazilian films because of a confusion over who is black, a proof if ever one was needed that race is a historically constructed category.

One way that Brazilian culture is figured as a mixed site is through the metaphor of garbage. For the late 1960s *udigrudi* (underground) film-makers, the garbage metaphor captured the sense of marginality, of being condemned to survive within scarcity, of being the dumping ground for transnational capitalism, of being obliged to recycle the materials of the dominant culture (Xavier, 1982). In an Afro-diasporic context, the garbage aesthetic evokes the ways that blacks in the New World, largely deprived of social and economic power, have managed to transmogrify waste products into art, whether through the musical use of throwaway metal (the steel drums of Trinidad), the culinary use of throwaway parts of animals (soul food, *feijoada*), or the use in weaving of throwaway fabrics (quilting). All these bricolage aesthetics have in common a notion of discontinuity – a quilt is made of scraps exemplifying diverse styles and materials – whence their link with artistic modernism as an art of discontinuity, and with postmodernism as an art of recycled trash and pastiche. At the same time, garbage can be seen as a polysemic signifier which can be read literally (garbage as a source of food for poor people, garbage as the site of ecological disaster, garbage as the diasporized, heterotopic space of the promiscuous mingling of the rich and the poor, the industrial and the artisanal, the national and the international, the local and the global). Or garbage can be read metaphorically as a figure for social indictment – poor people treated like garbage, garbage as the dumping of pharmaceutical products or of canned TV programs. Or garbage can be an allegorical text to be deciphered, a form of social colonics where the truth of a society can be read in its waste products.

Two recent documentaries literalize the theme of garbage. Jorge Furtado's *Isle of Flowers* (1989) brings the garbage aesthetic into the postmodern era. Described by its author as a 'letter to a Martian who knows nothing of the earth and its social systems', Furtado's 12-minute short uses Monty Python-style animation, archival footage, and parodic/reflexive documentary techniques to indict the distribution of wealth and food around the world. The 'Isle of flowers' of the title is a Brazilian garbage dump where famished women and children, many of them black, are gathered in groups of ten and are given five minutes to scrounge for food. But before we get to the garbage dump, we are given the itinerary of a tomato from farm to supermarket to bourgeois kitchen to garbage can to the 'Isle of Flowers'. Throughout, the film moves back and forth between minimalist definitions of the human – those bipeds with telencephalon and opposable thumbs – to the ideal of freedom evoked by the film's final citation from Cecília Meireles' *Romanceiro da Indonfidência*: 'Freedom is a word the human dream feeds on, that no one can explain or fail to understand.'

The title of another Brazilian 'garbage' video, Eduardo Coutinho's documentary *Boca de Lixo* (The Scavengers, 1992), is triply allusive: literally 'mouth of garbage', the phrase also evokes 'red light district' and 'garbage cinema'. The film centers on poor Brazilians, again largely black and *mestiço*, who survive thanks to a garbage dump outside of Rio. Here too garbage defines and illuminates the world; the trashcan, to recycle Trotsky, *is* history. But rather than take a miserabilist approach, Countinho shows us people who are inventive, ironic, and critical, who tell the director what to look at and how to interpret what he sees. Rather than outcasts or pathetic people, the film's subjects exist on a continuum with Brazilian workers in general; they encapsulate the country as a whole; they have held other jobs, they have worked in other cities. While for Coutinho the stealing of others' images for sensationalist purposes is the original sin of the documentary and TV-reportage genres,[3] the garbage dwellers repeatedly insist that 'Here nobody steals', as if responding to the accusations of imaginary middle-class interlocutors. Instead of the suspect pleasures of a condescending sympathy, the middle-class spectator is obliged to confront vibrant people who dare to dream and to talk back.

The trope of garbage is also symptomatic of the postmodern and postcolonial moment. If Third-Worldist discourse drew sharp lines between Europe/non-Europe, First World/Third World, oppressor/oppressed, contemporary discourse is less binary. With post-Third Worldism, such binaristic dualisms give way to a more nuanced spectrum of subtle differentiations, in a new global regime where First World and Third World are mutually imbricated. Notions of ontologically referential identity metamorphose into notions of a conjunctural play of identifications. Once rigid boundaries are now presented as more porous; imagery of barbed-wire frontiers have mutated into metaphors of fluidity and crossing. Colonial metaphors of irreconcilable dualism give way to postcolonial tropes drawing on the diverse modalities of mixedness: religious (syncretism); biological (hybridity); human-genetic (*mestiçagem*); and linguistic (creolization). The Tropicalist movement of the late 1960s, picking up from the Modernists' mix of futurism and primitivism, anticipated the 'posts' with its diverse tropes of mixing, its musical minglings of electric guitar and *berimbau*, its creative syntheses of bossa nova, traditional samba, and north-eastern music.

Latin America has been fecund in tropes of aesthetic innovation: García Márquez's 'magic realism'; Carpentier's 'lo real maravilloso americano' (Latin American Marvellous Real); Rocha's 'aesthetic of hunger'; the Underground's 'aesthetics of garbage'; Paul Leduc's 'salamander' (as opposed to dinosaur) aesthetic; Guilhermo del Toro's 'termite terrorism'; Espinosa's *cine imperfecto* (imperfect cinema); Arturo Lindsay's 'santeria aesthetics'; and Caetano and

Gil's 'tropicalia'. Many of these alternative aesthetics have in common the twin anthropophagic notions of revalorizing what had been seen as negative – even magic realism inverts the traditional condemnation of magic as irrational superstition – and of turning strategic weakness into tactical strength, teasing an aggressive beauty of the very guts of misery. The Brazilian anthropophagic movement called for an art which would devour European techniques in order to better struggle against European domination. And if we substitute dominant and alternative, or mass and popular, for Europe and Brazilian, we begin to glimpse the contemporary relevance of their critique. By appropriating an existing discourse for its own ends, anthropophagy assumes the force of the dominant discourse only to deploy that force, through a kind of artistic jujitsu, against domination, stealing elements of the dominant culture and redeploying them in the interests of oppositional praxis.

In Brazilian art, syncretism has been an absolutely crucial thematic and aesthetic resource. Historically, Brazilian architects and artisans, many of them black, tropicalized the Iberian Baroque church style, for example, by turning grapes into pineapples. The Afro-Muslim architect Manoel Friandes, as Henry Drewal points out, infused the austere Christian exterior of the Church of Lapinha in Salvador with an 'exuberant Islamic presence' through Moorish arches, decorative tiles, and Arabic script (Drewal, 1996, p. 266). Brazilian cinema, in the wake of this perennial tradition, also proliferates in the signs and tokens of syncretism, deploying 'multi-temporal heterogeneity' (Canclini) as a means for achieving a renovated aesthetic. The opening sequence of *Macunaíma*, for example, shows a family whose names are indigenous, whose epidermic traits are African and European and *mestiço*, whose clothes are Portuguese and African, whose hut is *mameluco*, and whose manner of giving birth is indigenous. The tensions between Catholicism and *candomblé*, in *The Given Word*, similarly, are evoked through the manipulation of cultural symbols, setting in motion a cultural battle, for example, between *berimbau* (an African instrument consisting of a long bow, gourd, and string, and played with wooden sticks) and church bell, thus synecdochically encapsulating a larger religious and political struggle. *Tent of Miracles* (1977) counterposes opera and samba to metaphorize the larger conflict between Bahia's white elite and its subjugated *mestiços*, between ruling-class science and Afro-inflected popular culture. Thus Brazilian cinema at its best orchestrates not an innocuous pluralism, but rather a strong cultural counterpoint between in some ways incommensurable yet nevertheless thoroughly co-implicated cultures. The final shot of *Terra em Transe* exemplifies this process brilliantly. As we see the film's protagonist Paulo wielding a rifle in a Che-Guevara-like gesture of Quixotic rebellion, we hear a soundtrack composed of Villa-Lobos, *candomblé* chants, samba, and machine-gun fire. The mix, in this feverish bricolage, is fundamentally unstable; the Villa-Lobos music never really synchronizes with the *candomblé* or the gunfire. We are reminded of Alejo Carpentier's gentle mockery of the innocuous juxtapositions of the European avant-gardists – for example, Lautréamont's 'umbrella and a sewing machine' – which he contrasts with the explosive counterpoints of indigenous, African, and European cultures thrown up daily by Latin American life and art.

Rather than merely reflect pre-existing syncretisms, Brazilian cinema at its best actively syncretizes cultural forces in ways which reflect the subterranean workings of Afro-diasporic energy. Also interesting in aesthetic terms is the link between African religions and magic realism, a link prefigured in Carpentier's earlier vodun-inspired notion of 'lo real maravilloso'. In their attempts to forge a liberatory film language, both African and Brazilian artists have drawn on popular religion and ritual magic, elements less pre-modern (a term that embeds modernity as telos) than para-modern. The question of cinematic magic illustrates the pitfalls of imposing a linear narrative of cultural progress in the manner of development theory, which sees people in traditional societies as mired in an inert pre-literate past, incapable of change and agency. Within a palimpsestic aesthetic, the artistic reinvoicing of tradition can serve purposes of collective agency in the present. In *A Deusa Negra* (The Black Goddess) and *Macunaíma*, as in many African films such as *Yeelen* (1987), *Jitt* (1992), and *Kasarmu Ce* (This Land is Ours, 1991), magical practices become an aesthetic resource, a means for breaking away from the linear, cause-and-effect conventions of Aristotelian narrative poetics, a way of defying the 'gravity', in both senses of that word, of chronological time and literal space. The values of African religious culture inform films like *A Força de Xangô* and *Amuleto de Ogum*. A film such as *A Deusa Negra* synthesizes the modern and the traditional through an Afro-magical *egungun* aesthetic, i.e., an aesthetic that invokes the spirits of the ancestors as embodiments of personal and collective history, in a transgenerational approach that mingles past (slavery, the *quilombos*) and the present.[4]

All of the world's cultures have washed up on the shores of Brazil. What triggers optimism even in this crisis-ridden period for Brazilian cinema is Brazil's constitutive multiculturalism, its chameleonic *disponibilité*, its permeability to Africa, Europe, and indigenous America. As a country both 'occupying' and 'occupied', as Paulo Emilio Salles Gomes once put it, no culture, ultimately, is completely alien to Brazil, whence its ability to play on a wide spectrum of cultural repertoires. Brazilian art reflects an ability to move between linguistic/cultural worlds, to negotiate multiple identities in a manner reminiscent of the playful dance of identities in carnival and *candomblé*. Although the country's class structures are ossified and sclerotic, its cultural structures, thankfully, are open and porous.

Despite substantial obstacles, Brazilian cinema has accomplished an enormous amount. It has given some voice to people of color and provided glimpses of Brazilian history from a multicultural perspective. Nonetheless, Brazilian cinema has not yet managed to achieve the proud and open-ended synthesis typical of Brazilian popular music. Indeed, it has yet to become truly and consistently, as opposed to superficially and sporadically, polyphonic, not only in cinematic terms (the contrapuntal call-and-response play of track against track and genre against genre), but also in cultural terms of the interplay of socially generated voices. The overall trajectory from the white cinema of the silent period to the undoubtedly multi-colored cinema of today does point, thankfully, to the progressive deployment of more social and cultural voices, even if that process has been less thoroughgoing than one might have hoped. The challenge now is to go beyond the mere inclusion of individual representatives of the diverse groups, to go beyond even a concern with positive and negative images, in order to present diverse community perspectives, to stage, as it were, the polyphonic clashes and harmonies of Brazilian cultural diversity. True cinematic polyphony will emerge, most probably, only with the advent of political equality and cultural reciprocity among the diverse communities. But until the advent of such a utopian moment, cultural and political polyphony can be evoked, at least, through the proleptic procedures of anticipatory texts, texts at once militantly imaginative and resonantly multi-voiced, with their eyes and ears always open to the long-term possibilities of change.

NOTES

1. Seminars and colloquia on Latin American cinema often lapse into ritualistic denunciations of Hollywood. What is lost is the sense that Hollywood is not a monolith, and that the natural allies of Brazilian and Third World film-makers, and in some cases their spiritual children, are the independent critical film-makers in the US and other First World countries, for example, Spike Lee, Julie Dash, John Sayles, Marlon Riggs, Isaac Julien, and so forth.
2. *Afinal*, 23 July 1985, p. 8.
3. Quoted in *Revista USP*, 19 (September/October/November 1993), 148.
4. *Egungun*, as practiced in Brazil, calls up representations of male ancestors. It was founded, interestingly, as a response to the preponderant role of women in *candomblé*. For a documentary presentation of *egungun*, see the Carlos Brasbladt film entitled, simply, *Egungun*.

17

Of silences and exclusions
Nation and culture in nineteenth-century Colombia
Patricia D'Allemand

The aim of this chapter is to explore some of the issues that structure the debates on the Colombian nation and culture that took place during the second half of the nineteenth century, with a view to arousing interest in the effect that these debates may have upon our understanding of the national literary and cultural histories that have since been constructed over the past hundred years. The text around which these reflections are woven, *Historia de la literatura en Nueva Granada* (History of Literature in New Granada) by José María Vergara y Vergara (1867), is conventionally recognised as one of the landmarks of the Colombian literary establishment, while at the same time no-one is in any hurry to actually read it. This typifies a general lack of interest in re-reading nineteenth-century literature, rightly attributed by Monserrat Ordóñez to the urge to erase 'versions of ourselves [in which we would not wish] to recognize ourselves because, at this moment, accepting their validity would mean coming to terms with very ambiguous aspects of our history and our literature' (Ordóñez, 1988, p. 11).

Perhaps we ought to add to this another reason: a particular paradigm for the valuing of literary production. Within this paradigm, now firmly rooted within Colombian criticism, the search for antecedents or pioneer manifestations of signs of modernity is of central interest, while any work perceived either as anachronistic or as somewhat unorthodox is to be treated with condescension, if not excluded altogether. Paradoxically, this yearning for modernity and for being part of the 'universal' movements of culture reproduces the yearning that the nineteenth-century creole elites had for leaving 'childhood' behind and for reaching 'maturity', a maturity that would allow them to take their place within the international community of nations on terms of equality. It is not very difficult to see how one of the consequences of this perspective is the undervaluing of this literary production, seeing it merely as a period of learning in which strenuous efforts were being made to become 'up to date' and a resulting vision of the nineteenth century as a desert from the point of view of literary discursive practices. In fact, this present-day vision of a nineteenth-century desert only mimics the image that the nineteenth-century elites also built in their foundational discourses – of the literary production of the previous (colonial) period as a desert.[1] The present *a priori* disqualification of nineteenth-century literary production, stems, to a certain degree, from the acritical appropriation of universalist paradigms on the part of critics. The multiple effects of this tendency, not exclusive to Colombian criticism, were subject to scrutiny and radical reformulations on the part of an important sector of continental cultural criticism, particularly during the 1970s and 1980s, generating fertile re-readings, especially of Andean and Caribbean literatures.[2] Curiously, however, a large part of Colombian criticism seems to have remained divorced from these debates.[3]

The work of which I invite a re-reading is, as mentioned, none other than Vergara y Vergara's *Historia de la literatura en Nueva Granada*, so to Ordóñez's question, 'who wants to re-read nowadays … the literature of the nineteenth century?' (1988, p. 11), we should probably add, and 'who wants to re-read literary histories?', and even more, 'who today wants to re-read Vergara, this conservative Hispanist, out-and-out Catholic?'

The national literary histories written in Spanish America in the second half of the nineteenth century follow, as Beatriz González Stephan points out, post-independence political nationalisms and, 'in one way or another, consolidate, at an ideological level, the republican foundational projects' (1985, p. 49).[4] Among the ideological functions taken on by these histories, the Venezuelan critic mentions their contribution to the fixing of 'imaginary representations of national political unity' and the legitimation of the existence of the 'Nation' on the basis of its 'History' and its 'Literature' (Letras) (González Stephan, 1993, pp. 16, 43). Vergara clearly conceives of his *Historia* as part of the project of legitimation of the new nation in the international context: his objective is to insert the nation into this context, but a nation with its intellectual profile and its own coherent version of its history; he wants to bring to the attention of other Spanish American countries, but even more so European countries:

> the intellectual reality of these nations [and not only their wars, which to the European mind] resonate as isolated and without foundation, [as the Europeans have no knowledge of] the spirit that moved those who fought from La Plata in the South to the Guayanas in the North. (Vergara, 1974, I, p. 20)[5]

However, the incapacity of republican politicians to achieve peace and to preserve national integrity, constantly undermined by the continuous outburst of wars and revolutions, obstructs and slows down this corrective task which, Vergara writes, had obsessed him for 16 years and which, he seems to suggest, makes all the more pressing the historians' intellectual construction of the nation, since against all these obstacles it is they who must now remedy the failure of the politicians (ibid., I, p. 20; see also p. 22).

Nation and culture in 19th-century Columbia 217

Vergara's *Historia de la literatura en Nueva Granada,* the first of its kind written since independence from Spain, is part of the intellectual production of the second republican generation of the country we know today as Colombia. As has already been mentioned, this *Historia* is part of the collective project of intellectual construction of the nation carried out by the postcolonial creole elites[6] and is specifically conceived as a contribution to the production of a literary tradition that should give meaning to Neo-Granadan letters, serving as an anchor in the search for a definition of a national profile.[7]

Vergara reconstructs the trajectory of Neo-Granadan erudite colonial writing from 1538 to 1820, in a book which in its original title is presented as *Parte primera: desde la conquista hasta la independencia* (Part I: From Conquest to Independence) leaving the period following independence for a second part which unfortunately he would never publish, as death took him by surprise in 1872. He gives his book a clearly foundational character, stating that, before his work, 'nothing had been written in this vein' (ibid., I, p. 18). With this gesture, Vergara indulges in the adamic myth which, needless to say, is general to the post-independence creole elites and through which, as has already been pointed out, 'the rich, heterogeneous colonial past [was ignored]' (González, 1993, p. 15). In fact, Vergara's statement might lead us to lose sight of the emergence back in the seventeeth century of discursive and classificatory practices (part of different types of systematisation of colonial erudite production) with functions to some extent comparable to those of the nineteenth-century literary histories (González Stephan, 1985, p. 48, 1993, pp. 18–19).

Aware of the fact that his proposal competes with others, Vergara clearly states his belief that all Spanish American literature originated from and grew around the literature of Spain. He puts forward his argument against the grain both of 'the three centuries of supposed ignorance which loom large … in all the patriotic speeches' and of those who like José Antonio de Plaza (1830), state that from the year of the Declaration of Independence, 1810, onwards:

> as if by magic, there stand out from among the foggy-minded rabble, rare geniuses who, in the dark corners of their studies, were raising questions about high politics as well as delving into the mysteries of science and drawing up grandiose projects. (quoted by Vergara, 1974, I, pp. 18–19)

Vergara distances himself somewhat from this foundational myth of the first republican generation, for which 1810 would split into two the history of Spanish American countries, cancelling the past as a time of absolute darkness and building the present as the beginning of an era of heroism and splendour. His objective is to give shape to an intellectual tradition that would have made possible the emergence of the intellectual generation of 1810, which was already disappearing:

> in order for the admirable Generation of 1810 to come into being a great deal of work was necessary beforehand, and indeed much earlier on ... Men such as Caldas do not appear overnight anywhere in the world ('Hombres como Caldas no improvisa la humanidad en ninguna parte del mundo'). (ibid., I, p. 19)

And this generation, for Vergara, is not the beginning of the Republican present, but the culmination of prior traditions. The Republican present, in which, 'our literature, after copying and imitating the English and French, closes in on itself and attempts to find its own shape', is the beginning of a new era that still remains to be defined (ibid., II, p. 203).

The narrative offered by Vergara attempts to make intelligible the processes of independence and the gestation of the bases of nationhood, themselves resulting from a cultural process derived from Hispanic tradition. Neo-Granadan literature is shown as a variant of Spanish literature, rather than as a specifically Neo-Granadan or 'national' literature. With the exception of the novel, in which it would be possible to 'glimpse an original expression, a national school', national literature is really still to come, as in fact nationhood is still to come, since the many '[human] types of the Republic have not as yet been fused into one' nor do the people have a truly national memory which gathers together 'the memories of all the classes of which it is comprised' (ibid., II, pp. 215, 219).

In his prologue to the first edition of Vergara's *Historia*, his contemporary Manuel Ancízar echoes Vergara's claim, stressing the importance of his work as an instrument to render national history comprehensible on the basis of the tracing of the evolution of ideas in Spanish America. As can be appreciated in the following extract, this perception is not very far from Vergara's:

> In my research, when I went up the stream of the three centuries which constitute our history, I viewed the landscape in reverse, without perspective and without explanation. Those research materials that I found along the way were milestones for me since they helped me to recognize that this – and no other – was the correct path. But once the materials were organized methodically and I had come back downstream from 1538 to 1820, I found everything could be explained; I viewed the landscape the right way. (ibid., I, pp. 23–4)

What for both Ancízar and Vergara consists simply in making visible something that was always there and would naturally lead to this conclusion, in reality involves a process of selection, ordering and construction of an intellectual tradition on which to found the nation that was being built by the mid-nineteenth-century generation. As González Stephan justly reminds us in her lucid analysis of colonial literary historiography, every literary history 'is a metadiscourse which constructs an order, which selects, hierarchizes [and evaluates] a previously established set of materials' (1993, p. 17), and this process obviously expresses different conceptions of what is defined as (or is excluded from) national literary heritage. As should be obvious by now, this process of selection and ordering of materials involves both exclusions of others and silencing of links to practices that are part of cultural circuits arising out of matrices other than the Hispanic one.

In constructing this tradition, Vergara is in direct opposition to the project of national literature that conceives of it as articulated to French literature, a project in which it is treated as an 'abandoned literature, an orphan without traditions struggling to break the golden ties which, despite such poor efforts, still keep us attached to Spain'. For Vergara, the only effect of this strategy is to weaken even further the nascent national literature (ibid., I, p. 167). However, taking into account the profound heterogeneity of Spanish American societies, one need not be too shrewd to realise that the colonial indigenous written production is excluded from the literary tradition that Vergara presents to us (and this is quite apart from the fact that we are focusing the discussion exclusively on erudite culture).[8] This exclusion is of course common to the literary histories of the rest of the continent. In fact, we will have to wait more than a hundred years for correctives to this kind of mutilation of the corpus of the Spanish American literatures to begin to appear (see Cornejo Polar, 1982b; Ángel Rama, 1982; Lienhard, 1991). However, to do justice to Vergara, it should be acknowledged that orality, the space *par excellence* of cultural heterogeneity in Latin American societies, is not totally ignored in his study: the last chapter of his book, which in more than one way is not entirely in harmony with the rest of his discourse, is dedicated to the examination of the popular poetry of tri-ethnic origin and to its contributions to the development of national culture. We will return to this point later.

The exclusion of the indigenous written production from the corpus of Latin American national literatures obviously stems from the creoles' perception of indigenous civilisations as a thing of the past, since the process of conquest and colonisation was thought to have sealed their destruction. Once independence was consolidated, the mobilisation of the Indian as an instrument for the justification of the emancipation movement lost its usefulness (Konig, 1994, pp. 234–45). If within the rhetoric of the generation of independence the Indian went from having been a symbol of barbarism to becoming an object of compassion due to the degradation resulting from 300 years of colonial slavery, in the mid-nineteenth century his image is once again associated with barbarism, since he is seen as incapable of contributing to the modernising ('civilising') project. As is well known, the Latin American elites put forward various solutions to this 'problem', from genocide, the Argentinean formula, to the elimination of the Indian through genetic assimilation, a formula favoured by the Colombian creoles. The times when the creole representations of the Indian had conferred upon him some status or had associated him with slogans of resistance or liberty, even if it was just at a rhetorical level, lay well behind. This change of perspective throws some light on Vergara's brief comments, in the second chapter of his *Historia*, on the 'nation which inhabited this vast territory [of New Granada]' and on the literature of those whom he blandly refers to as 'those who used this land before us'. Vergara contrasts the speed of their conquest by a handful of Spaniards with the vastness of the land and 'the thousands of men and hundreds of villages [ruled by the princes of Bogotá and Tunja]'. And even though he condemns the Spaniards for having decimated and degraded the Indians, for having destroyed 'the traces of their past' and for not having preserved any vestige of their literature, he concludes that in any case the latter could not possibly have been anything but 'uncultured' (*inculta*) and 'crude' (*burda*) (Vergara, 1974, I, pp. 37–9).

Even though Vergara vindicates Spanish tradition as the matrix of Spanish American tradition, he nevertheless regrets the poverty of origins of the latter, not only because of the intellectual limitations of the early conquistadors and the sheer shortage of men of letters, but also because the literary languages and tastes of those conquistadors would have been the most 'backward', untouched by the airs of renaissance renewal (ibid., I, pp. 27–36). The remedy for these limitations could only come with the boost to education, which would start to bear fruit in the seventeenth century, culminating in the intellectual richness of the generation of independence (ibid., I, pp. 61, 211). Vergara does not fail to remark on the fact that this remedy is only partial, and he regrets the fact that the project of creating schools for (noble) Indians was never carried out, since that negligence would give rise to what his class perceived as the total degradation and stultification of the Indian and of his loss of knowledge and skills for what Vergara catalogues as 'the mechanical arts' (*artes mecánicas*), in other words, artistic and craft traditions 'without any admixture of European science'. This cultural heritage, Vergara tells us, would have made possible the existence of a 'true nationality' (ibid., I, pp. 59–60).

The reader is left in no doubt that the present-day Indian has been left outside any such project and also recognises that Vergara is to a certain extent aware of the paradox of his own discourse, which in its denial of heterogeneity through his exclusive emphasis upon the Hispanic tradition, in fact excludes the possibility of a 'true nationality'. Attempting to resolve this paradox, the second republican generation will appeal to the mobilisation of the *mestizo* as the basis of its project of nationhood, as will be seen later.[9] But before moving on to this point, let us look at Vergara's complaint regarding the degradation of the Indian and what he believes to be the entire loss of his cultural memory, leaving recollections of neither their language nor their ancestors; Vergara concludes that, as a result, it is the task of the creole intellectuals to speak both for them and their history (ibid., I, pp. 128, 133). This *topos* is in fact common among his contemporaries. It can be clearly seen, for example, in the reflections of Manuel Ancízar on the Neo-Granadan population, which would first be published in periodical publications and then collected in the book

Peregrinación de Alpha (1853).[10] Here Ancízar offers an account of the exploration of the provinces of the north and north-east of the country, carried out between 1850 and 1851 by the Comisión Corográfica team, of which he is part.[11] The theme of the loss of cultural memory of the Indian is present in his description of the looting of the cities of Iraca and Tunja, where Ancízar deplores the conqueror's violence which leads to the destruction of the 'memories and traditions' of the Chibchas; he states that even though there are still 'pure Indians in Sogamoso ... it is useless to ask them anything about the Conquest [since] slavery has degraded them to such an extent that they have no memory of themselves' (Ancízar, 1984, II, pp. 27–8).[12] In fact, to the silencing of both indigenous voice and memory by the violent physical destruction inflicted by the Conquest is added the silencing of the same voice and memory by the violence of this creole rhetoric which assigns to creole discourse both the role of privileged interpreter and spokesman for the indigenous past, and the task of 'rescuing' that past. In Ancízar's text, this 'rescue' is often carried out on the basis of the signs of the past inscribed in the landscape; however, these signs can only be deciphered with the aid of the memory of the conquistador, in most cases by resorting to his chronicles, but also through documents such as Encomienda deeds, documents that in fact sealed the Conquest, as is evident in Ancízar's account of the Comisión's visit to the Salto de Olalla and to the Fúquene lake (Ancízar, 1984, I, p. 43).

This self-assigned task of ventriloquism is obviously part of the nation-building efforts of the mid-nineteenth-century republican elites, who embarked upon a project of modernisation to which, as has been mentioned earlier, the Indian constitutes an obstacle that has to be eliminated through genetic assimilation. As Frank Safford points out in his essay on the policies of integration of the Indian in Colombia between 1750 and 1870, the idea that by encouraging miscegenation it would be possible to change the racial profile of the nation's population and that it would also be possible to expect its transformation 'into something similar to a European phenotype', could already be found within Hispano-creole thought by the end of the eighteenth century (Safford, 1991, p. 2). As is clear in Pedro Fermín de Vargas's discourse, for example, the aspiration to whitening was directly associated with projects of economic development to which the Indian – because of his 'stupidity' – would not be able to contribute; in order to be able to rely upon a population able to make such a contribution, Fermín de Vargas recommends the extinction of the Indian, through his hispanisation by means of miscegenation with whites (Safford, 1991, pp. 7–8). No great effort is needed in order to establish parallels between Fermín de Vargas's recommendations and the analysis of the second republican generation, with its aspirations to the modernisation of society following the European and North American model and its concern with the main obstacle in the path of its project, the supposed ethnic 'deficit' of the population, a deficit which they believed could be overcome through the incentive to *mestizaje*. An eloquent example of the ideologeme of mid-century creole thought which processes *mestizaje* and whitening as underpinning both the project of modernisation and the construction of nationhood can be found in Ancízar's enthusiastic description of Guateque, where he seems to see signs of whitening that allow him to foresee the achievement of the yearned-for national prosperity:

> In this region, as in many others, the Indian race is a distinct minority, such that it is amazing how quickly it has been crossed and absorbed by the European race, since barely half a century ago the Tunja province possessed a compact mass of Indians with only very few Spanish families. Today the progressive improvement of the castes is evident in the new generation: the children are white, with fair hair, and they have delicate, intelligent features, and better formed bodies than their elders. If as the new generation grows up there were in existence an efficient municipal administration, along with well-run primary schools, there is no doubt that the population of these provinces would offer a firm basis for national stability and culture, and become the centre of the arts and the touchstone for our future moral and industrial prosperity. (Ancízar, 1984, II, p. 105)

This extract emphasises the exclusion of the Indian from the notion of national culture which we had already noted in Vergara's discourse. Although it is probably abundantly clear by now, let us insist that the project of nationhood building upon which Vergara's generation is embarked, is conceived of on the basis of the elimination of the memory and the voice of the other and on the aspiration to a homogeneous national subject, that ideal *mestizo*, the whitened *mestizo* which is still in process of gestation, but which will constitute the agent of the desired prosperity. We should not forget that another notable characteristic of this discourse lies in its continual reference to the future rather than the present: both whitening and prosperity are goals which are aspired to, as is illustrated in Ancízar's statement as part of his evaluation of the process of *mestizaje* in the Vélez province:

> when the absorption of the Indian race by the European has fully taken place ... there will be a homogeneous, vigorous and well-constituted population, capable of producing the greatest benefit to the 'sources of wealth' and the industries of the province. (ibid., I, p. 120)

It is almost redundant to say that this faith in the capacity of absorption of the coloured races by the white race (which is anyway common to Ancízar's generation), is part of an ideological construct within which the superiority of the white race over the coloured races appears as unquestioned: in fact, the possibility of a reverse process is never even considered by creole intellectuals. The *mestizo* mobilised by the said intellectuals rests upon a racist frame of thought within which the *mestizo*, in his continual process of yearning for whitening, is destined to dilute his deficiencies thanks to the acquisition of the supposed superior intellectual, cultural and, of course, physical characteristics of the white.

But let us return now to Vergara's comment on the poverty of the origins and on the slow 'evolution' of Spanish American letters: evidently, one effect of his view is to give the appearance of an even more monumental task for his own generation. At the same time it provides Vergara and his contemporaries with an alibi for the precariousness of Spanish American literature, apparently destined to this condition as a result of a lack of stimulation, given the material and cultural restrictions of the colonial world, a circumstance which leaves it with no option but to imitate the scarce and minor models arrived from Spain (Vergara, 1974, I. pp. 85–114). And the magnitude of the cultural task, it can be deduced from Vergara's evaluation, has been greatly amplified by the destruction of a major part of the generation of independence at the hands of the blind violence of the Spanish 'pacifiers': 'all the sap of previous generations, since 1538, had come together in order to produce these men, who were destined to be the delight of their country, but they became fodder for the executioner' (ibid., II, p. 36).

Vergara dedicates over a third of his book to the generation of 1810, that 'prodigious generation of wise men' (ibid., II, p. 64). However, against the grain of the majority of his contemporaries, this attention does not take the form of an epic account of their emancipatory exploits, but rather a meticulous examination of their scientific work and intellectual productivity and a lament for the waste of so much talent, owing to the 'stormy genius of freedom ... because all of them [Mutis's disciples] put on the warrior's helmet and some marched to the cares and turbulence of politics while others faced the dangers of battle' (ibid., II, p. 123). More than a glorification of sacrifice, what emerges is bitterness against war and the death and destruction it brought about, as well as a great nostalgia for the peace lost, as exemplified in his reference to the destiny of the members of the literary circles of Santa Fé:

> all those men who were extraordinarily endowed for peace and the world of letters, all of them, through the bitter twist of destiny, will one day file past, not crowned with laurels or dressed in white, but instead as ghosts dragging bloody shrouds along after them and revealing the deep wounds which fatal bullets traced on their chests, or shouting out for the earth of their beloved country, that they might die in it. (ibid., I., p. 36)

Later on, Vergara seems to suggest that if succeeding republican generations are indebted to the generation of independence for their sacrifice, the debt is really to their 'scientific and commercial enterprises', aborted by the stupidity and political and economic blindness of the Spanish regime; according to Vergara, it was this same stupidity and blindness that were the true cause of the revolution of 1810. Furthermore it would have been the brutality and stupidity of General Morillo that really led to the establishment of the Republic (ibid., I, pp. 146–7).

It is this vision within the discourse of Vergara that has undoubtedly earned him least friends: his resentment against the revolution of 1810 and his colonial nostalgia. In Vergara's text there is a longing for an alternative history in which somehow it would have been possible to continue to form part of the Spanish nation: after all, Vergara catalogues the war of independence as a war of Spaniards against Spaniards (ibid., I, pp. 173–4). To be more precise, his bitterness against the revolution of 1810 should be defined as the bitterness caused by the devastating ravages that the war of independence brought to 'the most glorious era' of Neo-Granadan letters. It would equally have to be said that his desire for an alternative history in which the divorce from Spain could have been avoided, is intimately linked to his idealisation of the colonial period as an arcadia of 'silence and ... peace' (ibid., II, p. 66); but at the same time that arcadia is derived from Vergara's dissatisfaction with more than one aspect of his present: on the one hand, in some way, the arcadia constitutes for him a refuge from the instability, disorder and civil wars that surround him. On the other, it constitutes a discursive strategy that allows him to solve at an ideological level the ethnic and social conflicts around him. It is obvious that the refuge of silence and peace imagined by Vergara could in any case have constituted a refuge only to those of his class; with his arcadia Vergara in fact attempts to gloss over three centuries of violence, exploitation and inequality under the Hispano-creole order, three centuries of ethnic and social conflict very far from having yet been resolved.

Vergara imagines a seventeenth century where once the Conquest was consolidated and the Neo-Granadan territory 'pacified', everything would promise only peace, prosperity and harmony between the worlds of the conqueror and the conquered. In his description, the violence of the Conquest, which actually includes mention of the extermination of those who resisted, would be confined to the first hundred years after the foundation of Santa Fé. However, he tells us that by then

> the dreams of El Dorado and the appetite for new conquests have calmed down, bringing peace to a nascent society ... With the tranquillity and firmness that the civil government is taking on coupled with the harmony already well established by the ecclesiastical authorities, the peace enjoyed by the people of New Granada is now assured. (ibid., I, pp. 66–7)

We can hardly miss the relationship between this construction of the past and Vergara's frustration with the confrontations between the liberal State and the Church in his society. Nor can we easily miss the contrast between the bucolic scene quoted below and the inequalities and fractures inherited from colonial society, still existing in Republican society:

> All the domestic animals of Europe graze in our pastures, and they are more beautiful and more robust than those in Andalusia; and the ducks from our lakes, now domesticated, are companion in the yards to the fowl brought here from Spain. European seeds burst into flower in the midst of Chibcha maize, and on the valley meadows the stately plaintain offers its golden fruit

> to a race to which it was unknown. The daughter of the cacique eats the white bread of doña Elvira Gutiérrez, the first person to knead flour in this land; and the Castillian lady, newly arrived with her husband to the Viceroyalty, has found our maize to be a worthy rival of her wheat. (ibid., I, p. 67)

In this scene there are no inequalities. There is no conflict either between the worlds of the conqueror and the conquered: on the contrary, the relationship between the two is complementary, the exchange productive and the co-existence harmonic and happy. Here there is no place for scars nor for traces of the acts of violence that Vergara refers to at the start of his account. In some ways, the miscegenating formula already discussed, conceived of by the creole elites as a pillar for the modern and prosperous nation on whose construction they are embarked, resonates in this image of idyllic co-existence, even if placed in a lost past. Through his agrarian metaphor for *mestizaje*, Vergara 'resolves' the contradictions of his society at an ideological level, bringing to mind the images of (demagogic) harmony proposed by the ideology of *mestizaje* within the Latin American cultural discourse.

Inequalities and fractures run through both the discussion on the silencing of the voice of the Indian and his exclusion from the sphere of nationhood and from the corpus of Colombian and, in fact, Latin American literature. They are also present in the elitist perspective that dominates not only Vergara's book, but in general, Latin American national literary histories. And, finally, they are clearly evident in the structure of Vergara's *Historia*, where the inclusion of a last chapter on popular poetry functions as a kind of appendix to a discourse which so far had been dedicated 'solely to the discussion of the development of the literature of the cultured échelons of society'. This erudite class, let us not forget, means of European origin. But Vergara feels obliged to '[reserve] some space in the last section for an examination of our lamentably poor popular poetry', which, however, 'is not devoid of interesting phases and which shows evidence of intellectual qualities among the lower social classes of New Granada' (ibid., II, p. 205). We should remember that for Vergara both national literature and nationhood are something still to be built, and that for '[all] types of people in the Republic' to melt into one, and for a truly national memory to emerge, one or two hundred years would have to go by (ibid., I, pp. 215, 219). In spite of his effort to lay the foundations of a national literature on the basis of a Hispanic colonial writing tradition, and in spite of all the erasures that this effort implies, there is nevertheless an ambivalent and tacit acknowledgement of the vital role that popular culture (no matter how poor he may consider it) would have to play in the republican construction of the nation. This is a well rehearsed paradox among nineteenth-century Latin American elites, and in no way, exclusive to Vergara: while on the one hand they are committed to the eradication of the heterogeneity of their societies – the realm of popular cultures – from their projects of nationhood, on the other hand, they are forced to acknowledge that without those heterogeneous popular cultures there is in fact no nation. Vergara is actually quite explicit when it comes to acknowledging the heterogeneity of popular culture, when he emphasises not only 'the multiplicity of its origins', but also (and in sharp contrast with his agrarian metaphor) the conflictive and unfinished nature of the mix between whites, blacks and Indians (ibid., I, pp. 205–6).

For Vergara, it is the imperfection of this process of mixing that constitutes the main obstacle to the formation of a unified and homogeneous popular tradition, and this same deficiency would in some way act as the main obstacle for the formation of a national literature. Let us remember that homogeneity is one of the ideals of the liberal nation-building project and that this paradigm is central to Vergara's discourse. The ideology of *mestizaje*, which, as has been suggested, meets the great yearning for homogeneity, also supports Vergara's national literary project (and, for that matter, many other Latin American national literary histories); in spite of its deceitful promises of harmony and equality, it in fact secures the marginalisation and subordination of the expression of popular cultures.

NOTES

1. For a discussion of this effect of nineteenth-century foundational discourses upon colonial literary historiography and for the re-reading and re-evaluation of the latter, see González Stephan (1993).
2. For a discussion of these debates, see D'Allemand (2000).
3. An example, among others, of work ruled to some extent by these paradigms, is David Jiménez's book, *Historia de la crítica literaria en Colombia* (1992); it is mentioned here, because in one of the early sections dedicated to nineteenth-century critical discourses, José María Vergara y Vergara's *Historia de la literatura en Nueva Granada* is reviewed; the discourses of Vergara and his contemporaries are relegated to a 'pre-history' of Colombian criticism.
4. For references specific to New Granada, see Janik (1998, pp. 202–3).
5. The 1974 edition used in this chapter was published in two volumes.
6. Vergara's contribution to this project goes beyond his *Historia*, to his active participation in the development of national literature as an author of *cuadros de costumbres* (vignettes), plays, poetry and novels. He was also the founder and editor of several newspapers, co-founder of *El Mosaico* (The Mosaic) the most notable literary and cultural publication of its time, and co-editor of the *Museo de cuadros de costumbres, variedades y viajes* (The Museum of Vignettes, Varieties and Voyages), one of the most important anthologies of the *costumbrista* genre to date. *Parnaso Colombiano* and *Lira Granadina* are also results of his work as a cultural disseminator.
7. For an analysis of the role of periodical publications in the process of construction of the notion of national literature during the early Republican period, see Janik (1998). It is worthwhile remembering that the notion of literature that supports Vergara's *Historia* differs greatly from the modern notion of literature, since while

Nation and culture in 19th-century Columbia 227

the latter distinguishes poetic genres from other fields of intellectual activity, the former includes, besides the poetic genres, sacred and profane oratory, and the production of historical, philosophical and scientific knowledge.

8   For an interesting compilation of representative indigenous texts, see Lienhard (1992).
9   Even though the marginalisation of the Indian from the construction of nationhood constitutes the focus of this article, the mobilisation of the *mestizo* also implies the exclusion of blacks. In fact, blacks are mentioned by Vergara only in the last chapter of his book, where he tackles popular poetry. The most important study of the erasure of blacks from the space of nationhood in Colombian history is Wade (1993).
10 In this chapter the 1984 edition in two volumes is used.
11 The Comisión Corográfica, as is well known, was constituted by the government of José Hilario López in order to carry out the first systematic geographic study of the country. For the most thorough and fascinating study of the work, history and vicissitudes of the Comisión, see Sánchez (1998). For a discussion of the ethnographic descriptions of the Comisión as constructions of the imaginary of the nation, see Restrepo (1999).
12 This theme is also present in the watercolours that illustrate the descriptions of the territories surveyed by the Comisión Corográfica: as Restrepo points out, indigenous civilisation is represented by its indecipherable written signs, as in *Piedras con jeroglíficos*, which act as mute witnesses of the past (1999, p. 44).

18

Testimonio and its discontents
Francesca Denegri

HISTORY

A *testimonio* is an oral narrative told in the first person by a narrator who is also the real protagonist of the story. As the narrator is by definition illiterate, the narrative is recorded, transcribed and edited by an interlocutor who is normally a university-trained intellectual, or *letrado* (lettered). For many critics, it is a genre which represents the struggle for hegemony between illustrated elites and the subaltern classes (Yúdice, 1991) or more generally, the struggle between Third World postcolonialism and Western postmodernism (Jameson, 1996). Other critiques centre the discussion in the perception of *testimonio* as a discourse principally configured through and for the lettered (Achugar, 1989).

The use of testimonial practices in Latin American literature is as old as the Conquest. Early forms of *testimonio*-based texts appeared in the sixteenth century with the *crónicas*, or non-fictional first-person narratives which typically tell the experience of soldiers and priests who followed the conquistadors in their expeditions to the New World. The role of testimonial witnessing played by native Indians is significant in the representation of the unfamiliar landscape and history which the chronicler endeavoured to convey to the European reader, as illustrated in Bartolomé de las Casas' *Brevísima relación de la destrucción de las Indias*, Bernal Díaz del Castillo's *Historia Verdadera de la Conquista de la Nueva España*, Pedro Cieza de León's *La Crónica del Perú*, Francisco López de Jerez' *Relación* and Fray Bernardino de Sahagún's *Historia de las cosas de la Nueva España*, among others.

This non-fictional tradition was revived throughout the nineteenth century by creole elites whose nationalist, Americanist discourse was developed in forms which included the autobiography, the epistolar and a hybrid form of the essay, as is the case of Domingo Sarmiento's *Facundo* and Euclides da

Cunha's *Os Sertões*. An interesting case that prefigures the way in which the illustrated progressive citizen and the subaltern would participate in the twentieth-century Latin American *testimonio* is that of the Cuban slave Juan Francisco Manzano's *Autobiografía*. Manzano was first encouraged to tell the story of his life as a slave in a Cuban plantation by his protector, the Cuban liberal reformer Domingo Del Monte, who subsequently used Manzano's testimony in order to publicise the cause of abolition abroad. Later, as Manzano became a self-taught writer, he wrote his full life story which, however, was subsequently corrected and edited by a member of Del Monte's group, and then translated into English, ready for inclusion in an anti-slavery dossier to be presented to the General Anti-Slavery Convention held in London in 1840. It is worth noticing how, despite the fact the Manzano was in the latter part of his life functionally literate, his manuscript was still manipulated, altered and interfered with by a series of *letrados* who used it in order to further their own political cause (Molloy, 1991).

With the rise of ethnography and anthropology as academic disciplines in Latin America, the genre was invigorated and its boundaries pushed further to include the urban poor and the Indian campesinos. Ricardo Pozas' *Juan Pérez Jolote: biografía de un tzotzil* (1952) and Oscar Lewis's *Los hijos de Sánchez*, both published in Mexico in the 1950s, were to inspire key *testimonio* writers like Elena Poniatowska, author of *Hasta no verte Jesús mío* (1969) and *La noche de Tlatelolco: testimonios de la historia oral* (1971). With the struggles for national liberation in the 1960s and 1970s in South and Central America *testimonios* were produced in great numbers to record the stories of *guerrilleros*, resistance fighters, organised workers, community leaders and miners in Bolivia, Peru, Nicaragua, Cuba, Chile and Brazil. In this respect, Fidel Castro is considered by some critics to have acted as an inspirational force to *testimonio* compilers when in his speech 'Words to the Intellectuals' (1961) he confronted his largely middle-class audience, suggesting that no one could describe life under slavery better than a slave herself (Sklodowska, 1994). In Cuba, Miguel Barnet's *Biografía de un cimarrón* (1966) and *Canción de Rachel* (1967) claimed to add a literary dimension to the ethnographic documentation provided erstwhile. Barnet's (1973) critique of the genre as a revolutionary alternative to the creole elite literary tradition is considered by some as the definitive 'poetics' of *testimonio* (González Echevarría, 1985). The genre was finally given its institutional legitimation with the inclusion of *testimonio* as a literary genre in its own right in the Casa de las Americas' prestigious literary contest.

In US and European academia, the emergence of *testimonio* in the 1960s provoked great interest. It coalesced with the consolidation of testimonial journalism that US journalists, especially women, had been practising in Central America, in their endeavour to look for 'other ways to tell the story', ways which would give space to those voices which had been historically silenced or altered by official interpretation (Randall, 1991). Viewed as the narrative produced by the Third World subaltern campesino, miner, domestic worker, revolutionary, or urban poor, it would later seem to provide an optimistic answer to Gayatri Spivak's suggestive question 'Can the subaltern speak?' (Spivak, 1988). *Testimonios* produced in the 1970s and 1980s in Latin America or by Latin Americanists and which circulated among metropolitan readers proved that indeed the Third World Other not only could speak but also that s/he could speak as a subaltern, i.e., from within his/her own cultural difference and therefore keeping its unfamiliar, transgressive edge and avoiding the domestication of its alterity.

Unlike the (postmodern) university-trained intellectual/editor, and the *testimonio* reader, this new (postcolonial) Latin American subject had orality and not writing and the printed culture as a primary cultural referent. Moreover, at the heart of testimonial discourse there was a clearly formulated suspicion of the Western unquestioning respect for a humanist education. As Rigoberta Menchú, author of the now classic *Me llamo Rigoberta Menchú y así me nació la conciencia* (1983) points out in her *testimonio*, going to school and reading books are not necessarily an instrument of liberation but one of oppression: 'For the Indian, it is better not to study than to become like ladinos' (1983, p. 205). In this respect, some critics believe that *testimonios* might tell not only why the revolutionary movement of the 1980s failed to crystallise, but also when and how future modes of resistance might begin (Zimmerman, 1991).

ORALITY AND WRITING

The tension between orality and writing is at the heart of an unresolved conflict between native and European cultures which *testimonio* enacts. As the European technology of power which included ships, horses, gunpowder and writing became rooted in colonial America and the representational systems developed by indigenous civilisations were ignored or misinterpreted, the Eurocentric concept of *écriture* became entrenched in the colonial and creole elites (Greenblatt, 1991). In the nineteenth century, as the institution of literature became an instrument of nation-building, the canon developed in close relation to the state (Rama, 1984; Molloy 1991; González Echevarría, 2000). The prestige of the *letrado*, which was based on the Eurocentric overvalorised concept of writing, became part of the ideology of progress as illustrated in the work of statesmen who were also writers, i.e., Sarmiento, Mitre and, later, Gallegos.

The rise of *testimonio* as part of the movements of liberation of the subaltern created great expectations of successful resistance to this oppressive overvalorisation of printed culture which excluded the majority of the population. Books like Domitila Barrios's *Si me permiten hablar*, or *Somos millones: la vida de Doris María* were read as part of a culture of postcolonial resistance to dominant forms of communication. In this sense it was viewed as a kind of resistance literature (Harlow, 1987; Sanjinés, 1996) which offered a new cultural model, horizontal instead of vertical, in terms of the relationship established between writer and speaker which seemed to question the situation of structural inequality between representatives of dominant and subaltern cultures. They were also read as enacting new forms of solidarity between college-educated intellectuals and subaltern communities who were allowed to speak for themselves, and therefore become audible and visible in their own terms (Beverley, 1993a). In this process in which the subaltern made explicit the political agency of his own community, the *letrado* was forced to unlearn the privilege of his/her own class.

One of the many and diverse debates that *testimonio* provoked was around the issue of the politics of representation. It was argued that Boom novels which used the voice of the subaltern did so, to some extent, by deforming it and making it the Other of the culture which the writer represented. In the new genre, this problem seemed to be addressed successfully as it was the subaltern who constructed his own story, in his own terms and with little mediation from the *letrado*. The process of making the subaltern audible, however, is flawed with contradictions which themselves reflect the unbalanced power structure of postcolonial societies. For the two subjects who participate in the process of *testimonio* production, i.e., the interviewer/editor/addressee/researcher and the interviewee/narrator/speaker/witness represent the cultural groups of the dominant and the subaltern respectively. Moreover, the process of production involves two different stages in which interviewee and interviewer participate unequally. In the first stage, the interviewer/editor/writer, having warranted the story's tellability (Bruner, 1991), must facilitate its narration and record it. In the second stage, it is the interviewer who organises this oral material and writes the story, albeit from the perspective of the informant. It is in this second stage where the editor must confront ethical dilemmas regarding the use of the voice of the other in the act of translating the original orality into writing.

In the first stage, the informant subaltern articulates his/her personal testimony within a horizontal, dialogical model of representation in which s/he enters into direct relation with the *letrado* interviewer in conditions of trust and intimacy. The second stage, however, enacts aspects of a politics of representation which might be seen as reflecting a more vertical model. The task of organising the recorded oral material and submitting it to literary conventions alien to those of a conversation or an interview falls largely on the editor, even if s/he allows the informant a degree of control over the production of the text. The editor must, first of all, establish the veracity of the facts told. He must then organise the transcripts according to a criterion of verisimilitude acceptable to a reader whose concept of what is and what is not credible might be entirely different to that of the narrator.

As the original voice is that of a narrator whose language does not always conform to grammatical norms established by the academy, the editor must decide how to use that voice, whether s/he must 'correct' it or not. A number of editors of Latin America *testimonios*, guided by the politics of solidarity mentioned above, opt to 'improve' the incorrect language of the narrator for fear of presenting a caricaturesque image of the informant's language. Despite the good intentions, this practice assumes the editor's own language forms as normative. The prologue to Menchú's testimonio is revealing in this context. The book tells the story of a Maya Quiché woman whose community, trapped between the guerrillas and the military, was murdered by the counter-insurgency campaigns mounted by the Guatemalan army during the presidency of Efraín Ríos Montt. The editor, the Venezuelan anthropologist Elizabeth Burgos Debray, in a move which suggests the kind of impasse foreseeable in the management of that 'other' voice, points out that Menchú's language was corrected to avoid a folkloric image of her informant, and to protect her dignity. The corrections result in a grammatically correct language which, however, it might be argued, risks losing its own rhythms and vitality, and becoming neutralised and whitened in that process.

Other practitioners of testimonial forms opt for not editing out the informant's peculiar grammar, in the belief that productive alliances respect rather than obliterate linguistic differences. Such is the case of José María Arguedas, who relied heavily on Indian and *mestizo testimonios* for his ethnographical and fictional texts. He assumed, in agreement with his informant Joaquín López Antay, that 'we all say it in our own way' ('cada unos tenemos nuestro hablar') (Arguedas, 1975, p. 160). An Indian Quechua's own way of saying it would include, for example, 'encomillados'. These are made up 'quotes' which structure the text and which represent a plurivocal memory, i.e., one which includes the voices of others. The past is in this case represented through the direct, theatrical evocation of voices which entered the subjectivity of the informant at a time previous to that of enunciation, through conversation, pleading, disagreement, interpellation, confrontation, etc. The meaning of the text in these instances emanates from the permanent dialogue between the speaker and other absent and, more often than not, contradictory voices. This is clearly not a discourse which organises sequences and meaning according to a master narrative. To neutralise these theatrical marks would imply devaluating the aesthetic standards of the informant's original culture. Other texts that centre their poetics in the specificity of the subaltern's language are *Hasta no verte Jesús mío* (1969), *Gregorio Condori Mamani* (1977) and *Soy señora* (2000). The assumption is that these textual marks themselves represent five centuries of struggle to speak the language imposed by the colonial institutions. The 'incorrect' indianised Spanish in which the story is originally told, is precisely the fruit of that old struggle, so the argument goes, because language is not just a vehicle for communicating prefabricated thoughts and ideas, but the instrument which gives its distinct shape to them (Denegri, 2000).

The reading strategies demanded by the first group and those of the second are quite different. The story narrated by a Maya Quiché peasant, that narrated by a Bolivian miner, or that of a Peruvian organiser of housewives committees are aesthetically homogenised and familiarised and thus easily consumed by the reader. If the editor corrects and neutralises the language of the informant in order to nuance its linguistic peculiarities and make it more familiar to its public, it is, logically, because the text is not addressed to a local reader who is competent in the informant's codes, but to a metropolitan reader, who does not know those codes. Following this logic, the interest of the metropolitan reader would be based mainly on the content of the story. The contents would confirm stereotypical notions of the Third World subaltern as Other, and would thus facilitate the appropriation of that Other and its assimilation into understandable, universal (i.e., Western) categories. The fact that *testimonios* like Menchú's or Barnet's circulate in cosmopolitan centres of the Spanish-speaking editorial market (and not, say, in Guatemala or Cuba), would confirm this view. The corollary is that the aesthetic and cultural specificity codified in the informant's language does not provoke the interest of the metropolitan reader precisely because of its unfamiliarity, its alien quality, in other words, because of its alterity.

The competent reader would be, in theory, the local reader, i.e., the Maya, the Quechua, the Aymara reader. However, none of these are readers at all. Moreover, as has been argued above, their survival as a distinct ethnic community depends on their successful resistance to the Spanish language and education system (Sommer, 1996). This alleged partial incompetence of *testimonio* readers, then, takes us back once again to Spivak's question: Can the subaltern speak? One of the common definitions of *testimonio* is that it is a narrative genre which opens up a space to make audible the voice of those who are silenced by the dominant printed culture. However, bearing in mind the above discussion, it becomes imperative to examine the conditions under which the transaction is made, what exactly this voice gains and what it loses, in this process of finding a space in the *letrado* culture.

Finally, and to close the issue around *testimonio*'s politics of representation, there is the question of whether the informant's story represents the experience of the collectivity or that of the subject. If it is a story focused on the development of the inner self, along the lines of the autobiographical narrative, then *testimonio* would be just another form of autobiographical genre. Again the answer depends on which *testimonio* one chooses to study. In the case of Barnet's *testimonio*, for example, the protagonist, Esteban Montejo, is socially isolated from the Cuban people, so it is generally agreed that he cannot be considered to represent a communal experience (González Echevarría, 1985). The same has been argued for Poniatowska's testimonial novel *Hasta no verte Jesús mío*, where Jesusa Palancares (fictional name of Josefina Bórquez) claims to represent no one but herself. The opposite can be argued for Menchú's or Barrios' *testimonios*. As the informants themselves warn that no reader should forget that what has happened to them has happened to the entire community

(Barrios and Viezzer, 1977, p. 15; Menchú, 1983, p. 30), critics argue that part of the contract they establish with their readers involves the confrontation with larger issues of social justice and subaltern communities (Beverley, 1993a). Finally, and in this context, it is also suggested that *testimonio*, unlike other forms of literature including the autobiography, offers 'decentered subjects' (Jameson, 1996), i.e. subjects who do not share the bourgeois' privilege of 'personal identity' or even 'plural subjects' (Sommer, 1996). To emphasise the difference between the two modes of narrative, it is also argued that even in those stories which involve a personal development narrative there is no continuity, but a collective denunciatory tone defined by rupture such as genocide, economic or political migration, persecution, war, imprisonment, etc. (Beverley, 1993a).

TRUTH OR FICTION?

Beyond the difficulties inherent in the transmutation of the word from its original medium to a derivative form, the issues related to the subjectivity of the editor and the form chosen to represent the narrated story must be addressed. In order to organise the recorded material, the editor must aim to capture the 'essence' of the informant and his/her language. This 'essence', however, is nothing more that the editor's personal and limited impression, from their own perspective, of the heart and soul of the narrator.

The informant's language must be systematised, which implies having to opt between eliminating or keeping linguistic structures which appear asymmetrically in the narrative. Which structures are whitened, and which are left intact? In terms of the content of the story, which anecdotes and episodes are maintained and which are obliterated? The decision will be made depending on the aesthetic and ideological criteria which are used in the editing of the recorded material. Generally these criteria are dictated by the cultural referents which arise from the subjectivity of the editor. This is, therefore, not an objective genre, even if it is considered by some as 'documentary literature' or 'authentic narrative' serving as an instrument of truth that can set aright official history (Yúdice, 1991).

The text represents one version of a multiplicity of possible versions. This has given rise to a heated polemics in recent years. A *testimonio* could be used as a judiciary, anthropological, ethnographic, historical or political document. In these cases the text purports to represent an event in order to inform those involved in the judiciary process and to establish the truth. And yet, it is universally agreed that any verbal discourse is a construction where reality is perforce reinvented. For a start, the narrative text has a chronological order, whereas the story told orally arises from memory which contains images in simultaneity, not consecutively, particularly when the events recalled are of a traumatic nature. The logic of memory does away with the linear ordering of time. Likewise, the reality of pleasure or pain which is enacted through memory overflows the rims of language, which is linear and syntactical by definition, and therefore it overflows the boundaries of the literary text. In this game of opposites literary truth, i.e., verisimilitude, imposes itself on the speech act, just as in fiction, literary truth imposes itself on the reality of experience (Denegri, 2000).

Moreover, between the events narrated and the act of narration there are a number of mediations that one must take into account (Degregori, Blondet, and Lynch, 1986). The power of a *testimonio* depends on the art of storytelling, one in which the self is projected in a number of different possible ways. This requires artifice, i.e., an emphasis on *dispositio* over *materia*, as defined by the neo-Aristotelian literary theory of the Renaissance. It is an old and demanding art which asks the narrator to confer upon its material the sense of temporal fluency, even if reality was not experienced as fluent. The narrative also requires the construction of a verisimilar 'I' even if the real 'I' is contradictory, improbable and fragmentary. It is also important to inject the narrative with a precise dose of suspense and surprise. And the catalogue of musts goes on.

Concerns about the text's 'authenticity' and truth have been voiced especially among critics who might not be so sympathetic to the genre and who are more interested in examining the informant's manipulation of the text for personal or political purposes (Stoll, 1998). Other critics with greater solidarity for *testimonios* have also reflected on the informant's strategic interventions and the deliberate textual resistance that s/he might perform, for example in the famous 'secrets' withheld purposely by Menchú in her story. These 'secrets', some suggest, might be 'more literary than real', i.e., they might be read as protests of silence (Sommer, 1996, p. 142), which might explain why, despite the 400 pages of rich information about her community's history, ritual practices, and struggle against oppression, the informant still insists that she is covering up, and that she is not going to give essential information away. 'Not even anthropologists or intellectuals, no matter how many books they have, can find out all our secrets' (Menchú, 1983). These secrets could be read as a strategy for self-authorisation in a scene of potentially humiliating interrogation, or as a rhetorical move to frustrate the interrogator's control (Sommer, 1996).

Authenticity and truth remain a central point of reflection and concern in the genre. Quite apart from strategies for empowerment, there is the question of how to 'speak the truth'. To convey the truth which the informant has glimpsed through vital experience, s/he must first refract it in order to then reconstruct it and submit it to a new form, which is that imposed by the art of narrating, or *dispositio*. What is thus produced will never be the entire truth. Parts of that truth experienced in real life is lost, but in the act of refracting and reconstructing it, a new truth, more intense, clearer and more revealing is discovered. This issue is relevant today, bearing in mind the questioning of the veracity of Menchú's testimonial and hints at her unreliability as a narrator, formulated with respect to several episodes of her story, especially with regards to the torture and death of her brother (Stoll, 1998). As Beverley notes (1993a), granting testimonial narrators the role of witnesses but not the authority to negotiate their own conditions of truth and representativity is but another turn of the colonialist screw. It seems, therefore, that the dichotomy of truth/false or that of transparency/opacity might not be entirely useful to the examination of *testimonios*. What the story allows the reader to glimpse is not the objective truth, but, rather, the subjectivity of the informant.

To complicate things further, it must be pointed out that the 'reality' of the narrated story is mediated at least twice, and therefore twice submitted to the game of contraries. In the first mediation the story is subjected to the subjectivity of the testimonial narrator, and in the second mediation, it is submitted to that of the editor. In this respect this is a dialogical process in which two perspectives, two interferences, two strategies and possibly two agendas, are at play.

POWER AND EMPOWERMENT

It should be noted that it is not a mere coincidence that *testimonio* as a literary genre became visible in the 1960s when the movements of liberation, national as well as women, blacks, gays, and others, picked up momentum. These movements empowered people who had been silenced before, and who henceforth would begin to express their will to take control of their lives and that of their families and communities. As the subaltern reasserted himself/herself publicly, his/her voice became more audible, and, in terms of the Latin American subaltern, despite a lack of formal education, s/he began to vigorously develop their own strategies of effective communication. *Testimonio*, as discussed above, can be used, among other things, as an opportunity for self-authorisation and empowerment.

But it is important to examine how the relations of power between the written word and speech rule in a testimonial narrative. Although the narrator is almost by definition someone who has been empowered by their participation in communal struggles, the testimonial contract implies that s/he must entrust their narrative to a *letrado* interlocutor. It is the latter who ultimately decides what to add and what to eliminate, how to shape the story into sequences and chapters, how to present the informant. The image that the narrator has of himself/herself or their struggle might not coincide with that which the editor has construed of him/her in the act of speech. The versatility of the genre is such that the final text could just as well be a hagiographic representation of the testimonial narrator or a neorealist, picaresque representation, going through all intermediate stages. The final portrait is the result of a juxtaposition of two outlines: that elaborated by the narrator, and that of the interviewer.

Despite the local prestige and social authority that the informant might enjoy, he/she asks the editor to intervene and decide for him/her because he/she accepts the fact that their language is devalued. Evidently the interlocutor's interference can never be neutral, the translation from *oratura* into *escritura* is carried out in a field of unequal forces, where the editor's aesthetic criteria ultimately reigns over his/her informant. This is an imbalance which needs to be examined more closely by future *testimonio* practitioners. It is true that the informant can use textual strategies in order to secure the representation of cultural identity by, for example, calling the attention of the reader to an unknowable subtext, the secrets, or she might dismiss her interlocutor like Jesusa Palancares, but these are all responses to the privilege that the inquisitorial *letrado* has 'to demand the narrative of the other, to extort it from him like a secretless secret' (Derrida, 1976). Some argue that *testimonio* is a true popular form of communication (Sanjinés, 1996) which tends to either erase or make evident the tracks of privilege of the editor who is mediating the narrative. However, empathy and curiosity, the feelings generally associated with the *letrado* mediator, can be seen as just covering over a controlling disposition. Subaltern empowerment in the genre is then, unclear.

TESTIMONIO, THE CANON AND LATINAMERICANISM

As *testimonio* increasingly became an intense source of interest in US and European academia in the 1980s, questions about the specific literary form which it represented were raised. It was generally agreed that it corresponded to the postcolonial processes of cultural disalienation and appropriation, and that, as such, it was an unclassifiable genre and therefore outside the canon. In this context, *testimonio* galvanised those who saw themselves as defenders of the traditional literary canon, and therefore questioned the value of *testimonio* (Dinesh D'Souza, 1991), and conversely, those who celebrated this form of literature because of its anti-canonic, anti-hegemonic qualities. In this respect *testimonio* was regarded as a negation of the literary and as an affirmation of non-literary forms of cultural practice (Beverley, 1993a; Gugelberger, 1996; Zimmerman, 1991).

If it is true that *testimonio* created expectations precisely because of its apparent gesture against literature (Beverley, 1993a), the widespread interest it generated in the 1970s and 1980s resulted in the inevitable canonisation of the genre, especially with regards to some key texts like Menchú's, which have now become classics. When *testimonio* became canonic, some argue, it lost its otherness, its transgressive edge, and henceforth its value within Latinamericanism was questioned. Critiques of *testimonio* as a devalued genre coincided with Menchú's winning of the Nobel Peace Prize in 1992, and her instant accession to celebrity status. With the inclusion of the genre in the Latin Americanist canon, and with the newly acquired star status of Menchú, some suggest that the genre became re-authoratised and re-territorialised, in short, that its institutionalisation as cultural capital became all too visible for comfort (Gugelberger, 1996).

A question which needs to be addressed, however, is why in Latin America the testimonial genre is thriving despite the widely announced demise of the genre by Latinamericanists in the USA. The past tense is commonly used now with reference to *testimonio* as in the following statement by one of *testimonio*'s most distinguished critics:

> The desire called *testimonio* was the desire called Third World literature. With the replacement of the Third World metaphor by the metaphor of postcoloniality, *testimonio* critics could not remain unaffected. When the margin moves to the center and loses its counterhegemonic quality, a different assessment is required. (Gugelberger, 1996, pp. 1–2)

In the present world of globalisation, so the argument goes, *testimonio*, which was born as documentary support for the Latin America armed struggle in the 1970s, has rather lost its relevance. Furthermore, as the new social structures imposed by globalisation within Latin America require new forms of narrative representation and communication, *testimonio* risks becoming a new form of *costumbrismo* (Sanjinés, 1996). *Testimonio* is seen in this context as yet another progressive utopia thwarted by the political and economic neoliberal reforms of the turn of the century. This diagnosis which announces the demise of the genre ('the euphoric moment of the *testimonio* has passed', Gugelberger, 1996, p. 1), however, could be more revealing about a possible crisis in Latinamericanisms, than about the actual health of the genre, which is still thriving in Latin America, despite and perhaps because of the fact that it never made that move into the literary canon.

19

Nicomedes Santa Cruz and the vindication of Afro-Peruvian culture

Martha Ojeda

> Colonialism is not satisfied merely with holding a people in its grip and emptying the native's brain of all form and content. By a kind of perverted logic, it turns to the past of the oppressed people, and distorts, disfigures, and destroys it. (Fanon, 1963, p. 210)

Nicomedes Santa Cruz (1925–92) is one of the most important exponents of the African legacy and its contribution to Peru's cultural hybridity. The aim of this chapter is to show the important role he played in the political process of vindication of the African legacy in Peruvian culture. Before Santa Cruz's work the contribution of Afro-Peruvians had been downplayed, ignored and even negated by thinkers such as José Carlos Mariátegui. By targeting prevalent negative attitudes towards blacks in Peru and their erasure from official discourses about *peruanidad* (Peruvianness), Nicomedes Santa Cruz in effect rescued his African heritage from cultural and political oblivion. Through his journalism and literature he challenged Peruvian intellectuals to re-think and re-define their conception of what it meant to be Peruvian. He also brought to the fore prevalent Peruvian cultural practices such as the procession of *Nuestro Señor de los Milagros* (Our Lord of Miracles) and *la marinera* (Peru's national dance), which are manifestations of the African cultural legacy.

In order to fully understand Santa Cruz's work it is important to provide some context and background information.[1] Although Santa Cruz has been credited specifically with recuperating the *decimista* tradition, his most significant contribution has been the legitimization of Peru's vibrant African cultural legacy.[2] In 1982, he published his seminal work, *La décima en el Perú* (The Decima in Peru), where he brought together the poems of forgotten *decimistas* and traced the history of the *décima* tradition in Peru. Santa Cruz not only compiled and recorded the poems that had been circulating orally but also wrote several hundred new, original *décimas*. In 1959 he published his first collection. In the Introduction to his *Antología: décimas y poemas* (1971), he wrote: '[m]y first ten-line stanza poem dates back to 1949 (I was about 24 years old). When I was a boy my mother would put me to sleep singing *décimas en socabón*. My childhood friends – in my native district of La Victoria – were children or grandsons of *decimistas*' (ibid., p. 11). Santa Cruz continues this artistic tradition in Peru and, by exploiting this poetic form, he recreates the plight of black Peruvians and Indians, condemns racism, and calls for an alliance between the races. Moreover in his *décimas* he undermines traditional stereotypes about blacks, replacing them with positive and complex representations of Afro-Peruvians and their contribution to Peruvian culture.

In the 1960s and 1970s Santa Cruz published four collections of poems, a collection of short stories, and two anthologies: *Décimas* (1960), *Cumanana* (1964), *Canto a mi Perú* (Song to My Peru) (1966a), *Ritmos Negros del Perú* (Black Rhythms of Peru) (1971), *Antología: décimas y poemas* (Anthology: Decimas and Other Poems) (1971, 2nd edn 1973) and *Rimactampu: rimas al Rimac* (Rimactampu: Rhymes to the River Rimac) (1972). He was able to reach mass audiences through his radio and TV programs, *Así canta mi Perú* (This is How Peru Sings), and *Danzas y canciones del Perú* (Songs and Dances of Peru), which were broadcast in the late 1960s and early 1970s. In his widely circulated poems such as 'De ser como soy, me alegro' (I'm glad to be who I am), 'Soy un negro sabrosón' (I'm a tasty black), and 'Cómo has cambiado, pelona' (How you've changed, baldy) he affirmed his negritude and criticized those who rejected their African roots. During these years he also recorded numerous musical albums, one of the most famous being *Cumanana*. Martínez and Jarque made the following observation about Santa Cruz's contribution to the renaissance of Afro-Peruvian music:

> One of the undisputed pillars of the Afro-Peruvian musical resurgence was the poet, composer and musicologist Nicomedes Santa Cruz. In the 1950s, he began compiling and rejuvenating Afro-Peruvian cultural forms; later, as a student and a supporter of the black consciousness movement, he used radio and television as forums for bringing many unknown Afro-Peruvian musicians to the attention of the public. (1995, p. 4)

Although it is true that Santa Cruz composed a remarkable number of poetry collections, his journalistic work cannot be underestimated. He published hundreds of articles about the influence of African culture on Peruvian popular customs, history, philosophy, sports, education, language, culinary art, dance and religion. Some of his most important newspaper articles were: 'Tondero and Marinera' (1958), 'La décima en el Peru' (1961), 'Cumanana' (1964), 'Festejo' (Celebration) (1964), 'El negro en el Perú' (The Black in Peru) (1965), 'El racismo en el Perú' (Racism in Peru) (1967), 'De Senegal a Malambo' (From Senegal to Malambo) (1973) and 'El negro en Iberoamérica' (The Black in Latin

America) (1988). These articles were published in major newspapers and magazines such as *Caretas*, *El Comercio*, and *Expreso* – the latter newspaper is the most widely read among the popular classes. These articles, as well as uncovering the African heritage, were a vehicle for raising awareness of the social situation of blacks in Peru and the Americas. He used his articles as a vehicle to denounce racism and the oppression of marginalized classes and ethnic groups in Latin America. In 'El negro en Iberoamérica' (The Black in Latin America), he wrote about the unrecorded and forgotten history of blacks and their contributions to the Hispanic world. Fortunately, current history books, such as Burkholder and Lyman (1994), now are starting to allude to the important role that blacks have played since their arrival in America alongside the Spanish conquering troops. With respect to the work of Santa Cruz, Romero asserts that 'the process of reconstruction in itself did succeed, but it did not help *at that time* to confirm black identity in Peru' (1994, p. 323; my emphasis). Romero rightly notes that the initiative taken by the poet was the first step towards recuperating the African legacy. This first step has encouraged many to explore the situation of blacks and their culture in Peruvian society. For example, the growing interest in literature, language, culture, the experiences of blacks and their contributions to Peruvian national culture, is evident in recent studies by Fernando Romero (1987, 1988), Carlos Aguirre (1993), José Antonio del Busto Duthurburu (2001) and Martha Ojeda (2003).[3]

MISCONCEPTIONS ABOUT THE CONTRIBUTION OF BLACKS TO PERUVIAN CULTURE

Writers such as José Carlos Mariátegui, Víctor Andrés Belaúnde, José María Arguedas and Antonio Cornejo Polar, among others, have studied, analyzed and theorized about the hybrid and heterogeneous nature of Peruvian culture and literature. However, these critics have often failed to acknowledge the African legacy or to incorporate it into the heterogeneous equation of Peruvian culture. Unfortunately, Mariátegui, despite his commitment to the vindication of the indigenous peoples, is complicit with the racist and exclusionary ideologies of his times. He negates the contribution of blacks to the formulation of a Peruvian national culture:

> The contribution of the black, who came as a slave, almost as merchandise, appears to be even more worthless and negative. The black brought his sensualism, his superstition, and his primitivism. His condition not only did not allow him to help create culture, but the crude, vivid example of this barbarism was more likely to hamper such creation. (1971, p. 280)[4]

It is evident that the contributions of Afro-Peruvians have been systematically distorted or even negated. What is more Belaúnde, in his study on *peruanidad*, completely ignores the African contribution to Peruvian culture. He says that '*la peruanidad* is born of the conjunction of the two races [indigenous and European] that not only juxtaposed but began to merge' (1965, p. 56). This is a clear example of the exclusionary policy and the invisibility to which Afro-Peruvians have been subjected. These are merely a few examples of the kinds of rhetoric and discourses widely spread during the early and middle part of the twentieth century. Hence, under these circumstances, the work of Nicomedes Santa Cruz becomes crucial in redefining the heterogeneous nature of Peruvian culture.

Nicomedes Santa Cruz and other 'afroperuanistas' such as Carlos Aguirre, Fernando Romero, José Luciano, and Edgar Montiel have questioned and challenged these racist assertions. In contrast to Mariátegui's claims, Dobyns and Doughty draw attention to the existence of cultural and racial hybridity in Peru:

> Biological mixing of peoples produced a parallel cultural fusion. The Lima urban area in particular showed the effects of the process. In the post-independence generation, this emergent culture increasingly came to be identified with that which was 'Peruvian'. Creole food, music and popular dances, which owed much to the Blacks and Mulattos, became representative of coastal culture. (1976, p. 176)

Few studies, such as the one mentioned above, recognize the African influence in music and popular dances. In this process of recuperation Santa Cruz demonstrates that Peruvian culture is hybrid due to the convergence and coexistence within it of diverse ethnic groups, so that it is possible to speak of a legitimate hybrid culture in Peru. Cultural manifestations like art, religion, and language show the undeniable influence of the African legacy. The official culture has reappropriated these cultural manifestations, in some cases as symbols of *peruanidad*, without taking into account or acknowledging its African roots. Santa Cruz's journalistic and artistic productions demonstrate that, in fact, the African legacy is an integral part of Peruvian culture.

ART, LITERATURE AND MUSIC

Literature and the fine arts in Peru have had several Afro-Peruvian representatives. During the colonial period, for example, the poet and protomedic Juan Manuel Valdés (1767–1844) was well known, and the painter Francisco Fierro Palas, known as Pancho Fierro, (1809–79) was famous for his representative watercolors of daily life in Lima; the latter is now considered the most important *costumbrista* painter of the nineteenth century. Likewise Peruvian literature has had many writers of African ancestry such as Ricardo Palma (1833–1919) and, in the twentieth century, Enrique López Albújar (1872–1966), as well as poets (apart, of course, from Santa Cruz) such as Manuel Aparicio (1902–71), Higinio Quintana (1881–1944), and Juan

Urcariegi (b. 1928). Also worth mentioning are the novelists Gregorio Martínez (b. 1942), Delia Zamudio (b. 1943), and Lucia Charún-Illescas (b. 1967); the latter's first Afro-Peruvian novel, *Malambo*, was published in 2001. There has clearly been a distinct presence of Afro-Peruvians in the arts since colonial times even if it has been downplayed in official literary histories.

The reconstruction of songs and dances of African roots undertaken by Nicomedes Santa Cruz and his sister, Victoria, encouraged, however slowly, the creation of a conscious sense of Afro-Peruvian identity. Raúl Romero (1994, p. 314) analyzes the implications and the repercussions of their work and attributes the resurrection of Afro-Peruvian music in the late 1950s largely to their efforts. However, he also points out that Santa Cruz was unsuccessful at the ideological level because the Afro-Peruvian population did not consider itself a unique ethnic group, as the indigenous people do (Romero, 1994, p. 325). He also adds that people of African ancestry in the Americas have always sought to integrate themselves into the dominant culture and that this route of integration was thought of as a way of escaping oppression. While Romero's assertion is accurate, it is important to note that Peruvian blacks and other ethnic groups were encouraged to undertake cultural and biological 'whitening'. Cuche emphasizes this point:

> From colonial times [the whites] had insisted on suppressing all the cultural manifestations of Africans. This 'civilizing' repression had created a tremendous cultural vacuum within the black population. Blacks, who wanted to be recognized by whites as persons, had to adopt as much as possible the culture of their masters and to identify themselves with them. (1975, p. 64)

In addition, Romero views Santa Cruz's work as nothing more than a musical renaissance that could not transcend the commercial sphere because Santa Cruz did not share the philosophy of the movement with the young people who participated in the diffusion of Afro-Peruvian music:

> the movement did not address the social and political problems of Peruvian blacks as a whole, and it only focused on the artistic aspect. Peruvian blacks, thus, did not identify themselves deeply with the movement, because their problems went further than these artistic interests. (1994, p. 323)

Romero's observation does not take into account Santa Cruz's poetry which *does* address the social and political problems of the black population and the marginalized social classes in general. Santa Cruz's socio-political commitment is evident in the hundreds of poems that condemned the marginal situation of blacks and other oppressed groups. Furthermore, the leaders of NGOs such as the Francisco Congo Black Movement and ASONEDH (Black Association for the Promotion of Human Rights) credit Santa Cruz for raising self-esteem among his own people and for demanding respect for, and appreciation of, the African cultural legacy.

Cuche's point about the desire for cultural whitening is undeniable. Nonetheless, this critic does not take into account the passive resistance put up by these marginalized groups, a strategy which allowed them to survive in an oppressive atmosphere while maintaining their cultural identity. It is crucial to emphasize this phenomenon of adaptability in an alien milieu because the strength of the so-called marginalized cultures resides, precisely, in its ability to adapt and remain flexible in order to infiltrate and to become a part of the dominant official culture. García Canclini has argued that pre-modern cultures have been able to survive thanks to their flexibility and adaptability (1990, p. 222). The same is true of Afro-Peruvian cultural traditions because, like indigenous cultures, they have undergone a process of adaptation (cultural syncretism) and an ongoing reconstruction within the traditions established by the dominant culture. Gramsci along with a number of cultural theorists have underscored this characteristic of subordinate cultures; marginalized cultures are not simply victims of the dominant one, rather it is in the cultural arena where dominant practices are negotiated and contested (García Canclini, 1990, p. 243; Agger, 1992, p. 9). The risk here is that the official culture appropriates the symbols of the oppressed culture, as is the case with *la marinera* (a dance which then came to represent 'lo peruano') without giving due credit to its African roots. Nicomedes Santa Cruz, in his book *Tondero y marinera,* traced this dance back to its origins in African culture. He also reconstructed other songs and dances such as *panalivio* and *saña* which are artistic expressions that were born in an atmosphere of oppression and slavery.

Panalivio, Santa Cruz tells us, was a type of sad labor song, a kind of 'lament' through which blacks voiced their troubles and pains (1973a, p. 108). According to Santa Cruz, the word *zambé* that is repeated throughout the *panalivio* is the name of a drum used in the ceremony dedicated to the African God, Changó (Romero, 1988, p. 219). For example, in the poem 'Panalivio' from the collection *Canto a mi Peru*, dedicated to Nicolas Guillén, the slave expresses the suffering he experiences as a result of mistreatment by his oppressor:

Bajo el látigo español	Under the Spanish whip
('¡Párate, negro mojino!')	('Stand up, you lazy negro!')
sudando de sol a sol	sweating from dawn to dusk
cantaba mi aliento tibio.	I sing my warm breath song.
Si fumo	If I smoke
paentro me como el humo.	I take the smoke down inside.
Si aguanto	If I put up with it
paentro me trago el llanto.	I swallow my pain up inside.
Si vivo	If I live
paentro busco motivo.	I look for a reason deep down inside.
Si muero	If I die

paentro morirme quiero.	I want to die deep down inside.
Sólo es pajuera que canto	I only sing on the outside
cantando mi pena alivio	singing I relieve my pain
¡m'alivio, mi pena alivio,	I feel relief, I relieve my pain
m'alivio zambé;	I feel relief, *zambé*;
panalivio pa mi pena,	*panalivio* for my pain,
mi pena alivio	I relieve my pain
m'alivio zambé! ...	I feel relief, zambé! ...

(Santa Cruz, 1966a, pp. 147–8)

The poem illustrates clearly the oppressive atmosphere in which slaves lived; every instant of human activity like smoking, crying, living and even dying were limited by their enslaved condition. The repetition of the word 'paentro' (down inside) associated with basic survival conditions such as living and dying emphasizes the restraints placed on the slaves denying them basic human rights. They were only allowed to sing: '[s]ólo es pajuera [para afuera] que canto / cantando mi pena alivio' (I only sing on the outside / singing I relieve my pain). Although it is not recognized as such by the oppressors, the act of singing becomes an act of vindication since it is the only thing the slave can express openly.

The third stanza of 'Panalivio' points quite explicitly to the poet's political and social disenchantment:

Hoy no es España quien manda	Nowadays it's not Spain in charge
pero sufrimos igual:	but we suffer just the same:
Sutil segregacionismo,	subtle segregationism,
sordo racismo;	deaf racism;
discriminación racial.	racial discrimination.
Si estudio	If I study
la clase me da repudio.	The class repels me.
Si como	If I eat
el maitre me escupe el lomo.	The master spits on my back.
Si grito	If I shout
me dicen negro maldito.	They call me an accursed negro.
Si callo	If I keep quiet
me pegan como a caballo.	they beat me like a horse.

(Santa Cruz, 1966a, p. 148)

The dominant image here is that of oppression and abuse which is obvious in the choice of words: 'sufrimos', 'discriminación', 'repudio', 'escupe', and 'pegan' (we suffer; discrimination; repudiate; spit; and hit). This stanza is juxtaposed to the second one where it shows the past injustices endured by the slaves during colonial times. The line, 'Hoy no es España quien manda / pero sufrimos igual' (Nowadays it's not Spain in charge / but we suffer just the same), suggests that, even after the abolition of slavery and independence, the problems of discrimination, racism and segregationism are still alive. The present has not changed their oppressed condition; slavery has only modernized itself. It is surprising that some sociologists have denied that racism exists in Peru. McLean y Estenós, for example, states the following:

> Blacks in Peru nowadays, given the characteristics of their lives, do not constitute nor give rise to any problems. Neither pertaining to minorities, nor discrimination, nor segregation of any type or expression whatsoever. Our country is mercifully free of prejudices and racial hostilities, brought about by barriers of color, and the unavoidable incompatibility between different ethnic groups. ... In Peru our sense of equality and human dignity is not solely limited to men with white skin. (1948, p. 1)

Although this observation was made in 1948, similar attitudes are still prevalent nowadays. Cuche makes this point eloquently: 'that a sociologist, the most senior university professor of sociology in the National University of San Marcos, was able to write such a thing, reveals the blindness of Peruvian society with regard to the problems of blacks' (1975, p. 10). In the light of this remark, the lines 'Sutil segregacionismo / sordo racismo' (subtle segregationism / deaf racism) are particularly important because they allude to racism in contemporary Peruvian society, in effect contesting the myth of racial harmony. In addition, the alliterated 's' accentuates the hidden and silenced manner in which discrimination occurs in contemporary Peruvian society.

Saña is a type of dance-song which was performed by the slaves to mock the incongruous practices of Catholicism. Santa Cruz composes his poem 'Dios perdone a mis abuelos' (May God forgive my ancestors) to describe the genesis of *saña*. He refers to it as a type of 'irreverent song' because it satirized unjust religious practices. However, the lyrics reveal the questioning, revolutionary spirit of the slaves who were well aware of the double standards religious institutions used in order to oppress them. Contrary to popular belief and the ideologies of the dominant class, these African slaves were not humble and submissive people who served their masters with a smile. Slaves resented the fact that the church preached equality to them while they were being refused access to the centers of worship. Thus, the message of *saña* questioned the practices of the church that reinforced stereotypes, dehumanized blacks and sought to reduce them to passive, perpetually immature human beings.

The poem 'Dios perdone a mis abuelos' describes the punishments meted out to those who dared transgress the boundaries established by dominant ecclesiastical powers:

> Tan negro como el hollín
> un negro asomó su cara
> al Templo de Santa Clara
> o al de San Agustín.

> Though as black as soot
> a negro once stuck his foot
> in the Church of Santa Clara
> or was it St Augustine?

La misa y su retintín	The smells and bells
le resultó cosa extraña,	were to him a strange thing.
y la palabra '¡patraña!'	'What nonsense!' he said,
fue la póstuma en su labio:	and soon he was dead.
su muerte pagó el agravio	Before you could say one-two-three
por herejía tamaña.	he paid the price for his heresy.
'Ante Dios somos iguales ...'	'Before God we are all equal ...'
proseguía el señor cura,	droned on the priest
en tanto, la gente oscura	meanwhile the black people
llevó sus restos mortales.	carried off his mortal remains.
Después de los funerales	After the funeral
los esclavos, sin recelos,	the slaves, with no inhibitions,
sopesando sus flagelos	weighing up their whippings
con las frases de la misa,	with the words in the mass,
entre llantos y sonrisas	amid tears and smiles
se burlaron de los cielos ...	they made mockery of heaven ...

(Santa Cruz, 1966b, p. 22)

This *décima* adopts an ironic stance with regard to some Christian practices and underscores the existence of discriminatory practices within the church. In the second stanza, the line 'Ante Dios somos iguales ...' (Before God we are all equal ...) shows the hypocrisy of those priests who condoned the unjust treatment suffered by slaves. The sermon of equality before God repeated by the priest stands in stark contrast to the realities of the everyday inhumane treatment of slaves. This incongruence between the preachings and the practices lead the slaves to ridicule Catholic rites. The last stanza functions as an apology since it vindicates this 'irreverent dance', and concludes on the following note:

De este modo tan austero	In this most austere way
nació en Zaña aquel cantar,	that song was born in Zaña,
satírico renegar	a satirical snub
a la liturgia y al clero.	to liturgy and the clergy.

(Santa Cruz, 1966b, p. 22)

José Mejía Baca has pointed out that *saña*, in which satire and social protest are combined, is a song form originating in Zaña, a city to the north of Lima (Toro, 1995, p. 338), and Santa Cruz's poem echoes this idea. Santa Cruz, once more, rewrites the history of slavery during colonial times, uncovering the origins and cultural context of this ancient practice. As we can see, dances and the songs, besides allowing Peruvian blacks to express their feelings and their frustrations, served as ways of preserving ancestral cultural knowledge and inscribing the invisible history of their people within the exclusionist rhetoric of 'official' Peruvian history.

RELIGION

As suggested above, religious syncretism has functioned since colonial times in Peru as a vehicle of passive resistance allowing slaves to maintain some of their ancient religious practices. For example, every October, the procession of Our Lord of Miracles is celebrated in Peru where thousands of devotees fill the streets of Lima to participate in a very important popular cultural ritual, one which originated in a brotherhood of African slaves in the seventeenth century. Although the vast majority of the devote population is ignorant of this fact, it is now an integral part of popular religiosity in Peru. Dobyns and Doughty point out that

> The largest probably and most popular cult in Peru today, that of Our Lord of Miracles, is a major cultural and spiritual [Afro-Peruvian] legacy of colonial times. Colonial policy precluded Blacks and Indians from even entering the sumptuous parish churches and the Cathedral of Lima. Largely converted to Christianity, many Angolan and other slaves sought to emulate the Spaniards by forming their own sodalities. (1976, p. 110)

At first glance this practice appears to indicate cultural assimilation; however, it can more appropriately be seen as an example of the passive resistance of marginalized groups which, in spite of the repressive environment in which they lived, managed to transform official religious cults, thereby cleverly adapting them to their own needs. This event is worth highlighting because, during colonial times, slaves, although officially Christianized, were forbidden to enter the churches. In essence, Afro-Peruvians became agents of reform with regard to the official religious rituals of Catholicism. With this act, they not only participated in the rituals of the dominant culture but also had an active role in reconstructing and adapting them.

Cofradías (brotherhoods) were organizations that played a very important role as spaces for resistance and liberation. Documents exist which prove that these groups often collected funds to buy the freedom of congregation members (Cuche, 1975, p. 143). César Toro writes:

> The set-up and operation of the brotherhoods, which originally were mechanisms of economic control for the Church as well as the spread of Christianity, became – especially in rural areas – a space of refuge for slaves, a place where they were able to recreate their native idiosyncrasy. That is, beneath the apparent devotion towards Christian symbols, they hid cults and rituals which had African roots. (1995, p. 577)

The ability of these groups to adapt to the norms of the oppressors by an act of passive resistance was remarkable. Slaves astutely inserted their native rituals into those of the official culture, thereby creating an impression of religious assimilation. Cuche explains that, before abolition, the cult to the African Gods was common among Afro-Peruvians and these deities were identified with

Catholic saints. For example, Afro-Peruvians prayed 'indistinctly to Zambi (Bantu God) or Our Lord of Miracles, Yemanga or the Virgin of the Rosary, Omolu or San Benito' (1975, p. 165). This adaptability implies a process of transculturation that allowed Afro-Peruvians to maintain certain elements of their African heritage. Raúl Romero notes that ACEJUNEP (Cultural Association for Peruvian Black Youth) considered cultural resistance of Peruvian blacks as a key practice since this resistance allowed them to disguise their religion, to impregnate music and Creole dances with spirits and African deities, and to influence popular medicinal and culinary practices (1994, p. 321).

Religion is a common theme in Santa Cruz's poetry. In effect, he imitates this same process of religious syncretism when appealing to Yoruba Gods and when chronicling the cult of Our Lord of Miracles. Once again it is clear that his artistic creation is closely linked to the process of cultural legitimization. In the poem 'A la hermandad de cargadores' (To the brotherhood of bearers), for example, by recording the history of the origins of the cult of *Nuestro Señor de los Milagros*, Santa Cruz seeks to highlight the contribution of Afro-Peruvians to popular religious rituals:

> Un moreno pintó a Cristo,
> Cristo quiere lo moreno
> y a los pies del Nazareno
> moreno malo no he visto.
> En hombros va Jesucristo
> el Señor de los Temblores;
> son morenos pecadores
> que portan las angarillas
> conformando por cuadrillas
> la Hermandad de Cargadores.

> A blackamoor painted Christ,
> Christ loves the blackamoor
> and at the feet of the Nazarene
> I've never seen an evil blackamoor.
> Jesus Christ, Lord of the Earthquakes
> is carried along on the shoulders
> of blackamoor sinners
> carrying the platform
> making up the company
> of the Brotherhood of Bearers.
>
> (Santa Cruz, 1971, p. 174)

The repetition of the noun 'moreno' (blackamoor) four times underscores the close association of blacks with this religious ritual. In fact, to this day, the brotherhood of bearers is comprised mostly of blacks; today it is still the 'morenos ... / que portan las angarillas' (blackamoors / carrying the platform).

The cult of San Martín de Porres (1579–1640) is another example of Afro-Peruvian contribution to religious rituals. Being a mulatto, San Martín could only be considered a friar in spite of his obvious service to the poor and, more importantly, the well-documented miracles he performed that would have merited canonization had he not been a mulatto. The poem 'Santo de mi devoción' (Saint of my Devotion) vindicates San Martín and condemns the ecclesiastical bureaucracy for discriminating against him; indeed, it took over 400 years for San Martin to be canonized.[5] Santa Cruz wrote this poem in 1959, namely, three years before the saint's canonization; and the use of 'santo' in the title is significant since it is, in effect, an *avant la lettre* vindication of the cult of San Martín. The introductory stanzas summarize one of the miracles most commonly attributed to this saint, that is, his ability to feed a cat, a dog and a mouse from a single plate:

> Santo de mi devoción,   Saint of my devotion,
> a tu divino mandato   following your divine command
> perro, pericote y gato   a dog, cat and mouse did not
> no hicieron segregación.   practice segregation.

To Santa Cruz, this act becomes symbolic of the racial harmony that he longs for. The first *décima* acts as a profession of faith as well as a hagiography of San Martín:

> Quien desconoce tu historia   Whoever doesn't know your history
> puede no creer en ti,   may not believe in you
> pero yo que la aprehendí   but since I learned it
> glorifico tu memoria.   I glorify your name.
> Fue tu vida expiatoria   Your life was an expiation
> y de total sumisión.   and an expression of submission.
> Por tu conmiseración,   Because of your compassion,
> por tu humanitario exceso   and your deep humanitarian love
> a ti consagro mi rezo,   I consecrate a prayer to you
> *santo de mi devoción.*   The saint of my devotion.
>
> (Santa Cruz, 1966, p. 65)

The poetic I 'glorifies' and 'consecrates' San Martín, giving him the recognition that he failed to obtain from the official clergy:

> ¿Milagros? ... El hizo tantos   Miracles? ... He performed as many
> como peces tiene el mar;   as there are fish in the sea;
> de empezarles a contar   If I began to tell you about them
> no acabarían mis cantos.   My song would never end.
> A su canonización   When he's finally canonized
> Que aguarda el mundo cristiano   which Christians eagerly await
> Sabré que en el Vaticano   I'll know for sure that in the Vatican
> No hicieron segregación.   there was no trace of segregation.
>
> (Santa Cruz, 1966, p. 66)

Santa Cruz, while remaining optimistic about San Martín's eventual canonization, contests the politics established by the Vatican. In this poem, he projects an Afro-Peruvian culture of resistance that reformulates itself continuously in order to survive. Often this process of legitimization takes place within the parameters of popular culture, which the official culture is subsequently forced to accept.

HYBRID CULTURES

The contribution of Afro-Peruvian culture to national cultural hybridity demonstrates how subordinate culture uses the terrain of the popular to contest and to negotiate hegemonic exclusionary practices. According to cultural theorists:

> culture is one of the main sites where this division is established and contested: culture is a terrain on which there takes place a continual struggle over meaning, in which subordinate groups attempt to resist the imposition of meanings which bear the interest of the dominant groups. (Storey, 1996, p. 4)

García Canclini, in his famous study *Culturas híbridas: estrategias para entrar y salir de la modernidad* (1990; English translation 1995), analyzes the dialectic and dynamic relation between modern and pre-modern or indigenous cultures. Paradigms of analyses similar to the ones established by García Canclini can be used to study the process of transformation and hybridization present within the diverse cultures of Peruvian society. The official discourses on national culture incorporate manifold cultural manifestations with the purpose of unifying the nation, but without recognizing the African component. For example, *la marinera*, a dance of African roots, became representative of *peruanidad*. Furthermore, alongside songs of a nationalistic nature that incorporate African rhythms, Peruvian 'criollo' cuisine is an adaptation of many African dishes popularized by black urban and domestic slaves.[6] García Canclini criticizes the process of cultural nationalization from which, he believes, subaltern groups are excluded:

> The liberal oligarchies of the late nineteenth and early twentieth centuries acted as if they constituted states, but they only ordered some areas of society in order to promote a subordinate and inconsistent development; they acted as if they formed national cultures, and they barely constructed elite cultures, leaving out enormous indigenous and peasant populations, who manifest their exclusion in a thousand revolts and in the migration that is bringing 'upheaval' to the cities. Populisms acted as though they were incorporating those excluded sectors, but their distributionist policies in the economy and culture, made without structural changes, were reversed a few years later or were diluted into demagogic clientelisms. (1995, p. 7)

Although Canclini has a valid point, he does not take sufficiently into account those latent cultural manifestations from the so-called subordinate cultures. He also makes an ironic interpretation of the paternalistic ideology of the liberal oligarchies and demonstrates that the official culture refuses to accept cultural hybridization, and their distributionist economic system produces winners and losers (dominant versus subaltern) and, in this way, subordinate cultures. Nicomedes Santa Cruz demolishes the distributionistic logic of the liberal oligarchy; his works obviate the existence of a genuine, although ignored, cultural hybridization. The poet, aware of this process of appropriation, uses his poetry to recover and historicize the contributions of Afro-Peruvians. He calls for the legitimation of the African cultural contributions while criticizing discourses that undermine the contribution of his ethnic group to the formation of a national culture.[7] Most of his artistic and journalistic work shows Santa Cruz's efforts to recover and portray a complex and syncretic national reality. Despite its exclusion from the official discourses of *peruanidad*, the African legacy remains an integral part of Peruvian culture.

NOTES

1. For more background on this author consult Ojeda's *Nicomedes Santa Cruz: Ecos de Africa en Peru* (2003) and the excellent web page created by Pedro Santa Cruz, his son [http://es.geocities.com/nicomedessantacruz/]. This web page also includes the poet's work in Spain during the last ten years of this life. I do not deal with this information here because of the scope of this chapter.
2. A *décima* is a poetic form of ten-line stanzas with abbaaccddc rhyme scheme. The *decimista* is the person who uses this poetic form. Santa Cruz is mainly known as a *decimista* but he also used other poetic forms.
3. I should add that the process of recognition of the Afro-Peruvian presence in Peru, however slowly, is under way. In 2001, at the request of several Afro-Peruvian NGOs and cultural organizations such as ASONEDII (Black Association for Human Rights) and 'Todas las sangres' (All Bloods) they were included by Congress in the 'Commission for indigenous and Afro-Peruvians Affairs'.
4. Santa Cruz, in 1967, published 'Mariátegui y su preconcepto del negro' (Mariátegui and his Preconception about the Black) where he questioned claims that Blacks gave preference to Spanish customs and did not try to form an alliance with Indians. However, current research shows that Blacks and Indians did form communities together and that intermarriage was common during the colonial period. In fact, José Campos, a black sociologist, describes the relationship among these groups as follows: 'the zambo (Indian-black) is the product of love, while the mulatto is a product of violence'.
5. For a detailed information on the politics of canonization, see K. Woodward (1990). For an interesting study on this topic, see Luciano (1993) and R. Romero (1994).
6. For an interesting study on this topic, see J. C. Luciano's article 'Comida afroperuana: resistencia y aporte' and F. Romero's 'Afronegrismos en la cocina peruana,' in *Cultura, identidad y cocina en el Peru* (1993).
7. It is important to point out that, in February 2002, the Instituto Nacional de Cultura finally recognized Nicomedes Santa Cruz as the 'digno representante del patrimonio cultural de la nación' (worthy representative of the cultural patrimony of the [Peruvian] nation).

20
Queering Latin American popular culture
David William Foster

> By publicly articulating our queer positions in and about mass culture, we reveal that capitalist cultural production need not exclusively and inevitably express straightness ... Indeed, the more the queerness in and of mass culture is explored, the more the notion that what is 'mass' or 'popular' is therefore 'straight' will become a highly questionable given in cultural studies – and in culture generally, for that matter. (Doty, 1993, p. 104)

The title of this chapter exploits a clear structural ambiguity in the English language, one in which the right-posed noun phrase can be interpreted to function as either the subject or the object of the left-posed present participle. Thus, the (at least) two interpretations that may be extracted from the phrase are: (1) the process whereby one queers popular culture; and (2) the process whereby popular culture produces a queering effect.

The need to queer popular culture, in the sense of producing a queering of popular culture in a deliberate and agentive sense, is certainly an imperative ideological undertaking, one that accompanies a commitment to the deconstruction of compulsory heterosexuality or heteronormativity.[1] If modern bourgeois society has, as a consequence of what Jonathan Katz has called the 'invention of heterosexuality', worked diligently to impose a notion of social normalcy whereby heteronormativity is the ground zero of human experience – whether in the sense of being always and ever naturally so, or whether in the sense of our wishing to enforce it as historically desirably so – cogent exceptions to the reign of that heteronormativity would want to see every opportunity to deconstruct it, along every possible axis of cultural production. By its very nature, popular culture, because it is majoritarian, egalitarian, democratic, and, quite simply, all-pervasive, offers itself as an important arena for this deconstructive effort.

Indeed, as Alexander Doty has brilliantly shown in *Making Things Perfectly Queer*, such an effort of queering is inevitable in popular culture, first, because popular culture stands as something like a perverse antiphony to the realms of decency enforced by heteronormativity (the rules of the patriarchy work from the top down, and down toward the bottom flatland of popular culture, the reins of the patriarchy are slack, which is why there tends to be, from on high, a disdain for the messiness of popular culture and the recurring belief that it is morally corrupting) and, second, because popular culture, since it is frequently driven by rather transparently crass commercial motives, must always be probing the fringes for new creative opportunities. The very mass nature of popular culture results in a voracious machine of representational opportunity, where anything and everything are potentially permissible to see if mass audiences will 'buy' into it in every sense of the word: the only impediment is the perception that 'the public is not quite ready' for something, which brings with it the implied belief that in time it will be. The point I am making here is that the arena of popular culture lends itself very well to undertaking a queering of the patriarchy – that is, to defying the patriarchy with queer signs – whether it is done out of a sheer need to pursue unrestrainedly new creative impulses or out of a commitment to using the 'indecency' of popular culture to defy patriarchal restrictions.

One thinks immediately of someone like Madonna, who pursues very effectively both options at the same time. The moral ditherings of the guardians of virtue over her efforts demonstrate how popular culture can get away so relatively easily with underscoring the limited attractions of patriarchal soberness (see Robertson, 1996, on Madonna and feminist camp; also Frank and Smith, 1993). Yet, in this understanding of the relationship between patriarchal heteronormativity and popular culture, there is an implied adherence to the idea of the form as a norm that must and can be challenged, with the interesting possibilities of popular culture deriving from the relative success in effecting that challenge. As part of the logic of the binary, what popular culture is doing in this regard would not be particularly interesting if it were not for the fact that the patriarchal norm remains centered as the reference point for the endeavors – as much unconscious and unreflective as deliberate – of the former.

In the second construal of the phrase 'queering popular culture', it is popular culture, rather than its creative agents, that provides the instance of queer effects. The creators of popular culture, rather than organizing a production that is ranged specifically against a bulwark of patriarchal heteronormativity, channel the very nature of lived human experience that makes that heteronormativity such a remarkable (for many, terrifyingly remarkable) invention: lived human experience is, in the terms of that normativity, fundamentally queer, and the need to control that queerness (the Freudian civilization *versus* Eros) and the elaboration of a draconian fear of a queer planet (see Warner, 1993) have the effect of distracting attention from our essential queerness, our essential polymorphous perversity. High bourgeois culture is able – or, at least, for a couple of centuries, has been more or less able – to enforce a heteronormative premium, but the very messiness, the uncontainability, and the excessiveness of popular culture have always been there to constitute an arena where the heteronormative either does not hold sway or only barely does so. The very way in which queer scholarship now is able to read so much of apparently normalizing Hollywood film-making against the grain and to demonstrate, over and over again, how the queer is hardly contained by Hollywood's Main Street fantasies, is an eloquent index of how even what we may tend to think of as the pinafore and candy-stripe normalcy of mainline film-making is also a realm of only tentatively contained queerness (see Richard Dyer, 1990, 1992; Alexander Doty, 2000; Ellis Hanson, 1994; Chris Straayer, 1996). (I understand that I am basically speaking here of popular culture as synonymous with a straightforward commercial culture, a meaning that excludes popular culture in the artisanal or folkloric sense of the word. As theorists like García Canclini have shown, it is no longer very easy to distinguish the two. But even where it is, artisanal and folkloric popular culture is equally on the margins of the bourgeois patriarchy, which is why a lot of it is hidden away in 'secret museums' [such as the Kinsey collection].)

Such an understanding of the possibilities of popular culture is, in many ways, outrageous, both because of the importance conferred on an arena of cultural production that is – at least from the perspective of bourgeois values – considered aesthetically unsatisfactory and frequently morally and politically disdainable. Because of the alarming confirmation of the power of that arena to undermine the pillars of heteronormativity that bourgeois society undertakes so energetically to maintain, the image becomes one of forms of cultural production that are all over the place and lack any principled commitment to maintaining heterosexual decency. Moreover, in the formulation by Doty and others (1993), even when popular culture appears to be enforcing heteronormativity, as in classical Hollywood film-making, the veneer of decency is very thin indeed, and what is often most interesting about these films is the free-wheeling queerness that bursts through, even if it is routinely condemned and punished in the last reel. This is, after all, the essential fascination of the double discourse of *film noir*, where we get to enjoy the titillation of all that raunchiness and nastiness, even if the 'right values' reaffirm themselves in the end. Or do they?, since often the agents of the right values – i.e., bourgeois heteronormality – are often just as nasty and raunchy as those who get punished.

Thus, when one turns to popular culture, one finds, among many other things (i.e., the representation of a wide range of social subjects systematically excluded or marginalized by high bourgeois culture), a display of erotics that can rarely sustain the normalizing gaze of bourgeois heterosexuality. My aim in this chapter is to explore an example of Latin American popular culture to show how this arena of cultural production is particularly important because of the ways in which it furnishes such a counterpoint to bourgeois hegemony and how this cultural production cannot but be anything other than a site for the display of the essential queerness – i.e., the nonheternormativity, the impossibility of the heteronormativity – of lived human experience (see Foster, 2000, for my specific formulations of the queer with reference to Latin America). I will not be maintaining that the producers of this popular culture are queer in some essential way or that they are even conscious of unleashing – or enabling the unleashing of – queer interpretations of lived human experience: indeed, many of them might be quite concerned at such a suggestion, particularly those artists who adhered to leftist positions that have seen in popular culture a radical or revolutionary alternative to bourgeois art and the social ideology it embodies, while at the same time refusing to acknowledge queerness as itself a radical, liberating political position (this is less of a possibility as of this writing than it was in the 1960s and 1970s, when many social revolutionaries who were, nevertheless, firmly homophobic, invested in the ideological potential of popular culture modalities).

Nor will I be maintaining that popular culture is solely or exclusively an arena for opposition to bourgeois heteronormativity, even if it is true that one need not be primarily a sexual dissenter in order to oppose heteronormativity: because of the redundant homologies of social life, when sexual definitions (such as the unimpeachable division of the universe into masculine and feminine) are taken as the ground zero of the social semiotic, any deconstruction of social primes becomes a deconstruction of everything else and thus necessarily refers back to the sexual. But what I will be maintaining – keeping this last statement firmly in mind – is that popular culture meets, in a far different and expanded register (that is, of course, the popular one), elite vanguard culture in constituting an implacable demonstration of the inconveniences of bourgeois values and, with that, of its sustaining compulsory heterosexuality.

THE GRAPHIC ART OF QUINO

I would like to devote the remainder of this chapter to modeling an understanding of the queering of popular culture by focusing on the graphic art of Quino (Salvador Joaquín Lavado; b. 1932).[2] Quino, who left his native Argentina in 1973 at the time of a deeply disturbing cross-fire (literal as well as metaphoric) involving right-wing cultural nationalists who saw his work as subversive (during the period of the neofascist tyranny [1966–73; 1976–83], there was a dense and uncontestable discourse of what was to be considered subversive) and left-wing militants, who saw his work as too 'light', too 'entertaining', and too grounded in 'US/internationalist' artistic codes to constitute a satisfactory and appropriate 'contestatorial' artistic production – i.e., it was insufficiently committed and inadequately dialectical (once again, those who exercised cultural power from the left, if only symbolically, adhered to a tight and uncontestable standard of sociopolitical commitment) (see Hernández, 1975, whose title evokes the by-now classic anticapitalist work on cartoon art by Dorfman and Mattelart). Less from the left (although there were some cases of acts of violence from the left directed against cultural producers who came up short in the area of adequate commitment), there was unquestionably a climate of violence – and, frequently, assassination – of cultural producers at the hands of the right, which usually counted directly (through dictatorial regimes) or indirectly (through the tacit and implicit support of nominally or precarious democratic governments – e.g., the Peronista presidency, 1973–6) on the apparatus of state terrorism to impose their way of viewing things. Quino decamped for Italy, ceased drawing his signature strip *Mafalda* (created in 1963, and published in ten collected volumes between 1966 and 1967; see the memorial volume, Lavador, *Toda Mafalda*), and has devoted himself since to single-panel drawings that are increasingly bleak and biting (he has published a half-dozen volumes of collected single-panel cartoons or one-time cartoon strips since 1973), and his new work is carried by numerous publications throughout the Spanish-speaking world.

It might be difficult at first to associate queer elements with the work of a humorist whose principal fame has been in terms of a production centering on a pre-teen middle-class girl and her paradigmatically *porteño* neighborhood family and friends (see my own work on Mafalda, Foster, 1989b, 1998). As is well known, Mafalda always assumed a very critical stance toward the bourgeois values of her parents and friends, and she criticized unrelentingly an entire spectrum of hypocritical attitudes that are often viewed as paradigmatically Argentine (even when, of course, they intersect with those of other Latin American and world societies, such as the treacly idealization of the maternal figure in the postulation 'Madre hay una sola' [You only have one mother]); these attitudes also included the propositions that Argentina was the most civilized, the most sophisticated, and the most prosperous country of Latin America. Someone once remarked that if Quino had continued to draw *Mafalda* and if he had had her grow up during the course of his strips, she would have become a *desaparecida* (missing person) during the period of the so-called Dirty War against subversion in the late 1970s (by which time she would have been around 20 years old; young people who were deemed disrespectful of established society were a particularly preferred group of those viewed, first, as subversives and subsequently detained, tortured, held in concentration camps, and murdered by the apparatus of state terrorism).

This may be a matter of inconsequential speculation, because left-wing criticism of *Mafalda* centered, precisely, on the degree to which no effective sociopolitical criticism was going on in the strip – certainly nothing approaching the ground-breaking politically focused material in publications such as *Satiricón*, *Humor registrado* and *Superhumor*, to refer to publications that emerged subsequently as unremittingly trenchant commentaries on national life via the vehicle of graphic humor (see Trillo and Saccomanno, 1980, pp. 163–71) or the various strips by Roberto Fontanarrosa (*Boogie, el aceitoso* and *Las aventuras de Inodoro Pereyra, el renegau*) (see my discussion of Fontanarrosa: Foster, 1989a).

Mafalda does engage in a modicum of pithy observations on the institution of patriarchal matrimony and the sacred bourgeois family, but there is no significant critique of their ideological premises, and the scandalous reactions of parents, friends, and neighbors to some of Mafalda's observations are more the corrective horror of the bourgeois (for whom any dissonance is scandalous) than the site of a perception that something incisively subversive or deconstructive has been uttered. For this reason, it is necessary to view the *Mafalda* material as something like a bemused mocking of patriarchal institutions, and from there to see it as foreshadowing the ways in which Quino will, in fact, more subversively and deconstructively address heteronormativity in the one-time graphic production to which he devotes himself exclusively after, in his own words, 'sending Mafalda on vacation' (and there is no sign that she will ever come back again).

Allow me to begin with a survey of some examples of queering in Quino's single-occasion cartoon art. In *Déjenme inventar* (Let me Invent) (1983), a scowling hypermasculine type stands before a full-length mirror with a sledgehammer in his raised hand; in the mirror, there is an attractive and smiling woman, also holding a sledgehammer in the same raised hand. Does the man wish to destroy the feminine he sees inside him? The woman may be as equally real as the man, and the man may be her mirror image, although one would, in this case, be more inclined to believe the woman wishes to counter-attack the male aggressor.

The following cartoon also involves mirror images, and focuses on a grandfather who selects, to wear out on the street, a hat that shows up in the mirror as a woman's; his granddaughter convinces him to wear one that is 'translated' correctly by the mirror. After the grandfather has departed, somewhat befuddled by the experience, the woman looks at herself in the mirror and sees an old man; she walks away wondering if she will, in time, be an old man like her father/like the man in the mirror. This interplay between masculine and feminine speaks to the instability of gender identity and, surely, to how it is/may be less and less important for the elderly individual.

In *Humano se nace* (We are all born human) (1991), a sober man of means is dressed by his valet in an impeccable business suit. As he makes his way through the streets – through a public space which his disdainful look insinuates he wishes he could control – he encounters a sloppily dressed hippie and an extravagantly dressed New Age-type woman. Arriving at his destination, another valet takes his hat, his gloves, and his briefcase, and then we see him entering a courtroom, decked out in the curly-locks wig, starched bib, and flowing robes of a judge. All dress is drag, all dress is the performance of social identity. During the military regimes, men in hippie dress were severely persecuted, since their loose clothes, inappropriate colors, long hair, peacenik jewelry marked them as 'women', traitors to their gender. Equally, women whose clothes, although feminine, were gauged as hippie-like, were homologated with hippie men, and read as insufficiently feminine and perhaps (although it would not be the case with the woman in Quino's cartoon) even masculine; this, too, was viewed as a form of gender betrayal: anything smacking of the blending of the genders, of the confusion of the absolute God-given primes of Adam and Eve, was understood to be subversive. But, of course, the feminine apparel of judges (feminine because of the wig and flowing robes) is the neutralized marker of an establishment institution. This institution – which is masculinist in nature and becomes unisex with the incorporation of women judges – is questioned here for presumably lying outside the realm of gender enforcement based on an imperious coherence of the secondary features of dress.

In another cartoon sequence in *Humano se nace* (all of the strips deal, evidently, with issues of human identity, sexuality being one of them), Adam and Eve, along with the serpent, are thrown out of the Garden of Eden by an infuriated angel, who brandishes the flaming sword of the Law. As they bewail their expulsion – one assumes, for having tasted of the fruit of sexual knowledge – they see another man and a monkey being expelled by the angel in the same fashion. One perceives that their sin has been inter-species sexuality; since inter-species sexual contact is of a higher order of proscription than same-sex sexuality, it is immaterial whether the monkey is male or female.

One single-panel, full-page cartoon in *Humano se nace* is the setting of a gay/punk/rock/countercultural bar. It is difficult to be sure, but one has the sneaking suspicion that the extravagant gender-bending denizens are based in large measure on the children who are the cast of characters of *Mafalda*. Unquestionably, the waiter, who uncaps a bottle with an opener attached to a chain that is attached on the other end to a nose ring, is a dead ringer, twenty-some years later, to the bonehead Manolo of the earlier series, down to the crewcut and the protruding tongue that marks his efforts to concentrate on the task at hand. In any event, this antiestablishment and antiheterosexist environment is far removed from the petit-bourgeois family-oriented world of *Mafalda*.

One of Quino's most wicked cartoons appears in *¡Yo no fui!* (It Wasn't Me!). The automotive garage is easily one of the most masculine spheres of any society, and it remains particularly so in Argentine, where small neighborhood shops are the norm, staffed by men who resolutely enforce an all-male zone in which women are clearly unwelcome. Oscar Viale's and Alberto Alejandro's play from the 1983 season, *Camino negro*, makes this brutally clear, where the garage, complete with a rape scene, becomes a terrifying metaphor for Argentine machismo. One of the features of such *outré* masculinism in such a space is the girlie pin-up as a stand-alone (or better, lie-alone) image, as the vehicle for an advertisement of an automotive product, as a calendar, or as both. In Quino's panel, which carries no dialogue, a middle-class man and a woman are in the garage, where a mechanic of paradigmatic masculine aspect, is working on their car. While the man watches the mechanic work (the male–male circuit of communication, whereby the man is supposed both to understand what the mechanic is doing and to be making sure he is doing it right), the woman's gaze has wandered the walls of the shop. Typically, what the woman would see are pin-ups of curvaceous women, and there are five in full view. But there is a sixth.

The sixth one, which adheres to the language of the girlie pin-up, which includes a naked figure in a provocative pose, with an automotive part that bears suggestive sexual, preferably phallic, symbolism (in this case, a large wrench strategically overlaying the region of the anus), is of the mechanic himself, complete with full moustache, glasses, mechanic's cap, and tight-lipped smile; they are the same features we see as he leans over the couple's engine under the man's gaze. The fact that the man's body contrasts so graphically with those of the female models – not only is he a man, but his body mass is that of a middle-aged man who has eaten as befits his name (the pin-up is an advertisement for Car-Service Ivan Moncucco) – makes the shock of the juxtaposition and the violation of the cultural code of hypermasculinity all that much more hilarious. The disconcerted look on the woman's face is the trace of the bourgeois gaze directed at the queer.

Far less hilarious, but equally focusing on gender bending, is a panel included in ¡Qué mala es la gente! (How Awful People Are!). The boss of an enterprise is saying to a portly middle-aged woman, '–¿Puede pasar un momento, Señorita Dolly? Habría un cierto tema a tratar con usted' (Can you step in[to my office], Miss Dolly? There is a certain matter I need to discuss with you). The certain matter her supervisor wishes to discuss with Miss Dolly is that not only is her dress not in concert with the hyperfeminine dress, hairdo, and accessorizing of the other five female employees one can study in the panel, but that she is dressed in a skirted version of her supervisor's three-piece suit, down to the flower in her buttonhole, a matching tie, identical glasses, and matching shoes; her breasts, her earrings, and her longer hair (but not as long as that of her female companions), which serves her to hold a pencil, are all that distinguish her from him. One could read the panel as to imply that the conflict is that the woman aspires to the man's job, and so she dressed to merge with him: in this sense, sexism is involved, especially since the Argentine workplace still has virtually nothing in the way of safeguards against sexual harassment. But it is also possible to view it in the specialized sexist way of addressing the even less protected homophobia of the workplace. The fact that the woman is unmarried is a significant marker; Argentine popular culture assumes unmarried women to be lesbians (as it does any woman with what can be taken as a 'feminist' agenda), and this is even more the case with a portly middle-aged woman. The fact that she affects masculine dress is, therefore, iconic of her presumed deviant sexuality. This is reinforced by the way that two of her female co-workers are looking very much askance at her as she is being called into the supervisor's office.

I would like to round this discussion off with a detailed analysis of a cartoon taken from Quino's most recent production, a drawing from 2001 (as yet not collected into a published volume) that illustrates very well where he has gone with his social commentary. One of the staples of Quino's cartoon art is the 'well-constituted' bourgeois family, Argentina version: this is not surprising, since for heteronormative societies, the family is what it is all about. Argentina is no different in this regard, although one ought to note that the rather hysterical enshrinement of the family (at least when viewed from the perspective of those who sought to challenge patriarchal hegemony) was high on the list of the neofascist dictatorships that served as the backdrop of Quino's first successes as a cartoonist. Indeed, from a broader perspective than the issue of just how critical of the family and patriarchal society *Mafalda* is, the mere fact of having centered clever and often rather mordant observations around – and therefore, about – the bourgeois family in Argentina was sufficient unto the day to bring censorious scrutiny upon Quino, even though he may not have risen to the level of the subversive as, for example, in the queer fiction of Manuel Puig, the dirty realism of Enrique Medina, or the feminist deconstructions of Griselda Gambaro, Reina Roffé, and Cecilia Absatz, to mention only a few of the cultural producers who suffered concrete persecution (see Foster, 1985). Any version of the family other than sentimentalized evocations necessarily contains a germ of critical analysis, and the forthright critique of the institution of the family, by virtue of its challenge to the heterosexist patriarchy, contains perforce a germ of queer analysis.

In the cartoon at hand, the typical middle-class Argentine family is assembled for dinner. The earrings of the mother, her hairdo, and the wine goblets – even if they are only being used for water – indicate a level above that of the working class; both mother and father manifest the physical traits of the characters found in Quino's cartoons who are most likely to be associated with the mid-level bureaucrat. The typicalness of this family is signalled by the fact that they are eating a basic Argentine meal, *pasta* (here, specifically, spaghetti), which in itself is a subtle sign of the changes in the Argentine middle class: if before they might be eating meat, during the past decade the changes in their status have made *pasta* the main meal preferred for reasons of economic necessity; they are also drinking water rather than wine (and the working-class syphon, used to cut cheap wine, has been replaced by the plastic bottle).

With his wife looking on benevolently, the father asks the son: 'Bien, ¿y cuando llegue a grande qué quisiera ser nuestro hombrecito' (So, then, what would our little man like to be when he grows up?). There are three patriarchal details about this innocuous dinnertime question. First, it is formulated by the father: the father speaks, while the mother listens, and it is the father's right to demand information, even if it is framed as family chit-chat. Second, the information demand has, in addition to implying the right of the father always to know (one family-centered campaign of the military dictators was to exhort families to know where their children were, especially at night), carries the sense of enforcing patriarchal constraints on the life-choice decisions of his children. And, finally, the question is directed to 'nuestro hombrecito': the pride of the patriarchal family is the male child, who is sustainedly viewed in terms of his conversion into an agent of the patriarchy – the *hombrecito* will, with proper guidance, become an *hombre*, and he will, in turn, have his own son to enquire after and guide in a proper (that is, heteronormative) subject formation.

One can well imagine what sort of responses the father might be soliciting, what sort of responses would retain the happy look on his face, the benevolent gaze of the mother, and their continued joy over their son. We should well speculate on what response is appropriate because we, as the reader of the panel, occupy the subject position of the two parents: is our career choice appropriate to the implied ideological position from which they are coming? Certainly, for the Anglo-American reader as well as the Argentine one, any professional option is 'correct', although for Argentina the desire to be President might seem odd, given the pox on many of the occupants of that office throughout Argentine history. And in Argentina, depending on the politics of the family, the desire to be an army officer is a bit dicey, as would also the desire to be a policeman – and even more so in Argentina, given sharper class prejudices. Concomitantly, an expression of career choice – and this is always supposing that what the father is after is career choice, rather than any other social category that might occupy the nominal predicate to answer the *qué* (what) of his question – that would be inappropriate to the presumed 'normal' patriarchal expectations can also be imagined: say, torturer, garbage collector, CIA undercover agent. Yet, what the son provides is, indeed, an inappropriate answer.

The second panel of the cartoon brilliantly exemplifies Quino's artistic genius. First of all, the gaze is reversed: the reader is no longer the direct object of the parents' gaze, as well as the neutral observer of that gaze. The reader becomes the active subject of a gaze directed at both the child (i.e., the perspective shifts 180 degrees) and at the parents, as the reader engages in a calculus of interpretation between these two separate objects. Indeed, the way in which some languages distinguish between a third and fourth person is appropriate here: having been, in a displaced sense, the second person of the parents' gaze in the first panel, the reader becomes the first person of the second panel, and the parents become the third person of this shifted gaze: the third person is the immediate non-second person direct object of the discourse formula. Thus, the son becomes a fourth person (also called the 'obviate'; see Crystal, 1992, p. 240), an individual in the third person position, but further removed (often nonpresent) than the immediate third person (Spanish, but not English, captures this four-person scheme with the distinction in the deictics between *éste, ése, aquél/[aqu]él de más allá*).

The son's response – *gay*, which essentially means only 'male homosexual' in Spanish – is problematic in a number of ways. In the first place, it is 'incorrect' because it is a predicate adjective or nominal (it could be either) referring to something like a lifestyle, but not the career noun being implicitly sought. As a noun, *gay* refers to a social identity that is still intensely pariah in the view of most middle-class Argentines (and Anglo-Americans, of course). As an adjective, it is doubly problematical, because, in addition to having nothing to do with careers, it serves to characterize traits and behaviors that are pariah-like. Some adjectives might properly respond to the patriarchal inquisitiveness – such as 'rich' and/or 'famous', but *gay* is undoubtedly not among them: no one is brought up to be gay. It's not so much that gay parents don't bring their children up either to be gay for whatever homophobic reason one might suppose, but that, precisely a tenet of queerness is that children should, as in everything else, find their own sexuality: straight, gay, whatever. Obviously, straight parents are categorically constrained to do everything possible to ensure that their children grow up to be straight.

The seizure-like look on the father's face is continuous with the realization that he may have failed to comply with the patriarchal imperative to ensure his son's heterosexuality. His seizure is accompanied by the objective correlative of the utter chaos that is imposed in the domestic microcosm – the dinner table – by the son's declaration (most middle-class Argentine households are dominated by the *living-comedor*, the combined living/dining room, the patriarchal center of the household, which is in turn dominated by the television set, which is frequently viewed while eating, and serves as the vehicle of the transmission into the household of a fundamentally patriarchally dominated popular culture, not to mention direct and indirect propaganda during neofascist military regimes). The objective correlative of the chaos of the dinner table involves the mess created by the father's panic-striken gripping and dragging of the tablecloth toward himself and the food that has been spilled in the process, some of which falls to the floor, along with broken crockery. Particularly hilarious is the way in which his plate of spaghetti ends up all over his lap and crotch (are the strands of spaghetti icons of the diminishment of his phallus in the face of his son's declaration?). And of particular note is the spilled salt from the unstopped shaker: in Western culture spilled salt is considered bad luck, something like the curse on a family that has produced a gay child.

The father's shock is complemented by the startled look on the child, who is standing on his chair, gripping its side (just as the father is gripping the tablecloth). The mother is fanning the father with a napkin and, with tears in her eye, reading aloud from the dictionary. She is shown to be upset (the tears) and fulfilling the paradigmatic maternal role of conciliation by attempting to defuse the situation with an alternative reading of *gay*. In the first place, *gay* is a word only recently incorporated into the Spanish language, with varying degrees of success in different dialects. In Argentina it has become widely known, especially in urban settings, because of the ways in which redemocratization following neofascist tyranny has meant a measure of 'tolerance' for personal, including sexual difference (confirmed by Article 11 of the 1996 constitution of the city of Buenos Aires). It has also meant an often uncritical assimilation of what is perceived to be the vanguard of American life, which includes the rights of women and sexual difference. Certainly, it is the younger generation that is more likely to adopt postdictatorship parameters, including an acceptance of – if not an adherence to – queer issues. Of course, the son in the cartoon is far too young to have exercised much of a discriminating choice, and so one is left both to assume how he has acquired the word and exactly what it means. Young children often use words they have heard but of whose meaning they are unsure or ignorant.

The mother's verbal attempts at conciliation play on the way in which children often do not know what words they use mean. Thus she consults an English-Spanish dictionary, and she reads a definition that insists on the primary meanings of *gay* – to wit, the Spanish equivalents of 'happy', 'festive', 'carefree', 'delighted', 'good-humored', 'catchy' (it is doubtful there is a Spanish-English dictionary that contains the word *gay*). Homophobic decrying of the expropriation of 'good, normal' words is very much of a willful ignorance of how the lexicon of a language evolves, and it is in evidence here as the mother wishes to distract attention from the current primary meaning of the word to designate gay male (at least in Spanish), while it is certain that the father knows all too well what that primary meaning of the word is as it has become incorporated into the everyday vocabulary of Argentine (or, better, Buenos Aires) Spanish. And, too, even if the son does not really know the meaning of the word he is using, it is highly unlikely he has heard it used in Spanish in any way other than with the meaning of which the father is emphatically conscious.

Quino's strip queers Argentine bourgeois values in its perception of the way in which the word *gay* means (its very use in a self-attributory fashion is enough of a bombshell), what it means, and what it means to subscribe to it as something to be when one grows up. It queers Argentine bourgeois values in the demonstration of how it cannot yet, despite a public ideology of tolerance, be really assimilated into everyday life: this is demonstrated by the need for the mother to attempt to divert the father's attention toward alternative and nonthreatening meanings. It also queers Argentine bourgeois values in the way in which it constitutes one more example of the system of hypocrisy that controls all aspects of Argentine social life. The major goal of Quino's graphic humor is to demonstrate this truth; in recent years his work has become bleaker and bleaker, more mordant, and, I would insist, therefore more eloquent in the coherence of its critique.

Quino, to the best of my knowledge, never publicly defended any version of queer culture, and he has never aligned himself with any political or social movement; it would be unreasonable to view him as anything of a spokesperson for lesbigay liberation – even if it is reasonable to assume that his manifest commitment to human dignity would include such support, if only implicitly. Additionally, none of his cartoons really addresses anything that is part of the lesbigay agenda in either the West in general or in Argentina specifically.

Yet, what I have done here is to show that this one medium of popular culture, graphic humor, can pursue its analytical critique of social issues via utilization of a queering perspective – that is, a perspective that questions in a principled way the closed system of patriarchal and heteronormative values. In the case of the cartoon that I have analyzed so extensively, Quino might not recognize all of the elements I have identified: the critic necessarily sees beyond what the creator may claim to 'have meant', which is part of the critic's function and part of the critic's contribution to the semiotic process of culture. But the point is that, by seeing a queer perspective in this cartoon, one can see how effective it is in questioning one iconic example of patriarchal attitudes, those relating to career choices, in Argentina.

NOTES

1   By 'heteronormativity' I understand the imperative of straight reproductive sexuality, sustained through the confluence of monogamic fidelity, romantic love, exclusive sentimental investment, and multiply binding matrimony; by 'compulsive' I understand the unquestioned and unquestionable imperative for all members of society (with the exception of a few who are – i.e., prisoners – punished by being excluded from it) to engage in straight reproductive sexuality. For some sectors, it is possible, under unique circumstances to opt out of compulsory heteronormativity (i.e., some religious people, such as Catholic priests and nuns), although for large sectors of society those who opt out through religious orders, through the decision, even if duly married, not to have children, or by refusing to marry are considered pitifully 'abnormal' or even 'queer'. Obviously, in Latin America religiously driven opting out of compulsory heteronormativity for religious means becomes a particularly complex issue. Finally, one understands that the queer, as the counterpoint to compulsory heteronormativity, does not only include sexual matters or matters of sexual desire, but rather an entire range of social dynamics – dress and body appearance, language, ways of being in the world, professions, regionality, ethnic and social class, race – that are homologously correlated with sexuality as the dominant discourse of our society.
2   The best information available on Quino is to be found on his website: www.clubcultura.com/clubhumor/quino/espanol/intro.html

PART 5
Cultural practices

21

Food in Latin America
Mike González

CONTINUITIES

Conflict, conquest, seduction, ethnicity and nationhood, dreams and disillusionments; all these have their place at the dinner tables of Latin America. Eating itself may be an act of conquest or a gesture of tribute and reverence, the meal an affirmation of hierarchy or a kind of abnegation. And food may hide poison, or tears, or the ingredients that stimulate love or induce forgetfulness.

But all histories agree on the beginnings. First, the gods made men of clay – but they fell apart. Then came the men of wood – 'but they had no blood or substance, no memory or purpose'. Then the gods made men and women out of corn 'and they saw as much as the gods'. The legend announces an end to hunger with the first cultivation – somewhere around 5000 BC – of maize, or Indian corn. By whatever route, maize spread south, until it appeared in the Andes some three and a half millennia later, with added black and purple as it married with the local grasses.

Why is maize so significant? Because it lent itself to two to three annual harvests and supplied protein in a highland world without meat. It was as precious to the pre-Columbian civilizations of the Americas as the goats and sheep and cattle of Europe and the Middle East. And today it remains at the heart of Latin American cooking, in its many versatile forms. In Mexico, the slapping sounds that announced the making of the *tortilla* are now replaced by the droning of the machines that transform the maize dough (*nixtamal*) into tortillas sold by the kilo. But it is present in hundreds of other manifestations – rolled around meat or chicken as *tacos*, flattened as *sopes*, fried as *tostadas*, eaten with chile or cream as *elote*, drowning in soup as *chilaquiles*. It may be steamed or baked in banana or maize leaves and emerge as *tamales*. In its peregrinations across the continent, maize became *arepas* in Venezuela, or was liquified into the *chicha* of the Andean highlands.

The other characteristic taste of the Americas has an even longer history – and a presence in global taste as ubiquitous as it is continuous. The *chile* pepper (*Capsicum annuum*) was misnamed by an overenthusiastic Columbus – in fact it is not a pepper at all but a member of the nightshade family (*solanacae*). Columbus's mistake was an indication of the central role played by spices – pepper, cloves and cinnamon among others – in the global trading economy of the late fifteenth century. Spain came late to an international commercial activity already dominated by the Portuguese. The Spanish Crown's sponsorship of Columbus's voyages reflected their desire to find an alternative (and quicker) route to the Indian Ocean and the sources of spice. In this, as in many other things, Columbus distorted the reality he found to please his masters (and ensure their continuing patronage).

There are around one hundred edible varieties of the *chile* pepper (experts disagree on the count), ranging from the simply hot to the unbearably fiery. Cultivated in Mexico from 7000 BC onwards, Columbus brought it back to Europe from where it spread south and east to become a staple of almost every spicy cuisine. The Andean varieties of *ají* ('chilli' was the Náhuatl or Aztec word), the yellow *mirasol* and the bright red *rocoto* did not spread in the same way.

Then as now, *chile* in its extraordinary variety colours the whole map of the food of the Americas. Then as now it colours and nourishes; perhaps it also warms and fills out the limited diet of maize and potatoes on the bitter cold nights of the highlands. And in an unequal twenty-first century, where it is still a key component of the food of the poor, it can, with salt and tortilla, allay the pangs of hunger and embellish poor quality meat. So *chile*, the archetypal mark of Latin American taste, is both exotic and basic, decoration and necessity, a mark of cosmopolitan consumption and a sign of hunger.

On the Bolivian highlands the dried and blackened pieces of *chuño* may not immediately recall the potato, *la papa*, whose presence or absence has drawn the line between plenty and famine. Yet these strange, naturally freeze-dried potatoes do identify the point of origin of the ubiquitous potato. Although with time it has become associated with the stolid diet of the European peasantry, the potato too is another Latin American gift to the world's kitchen. In Latin America its flesh is multicoloured – yellow, purple, black; and its most adventurous uses are in Peru, Bolivia and Ecuador, where potatoes and cheese are merged in the thick *locro* soup.

The sweet potato (*Ipomea batata*) is misnamed – presumably because of its appearance – as a sweet potato. The orange flesh of the tuber is widely eaten – from Brazil to Cuba. So too was manioc or cassava, whose cultivation probably began, like the potato and the sweet potato, sometime during the third pre-Christian millennium. Squash, courgette, pumpkins, avocados were also cultivated first in the Americas.

Almost as ubiquitous today are the beans or *frijoles* (*Phaseolus vulgaris*) which joined the banquet of the Americas some time around 5000 BC. These legumes (black, red, pinto, haricot beans) have had several rebirths or rediscoveries, most recently perhaps in the burgeoning vegetarian cuisine. But, unimaginably, they were absent from European food until Columbus made his transatlantic journeys from 1492 onwards.

ENCOUNTERS

The conquest of the southern Americas that began with the first of those voyages was, as many commentators have discussed, not merely an appropriation of territory. It was also a cultural crusade. It first demonized and then suppressed native religions as barbarisms; it was, of course, a necessary antecedent to the enslavement of indigenous labour – even as the theologians were debating the status of these people in the hierarchy of human evolution. It was, also, a sexual conquest – a transformation and absorption of a whole range of ethnicities. Yet in some respects it was also a symbiosis, a combination of ethnic and cultural histories and practices which could deserve the name of hybridization – were that term not so anchored in contemporary experience. The Spanish *mestizaje* has none of the odious racist connotations of the English 'miscegenation' – though it does define the product of a cultural encounter that was unequal and attended by violence and oppression.

The Indian voice went unheard for centuries; the history of Maya, Aztec and Inca America (not to mention Kogis, Guaranies, Mapuches and a thousand other nations) was buried and denied. And yet it survived the demographic catastrophe, the colonial denial, the oppression in some subtle and unexpected ways. There were cultural sites within the colonial order in which the indigenous presence made itself felt – in the School of Cuzco painters, in the high spires of cathedrals where the artisans left a mark, in the popular oral tradition, and in the culture of the everyday, in dress and music, and in food.

Food was a meeting place of traditions. What had nourished and sustained pre-Columbian America now merged and married with tastes and customs brought from a Spain and a Portugal which had themselves been places of encounter. So garlic and olives were cultivated in the Iberian peninsula by the occupying Romans; and the Moorish occupation brought the delicate and fragrant saffron, citrus and almond flavours that were in turn transported to the Americas. The slave trade carried tens of thousands across the nightmarish Middle Passage to work the sugar plantations of the Caribbean and Brazil. It was the tastes and scents of Africa, then, which were transmuted on the transatlantic soil to produce *cocinha baiana* which merged dende oil, coconut (another American fruit though its origins may arguably lie on the African shore), coriander, shrimp, nuts and farofa – the meal made from manioc. In Minas Gerais, on the other hand, or in Rio, the favoured dishes are stronger, warmer like the *cozidos* (stews).

The point here is that the table is often a place of exchange – though it is also true that the pace of infiltration between the foods of the poor and the table of the colonial elites may well have been uneven over time. Yet adaptation was a matter of survival for every layer of this divided society; the preservative properties of *chile* were presumably significant for a colonial elite not always able to maintain its tastes, its capacity to allay hunger central for an impoverished worker and peasant class for whom then – and now – the basic diet consisted of salt, tortilla and *chile*. Equally we may assume that the plantation slaves did not share the nut-laden stews, the spiced meats, the dairy products (cheese, butter, cream) that adorned the table in the big house.

Yet for all the merging and combination that occurred, class still divided the dinner table. In the grand houses of the cities – of Lima, of Mexico, for example – the locally exotic shared table space with the recognizable fare of Europe. Garlic and nuts sat beside the papaya, the avocado, the maracuyá, the passion fruit; peninsular recipes dressed the *huachinango*, the *jaiba* (crab), the shrimp and the *congrio* (not eel, despite the common Spanish name) of the Chilean coast. The result was fish *a la veracruzana* or the *pescado en escabeche* that originated in Peru. The encounter was most imaginative and dramatic, perhaps, in Brazil, in the *vatapá* of Bahia, which mixes shellfish and nuts, coconut milk and dende oil. The *moquecas* of Bahia were probably originally cooked over charcoal leaves and wrapped in banana leaves by Brazil's indigenous nations, until they were transformed by the tastes and scents of Africa and Portugal by the black plantation cooks.

PARADOXES

But in the shacks and shanties of the poor, or the impoverished and windlashed communities of the high sierra, there was neither such quantity and variety nor much in the way of fusion. For centuries the poor survived on the basic ingredients inherited from pre-Columbian America – maize, chile, salt in the highlands; the fruits of the rain forest; the fish of rivers and coasts.

The colonial classes, by contrast, introduced the European crops that corresponded to their own taste; wheat was grown plentifully and bread vied with the products of maize and cassava. Rice was introduced in the sixteenth century and was soon widely grown. And sugar, brought to Cuba before the end of the fifteenth century, proliferated through the Caribbean and Brazil along with the enslaved black population who hacked down the ripened sugar cane. It sweetened the chocolate that the Aztecs had drunk with maize flour as a bitter beverage; it entered the cuisine of the city and the plantation house; it was rolled with butter and cream into the sweetmeats that graced colonial markets. But it was not, by and large, available in any consistent quantity to the poor. In the same regions where the cane grew, however, the banana was introduced and spread in its many forms (*guineo, plátano, banana*) across Latin America where it was used with extraordinary versatility – fried and crushed and dried and eaten raw.

So while the conquest of Latin America had the catastrophic consequences that are now well rehearsed, there were also unintended consequences. The surviving populations, whether hunter-gatherers, fishing communities or the still isolated communities of mountain or rain forest, survived well in their original habitats. While there is still debate on the matter, it would seem that a continuing diet of beans, maize, unrefined fish and fruit was balanced and nutritious and adequate in protein content. For the indigenous peoples indentured to labour on mines or estates, however, an inadequate diet added to other negative conditions led frequently to hunger and death. So much so, that both Portuguese and Spanish colonial regimes rapidly enacted fair price legislation and other protections to ensure the survival of their labour force. The slave labour population of Cuba and Brazil, on the other hand, suffered in high numbers from the diseases of malnutrition – yaws, pellagra and others. They, after all, had experienced the complete disruption of their foodways, their access to the components of a traditional diet – though these groups incorporated local produce into their diets too.

Over time, however, the picture began to change, as rising numbers of indigenous Latin Americans were pressed into the labour force, as the latifundia expanded and deforestation spread. The gradual replacement of traditional foods by European imports like rice, wheat and the meat of pigs, goats and cattle undermined the traditional diet; by reason of taste and of cost, these foods were disproportionately eaten by the colonial *criollo* and *mestizo* classes – but they did not become the food of the poor. By the nineteenth century, and from then on, hunger stalked the continent.

As calorie intakes rose in the metropolitan countries, the demand for sugar, coffee, bananas and the fruits of the tropics, meat, rice and so on increased as a result. The estates, plantations and latifundia expanded in response to the international market, encroaching on the food-producing lands (*tierras de pan llevar*) and communal properties. In El Salvador, the result was a violent expulsion; the indigenous peasantry found themselves landless as the 'fourteen families' took their lands to cultivate coffee; in Mexico, the sugar estates invaded the peasant communities of Morelos and provoked the first Zapatista movement in 1911. These are just two examples but they typify the processes of economic growth of the time, and their consequences. As more and more rural inhabitants were driven to work on plantations, in the expanding mining industry, or to seek a future in the marginal communities on the edges of cities, their access to nutritious food grew increasingly difficult. By the mid-1930s, malnutrition was affecting 25 per cent of the regional population. The wage-earners of Latin America spent over two-thirds of their income on food, on average, by the late 1930s, compared with one-third in the United States, according to an International Labour Organization Survey of 1939.

This is not to say that some rural communities with access to wild or natural food were not able to maintain a balanced, if limited diet. But the overall picture exposed a widening gap between the urban and rural poor, who experienced hunger and inadequate nutrition, and the middle class and the bourgeoisie of those same cities whose patterns of eating became more varied and whose calorie consumption rose in step with other areas of consumption. In this as in so many other things, the property-owners and their professional advisers mimicked the patterns of eating of Europe and the United States.

That was the paradox of growth and modernity.

THE RAW AND THE COOKED

The pre-Columbian diet was not meatless; but its chosen flesh for consumption did not sit easily with the European palate. The flesh of the llama was dried into strips of *charqui* still eaten in Peru and southern Brazil; the guinea pig (*cuy*) still startles unsuspecting diners (like the present writer). Insects, snakes, lizards were eaten too – iguana can still be bought on the roadside in southern Mexico. But they were not the principal source of protein, as they were for many Europeans – after all, there was maize, there were beans, there were the ample fish stocks on Latin America's coastlines, there were the small animals, insects, snakes to be gathered by the hunter-gatherers.

The introduction of cattle, sheep and particularly pigs transformed the food ecology of the continent over time. Meat remained a food of the wealthy, while the alternative sources of protein became scarcer for their arrival. An exception was the southern cone, particularly the wide pampas of Argentina, Uruguay and southern Brazil. Here the cattle and horses abandoned by the first abortive Spanish expeditions to the River Plate in the mid-sixteenth century procreated prolifically in the sparsely populated grasslands and roamed freely under the guidance and control of the *gauchos*. This peripatetic group ate meat roasted over open fires; there was little to attend the *asado* in the way of vegetables and fruits. But the meat was plentiful at least; and there was income to be gained from the hides and *charqui* that remained.

By the end of the nineteenth century, the enclosure of the pampa and the industrialization of the beef industry had cleared the gaucho from the land as a kind of yeoman class, though the name was easily transferred to the wage-earning cattle men of the new, beef-producing agricultural sector. Buenos Aires grew exponentially as the metropolitan craving for meat and the first refrigerated ships took fresh Argentine meat to Europe and America. As the population was urbanized and the economy grew and modernized, the only remaining vestige of that now lost form of production was cultural. The songs of rural Argentina, the eternal popularity of Jose Hernández's great poem of rural exodus, *Martín Fierro*, the transformation of the gaucho into a symbol of nationhood (in Borges or Güiraldes' writing for example), had their ceremonial reflection in the preparation and consumption of food. The per capita consumption of beef in Argentina – of every part of the animal in rigorous succession – surpassed even that of the United States by the mid-1960s.

But meat-eating was more than mere protein-guzzling. In its manner and rituals of both preparation and eating, meat occupied the space between the kitchen and the open range, between the hunter and the cook. On most Sundays in most of Latin America, men cook; but not in the kitchen. From Mexico to Argentina, Sunday is the day of the *asado*. It is as close as the urban middle class will normally get to hunting. The raw meat sits like a trophy on wooden slabs, metal trays or – like Brazilian *churrasco* – on long skewers with handles much like swords. The barbecue, the contemporary equivalent of the camp fire, flames for a while before the embers sit menacingly red hot under the grill grid. The meat is cast onto the metal, it sizzles and groans as it is turned and thrown by the cook and removed still in a state closer to raw than most Europeans would tolerate. It is then eaten, as often as not carved with bone-handled knives on wooden blocks. The cook dresses as hunter – with boots and heels and Western hats – wielding knives that represent the hunter's instruments. This then is Sunday cooking – the reenactment of a primitive ritual of transformation from raw (nature) into a sort of transitional state, midway to the cooked (the domestic). It is not to be confused with the preparation of food in the kitchen, a realm even at the beginning of the twenty-first millennium still almost exclusive to women – albeit often cooks and servants. This is weekday cooking; a second transformation – of the natural into the refined – which in a sense reproduces the subjection of women to the stricter gender divisions of domestic life. (Rosario Castellanos, the Mexican writer, evokes that contradiction brilliantly in her short story 'Lección de cocina' [The Cookery Lesson].) The bold hunter may wear an apron – but it is like the leather apron of the pampa slaughterer, not the pretty affair that indicates a domestic realm.

In a more general sense, the ritual of eating is – as Jack Goody suggests – one of the rites of modern life most resistant to change. The long lunch followed by a siesta – the Spanish habit – may be increasingly disappearing in the real conditions of the contemporary city, where the poorest travel furthest to work and in the most intolerable of conditions. When the occasion presents itself, however, the family meal is still a hierarchical affair with the man at the head of the table and the women bringing the multiple dishes to the table. In a society where even the modest middle class has servants, it is still the women of the household who serve (deliver) the food, even though the usually labour-intensive preparation has been devolved to the cook and her assistants. The order of things is maintained.

On working days, however (whether that work is in industry, services, or the informal economy), the streets of every Latin American town and city become suites of ambulant eating. The picture of indigenous women sitting at the pavement's edge delivering tacos or papusas or empanadas from a wicker basket covered in a dishcloth, or from a makeshift stall at a market, is stereotypically familiar. But this is eating without ritual – distinct from fast food but fulfilling a similar fuelling function. And yet street food is as clearly differentiated by class and ethnicity throughout most of Latin America as all the other ceremonies of daily life. And it is not just a matter of price; food is also identity, solidarity and comfort; it is a connection with a past, a tradition rural in its origins and enduring in character. Strangely, in a world dominated by McDonald's and Taco Bell, the tortilla, the potato, chilli, the banana, salt, coffee and fish survive. Fried sweet potatoes, *farofa* (the crumbled cassava), the freeze-dried *chuño*, the purple *chicha* drink, still sustain the poorest people of the continent.

HOW NATIONS EAT

In the era of national movements and revolutions, from Mexico in 1910 through the struggles of Sandino in Nicaragua and Martí in El Salvador, to Bolivia in 1952 and Cuba in 1959, the cultural symbols have represented resistance against the empires of the north. Music changed, the written word described again the forgotten worlds of Latin America, the new Brazilian artists of the 1920s recommended cannibalism – *antropofagia* – eat the enemy, eat all that there is to eat, and make it your own. In rediscovering the Latin American past, and the present of the indigenous peoples, the crafts and monuments of the other America, so its tastes were recuperated too. Now, however, it became a cuisine, a national style, a mark of difference.

Urban culture in the period of independence defined culture as European civilization, taste as European taste. Cuisine was as French as the word itself, though Italy might attend the banquet too in a subordinate role. Cuisine was butter and cream, rich sauces over tender meat and attended by French wine. It was the third decade of the 20th century before the extraordinary culinary achievements of Peru, Mexico and Bahia were recognized and acknowledged as a *style* (though there were rare pioneering works of regional cooking like Rivera Galván's *El cocinero mejicano* of 1831). Now, however, nationalism produced tastes and smells as well as movements and manifestoes – chilli, *asados*, the national dishes of the continent. And each of them were cultural landscapes, histories of the encounters and dissonances at the heart of Latin America on a plate.

Argentine *carbonada* marries cuts of beef with Spanish paprika, rice, green peas from Europe, potatoes from the Andes, pumpkin and maize. Colombians breakfast on *humitas* – maize *tamales* with chocolate, bread and cheese. In Peru, *comida chifa* merges the food brought by Chinese labourers in the late nineteenth century with pasta and potatoes. But the potato re-emerges in a thousand manifestations – *papas a la huancaína, causa* and many more. In Nicaragua, *gallo pinto* cooks rice and beans in coconut milk – a development of Spain's *moros y cristianos*, which lacks the coconut. Colombia's *sancocho* is almost itself a metaphor for Latin American cooking – beef, garlic, onions, tomatoes, yucca, chicken, bananas, maize and limes cooked in the course of a week. It is almost instant when compared with Guyana's *pepperpot*, however, a dish of indigenous origin made from a cassava and sugar base to which is added a combination of meats; it can keep cooking for years by adding cooked meats. Peru's *pachamanca* has restored the ancient methods of cooking in earthenware and *under* an open fire. Ecuador's *llapingachos* are potato pancakes stuffed with cheese and served with *chorizo* and tomatoes and avocado. Brazil's *feijoada*, with its bean base, exuberantly absorbs almost any and every ingredient. And Mexico's wonderful, varied and exciting cuisine has its reference point in the hundred or more varieties of chile, in maize in its myriad expressions, in beans and tomatoes and chocolate. Perhaps *mole*, that exquisite marriage of chiles and chocolate so beloved of the Aztec emperor Moctezuma, might serve as its reference point.

THE CHILLIBURGER: FIGHTING BACK?

The century ends and the new millennium begins with a contradiction. On the one hand, the majority of Latin Americans are experiencing hardship – and many are facing hunger. The neo-liberal decade that began in the 1990s brought with it new privations; the loss of land to a rapacious export agriculture, the removal of protective tariffs which made many local products unprofitable to produce, except perhaps for the coca leaf. Debt spiralled and the consequent rising unemployment sent many more into a realm of poverty and need. The outbreak of cholera which began in Peru in 1991 had begun with *ceviche*, raw fish marinated in limes – but only because the *water* used had been polluted with sewage. The disease spread; yet cholera can be arrested with ample provision of clean water! Ten years later, the people of Cochabamba, Bolivia, occupied their city to prevent the privatization of their water supplies.

In January 1994, in Chiapas, southern Mexico, the communities led by the Zapatistas rose in protest at the implementation of the North American Free Trade Agreement. They had experienced decades of pressure on their land, of expulsion by the big landowners supplying cattle for the world hamburger trade. In preparation for the implementation of NAFTA, government subsidies on their crops were removed; their maize would now be more expensive than the corn imported from the USA. And most of their homes lacked access to clean water.

In Cuba, the fall of the Berlin Wall in 1989 precipitated a crisis in an island still subject to a ferocious economic embargo first imposed after the revolution of 1959. In the next two years, an epidemic of neuritis signalled the arrival of malnutrition after 40 years of a generally high level of health and basic nutrition among its population.

In Mexico City, Rio, Lima, La Paz, the labour-intensive preparation of traditional foods becomes less and less possible except on feast days and holidays. People eat on the street – or in the cheap *cocinas económicas* or *fritangas* (each country has its own version) where the ingredients and tastes of their own history may still be found and eaten with enamel spoons from cheap plates. For the rest of the urban population, the lower middle class anxious to participate, albeit peripherally, in modernity, there is always the ubiquitous fast food. There are VIPs, McDonald's, Burger King and all the rest. These flagbearers of globalization have reached into every corner of the world and 'plastified' (the word is Eduardo Galeano's) our palates. There is something forbidding about the absolute, relentless global uniformity of the Big Mac. The irony, as Galeano explains, is that the graduates of the McDonald's University at Elk Grove, Illinois, elected very different food for their graduation meals.

They, like most of the urban dwellers with some money to spare, preferred the ethnic restaurants that were springing up throughout the world from the 1980s onwards – coinciding with the success of World Music. As the fast foods of the West ruthlessly invaded the foodways of Latin America, more and more people in the richer countries – *and* in the expanding modern cities of Latin America – were discovering the taste for Latin American foods. The reality is that the Latin American variant of 'ethnic food' was largely Tex-Mex, the *nachos*, *tacos*, *chimichangas* to accompany the newly popular Mexican beers (from breweries largely established by Spanish and German immigrants). This was already an adapted version of Mexican food, toned down and cooled down to be acceptable to the sensitive palates of Europe and the United States. The magnificent cuisines of Peru, of southern Mexico, above all of Brazil, have yet to reach that level of acceptability – though it is now possible to eat *vatapé* or *feijoada* somewhere in most US and European cities. And in Latin America, a sort of parallel but equal process takes place; the chilliburger marks the intimate encounter between the universal arbiters of taste and a palate that is, at least minimally, still different.

Globalization levels and makes uniform; it imposes universal tastes and desires to make possible the highest level of economies of scale for the worldwide producers of hamburgers and Coke. The paradox is that the drive for global dominance produces deepening poverty, a widening gap between the beneficiaries and the victims of globalization, and a growing incidence of hunger. Latin American cuisine is a refinement, an adaptation perhaps, of those combinations and fusions that Europe found in the Americas; or it is the defiant survival of the tastes and smells of a continent forcibly abandoned by a black population that refuses to forget its music or its food.

If the patterns of eating and cooking are a faithful representation of the physical and social landscape, then the struggle for self-expression, for independence from the global economic tyrannies, may well find their unexpected symbol in the *feijoada, tacos de huitlacoche, pupusas, ajiaco, llapingachos, ropa vieja* – dishes that refuse to disappear.

22

Capoeira culture
An impertinent non-Western art form
Floyd Merrell

PRELIMINARIES

Capoeira plays havoc with our need for a world conveniently classified into blacks and whites. Say what Capoeira is, and you say what it is not. Say it is slam-bam, in-your-face rumbling, and it is not; it is good-natured play. Say it is music and dancing, and you're wrong; it is ludic struggle. Say it is frivolous play, and you're off the mark; it is serious business. Say it is fine-tuned acrobatics, and it's also something else; it is on-the-spot creativity. Say it is a matter of brute strength, and, you guessed it; it is more than that, it is finesse. Say it is just a lot of roughhousing, and that's not what it is at all. Say it is rule-governed, and it is, but not quite, for it also involves constant spontaneity. Well, then, you say it is nothing but improvisation, and you're both right and wrong, for there are rules that must be followed within the improvisation.

What is this poetry in motion called Capoeira? On the surface it seems like a scrappy, ritualized ballet, an embattling confrontation of physical ability and mental agility practiced to the rhythm of instruments and chants. Everybody who has been a capoeirista for years and has reached the venerable status of *Mestre* or *Mestra* (male or female Master) is ready to tell the tale of its history at the drop of a hat. It's in her blood. She relives its history constantly; every time she enters the *roda* (Capoeira ring), she relives it. But every capoeirista's history of Capoeira is different. Who is the person to be believed? This *Mestre* or that one? Any one of a number of books on the topic? It's difficult. The tradition is complex, with many side streets and blind alleys.

ENIGMATIC WORDS

One of the key words linked to Capoeira is *malícia*. This word comes with the same roots as the English 'malice'. *Malícia* is more subtle than its English counterparts, however. *Malícia* is a little bit of 'malice', but with a sly, clever, ingratiating roguish gesture. It involves awareness of what's going on under the surface appearance. *Malícia* is cunningly putting something on someone before she does it to you. It might involve a dose of double-dealing, but with a wily, jocular twist. It might involve deception, but with a big smile. It might involve duplicity, but with the appearance of honesty; it is cheating without taking it seriously, guile with a little ironic humor, pretense for the purpose of catching you off guard, trickery that is honestly revealed to you when you are taken in by it, a show of trust and then you are slammed when you accept it.

Malícia is one person's creation of expectations in the mind of the other person and then acting contrary to those expectations. The intent is in a good-natured way to make the other person out to be a fool, a clown. The act is brought about by deception, or as they sometimes put it in Brazil, by an *indireta* ('indirection'). The person putting himself up for the deception is led along a tangent. Then, at an unexpected moment, the tables are overturned, and he falls into the trap. The slaves in Brazil developed *malícia* into a carefully honed instrument by means of which to generate subversive acts against their masters. *Malícia* became their way of coping with life, a way of life, the heart and soul of which is found in Capoeira.

Malícia always appears to be what it is not. In order to practice Capoeira *malícia*, you must take on the appearance that you are one thing and then suddenly reveal yourself in a different mask. The accomplished capoeirista must become a master of deception. She must pretend she is angry when she is not; she must act as if she is injured when she is OK, she must feign fear when she is as confident as could be. She creates an *indireta* that sets your senses and your mind off in a circuitous route. The Capoeira master of the *indireta* leads you to expect she will do one thing and then she does something else. She tricks you, subtly. She plays you for a fool, then laughs with you when you take the bait. She brings you to an awareness that the world is never as it appears. You become aware that surprises are always just around the corner. Capoeira *malícia* always has yet another surprise in store.

Deception and discernment of deception are the beginning of an understanding of Brazilian Capoeira. The capoeirista is adept at the act of deception, and she is keen at perceiving deceptive acts thrown his way. The ability to dissemble out of innocence or with ulterior motives in mind is part of what makes us distinctly human. In this manner, Capoeira is germane to our very humanity. Deception became part of the slaves' practices *vis-à-vis* their masters during the longest period of slavery in the Americas, Brazilian slavery (1538–1888). In the course of three and a half centuries about 3.5 million Africans (six times the number taken in captivity to the United States) survived the brutal ordeal of the Atlantic crossing to Brazil. Then they experienced all the cruelty inherent in an institution charged with the duty of subjugating one race by another.

Those who managed to survive did so by their wits, by deception and evasion, and in part perhaps through Capoeira. According to the story among most Afro-Brazilian capoeiristas, Capoeira played an important role in the game of survival, which was not really just any game, mind you: it was a way to stay alive, a way to assert one's humanity with some form of dignity. When the slaves practiced Capoeira, the masters from their mansions likely saw what they wanted to see regarding the slaves' activities outside their shanties: they saw the folks having a good time. Fine and dandy. Let them enjoy themselves in whichever way they could, for tomorrow would be another hard day. The capoeirista slaves, however, were busy practicing deception. They were enacting one thing that was actually another thing. There were instruments making music, and there was singing and dancing and gaiety. That's usually what the masters saw and heard. The slaves, however, might have been singing something like: 'Freedom / dreamt so many times / was now reality / the final goal was reached, my companion! / freedom … freedom' (Bola Sete, 1997, p. 84). Capoeira was their symbolic act of liberation, as well as physical preparation for a day of rebellion, when they might be called upon to defend themselves against their oppressors.

Capoeira is played in a circle of some four yards in diameter called a *roda*. The *roda* was for the slaves and is today for the capoeirista a protective circle. It was and is a metaphor of the world, and Capoeira within the ring is an allegory for life 'out there'. Within the *roda*, the slaves engaged in their acts of deception, as they played out their role in the bigger world; the *roda* was a world upside-down. One of the most notable characteristics of Capoeira action is body inversion, the amount of time spent on the hands, with feet in the air while either making a 180-degree cartwheel (*aú*) move, or with feet cocked and ready to lash out. Either that, or the capoeirista might stand on the top of his head and do a spin like a spinning top (*apião*) (an act that has led to speculation that 'break dancing' in the United States might have been influenced by Capoeira). These aspects of Capoeira play give it an acrobatic look. Another inverted stance is the *queda de rins* ('falling onto the kidneys'), that finds the capoeirista supported on his head and one hand with his elbow against the kidney area for support, or he might support his entire body with one hand and elbow against his kidney section. The object is for the capoeirista to feel comfortable in the most bizarre and unaccustomed positions. For the slave, caught in the most humanly degrading and unaccustomed situations imaginable, found in Capoeira a world turned topsy-turvy, practice for survival value. (In fact, in Capoeira action the hands are rarely used as an offensive measure, which is quite natural for the slaves, in chains and forced to use their forearms, head butts, and their feet to trip up their opponent.)

The topsy-turvy Capoeira world is symbolically a deceptive world. Dissemble, and you present yourself as someone you are not. You pretend a role you do not feel, while you are aware of the distance between your performance and your true self. You present another self, not necessarily a false or fake self, but a self other than what you would otherwise present and other than what would otherwise be expected in a given situation. You give your partner a smile when in pain. You put on a face of pain while readying yourself for an attack. You make a fake attack to the left and get your partner to draw back so that he becomes vulnerable. You extend your hands, pleading for mercy, when you know you can get the better of your partner whenever you wish. You are also adept at reading your partner's deception. It is a matter of becoming aware of somebody else's dissembling practices, while at the same time engaging in your own dissembling practices for the purpose of duping that somebody else (Lewis, 1992).

I've heard male capoeiristas say women are by nature superior at the fine art of Capoeira, since for survival value in a male-dominated society they have been forced to become adroit dissemblers. They have had to learn deception in order to become competitive (Bruns, 2000, pp. 39–46). Whether this is the case or not, I admire the tactic adopted by Mestra Jararaca of Salvador, in the Brazilian state of Bahia. 'Jararaca' is her *nome de guerra* ('warrior name', the name she goes by in capoeirista circles). It is also the name of a venomous snake found in Brazil. That should give you an idea. Jararaca tells the women in her class that the days are over when they can whimper and moan and claim incompetence because of their sex. The female capoeirista must be a warrior, equal to the best men on the block. If not, she might as well give it up here and now and be done with it, for she will get no pity in the Capoeira ring. When young ladies in her class complain that they can't make a move according to the model Jararaca presented, I've known her to run over – not walk mind you – and give the student a swift kick in the *bunda* (butt). Capoeira moves are neither a man's nor a woman's thing. They are a Capoeira thing; they know no gender; they know no age – and yes, I've received a few unexpected blows to my *bunda* when I wasn't putting out the effort she demanded.

BUT WHAT, REALLY, IS CAPOEIRA?

Capoeira has been qualified as fortuitous play, serious struggle, game and sport, a martial art, dance, ritual, a musical performance, theater, drama, philosophy, and life. Actually, Capoeira is all of the above. And at the same time it is none of the above. But this vague description simply won't fly. It creates even greater confusion. So, if I can't define Capoeira outright, let me give you a Capoeira scene.

A man and a woman are squatting, face toward an elderly man, the *Mestre*, playing a one-stringed instrument (*berimbau*) and voicing the initial song, a *ladainha*. The *ladainha* sets a mood the Mestre feels at the moment. The moment is crucial, for every moment is unique; every act of Capoeira is to an extent improvised and hence it is one of its kind. I might also add that the Mestre plays the lead berimbau, called the *gunga*. There is a second, smaller berimbau, usually called a *médio*, and a third even smaller one, the *viola* (Capoeira, 1992, p. 123).[1]

To the Mestre's right there are two younger individuals, male and female, playing the smaller berimbaus. To their right, two people are playing tambourines (*pandeiros*). Then there is somebody holding a gong with two bells (*agôgô*) in his hands, and following him a woman has a bamboo scraper (*reco-reco*). They are not playing, yet they are ready for action when the proper cue is given. Finally, a man is sitting behind a tall drum (*atabaque*), also awaiting the moment to initiate his rhythm. The solo chant (*ladainha*) ends. The *agôgô*, *reco-reco*, and *atabaque* begin creating their own variations of the beginning rhythm, and all eight people enter into another song (the *entrada* or *chula*). This song consists of a call by the leader playing the large *berimbau* followed by a chorused response. After the *entrada*, the Mestre belts out the third type of chant, the *corrido*. The two people squatting have now crossed themselves, and, facing each other, for a second or so, they stretch their bodies out horizontally and less than a foot from the floor, balanced in a seemingly impossible way on one hand and supported by an elbow at the lower portion of their rib cage (a *queda de rins*) (Almeida, 1986).

Then they slowly, cautiously, begin moving toward the center of the *roda* around which there are about 15 people seated on the floor with legs crossed and clapping their hands and chanting. With her body in the lowest possible position, the person to the right slowly arcs her leg over the back of her partner, while he is at the same time gyrating his body away from her and bringing his left leg around and over her. They continue, apparently entangling their bodies together, but not quite, since at the point where they could lock their partner's torso in a leg or arm hold, they slither out. At the same time they are gradually directing their movements to the midpoint of the *roda*. When they are at the center, they slowly rise and begin what appears to be a dance step (*ginga*). This step consists of alternating shifts of body weight from the right to the left leg, backward and forward and to the right and the left, in a rocking motion. It is all done to the rhythm of the instruments and songs. The rocking and swaying motion reminds us of a fisherman in his small boat, trying to maintain his balance while the boat is bounced to and fro by the waves. At the same time the person's arms are moving back and forth and forward as if in a sculling or rowing motion.

(The *ginga* is the most basic of Capoeira moves. If the lead berimbau sets the mood, the *ginga* initiates the action. It is neither an attack nor a defensive move, yet it contains the possibility for both. Any experienced capoeirista will tell you that, above all else, you must always engage in the *ginga*. It is always present, in the *roda*, and outside the *roda*. When you work and play you are *gingando* (creating a *ginga* rhythm); when you talk, your body is *gingando*; when you eat, you are *gingando*; when you sleep and dream and make love, you are *gingando*; when you defecate, you are *gingando* – in fact, there is a Capoeira position called the *cocorinha*, the word to indicate the squatting position. *Ginga* provides the flow of Capoeira play; it is the flow of life; it is life itself.)

Activity within the *roda* now picks up, as the chant takes a new form of calls and responses: 'Who taught me to navigate? / Who taught me to navigate? / It wasn't you, fisherman / It was a little fish in the sea.' The two partners in the ring are now in a prone position, *gingando*, always *gingando*, and, crouched low, they make swinging motions with their legs, to the right, to the left, a fake kick here, a head butt there, while the opponent is busy setting up a defense in order to set up a bit of counter-offensive.

And, what's this? The female capoeirist is actually singing along with the instruments, with a big smile on her face as she rhythms around the *roda*, looking directly into the eyes of her partner. Why, this is no fiercely competitive game at all. It's play. They are not fighting but merely going through the motions. They are engaged in mock fighting. It is a ritual, a joyous ritual they are playing out. They, along with the instrument players and the capoeiristas sitting round the *roda*, are in a theater, and the action is a play; it is an enactment of the human condition as it should be, a community of people in communion with one another. So this is what Capoeira living is about. The *roda* is a microcosm where the grand human drama as it should be at its best is played out.

Now the female partner abruptly turns and places both hands on the floor, still eyeing the other person from between her legs. Then she does a quick hand-stand with legs cocked as if ready to unleash them in the direction of her partner's belly. He quickly cart-wheels away from her, landing on one foot, and then he arches the other foot in her direction, but with his leg retracted just enough so as to make no actual contact. She quickly drops to the floor, supported with hands and legs. Then she turns, with back to the floor, and, supported with both hands behind her and one leg in front of her, she does a feigned jab with her other foot. He rapidly draws back and prepares to retaliate, as she rises to a prone position. Poised on one foot, he arcs his back and brings about his own jab with his right foot (a *benção*, 'blessing'), careful not to extend his foot too far so as to come in contact with her. All the while, they maintain close vigil on one another. Their eyes never take leave of the other's eyes. As the song comes to a close, the Mestre breaks into another one and picks up the tempo. All instruments follow suit. The *viola* sings; the *médio* does its thing; both of them following the *gunga*'s cadence. *Pandeiros* shiver and shake; *agôgô* dings and dongs; *reco-reco-* scrapes; *atabaque* dum-de-dum-dums. The rhythm is lively.

The male capoeirista breaks into a wide grin and gestures to the right, then he quickly does a pirouette to the left with his left leg arched high. She once again goes to the floor and does a quick hand-stand, and momentarily holds her inverted position, eyeballing him, with a sly smile. He circles her. She gyrates on her hands, then falls on her feet toward him and slips to the floor with her torso twisted and her legs extended in the form of a pair of scissors.

Then she rapidly locks his legs at the knees between her legs and tightens her grip. He extends both hands as if to say 'I give up', then looks to the sky and crosses himself in the form of a petition to the gods for divine guidance. The audience roars with approval. Both partners approach the head songster, the Mestre. They squat, pensively, then they slowly cross themselves, and begin anew. That's a possible scene from among the virtual infinity of scenes when playing Capoeira.

The *roda*. World within the world, metaphor of the larger society. It is the circle where the *ginga* begins. Circle where rhythm begins. After Capoeira play comes to a close within the *roda*, it never really ends, for:

> the capoeirista walks more lightly. He returns to his day-to-day reality, with the same problems he left aside during his brief time in the *roda*. But, as he nurtures and fortifies his outlook on life as a result of his times in the *roda* while *gingando*, things gradually begin to change. His problems are the same, but they no longer oppress him. It is not the problems that have changed, but the capoeirista himself, when in the *roda*. Capoeira has changed his outlook on life. (Capoeira, 1999, pp. 124–5)

That's Capoeira living. But where did this uniquely Brazilian art come from?

UNCERTAIN SOURCES

The origin of the term 'Capoeira' is up for grabs. Some claim it comes from the Amerindian language, Tupí-Guaraní. The sound in Tupí-Guaraní comparable to the Portuguese 'Capoeira' means 'bush', or in other words, what was once 'forest' (*'caá'*) but is now something else (*'puêra'*). In another interpretation, the suffix 'capo' of Capoeira might have the same origin as the English 'capon', or 'rooster'. This would seem quite natural, since the observation is often made that two partners in a Capoeira match exercise moves that look like a cockfight.

Some scholars allude to Capoeira's Angola origins (Kubik, 1979; Matias da Silva, 1994, pp. 102–4). Edson Carneiro (1977), Waldenoir Rego (1968), and Luiz Renato Vieira (1996) are of the opinion that Capoeira is exclusively a Brazilian creation by Africans, since nothing in Africa existed exactly like Brazilian Capoeira (in contrast, see Dossar, 1992). The term's slipperiness is quite appropriate, since Capoeira by its very nature breeds elusiveness. The adept capoeirista is himself elusive, an adroit ironist saying one thing when meaning something else, a clever magician creating visual illusions.

In 1932 Mestre Bimba (Manoel dos Reis Machado, 1900–74) of Salvador, Brazil set up the first 'official Capoeira academy'. In 1937 he offered a course registered as 'Physical Education' with the Secretary of Education. He gained a reputation for accepting only students who had a job or were studying (Vieira, 1996, p. 145). By this time, Mestre Pastinha (Vicente Ferreira Pastinha

1889–1982), also of Salvador, was gaining public attention. While Bimba adapted moves to the Capoeira play that reminded many of jiu jitsu and other martial arts, in addition to a massive dose of acrobatics that added a note of spectacularism, Pastinha became increasingly obsessed with the conservation of Capoeira purity. From that time onward, Capoeira branched off into two directions, *Capoeira Regional* following Mestre Bimba, and *Capoeira Angola*, promoted by Mestre Pastinha (Matias da Silva, 1994, pp. 103–5). Largely as a result of Bimba's and Pastinha's efforts, Capoeira came in off the streets and alleys. Gradually, it was no longer conceived as the pastime of vagabonds and scoundrels as its old reputation had it. It gravitated from the margins of society toward the center, ever so slightly.

Thick, powerful Mestre Bimba took special interest in making the art respectable, in contrast to the *malandro* (bad ass) image with which it had been shacked. Attracting light-skinned students from the middle and upper socioeconomic strata of Salvador, he began demanding strict discipline; he set codes of conduct for his students; he made his classes more intensive than anything previously known to the art; he endowed his students with diplomas and a *cordão* (a 'cord' to be tied around the waist) after completing a course. In time, he surrounded himself with many university students, and professionals. Soon his more dedicated students were taken to other parts of the Brazil and to foreign countries, where they began setting up academies. In the 1950s his academies were organized in Rio and São Paulo, and by the 1970s they were appearing in Europe and the United States.

Small, wiry, Mestre Pastinha, on the other hand, held onto the idea of Capoeira in its pure, uncorrupted form, and he kept to tradition according to what was known of it at the time.[2] Pastinha wanted to keep the art in its original form. However, Capoeira, even Capoeira Angola, simply couldn't stand still. It changed. Since Pastinha insisted in conserving the Capoeira tradition, Capoeira Angola's changing face took on an increasingly conservative look. Over the years, as a result, Capoeira Angola became even less regimented and rule oriented, as it distanced itself from Capoeira Regional. That is the downside. The upside is that Capoeira Angola allowed for more individual expression and greater freedom. Classes were less formal and they varied greatly, according to the group and whoever was in charge. However, even though Capoeira Angola moves became increasingly slow in comparison to Capoeira Regional, it was part of the disguise: when quickness becomes necessary, it is always there, like a bolt of lightning (Capoeira, 1992, p. 378).

Thus Table 22.1 should by no means be construed as a set of binary oppositions. In the first place, Capoeira Regional to a degree manifests all the Angola characteristics. In the second place, the *Angoleiro* is certainly no slouch. Both Capoeira forms are both game and play, creative and efficient, deceptive and aggressive, flexible and rigid. As a matter of fact, of recent, some capoeiristas prefer to mix the two styles into a hybrid form that has become

Table 22.1: Comparison and contrast between Capoeira Angola and Capoeira Regional

Capoeira Angola	Capoeira Regional
Traditional	Modern
Change primarily from within	Transformation within larger culture
Slow play (*jôgo lento*)	Rapid play (*jôgo rápido*)
Low movements (*jôgo baixo*)	High movements (*jôgo alto*)
Flexible rules, improvisation	Rigid rules, application
Personal strategies and techniques	Codified strategies and techniques
Deceptive, and with *malícia*	Aggressive, and without *malícia*
Creativity, individualized	Efficiency, regimented
Play, recreational	Game, sport

quite popular in southern Brazil, the United States, and Europe, to the chagrin of the purists.[3]

Yet, the two Capoeira forms are distinct. Above all, Capoeira Angola continued to stress *malícia* over raw power, subtle unexpected moves over a fixed repertoire of moves in invariant sequences, and deception over seriousness. It was more a matter of having a good time, singing a little, dancing a little, now engaging in some 'trash talk', now getting low and dirty, now just having fun. It remained more of a family affair in contrast to the club-like affair Capoeira Regional was becoming. Consequently, *angoleiros* were on the average more 'black' and less affluent, more folksy and less professional. This is not to say that they were not as dedicated. On the contrary. Racial memory of their slavery past was part and parcel of their art. It was the very spirit of their art. While dancing and singing and gesturing and mock fighting, they played the role of their ancestors, who were even less fortunate than they. And in incessantly evoking the memory of their ancestors, *angoleiros* relived their own personal past, replete with hardships, prejudice, repression, and brutality.

We can find an example of Capoeira's doing an ironic twist on slavery practices in the *benção*, or 'blessing', in the form of a kick made by extending one foot toward the other person, with body arching back. During the colonial period slaves customary received a 'blessing' from their master at any and all appropriate moments. The slaves, of course, knew this was no more than a show of hypocrisy. Following the 'blessing', they might receive a lashing for the purpose of keeping them in line. The Capoeira *benção* turns the tables on this practice: punishment comes first, and it is followed by a loving gesture and a wily smile (Lewis, 1992, p. 228). I must once again emphasize, however, that not even can Capoeira Angola lay claim to purity. There is no pure Capoeira that has existed intact since colonial times. Even though Capoeira Angola strives to maintain traditions, like all improvisational cultural practices, it is incessantly evolving (Bruns, 2000, pp. 24–31).

On the other hand, one might consider Capoeira Regional as an effort to rid the art once and for all of its image as a subversive pastime for *malandros* and vagabonds, and as a means to get away from the idea that Capoeira is just *brincadeira* (from *brincar*, play as in fortuitous activity). In other words, there was an attempt to 'modernize' Capoeira and give it a progressive, industrious work ethic. In this spirit, Capoeira must have a purpose; it must be useful for somebody in some capacity or other. The most appropriate purpose of Capoeira Regional is for personal defense. Capoeira, within the relatively more 'white' regionalists schools, are occasionally given that interpretation. In presenting this image to the public, Renato Ortiz writes, courses must be offered, with a fixed code of rules and in the best of all worlds a text outlying the advantages of preparing oneself for confrontation with all those undesirable elements out there that might waylay one (Ortiz, 1986, p. 105; also Vieira, 1996, pp. 158–71).

After all is said and done, the capoeirista: 'Should be a good fighter in the mode of the *capoeira regional* but without losing the spirit, rituals, and playful characteristics of the *capoeira Angola*' (Almeida, 1986, p. 43). Capoeira, like all vibrant cultural phenomena, evolves, following natural processes of change. For this reason, we sense with greater acuity that …

CAPOEIRA IS LIFE

The journey through Capoeira living is continuous, with no abrupt promotions. The student must follow a natural process that requires dedication, discipline, training, and cultivation of a profound feel for the art. There is no haste, nor is one expected to lunge into week upon week of furious activity. There is meditation and contemplation just as there is strenuous practice. Capoeira is not merely strength, acrobatics, or a striving for mechanical perfection. It is life, and it is philosophy.

The capoeirista must strive to be more than she thought she could be. When a 12-year-old student is playing against her Mestre, it gives him great pleasure to be able to guide his young pupil through her moves. He helps her along, but with a few subtle *malícia* maneuvers to keep things honest and let her know who's in control. If you are well past your prime, like I was, and wish to learn Capoeira, this is not seen as a disadvantage in the same way that would be seen in a competitive, ego-driven society. You are brought along, like everybody else. In whichever case, you must try to do what you thought you couldn't do. That's all. Who you are, where you came from, your education, your social standing, your sex and race, are of no consequence. Consequently, the capoeirista who bullies less experienced partners, the young lad who sets out to embarrass an older partner, or the *macho* male who wants to kick some female ass, is setting himself up for rebuke and perhaps even expulsion from the Capoeira family. And family it is. Capoeiristas in body, mind, and spirit compose a caring, protecting, compassionate, loving family.

The family has its roots in its cultural soil. Playing Capoeira, especially Capoeira Angola, is above all playing close to the earth, with limbs contracted, body compacted into a knot (*fechado*, closed) in pretzel fashion. Mind is in the flow; spirit is contrite yet full of *malícia*; all is close to the earth. That is where life begins and ends. You give your partner a *benção* and you do so in a hunched, seemingly contrite position. You make many of your moves from the lowest possible position. Your partner thrusts a foot in your direction and you twirl away like a pinwheel, with legs doubled up and body curved in a elegantly grotesque way. All, close to the earth, where your (the Afro-Brazilians') ancestors rested each day after 15 hours of labor, or where they fell, in their own blood after a flogging, where they came to rest after their last gasp of life-giving air. Your compacted body also affords you protection, and readiness for launching an attack. It makes you less vulnerable. You remain more enigmatic, mysterious, undecipherable, close to the earth.

While in the *roda*, you are often in an inverted, upside-down position, viewing the world in mirror-image form. The world is seen as if through a looking-glass, for sure. From your top-down vantage point you try to see another world, a world less painful, a world other than what it is, as did your (the Afro-Brazilians') ancestors. But even the looking-glass is twisted at a 90-degree angle, over to the side, such that everything becomes inverted. You see the world in an involuted, convoluted, inside-out way. But you must imagine it as it would normally appear, because that is the world within which your (the Afro-Brazilians' ancestors') survival is at stake. In this manner you can see the world as it might otherwise be.

The *roda* is the world; it is life. Playing within this inside-out world actually gives you (the Afro-Brazilians' ancestors) the advantage. It allows you a break from the pain; it gives you a different angle on things by means of which, through deception, you can get the better of those who hold you in contempt and derision. They might not know you actually have the advantage, because their world is an either/or affair. They know only black and white, dominance and subservience, good and evil, beautiful and ugly, playing and fighting. You, in contrast, close to the earth, know the reality is too subtle to allow for such distinctions. You, with your *malícia*, take irony, ambiguity, vagueness, contradiction, paradox, into your heart and mind and spirit. You know that whatever appears, will disappear in the next moment and then appear as something other than the way it was appearing.

That's because you're living Capoeira: it is you and you are it.

NOTES

1 There is something deeply sad and spiritual about berimbau music. Mestre Curió of Salvador, Brazil, once told me it is the appropriate instrument for communicating with the dead, because the pitch of each berimbau is always at

variance with that of the other berimbaus, because each berimbau is always very carefully slipping off into another world.
2 The irony is, of course, that since 'tradition' is always to a great extent invented rather than recovered or found, a culture can hardly hope to revive its past and maintain it intact. 'Tradition' is an idealized version of an irretrievable past (Serra, 1995).
3 I have often listened to Mestre Curió's tirades against those novices who call themselves 'Mestres' but actually are not, and teach a mish-mash they call 'capoeira' that has nothing to do with the Angola tradition.

23

Mama Coca and the Revolution
Jorge Sanjinés's double-take
Stephen Hart

Jorge Sanjinés is one of the foremost contemporary film directors of Latin America. His work enjoys an international reputation, especially in terms of its revolutionary praxis and its espousal of Amerindian cultural values. In this chapter I will be assessing the cultural politics underlying two of his films, *Yawar Mallku* (The Blood of the Condor, 1969) and *Para recibir el canto de los pájaros* (In Order to Receive the Bird Song, 1995), focusing in particular on the portrayal therein of Aymara cultural practices. I will be arguing that these two films grew out of the same political insight but needed two takes before the point could be fully expressed, hence this chapter's title.

Sanjinés's revolutionary principles are evident in the distribution praxis of his films. He shuns the globalizing circuits of international filmic culture – what Nelly Richard calls 'la lógica globalizadora de la massmediatización cultural' (the globalizing logic of the mass media take-over of culture; Richard, 2001, p. 186) – choosing instead to focus upon the more immediate cultural environment of Bolivia, and particularly its Amerindian population. It is for this reason difficult to obtain copies of his films outside Bolivia (even *Yawar Mallku*, despite its international acclaim). Sanjinés personally oversees the film festival of his work which, for a number of years now, has been held in July in the Casa Municipal de Cultura in downtown La Paz. Though entrance ticket costs are low (costing 10 bolviarianos in July 2001, or about US \$2), the theatre in which the film festival is held (the Teatro Modesta Sanginés) has a capacity of about 150 people, and during the two-week festival in which films such as *Yawar Mallku*, *La nación clandestina* (The Secret Nation) and *Para recibir el canto del pájaro*, for example, were featured, they played to packed houses; Sanjinés's films clearly have a broadly popular appeal.[1] It is difficult to think of a system which is more at odds with the Hollywood film production and distribution formula.

The film which made Sanjinés's name, *Yawar Mallku*, has been voted the

59th most famous film of the twentieth century by UNESCO. Soon after it was released in 1969 Sanjinés achieved a cult celebrity, and not only in Latin America. As Roque Dalton suggested, *Yawar Mallku* 'is more than just a film, [it] is a cinematic revolutionary event that poses profound and burning problems of living Latin American reality' (quoted in Pick, 1993, p. 120). According to Sanjinés, it was seen by 250,000 people in Bolivia alone, and had a wide-ranging political impact, as we shall see.

Yawar Mallku focuses on the living cultural practices of the Aymara, a large South American Indian community who have been living in the vast windy plateau in the Andes in a cluster of communities around Lake Titicaca for hundreds of years. The Aymara depend for their clothing on their herds of llamas and alpacas, and for their sustenance on local crops such as potatoes, oca, ullucu, quinoa and corn, as well as fish from Lake Titicaca. They have a form of government (the *ayllu*) which is centred on the community and does not include private or personal ownership, and which is focused on allegiance to a pantheon of spiritual deities ranging from the Apu (mountain gods) and Pachamama (Mother Earth) to Mama Coca (Mother Coca); access to the wisdom of the gods occurs in special religious ceremonies co-ordinated by the *yatiri* (soothsayer) such as the coca leaves ceremony in which the coca leaves are 'read'. Conquered by the Incas in the fifteenth century and the Spanish in the sixteenth, the Aymara have often felt their culture to be under siege. Divided between Peru, Bolivia and adjacent sections of Argentina, their population now numbers about 2,000,000, roughly the same as in the mid-1970s when *Yawar Mallku* was filmed. Many of the Aymara nowadays speak Quechua, a legacy of their conquest by the Incas.

Given the above, it is perhaps inevitable that *Yawar Mallku* should in places have a documentary feel about it. In effect, it produces a negative image of the racism which animates Bolivian society, exposing and reversing the colour coding which, since the Conquest, has ranked individuals according to their whiteness quotient. During the period 1972–76 the Indian Health Service in the United States sterilized high numbers of Indian women in reservations mainly in the west of the United States – in states such as Nebraska and Arizona – (England, n.d., pp. 1–3), and there also were reports of coercive sterilization in Colombia and Bolivia at the time. *Yawar Mallku* tells the true story of how, 'in Bolivia, a US imposed population control program administered by the Peace Corps sterilized Quechua Indian women without their knowledge or consent' (ibid., p. 4), and shows this happening in Kaata, a remote village some 250 miles outside La Paz. As Sanjinés comments: 'The film contributed to the expulsion of the Peace Corps from the country' (Sanjinés, 1983, p. 37).[2]

To some extent *Yawar Mallku* can be interpreted as an Aymara version of a whodunnit mystery. Ignacio Mallku (played by Marcelino Yanahuaya, the communal leader of Kaata, i.e., not a professional actor) realises that many of the women in his community, including his wife Paulina Yanahuaya (played by

Benedicta Huanca, a miner from Huanuni), are unable to bear children, and he decides to investigate. He goes on a fact-finding mission in adjacent communities and discovers that their women too are now sterile. The trail gradually leads him to the Maternity Clinic owned by the Cuerpo del Progreso (a thinly-veiled reference to the Peace Corps); one day he surreptitiously looks through the window of the Clinic and sees an operation in progress, realising the full horror of what has been going on. Backed by his community, Ignacio attacks the Maternity Clinic and confronts the gringos, threatening that he will do to them what they have been doing to his community; though this occurs off-screen we presume that Ignacio castrates or kills them.[3] At this point, Ignacio and his accomplices are captured, led to the top of a nearby hill, and shot. They all die except for Ignacio who, though just clinging onto life, is carried down the Andes and subsequently transported by truck to La Paz, where his brother Sixto (played by Vicente Verneros who, like Paulina, in real life, was a miner from Huanuni) tries to find him some blood. But Sixto can't afford to buy any (the blood necessary for a transfusion costs $350 and he only earns $200 a month from his menial job), and eventually Ignacio dies.

In other ways the film appears to fit the bill of a classic revolutionary thesis movie. Thus sympathy is elicited for the three Indians of the story (Ignacio, Paulina and Sixto) while the enemy are the gringos who first appear on screen when they try to buy Paulina's eggs while she is on the way to market (a poignantly ironic scene since – without her knowledge – they have already incapacitated her uterine eggs). The film also depicts those who have sold their souls to the capitalist West; these include the Superintendent who is often seen riding on his horse – note the connotations of Conquest – and who, as the outright villain of the piece, orders the execution of Ignacio and his accomplices, as well as Dr Millán, whose wife encourages her children to speak English rather than Spanish, and who has organised a banquet for four dignitaries visiting from the United States with all his Bolivian cronies in a hotel called Los Escudos (another allusion to colonialism; the Spanish defeated the Incas with their swords and 'shields'), this, it should be added, while Ignacio is slowly bleeding to death in a nearby hospital.

Part of the narrative strategy of the film is to focus on the political consequences of these two cultural options – the Aymara versus the West – and Sixto is a key figure in this respect. When we first see him – in a cross-cut sequence before Paulina arrives – Sixto is wearing Western-style clothes, he works in a textile-weaving factory, he has pin-ups of blond women on his locker door, and he even goes as far as to deny that he is Indian when challenged by a racist *mestizo* during a football game ('No soy indio, carajo'; 'I'm not an Indian, damn it'). But, as a result of this sobering experience of attempting to obtain some blood for his dying brother, he 'wakes up' to the exploitation his people are suffering, and he casts off his Western garments, instead preferring Aymara clothes, and he also – the final freeze-frame of the film suggests – joins the armed struggle. As John Hess has argued, in Sixto, 'we see a Quechua who has tried to assimilate into Spanish Bolivian society return to his Quechua identity – in a sense we see the decolonization of a mind' (1993, p. 114). Given the events which had recently shaken Bolivia when the film was released (while attempting to spread the message about the Cuban revolution in the highlands of Bolivia in 1967, Che Guevara had been captured and executed), the freeze frame at the end of the film featuring nine raised rifles can legitimately be interpreted as a invitation for the Bolivian people to embrace a Cuban-style revolutionary communism based on a return to Amerindian cultural values.

That the call to arms in *Yawar Mallku* is one based on Aymara cultural values as well as a revolutionary fervour in the Cuban mould is suggested by the way in which pivotal Amerindian cultural practices such as the coca leaves ceremony are portrayed in the film. *Yawar Mallku* is structured around a series of flashback sequences initiated by Paulina when she is asked by Sixto what happened to Ignacio. Although the first flashback is indicated by Paulina's words – 'I will tell you what happened …' – this point in the film sets in motion an osmotic shuttling between the past and the present; it is osmotic in the sense that the viewer is not warned at what point the editing indicates a past sequence of actions (i.e., pre-execution) or the present (i.e., post-execution). In fact, as Sanjinés has pointed out in a number of interviews, and which he confirmed to me in conversation, the first viewings of *Yawar Mallku* were not universally successful because many of the Amerindian viewers, despite appreciating hearing their native language in a film (something unusual in the 1960s and rare even nowadays), were confused by the abrupt temporal shifts.[4]

What is interesting about the way in which Sanjinés portrays Amerindian culture in *Yawar Mallku* is that, far from being a museum-like 'artifice of the archaic' to use Homi Bhabha's phrase (1997, p. 207), it becomes a locus of overt political resistance against Western colonisation. This is obvious in the various scenes featuring the coca leaves ceremonies. There are four ceremonies filmed in *Yawar Mallku* and they become progressively more radicalized. The first occurs as the culmination of the flashback initiated self-consciously by Paulina. The audience initially witnesses a communal celebration in which Ignacio is being fêted as the recently elected leader of the community. But he and Paulina have unfortunately just lost their three children to an epidemic, and we subsequently pass to the first *yatiri* coca leaves ceremony. The scene takes place indoors; the *mise-en-scène* is dark, lit by a sole candle, and in soft focus. As Zuzana Pick points out: 'The camera seeks out gestures and meanings of acknowledging the ritual's significance for the community. The poetic resonances of this scene accent solidarity and respect for the soothsayer's decision' (1993, p.119). The soothsayer allows all the leaves to fall into the bowl, and then gestures towards Paulina: 'Paulina, this leaf is for you' (in Quechua, with English subtitles). This first scene offers a rather mixed message to Paulina since while the soothsayer says – first that things look good ('You have lived a good life, Paulina'), then the message abruptly changes when he says – focusing on Paulina's leaf once more, but now in the context of her child-bearing capacities: 'Something's blocked inside her. It stops children.'

The full implications of the soothsayer's words have not dawned on the community, however, at this juncture of the film. The second coca leaves ceremony – this time without the soothsayer present – takes place immediately after the *yatiri*'s ceremony. Respected members of the community, including Paulina's grandfather, discuss the soothsayer's words, and, intriguingly enough, two at first glance radically different interpretations are proposed. Paulina's grandfather suggests that the mountain gods should be propitiated: 'I think they should go and make an offering to the gods. They must go up to the shrine and Paulina must offer food to the mountain.' This is the animist interpretation of sterility. But Paulina's brother disagrees and offers a political reading: 'I think the evil was brought to our community by the gringos. Gringos bring disasters!' It is important to underline that, at this point in the film, it is still not clear what is at stake; the picture is only emerging at this time. The two readings – the Amerindian-animist and the revolutionary-political – are, furthermore, projected as diametrically opposed at this point.

After this first classic flashback sequence, the film then takes on an energy of its own, and flashbacks occur more and more frequently (and, for some viewers, more and more confusingly, as suggested above). If we compare the sequencing it is clear why Sanjinés has adopted this technique for his film. Rather than tell the story chronologically he is interested in showing the ways in which people's lives can re-enact patterns of previous lives, re-live other people's destinies. After the indication by Paulina's brother that it may be the gringos who are bringing disaster upon the village, Ignacio then goes on an investigative mission in order to test this hypothesis (remember there is no proof at this stage, just a hypothesis), and we cut to various consecutive scenes in which Ignacio is asking members of his own village as well as in adjacent communities if their women are experiencing problems conceiving. This sequence is cross-cut with various scenes in which his brother (though at a future time) is asking for help from various members of his community in La Paz, beginning with the owner of the restaurant; he asks her for some money to pay for Ignacio's blood (to no avail). The two brothers – though at different points in time – are shown to be enacting a search which leads, in each case, to the realisation that the West – in that it promotes its own ideology under the guise of offering health care to other nations – is irredeemably corrupt. But at the same time that Sanjinés is breaking down the linear vision of reality entertained by the West, by hinting that lives are cyclical rather than sequential, he is also preparing the viewer for the final sequence of the film in which Sixto decides to turn against the mock-Western life he has adopted while working in La Paz, and puts on traditional clothes, and returns to his community with Paulina. The symbolism is clear: though Ignacio has died, the community will fight another day, now that Sixto has 'become' (rather than being scientifically 'cloned') the new version of Ignacio. Cross-cutting is used in a nuanced way in *Yawar Mallku*, providing subliminal hints about the future direction of the plot as well as introducing an Aymara cyclical thread into its skein.

Since we return soon afterwards to another coca leaves ceremony, it is clear that these rituals are being invested with deepening cultural significance in Sanjinés's film. In this third ceremony, the mood is more bleak and aggressive. The soothsayer's words are, now, more specific about who has been wronged, and edge a little closer to naming the perpetrators:

> Pachamama, earth mother, may the sacred crops and our song to fertility help to overcome this evil. O mountain gods, please make Ignacio's wife and all our women able to bear children again. Pachamama, mountain gods, help our race live on.

Though the North Americans are not mentioned by name, the viewer will have been made aware – through a comparison with the immediately preceding scenes – that Ignacio has been finding out more about the Maternity Clinic. The third ceremony takes place at night, and the darkness – lit up only by the torches – adds a distinctly ominous tone to the proceedings. It is in the fourth ceremony, however – which precedes the attack on the three North Americans – when all of the sinister undertones of the previous three ceremonies are brought to the fore. Here the wronged parties are named (the women of the various communities who are now barren), as well as those who have wronged them (the gringos) as well as how the act was committed (by sterilising them in the Maternity Clinic). The scene begins with a shot of the blackness of the night, and a tilt shot of a solitary torch burning against the night sky, before the ceremony begins. The soothsayer appears more menacing because of the low camera angle shots of his figure, matched by the much more compromising force of his words: 'Mama Coca, tell us what is happening ... The leaves of the women and children are always turned over. And the leaves of the gringos are always near to death. The leaves say clearly that the gringos are sowing death in the bellies of our women.' Unlike at the beginning of the film when the Amerindian and the political readings of phenomena appear to be at odds, by this point in the film, the Amerindian-animist and the revolutionary-political agendas are moving in the same direction. Mama Coca is now a fellow traveller with the Revolution.

The way in which the coca leaves ceremonies have been interspersed in the action shows that they have not been introduced simply for local colour. As a result of their visual insistence in the film, indeed, they become a pivotal space between the temporal zones of the past and present, and specifically between Ignacio's and Sixto's life stories. Given that the ceremonies are always future-focused – standing as they do on the boundary between the present and the future – their semantic force becomes gradually more intense, as the truth the coca leaves uttered in the first ceremony is finally revealed to be a true omen. Each one of the ceremonies becomes progressively more political and confrontational; the final and fourth coca leaves ceremony is the prelude to the physical attack on the three gringos in the Maternity Clinic, which itself becomes a revenge ceremony. The gringos are castrated, and the suggestion is that Mama Coca condones the Aymara people's action. Aymara cultural practices, as we can see, are being portrayed by Sanjinés in a way which is diametrically opposed to the mentality of those who keep the Aymara people's descendants in glass cages in museums in Lima and La Paz.

There are four coca leaves ceremonies portrayed in *Yawar Mallku* but, in a sense, there is one missing. When the Ukumau group – led by Sanjinés and his cinematographer, Antonio Eguino – went to Kaata in 1968–9, they found initially that it was impossible to persuade any of the members of the local community to participate in the project. The film nearly had to be called off because the villagers reacted very aggressively towards them, seeing them as intruders from La Paz; they laid siege to the hut in which the film crew were sleeping, shouting at them that they should leave, and smashing the windows with stones. The Ukumau group had made a crucial error, believing that, once an agreement had been made with the leader of the local community, the rest of the village would all fall into line, whereas the *ayllu* did (does) not function in such a top-down fashion. One last attempt was made to salvage the project: the soothsayer was asked to hold a coca leaves ceremony, which he did, and which – amazingly, in Sanjinés's view, since he thought all was lost – produced a favourable result for the project. Filming began almost immediately afterwards.[5]

It could be argued that all of these events are surplus to requirements and have no place in a film about a specific event which had just occurred in Kaata. Up to a point, this is true. One of the virtues of *Yawar Mallku* is its unencumbered, streamlined style which allows the political message of the film to emerge effectively. But the issue does emerge in a later film, *Para recibir el canto del pájaro*, which can be seen to some extent as a postlude to *Yawar Mallku*, since it addresses a silent ghost within the earlier film, that is, Sanjinés's own role in the process whereby the subaltern is captured on camera. As Sanjinés has pointed out in an important essay, when he filmed *Yawar Mallku* he 'chose' shots according to personal taste, 'without taking into account their communicability or cultural overtones' (Sanjinés, 1983, p. 35). As a result of the lessons learned, Sanjinés filmed *El coraje del pueblo* (The Courage of the People, 1971) in a more open way, and was therefore able to 'clarify the language of our films and to incorporate into them the creativity of the people themselves' (Sanjinés, 1983, p. 35). But it was in the much later film, *Para recibir el canto del pájaro*, that Sanjinés finally focused specifically on the pivotal artistic problem underlying his work – and, indeed, all revolutionary art – namely, the relationship between the language of the people and the language of the artist. In the later film, he took a fresh, bold and honest look at the dilemma, and produced a subtle, self-mocking film.

Figure 23.1 *Yawar Mallku*. Reproduced with permission of Jorge Sanjinés

Figure 23.2 *The Birds Singing*. Reproduced with permission of Jorge Sanjinés

Para recibir el canto del pájaro tells the story of a film director, Rodrigo (Guido Arce), and his actors and film crew who want to shoot a film about the Spanish Conquest in the *altiplano*.[6] The film director tries to entice a number of the local community to act in the film – offering them double their wages – but they simply ignore him. There is a wonderful scene in which he is on a soap box with a megaphone calling for actors for a new film; the camera cuts away and we see him surrounded by the immensity of the Andes, with not a soul in sight. And there are a number of scenes which specifically re-create what happened when Sanjinés was in the Andes some 30 years earlier when filming *Yawar Mallku*. The film director and his team are surrounded by the Indians who threaten to attack and, true to type, they hurl stones in through the windows. *Para recibir el canto del pájaro* takes the original event one step further, though, by portraying the Indians as throwing into the hut not only stones but also the dead bodies of the beautiful birds which the two cameramen – in a thoughtless act of aggression – had killed earlier on that day. This enhances the motif of the film since the projectiles represent not only an act of aggression but also constitute a message with more or less the following meaning: 'Do not destroy our natural world!'

Whereas in *Yawar Mallku* the camera took on the role of a neutral, supposedly ideology-free eye creating an untrammelled vision of the subaltern, in the later film Sanjinés draws attention to the ways in which – as a white *paceño* – he is also involved in the process whereby the subaltern is imprisoned within an image imposed from without. Suppressed from view in *Yawar Mallku*, and thereby digested in an Aristotelian sense, the camera itself is now foregrounded as part of the epistemological problem: the artistic conundrum, in other words, becomes a metaphor of the political dilemma. What Sanjinés successfully demonstrates in *Para recibir el canto de los pájaros* is that technique and cinematic form draw strength from an emboldened relationship between the artist and the people. For Sanjinés, as García Canclini puts it:

> Technique is no longer conceived as something which is neutral but rather as something engendered within specific social relationships. Technique then becomes the foundation and the limit-point creating a symbiosis between the film director and the community. The instruments and the way they are used become a means whereby a new type of content is created, one which did not previously exist either in the community or in the film director's mind. Quite the opposite of a technique based on spontaneity, a bonding with the people becomes a *sine qua non* which articulates technique, signs and verisimiltitude. (1999b, pp. 88–9; my translation)

Canclini's observation points to a dialectical relationship of give and take between *pueblo* and film director, one in which the latter takes on board some of the insights of the former, but then goes on to create a new revolutionary and artistic consciousness, one which is specifically engendered during the creative process. In *Para recibir el canto del pájaro*, indeed, this takes the form of a 'double-consciousness' (for further discussion, see Hart, 2002). Once the film director, Rodrigo, prompted by Cathérine (Geraldine Chaplin), realises that they had completely misunderstood the nature of political power in the community – they had assumed that it was the local cacique, Ubaldino (Reynaldo Yujra), who governed the decision-making process in the community – a coca leaves ceremony is held, and the omens are good. The film crew are, thus, allowed to film the bird ceremony but, unfortunately, despite having all their advanced audio equipment with them, they don't hear anything. For them, to use Spivak's words, 'the sender – the "peasant" – is marked only as a pointer to an irretrievable consciousness' (1997, p. 28). The audience, however, is able to 'hear' the sounds of the birds as they are transmuted into music, so that the film is effectively able to voice a double-consciousness with regard to the voice of the subaltern, hearing it and yet – at the same time – showcasing how it will never be heard.

NOTES

1. This was rather different from the situation at the Fundación Cinemateca Boliviana just up the road which, despite costing only slightly more (12 bolivianos), showed rather high-brow French or Soviet films, and hardly had any custom at all during the same period.
2. I tried to visit the Kaata community in the summer of 2001 in an attempt to verify the allegation, but was prevented from doing so by the civil rebellion engineered by Felipe Quispe 'Mallku' at that time, who was encouraging the Aymara communities to blockade the roads in and out of La Paz; stones were left on the roads and any vehicles leaving the city were attacked; see 'Las armas …' (2001). It is ironic that Felipe Quispe has taken on the name of 'Mallku'. Sanjinés informed me during an interview which took place in the Gringo Limón restaurant, La Paz, on 23 July 2001, that this gesture was inspired by his film since, the previous summer (2000), Felipe Quispe had brought a delegation into La Paz specifically to see *Yawar Mallku*, and from that point on he had adopted the sobriquet 'Mallku'. 'So, all of this is your fault, then,' I quipped. 'Not really,' Sanjinés replied. 'The problems go much deeper within our society.'
3. John King suggests that, 'The community takes a decision to castrate the North Americans' (1990, p. 194).
4. There was another problem as well: 'In certain scenes we put the emphasis entirely on sound, without paying attention to the needs of the spectators, for whom we claimed we were making the film. They needed images, and complained later when the film was shown to them' (Sanjinés, 1983, p. 35).
5. Interview with Sanjinés in the Gringo Limón restaurant, La Paz, 23 July 2001.
6. Despite a number of attempts, it has been difficult to get Channel 4 interested in broadcasting *Para recibir el canto de los pájaros*. It would play well with European audiences not only because of its political honesty and humour but because of Geraldine Chaplin who plays a leading role in the film.

24

Buenos Aires and the narration of urban spaces and practices

Richard Young

The sense of place and identity attached to Buenos Aires is derived in part from meanings associated with its material fabric, its monuments, buildings, streets, and social spaces: the Casa Rosada and the Plaza de Mayo, the Colón Theatre and the Congress building, *barrios* such as Palermo, Belgrano, San Telmo, and La Boca, the docks, the obelisk at the intersection of Avenida 9 de Julio and Calle Corrientes, and other notable monuments.[1] Each embodies events, stories and lifestyles that contribute to the history of the city, from first foundation to great metropolis.[2] Buenos Aires is also identified in the practices of everyday life it contains and is constructed symbolically in various forms of expression in words, images, and sound such as popular music, cinema, literature, photography, newspapers and other media.[3] These may be the sources of an essential Buenos Aires for both tourists and inhabitants, but they also affirm the multiple identities of a city as a dynamic space that is constantly changing. In the city of today we still recognize the urban milieu of the writings of Jorge Luis Borges (1899–1984) or Roberto Arlt (1900–42), but it is not the same as it was. It has endured material transformations and changes in the patterns of life, and has added the memory of more recent times to its history. Nor has it remained immune to the quickened global pace of change in urban environments of the past 30 years or so in architecture and planning, communication technologies and transportation, patterns of consumption, and a different economic order. Underlying it all, however, is the construction of the meanings and uses of city spaces by urban subjects in everyday lives, which is the phenomenon I propose to consider in the following commentary on three relatively recent novels.

MAPPING THE DAILY ROUND

The central figure of *El sueño* (The Dream; 1998), by César Aira,[4] is a newspaper vendor named Mario who works at a street corner kiosk with his father. His working life is spatially contained within the few city blocks of the kiosk's domain and is controlled by a regime set by the early morning opening and midday closing, the daily round of home deliveries, and the coming and going of regular customers. On one particular day, he is led to explore hitherto unknown territories within his otherwise familiar domain when he searches for Lidia, last seen in a shelter for single mothers, located on the same corner as the kiosk. When his quest takes him into an underground labyrinth beneath La Misericordia, a convent located in the next block, it leads him into something more gothic than everyday. It is resolved as farce, however, when the street around the kiosk is reduced to chaos and becomes a battleground for two electronic robots. One of them is El Monjatrón, a nun 4 metres high, controlled by the Mother Superior of the aforementioned convent, the other is El Dormilón, dressed in rumpled pyjamas, the same height as his adversary, built to publicize a local bed and sofa shop.

This synopsis will suffice to suggest an interplay between the mundane and the unexpected, between surface meanings and hidden depths suddenly revealed, a process metaphorically represented by a firework display in a prologue to the novel. Each firework is an unknown, ephemeral force that reveals a hitherto unseen quality when it explodes, like the later shifting of the categories of reality in the narrative that appears to open a door onto the fantastic, as in a story by Cortázar.[5] A similar effect is obtained by the oniric, first noted in the title of the novel and repeated throughout it in references to Mario's dream of the remote reality that Racing football club of Buenos Aires were champions. In the end, his dream is one of several revelations about life in the neighbourhood which are initially misread and eventually shown to have mundane meanings when they are clarified.

The first sentence of *El sueño* – 'At midnight the sky over Flores fills with fireworks' (Aira, 1998, p. 9) – grounds the novel in space at the same time that it suggests that there is more to it than meets the eye. The reference to fireworks has a metaphorical purpose, but Flores is real enough. It sits on the northern side of the 25 de Mayo freeway at a point just before it divides and continues north and west into the suburbs of greater Buenos Aires. Within this *barrio* the events narrated unfold in a rectangular space bounded by the Calles Bonorino and Lautaro on two sides and by the Avenida Bilbao and the Avenida José Bonifacio on the other two. The names of the streets and avenues and their spatial relationships are real and figure on street maps of Buenos Aires. Such a map would not show the kiosk on the corner, or Divanlito, the bed and sofa shop further along the street, although La Misericorida, a religious institution, might be marked, as might also the Plaza de la Misericordia occupying the city block immediately south of it. These landmarks are part of the everyday landscape for the inhabitants of the *barrio* and are easily discovered by a transient visitor. Yet, although the location of the kiosk and the convent may be identified precisely on a street map, where they would appear as contiguous, the spaces they construct are worlds apart. The kiosk is small, open to the street and the elements. Like a temporary structure, it is set against the building housing the women's shelter, with which it is said to have a symbiotic relationship (see Aira, 1998, p. 44). By contrast, La Misericordia is large and imposing, closed to the street, but with an architectural and structural autonomy, reflected in the styles of its buildings, that also mark the age of the institution and give it permanence.

Not only is this relationship lost on most conventional maps, but it takes a certain type of urban geography to recognize it. As postmodern geographers have emphasized, maps are neither objective nor comprehensive with respect to the reality they represent. They respond to ideology, politics and economics and are drawn in light of their intended function (see Harvey, 1989a, pp. 340–59). Underlying this perspective is the notion, central to Henri Lefebvre's *The Production of Space*, that space is a product, not a void or a container into which objects are placed or built, but a product of human activity and perception. Social space, the space created as a consequence of social activity and perception, is a social product: 'Every society', Lefebvre asserts, 'produces a space, its own space' (1991, p. 31). City maps, although they are images of spaces created by urban societies, are also rationalizations that show only what their makers decide to show us and refer us principally to built environments in order to provide a key to the labyrinth of the material city. They do not reveal the lived environment, the social space that embodies the kind of contrast represented in the difference between the newspaper kiosk and La Misericordia.

The geography of Mario, his father Natalio, and others who work at the kiosk has some similarities to a city map. Their conversation, like the narrator's discourse, is punctuated by references to streets and buildings from which a conventional map might be constructed and which affirm the spatial character of their vision of their world and their relationship to it. Nevertheless, their knowledge of spaces is limited, defined by their social interaction in the spaces with which they engage. Mario's knowledge of the *barrio* is confined to its morning activities. His routine is spelled out clearly and, like the references to location, also anchors the narrative. Underlying his routine is a practice: negotiation of a given set of actions within a determined period of time and a particular space. Moreover, Mario's routine interacts with that of others. His is a social practice, such as that sustaining the symbiotic relationship of the kiosk to the shelter for single mothers mentioned earlier. The relationship is not solely a matter of spatial contiguity, the physical attachment of one to the other, but of the intersecting routines observed by those who frequent each place. Beyond the shelter, however, Mario's practice engages an entire community, both through the distribution of newspapers to homes and his interaction with customers at the kiosk, whether they buy a newspaper or just pass the time of day.

Through a representation of the activity associated with the newspaper kiosk, César Aira's novel affirms that knowledge of space is a function of its use and perception. The text of the practice underlying this knowledge is inscribed primarily in the memory, in the minds and gestures of the inhabitants of the city. They have a map of sorts, consisting of a notebook kept by Natalio with the names, addresses, and orders of customers on home delivery. It is not easily deciphered, as Natalio realizes when looking for a particular entry. Yet, paradoxically, the notebook is more lucid than a street map. Although the latter seeks to provide an unequivocal guide, it suppresses the ambiguity inherent in any social space. By contrast, Natalio's notebook is filled with uncertainty. It shows spatial relationships by relating people to the spaces they occupy, and it introduces an historical dimension by also encompassing those who occupied them in the past. The identity of spaces and the processes of their configuration are therefore mediated by memory and owe as much to perceptions and experiences of the past as to the present.

Mario and Natalio map familiar urban spaces in accordance with their knowledge and prepare the daily newspaper routes from memory. Their familiarity with urban space and its social dimension is notably incomplete, however, limited to the actual places they service. There are buildings they have never entered and potential customers of whom they know nothing. Mario, for example, had never been inside La Misericordia before. Its space, as Natalio reflects, is 'a black hole on the surface of his business' (Aira, 1998, p. 63), not just because he sells no newspapers there, but because he knows no more of it than the rumours that circulate in the street, just as he knows little of the customers at the kiosk, even those with whom he has daily contact.

Although *El sueño* is grounded in a recognizable urban reality, the figures who inhabit it struggle with ambiguity and the elusiveness of certain knowledge. Their condition is no better illustrated than when events take a different turn in the second half of the novel. The pivotal moment comes when Mario, about to enter La Misericordia for a second time that morning, decides to reconnoitre before attempting it again by viewing the terrain from the roof of a nearby apartment tower where his friend Horacio works as a porter. Once on the roof, looking out over the ground he knows so well from below, his perceptions are challenged in a way comparable with what is described by Michel de Certeau in his chapter on walking in the city in *The Practice of Everyday Life*. De Certeau remarks that observers who walk the city streets write a text they are really not able to see, but when they view them from above they become a *voyeur* who 'transforms the bewitching world by which one was possessed into a text that lies before one's eyes' (De Certeau, 1984, p. 92). Such is the effect on Mario. His view from above and his reaction to what he sees distance him from the uncertainty of spatial and social relations on the ground, as if his everyday view of space has been replaced by the rationalization of a conventional street map.

Mario's new view of familiar spaces highlights the significance of perspective and subjective engagement with space. After descending from the tower, he will enter the convent grounds again. There, like Theseus meeting the Minotaur, he will encounter El Monjatrón, who will later do battle with El Dormilón on the street. Before then, after seeing the city from above, Mario must descend beneath it to rescue Lidia. This movement clearly entails a change from the kind of space in which events narrated so far have been predominantly located. Yet the change could have been anticipated right from the early pages of the novel, from the moment when the extrovert, everyday life of the street, of which the newspaper kiosk is the centre, is contrasted with the hidden, introverted existence of the unseen interior of La Misericordia. The change, however, is not solely a change in material space. It is also a move to a different level of being, from the open and apparent simplicity of the everyday to the underlying complexity of its meaning and deeper structures, as have already found a place in the traditions of modern thought and critical analysis: 'Both Marxism and Freudianism when applied to the everyday suggest an approach that in attempting to reveal the unconscious or non-apparent structures of everyday life uncover deep structures that are relentlessly gothic in their dimensions' (Highmore, 2002, p. 8). This is a space, however, which for the purposes of this chapter we will not enter.

WIDE URBAN SPACES

'From Sidewalk to Cyberspace', the title of one of the chapters in Michael J. Dear's *The Postmodern Urban Condition* (2000), in some ways characterizes the movement from the *barrio* of Aira's *El sueño* to the kind of metropolis represented in Fogwill's *Vivir afuera* (Living Outside; 1998).[6] Not to a view of Buenos Aires as a fully connected cybercity, but to a sprawling urban space on which the marks of modernity in its contemporary form are to be seen. The novel is based on relations and dialogues among six characters grouped in three couples: Susi and Pichi, the latter a veteran of the Malvinas War and now a small-time drug dealer and marihuana grower;[7] Guillermo Wolff, a dealer in unspecified goods, and Mariana, a prostitute, also known to Pichi and Susi; and a Jewish couple, Diana and Saúl, both professionals, the latter a doctor and medical researcher who works at a clinic Mariana has attended. Much of the novel follows the movements, conversations and thoughts of these couples in separate narrative threads unfolding in separate spaces from the early morning of one day to later in the morning of the same day.

The concept of marginality implied by the title of the novel and reflected in the condition of the characters is embedded in textual organization. There is no discursive centre, but repeated displacement from a basic narrator to the thoughts and speech of the characters, whose language is also ex-centric. Within the dominant code of Argentinean Spanish there are numerous idiolects related to particular social conditions or activities, including drug trafficking and use, sexual practices, the discourses of science and medicine, and the topical slang of everyday. Language usage also reflects marginalized linguistic practices and often diverges so far from a standard that characters occasionally find it necessary to explain their terminology to each other. Moreover, every shift in enunciation also displaces content. Although much of the narrative focuses on the present time of the characters, when they tell their stories, they not only narrate their own past and the lives of others, but engage a multitude of topics, with a randomness not unlike that of everyday speech, where matters addressed range from the most banal to the highly esoteric or arcane.

The mobility apparent in the production of discourse and its contents is paralleled by the representation of space. References to different places and the movement of the narrative among different sites of enunciation result in movement among different urban locations so that no single one dominates and events are spatially de-centred. The narrative takes place in and around Buenos Aires, but there is no single centre from which everything emanates and to which everything devolves. Through movement back and forth from the city centre to the suburbs and the periphery of the capital region, such as La Plata and Florencio Varela, the novel conveys the sense of a city as a vast metropolitan region in which, as commentators have also noted (see Sarlo, 1994, pp. 13–23), the importance of its central core is diminished. The city is thus reconstituted in comparison with how it has formerly been seen. Traditional Buenos Aires, with its history of growth from 'gran aldea' (large village) to cosmopolitan capital and the urban personality it acquired between the 1920s and the 1950s, which dominated the urban novel in Argentina during the second half of the twentieth century, is absent from *Vivir afuera*. In its place are a series of marginal sites in a wide urban space, which become temporary centres for as long as they are sites of communication.

This emphasis and its implications are already evident from the sense of dislocation of time and space conveyed in the first 30 pages or so of the novel. In 1994, Guillermo Wolff remembers a dream he had in 1958 or 1959 of a scene in a bar, and within the dream there is a further dislocation in the fantasy of one of its characters who imagines himself leading an assault against a Peronist stronghold in the city. Moreover, Wolff's recollection occurs to him while driving back to Buenos Aires at high speed through the darkness in the early hours of the morning after a class reunion in La Plata. He is periodically confused about whether the reunion celebrated 25 or 35 years, and his thoughts eventually alternate with the narration of the situation of another of the six main characters, at the same time as it is fragmented by his own mental meandering and snatches of conversation among passengers in the car. At one point, he turns on the radio: 'The FM picked up several superimposed broadcasts. Someone mentioned that the area had been invaded by clandestine radios so that every sect and even every rock band had its own transmitter' (Fogwill, 1998, p. 21).[8]

The novel begins, then, with images of a car hurtling through the night, the darkness broken by its headlights and the sudden illumination from approaching vehicles, amid a cacophony of voices, confusion between the real and the imagined, and the absence of a fixed time and space. Such images emphasize the transitory, indeterminate nature of space as a model sustained throughout the novel. Thus, the first part of a conversation between Diana and Saúl takes place in a car while driving through central Buenos Aires, initially for breakfast in a café and then to the clinic where Saúl works. The city spaces, however, are merely sites to navigate and are less significant than the interior of a car or a café where social encounter and exchange take place. A café is also where Wolff and Mariana first meet, and when they subsequently go to Wolff's apartment the significance of this new space is its function as a site where their temporary relationship is continued. Similarly, much of the encounter between Pichi and Susi occurs in a hotel room, a temporary site for their relationship where they eat, sleep, have sex, talk, and watch TV, and from which they connect to other times and places through their thoughts and conversation.

The narrative strategies in *Vivir afuera* are not new to fiction, of course, but are used to capture new conditions in urban life. No visitor to Buenos Aires who walks the length of Calle Florida can fail to miss the ubiquity of cell telephones or recognise how they have transformed the modes of production of social space by giving the phrase 'person to person' a more literal meaning that diminishes the centrality of space in communications. Although there are no references to cellular technology in the novel, comparable effects from other technologies are mentioned. Both Susi and Mariana are preoccupied by Walkmans, which have transformed the mode of consumption of popular culture and, like the proliferation of FM stations, have reduced the dependence of cultural diffusion on traditional spaces. In the case of Mariana, the effects are inscribed in her body language, as when she is described as 'moving her neck and head as if listening to the rhythm of a current hit on a disk' (Fogwill, 1998, p. 127) even when she is not wearing a headset. Wolff's use of a remote control to turn on a disk player is a further example of the alteration of spatial relationships in the consumption of popular culture, but, in his case, remote communication of a different kind is more significant. His apartment floor is littered with faxes and his computer is turned on continuously, allowing him to be in touch with world markets from within his own apartment. Similarly, Saúl relies on his office computer both as a tool in medical research and as a means of communication, and is understandably frantic when it is stolen. His predicament and what it says about spatial relationships are no less than Pichi's preoccupation that his marihuana crop may be detected just as easily by satellite surveillance as by discovery by the police or a rival on the ground.

SPECTACLE AND SURVEILLANCE IN URBAN SPACE

Surveillance and fear of its consequences are also factors in Ana María Shua's *La muerte como efecto secundario* (Death as a Side Effect, 1997) where Buenos Aires is represented as a vaguely futuristic, but very recognizable, urban dystopia.[9] The title alludes to the side-effects of medicines which alleviate pain, but hasten death. More specifically, it refers to the profitability of withholding medication in order to keep the dying alive, as occurs in the euphemistically termed *Casas de Recuperación* (Convalescent Homes). These are private institutions where the elderly and infirm are forcibly interned and required to pay the costs of internment. Thus, the novel focuses on the commodity value of life and death, allowing Shua to draw attention effectively to economic and social conditions in contemporary Argentina. Coincidentally, her vision of Buenos Aires has elements in common with that projected by Mike Davis for Los Angeles. In *Ecology of Fear: Los Angeles and the Imagination of Disaster* (first published, 1999) Davis examines what for him are the inevitable consequences of California's defiance of the natural environment, but his last two chapters focus on the literary destruction of Los Angeles, the tradition of annihilation of the city in pulp fiction and film. In the process, he is somewhat dismissive of the image of the postmodern urban condition constructed in films like *Blade Runner*: 'for all of *Blade Runner*'s glamor as the reigning star of sci-fi dystopias, its vision of the future is strangely anachronistic and surprisingly unprescient' (1999, p. 360). He asks: 'Instead of following the grain of traditional clichés and seeing the future merely as a grotesque, Wellsian magnification of technology and architecture, would it not be more fruitful to project existing trends along their current downward-sloping trajectories?' (ibid., p. 362). In reply he points to what he considers already as indicators of the future: the problems of security and surveillance, riots, racial tension and conflict, the deterioration of up-market residential areas, and the growth of prisons.

Urban growth Los Angeles-style has acquired a certain notoriety of late and is emblematic of the influence of North American culture and social practices around the world. In her essay on the city in *Escenas de la vida posmoderna* (1994), Beatriz Sarlo writes: 'Many Latin American cities, Buenos Aires among them, have entered a process of *angelinización*' (1994, pp. 13–14). Although referring to the loss of centrality of the heart of the city, not unlike that seen in *Vivir afuera*, she could have been referring to other phenomena, all relevant to Los Angeles and major urban centres in Latin America: growth by polynucleation, or the absorption of surrounding communities into an extended urban sprawl focused around satellite centres; the flight of business and industry from the centre to the periphery and the creation of so-called edge cities; a general loss of privacy and systematic privatization of public spaces; the mallification of commerce; the increase in gated communities and no-go zones; and the continuing fragmentation of urban populations, if not from racial or ethnic differences, then from economic and class divisions.

This is not to trace all current patterns of urbanization and their ills to Los Angeles, but to note that, alongside local problems, there is also a growing standardization in urban life for which Los Angeles is often perceived to be the paradigm. With respect to Buenos Aires, Shua pursues an approach akin to what Davis undertook for Los Angeles: the projection of 'existing trends along their current downward-sloping trajectories'. Her narrative centres on Enrique Kollody, a forty-something man who has led a rather lacklustre life. He is also the narrator and writes his story for an ex-lover who has long since left him. His immediate difficulties stem from the age and declining health of his parents, both interned in a *Casa de Recuperación* – his mother with dementia and his father with intestinal cancer for which he undergoes surgery. Although his mother's condition has no remedy, Enrique recognizes the deficiency in the care given to his father and responds to his plea for rescue. These actions make fugitives of them both and lead them to seek asylum in a controlled zone that has become a sanctuary for elderly runaways (*viejos cimarrones*). There are several themes embedded within this story – issues of gender, questions of artistic creativity, and the concept of social authority, for example. In what follows, however, I will focus on the privatization and control of public spaces, the spectacularization of the social, and society under surveillance.[10]

The parks, streets, squares, and market places where citizens and visitors can pass and assemble freely allow the average city to be considered a public space, but the version of Buenos Aires presented in *La muerte como efecto secundario* has no such connotation. It is fragmented into zones of exclusion between which movement is hazardous and within which self-interest has replaced the common good. At one end of the scale are gated communities, like the one visited by Enrique Kollody in Belgrano (see Shua, 1997, p. 188) with chain-link fences, security huts, shopping centre, and carefully tended gardens. They are products of a politics of exclusion based on elimination of the heterogeneous from a community united by a common race, social class, and income levels, and motivated by a desire for security from fear of the city at large.[11] Such communities appropriate the public for private purposes, change the conventional notion of the street, and, in the process, use laws intended for the common good as a means to regulate on behalf of a minority. The place Enrique visits is no different from many others already established in cities such as Buenos Aires and São Paulo (see Caldeira, 1999). At the other extreme there are controlled zones, where crime and gang warfare are endemic. Avoided by the average citizen, they also exercise a kind of exclusivity and operate by their own rules, in defiance of the law. Enrique enters one such zone looking for help to rescue his father and describes it as a cancer spreading on the body of the city (see Shua, 1997, pp. 165–6).

Regardless of their differences, gated communities and controlled zones are both products of a society that has yielded to free-market forces and is left without the resources necessary to maintain services or authority. The entire city is a no-man's-land that no-one really controls. The convalescent homes employ guards as a defence against gangs searching for drugs, and the companies that run the homes maintain a security force to round up the aged or track down fugitives such as Enrique's father. Whenever Enrique ventures out of doors he travels by armoured taxi with a driver who is known to him. Ironically, wherever he goes in public, he has to surround himself with private space in order to feel protected. By the same token, loss of public spaces is compensated by substitutes and simulations: 'there are many strollerdomes [*caminódromos*] in the city, protected spaces that pretend to be a particular *barrio* where for a modest entrance fee it is possible to walk till you drop passing through infinite – or limited – landscapes that are almost real' (Shua, 1997, p. 18). Deprived of direct contact, inhabitants of the city experience it as spectacle and pay for the pleasure. The strollerdomes are comparable to shopping malls where experience is protected and sanitized, as in a Disneyland theme park, in an interior private space. Not only is the experience of life as a spectacle consistent with aspects of our age, so is the development of cities as tourist attractions by exploiting their history, as in tango tourism in Buenos Aires or the promotion of heritage districts such as San Telmo.[12] One telling incident in the novel will make the point. Wanting to walk outside for once, not in the artificial world of a strollerdome or shopping centre, Enrique pockets his pistol and heads for the Plaza de Mayo, for one of the protest marches of the mothers of May Square, which have become ritualized as a tourist spectacle and operate daily.

The 'spectacularization' of reality is already anticipated in the first paragraphs of the novel in Enrique's contemplation of photos of his father's cancer. Nowhere is safe from cameras that invade even the body. As if to reinforce the point, Enrique turns on the television hoping to remove the image of the cancer from his mind – 'one image is erased with another image' (Shua, 1997, p. 10) – but the program he sees is the President's weekly broadcast, a further reminder that life is essentially about images. As the novel proceeds, there are repeated references to cameras and it becomes clear that the society of the spectacle is also the society of the panopticon.[13] The inhabitants of the city are under constant surveillance and therefore under constant threat. For the old and infirm, there is the possibility of denunciation and internment in a *Casa de Recuperación*. For Enrique and his father, as fugitives from one such home, there is the fear of being seen and his father re-institutionalized. The cameras are inside and outside the *Casas*, often operated by freelance photographers in search of a newsworthy story. Inside, they film the sick and the dying and sell their footage for television. Outside they complement surveillance cameras, and Enrique is not in the least surprised to see a film of his father's rescue on television. Reality TV at its extreme, it takes us back to the photograph of the cancer described at the beginning of the novel. It too is an extreme image, which is also a metaphor of the city. When Enrique describes the controlled zone he visits in order to contract his father's rescuers, he refers to it as a cancer and describes it with same vocabulary used to describe the photograph, as if the city and its society were afflicted with the same pathology.

CONCLUSION

Although the attribution of a human pathology to a city is evidently metaphorical, it may also be taken to suggest the closeness between urban space and its inhabitants, which each of the three novels considered here reveals in its way. The material city is recognizable in all of them, but the identity of the city is also a function of how the inhabitants live their lives. Whether in the everyday landmarks of the *barrio* in *El sueño*, the highways and hyperreality of the great metropolis in *Vivir afuera*, or the urban dystopia described in *La muerte como efecto secundario*, our comprehension of the city comes from a recognition of the interaction of the various elements it contains. Such is the context in which we may understand the notion of space as a product that is constructed and given meaning on the basis of its social dimensions. It is also a way of understanding the culture of a city, not just in its great monuments and landmarks, but in the patterns of every day, in the sense of place felt by citizens, in movements and routines, such as we find symbolically represented in the works of fiction like the three considered here.

NOTES

1 For a general discussion of the symbolic meanings of space and place in relation to social life, see Derek Gregory's *Geographical Imaginations* (1994).
2 For the period of transformation of Buenos Aires from town to city, see James Scobie's *Buenos Aires: Plaza to Suburb, 1870–1910* (1974). For its current condition as a 'world' city, see David Keeling's *Buenos Aires: Global Dreams, Local Crisis* (1996).
3 David William Foster, in *Buenos Aires: Perspectives on the City and Cultural Production* (1998b), studies a number of urban cultural phenomena.
4 César Aira is a translator, novelist, dramatist and essayist and has published over 30 books in the past 25 years. Among his works of fiction are *Ema, la cautiva* (1981), *La liebre* (1991), *Embalse* (1992), *Cómo me hice monja* (1993), *Los misterios de Rosario* (1994), *La abeja* (1996), *La serpiente* (1997), and *Un sueño realizado* (2001). On one prominent website dedicated to fiction in Argentina he is described as 'one of the best kept secrets of Argentinean literature' (www.literatura.org).
5 In conversation with Ernesto González Bermejo, Cortázar comments: '[the fantastic] is something very simple, that may happen in the middle of everyday reality under this midday sun, now between you and me, or in the Metro while we

were coming to this meeting' (González Bermejo, 1979, p. 48). (All translations from Spanish in this chapter are mine.)
6   Rodolfo Enrique Fogwill (who prefers to be known simply as Fogwill) has also published several collections of poetry and short stories, notably *Muchacha punk* (1992), and is the author of several novels, including *Los pichiciegos* (1983), *La buena nueva de los Libros del Caminante* (1990), *Una pálida historia de amor* (1991), and *En otro orden de cosas* (2001).
7   Pichi is also a character in Fogwill's *Los pichiciegos*.
8   The breakdown of authority in urban regions (another manifestation of a fragmented environment) is not only represented by clandestine broadcasting, but by lawlessness on the highways at night, and the pirating of electricity by illegally tapping into the power lines.
9   Ana María Shua has written for the theatre and the cinema and has also published poetry, short stories, and books for children. In addition to *La muerte como efecto secundario*, her novels include *Soy paciente* (1980), *Los amores de Laurita* (1984), and *El libro de los recuerdos* (1984).
10 For other discussions of contemporary urban conditions in Latin America, see *Espacio urbano, comunicación y violencia en América Latina* (2002) edited by Mabel Moraña.
11 For an overview of the history of urban fear, see the chapter on the city in Fu-Yi Tuan's *Landscapes of Fear* (1975, pp. 145–74). For a view of the product of fear and security in a modern city, see Davis's chapter 'Fortress LA' in his *City of Quartz* (1990, pp. 221–63).
12 For further studies on the city as spectacle, see Judd and Fainstein (eds) (1999) and Hannigan (1998).
13 The term is derived from a structure described by Jeremy Bentham in 1791, but was made more current by Michel Foucault's references to it in *Surveiller et punir* (*Discipline and Punish*; first published in 1975).

References

Acevedo Muñoz, E. R. 1997: *Los olvidados*: Luis Buñuel and the crisis of nationalism in Mexican cinema. Paper presented at the meeting of the Latin American Studies Association, Guadalajara, Mexico, 17–19 April. http://lasa.international.pitt.edu/LASA97/acevedomunoz.pdf (accessed 11 September 2002).

Achugar, H. 1989: Notas sobre el discurso testimonial latinoamericano. In R. Chang-Rodríguez and G. de Beer, *La historia en la literatura iberoamericana*. Hanover, NH: Ediciones del Norte, 278–94.

Achugar, H. 1997: Leones, cazadores e historiadores: a propósito de las políticas de la memoria y el conocimiento. *Revista Iberoamericana* 180, 379–87.

Adorno, T. 1997: *Aesthetic Theory*, translated by R. Hullot-Kentor. Minneapolis: University of Minnesota Press.

Agger, B. 1992: *Cultural Studies as Critical Theory*. London: Falmer Press.

Agrasánchez, J. R. 1997: *Carteles de la época de oro del cine mexicano (Poster Art from the Golden Age of Mexican Cinema)*, with introduction by C. Ramírez Berg. Harlingen, TX: Archivo Fílmico Agrasánchez; Guadalajara: Universidad de Guadalajara; Mexico City: Instituto Mexicano de Cinematografía.

Aguilar, L. 2002: Hispanic media accused of failing to serve community. *Denver Post* 30 June.

Aguirre, C. 1993: *Agentes de su propia libertad: los esclavos de Lima y la desintegración de la esclavitud 1821–1854*. Lima: Fondo Editorial de la Pontificia Universidad Católica del Perú.

Aira, C. 1991a: *Copi*. Buenos Aires: Beatriz Viterbo.

Aira, C. 1991b: El sultán. *Paradoxa* 6, 27–9.

Aira, C. 1996a: Cómo me hice monja. In C. Aira, *Cómo me hice monja*. Mexico City: Joaquín Mortiz, 8–108.

Aira, C. 1996b: La costurera y el viento. In C. Aira, *Cómo me hice monja*. Mexico City: Joaquín Mortiz, 109–229.

Aira, C. 1998: *El sueño*. Buenos Aires: Emecé.

Alarcón, N. 1983: Chicana feminist literature – a re-vision through Malintzín: Putting the flesh back on the object. In C. Moraga and G. Anzaldúa (eds), *This Bridge Called My Back: Writings by Radical Women of Color*. New York: Kitchen Table-Women of Color Press, 182–90.

Alarcón, N. 1989: Tradutora, traditora: A paradigmatic figure of Chicana feminism. *Cultural Critique* 13, 57–89.

Alarcón, N. 1990: Chicana feminism: In the tracks of 'the' native woman. *Cultural Studies* 4, 3, 248–55.

Alegría, C. and Flakoll, D. J. 1983: *No me agarran viva: la mujer salvadoreña en lucha*. Mexico City: Praxis.

Almaguer, T. 1987: Ideological distortions in recent Chicano historiography: The internal model and Chicano historical representation. *Aztlán* 18, 1, 7–28.
Almeida, B. 1986: *Capoeira: A Brazilian Art Form*. Berkeley, CA: North Atlantic Books.
Alvárez, L. 1992: Breve panorama de la comunicación en el Uruguay. In C. Rama (ed.), *Industrias culturales en Uruguay*. Montevideo: Arca, 37–56.
Ancízar, M. 1984: *Peregrinación de Alpha*. Bogotá: Banco Popular. Original publication (1853): *Peregrinación de Alpha (M. Ancízar) por las provincias del norte de la Nueva Granada, en 1850 i 51*. Bogotá: Echeverría.
Anderson, B. 1991: *Imagined Communities: Reflections on the Origins and Spread of Nationalism*. London: Verso.
Anderson, B. 1993: *Comunidades imaginadas*. Buenos Aires: Fondo de Cultura Económica.
Andrews, J. 1999: The emergence of corporate subjectivity: Literature, imperialism, and the transformation of American national consciousness, 1882–1910. Unpublished PhD dissertation, Department of English, University of Pittsburgh.
Anonymous 2001: Las armas cierran el paso al diálogo. *La Razón* 3777 (14 July), 1, 8–10.
Anzaldúa, G. 1999a: Toward a new consciousness (La conciencia mestiza). In *Borderlands (La frontera)*. San Francisco: Spinsters/Aunt Lute, 99–120.
Anzaldúa, G. 1999b: The homeland, Aztlán (El otro México). In *Borderlands (La frontera)*. San Francisco: Spinsters/Aunt Lute, 23–35.
Anzaldúa, G. 1999c: *Borderlands (La frontera)*. San Francisco: Spinsters/Aunt Lute.
Arbena, J. L. 1988: Sport and the study of Latin American society: An overview. In J. L. Arbena (ed.), *Sport and Society in Latin America: Diffusion, Dependency, and the Rise of Mass Culture*. Westport, CT: Greenwood Press, 5–32.
Archetti, E. P. 1992: Argentinian football: A ritual of violence. *International Journal of the History of Sport* 9, 209–35.
Archetti, E. P. 1994: Masculinity and football: The formation of national identity in Argentina. In R. Giulianotti and J. Williams (eds), *Game without Frontiers: Football, Identity and Modernity*. Aldershot: Arena, 37–63.
Archetti, E. P. 1996: Playing styles and masculine virtues in Argentine football. In M. Melhuus and K. A. Stølen (eds), *Machos, Mistresses, Madonnas: Contesting the Power of Latin America Gender Imagery*. London: Verso, 34–55.
Archetti, E. P. 1999: *Masculinities: Football, Polo and the Tango in Argentina*. Oxford: Berg.
Archetti, E. P. 2001: The spectacle of a heroic life: The case of Diego Maradona. In D. L. Andrews and S. J. Jackson (eds), *Sports Stars: The Cultural Politics of Sporting Celebrity*. London: Routledge, 151–63.
Arendt, H. 1958: *The Human Condition*. Chicago: Chicago University Press.
Arguedas, J. M. 1975: *Formación de una cultura nacional indoamericana*. Mexico City: Siglo XXI.
Arias Saravia, L. 2000: *La Argentina en clave de metáfora: un itinerario a través del ensayo*. Buenos Aires: Corregidor.
Aronna, M. 1999: *'Pueblos Enfermos': The Discourse of Illness in the Turn-of-the-Century Spanish and Latin American Essay*. Chapel Hill, NC: North Carolina Studies in the Romance Languages and Literatures.
Auerbach, E. 1953: *Mimesis: The Representation of Realism in Western Literature*, translated by W. R. Trask. Princeton, NJ: Princeton University Press.

Baddeley, O. and Fraser, V. 1989: *Drawing the Line: Art and Cultural Identity in Contemporary Latin America*. London: Verso.
Bakhtin, M. 1981: *The Dialogic Imagination: Four Essays*, edited by M. Holquist, and translated by C. Emerson. Austin: University of Texas Press.
Balderston, D., Gonzalez, M. and López, A. M. (eds) 2000: *Routledge Encyclopedia of Contemporary Latin American and Caribbean Culture*. London: Routledge.
Baricco, A. 1999: *El alma de Hegel y las vacas de Wisconsin*. Madrid: Ediciones Siruela.
Barnet, M. 1973: *Esteban Montejo: The Autobiography of a Runaway Slave*. New York: Random House.
Barragán, R. and Rivera Cusicanqui, S. 1999: *Debates post-coloniales: una introducción a los Estudios de la Subalternidad*. La Paz: Editorial Tercer Mundo.
Barrera, V. and Bielby, D. D. 2001: Places, races, and other familiar things: The cultural experience of telenovela viewing among Latinos in the United States. *Journal of Popular Culture* 34, 4, 1–18.
Barrios, D. and Viezzer, M. 1977: *Si me permiten hablar: testimonio de Domitila, una mujer de las minas de Bolivia*. Mexico City: Siglo XXI.
Barry, T. 1987: *Land and Hunger in Central America*. Boston: South End Press.
Barthes, R. 1957: *Mythologies*. Paris: Seuil.
Barthes, R. 1972: *Mythologies*, translated by A. Lavers. London: Cape.
Barthes, R. 1986: *The Rustle of Language*. New York: Hill and Wang.
Bartra, R. 1987: *La jaula de la melancolía: identidad y metamorfosis del mexicano*. Mexico City: Grijalbo.
Basave Benítez, A. 1992: *México mestizo: análisis del nacionalismo mexicano en torno a la mestizofilia de Andrés Molina Enríquez*. Mexico City: Fondo de Cultura Económica.
Baudrillard, J. 1981: *Simulacres et simulation*, edited by M. Delorme. Paris: Galilée.
Bazin, A. 1951 (1971): Cruelty and love in *Los olvidados*. In *What is Cinema*, vol. 3. Berkeley: University of California Press, 209–15. http://www.mip.berkeley.edu/cgi-bin/cine_doc_detail.pl/cine_img?5456?5456?1
Beardsell, P. 2000: *Europe and Latin America: Returning the Gaze*. Manchester: Manchester University Press.
Beasley-Murray, J. 2002: Towards an unpopular cultural studies: The perspective of the multitude. In S. Godsland and A. M. White (eds), *Cultura popular: Studies in Spanish and Latin American Popular Culture*. Oxford: Lang, 27–45.
Belaúnde, V. A. 1965: *Peruanidad*. Lima: Ediciones Librería Studium.
Benítez Rojo, A. 1992: *The Repeating Island: The Caribbean and the Postmodern Perspective*. Durham, NC: Duke University Press.
Benjamin, W. 1969: *Illuminations*, translated by H. Zohn. New York: Schochen Press.
Bergmann, E. *et al.* (eds) 1990: *Women, Culture and Politics in Latin America*. Berkeley, CA: University of California Press.
Bermúdez, S. 2003: Popular culture in Latin America. In Philip Swanson (ed.), *The Companion to Latin American Studies*. London: Arnold, 172–84.
Berry, E. E. and Epstein, M. 1999: *Transcultural Experiments*. London: Macmillan.
Betancourt, L. 1995: El bolero, el son y la salsa. Unpublished manuscript provided for consultation by author.
Beverley, J. 1993a: *Against Literature*. Minneapolis: University of Minnesota Press.
Beverley, J. 1993b: The margin at the center: On *Testimonio*. In *Against Literature*. Minneapolis: University of Minnesota Press, 69–86.

Beverley, J. 1996: Estudios culturales y vocación política. *Revista de Crítica Cultural* (Santiago de Chile) 12, 46–53.

Beverley, J. 1999: *Subalternity and Representation: Arguments in Cultural Theory*. Durham, NC: Duke University Press.

Beverley, J., Aronna, M. and Oviedo, J. (eds) 1995: *The Postmodernism Debate in Latin America*. Durham, NC: Duke University Press.

Bhabha, H. 1997: Cultural diversity and cultural differences. In W. Ashcroft, G. Griffiths and H. Tiffin (eds), *The Post-Colonial Studies Reader*. London: Routledge, 206–9.

Bogle, D. 1989: *Toms, Coons, Mulattoes, Mammies and Bucks*. New York: Continuum.

Bola Sete, M. 1997: *A capoeira angola na Bahia*. Rio de Janeiro: Pallas.

Borges, J. L. 1962: *Ficciones*, translated by A. Kerrigan. New York: Grove Press.

Borges, J. L. 1964: The sham. In *Dreamtigers*, translated by M. Boyer and H. Morland. Austin, TX: University of Texas Press, 31.

Borges, J. L. 1989: El simulacro. In *Obras completas*, II, 1952–1972. Buenos Aires: Emecé, 1676.

Bourdieu, P. 1993: *The Field of Cultural Production: Essays on Art and Literature*. Cambridge: Polity Press.

Bové, P. 1997: Should cultural studies take literature seriously? *Critical Quarterly* 39, 1, 51–8.

Brantlinger, P. 1990: *Crusoe's Footsteps: Cultural Studies in Britain and America*. London: Routledge.

Brockett, C. D. 1988: *Land, Power and Poverty: Agrarian Transformation and Political Conflict in Central America*. Boulder, CO: Westview Press.

Brotherston, G. 1997: Regarding the evidence in Me llamo Rigoberta Menchú. *Journal of Latin American Cultural Studies* 6, 93–103.

Bruce, J. 1953: *Those Perplexing Argentines*. New York: Longman.

Bruner, J. 1991: The narrative construction of reality. *Critical Inquiry* 18, 1–21.

Bruns, H. T. 2000: *Futebol, carnaval e capoeira*. Campinas, Brazil: Papirus.

Bueno, E. P. and Caesar, T. (eds) 1998: *Imagination Beyond Nation: Latin American Popular Culture*. Pittsburgh: University of Pittsburgh Press.

Buñuel, L. 1994 (1982): *My Last Breath*, translated by A. Israel. London: Vintage.

Burkholder, M. A. and Lyman, L. J. 1994: *Colonial Latin America*, 2nd edn. Oxford: Oxford University Press.

Burns, S. (curator) 1997: *The Art of Desire: Erotic Treasures from the Kinsey Institute …* (Kinsey Institute for Research in Sex, Gender, and Reproduction). Bloomington: School of Fine Arts Gallery, Indiana University.

Busto Duthurburu, J. A. 2001: *Breve historia de los negros del Perú*. Lima: Fondo Editorial del Congreso del Perú.

Butler, J. 1993: *Bodies That Matter: On the Discursive Limits of 'Sex'*. London: Routledge.

Cabrera Infante, G. 1997: Prólogo. In J. Martí, *Diarios*. Barcelona: Galaxia Gutenberg, 7–22.

Cacciari, M. 1993: *Architecture and Nihilism: On the Philosophy of Modern Architecture*, translated by S. Sartarelli. New Haven, CT: Yale University Press.

Caldas, W. 1989: *O pontapé inicial: memória do futebol brasileiro*. São Paulo: Ibrasa.

Caldeira, T. P. R. 1999: Fortified enclaves. In S. Low (ed.), *Theorizing the City: The New Urban Anthropology Reader*. New Brunswick, NJ: Rutgers University Press.

Calderón González, J. 1996: El bolero en el cine: ¡Ay amor, qué bueno eres! In L. Arduengo Pineda (ed.), *Los cien mejores años de nuestras vidas*. Xalapa: Universidad Veracruzana, 183–202.
Callois, R. 1996: *El hombre y lo sagrado*. Mexico: Fondo de Cultura Económica.
Canaparo, C. 1999: *El perlonghear*. London: La Protesta Ediciones.
Capoeira, N. 1992: *Capoeira: os fundamentos da malícia*. Rio de Janeiro: Record.
Capoeira, N. 1999: *Capoeira: galo já cantou*. Rio de Janeiro: Record.
Carneiro, E. 1977: *Capoeira*. Rio Janeiro: FUNARTE.
Carpentier, A. 1981: Conciencia e identidad de América. In *La novela latino-americana en vísperas de un nuevo siglo y otros ensayos*. Mexico City: Siglo XXI, 79–158.
Cascudo, L. de C. 1983: *Historia da alimentação no Brasil*. Rio de Janeiro: J. Olympio.
Casey, E. 1997: *The Fate of Place: A Philosophical History*. Berkeley, CA: University of California Press.
Castells, M. 1998: *End of Millennium*, vol. 3. Malden, MA: Blackwell.
Castillo, A. del (ed.) 1996: *Goddess of the Americas: Writings on the Virgin of Guadalupe*. New York: Riverhead Books.
Castillo Zapata, R. 1991: *Fenomenología del bolero*. Caracas: Monte Ávila.
Castro, J. de 1977: *The Geopolitics of Hunger*. New York: Monthly Review Press.
Castro, R. 1995: *Estrela solitária: un brasileiro chamado Garrincha*. Rio de Janeiro: Companhia das Letras.
Chanady, A. 2000: National reconciliation and colonial resistance: The notion of hybridity in José Martí. In R. de Grandis and A. Bernd (eds), *Unforeseeable Americas: Questioning Cultural Hybridity in the Americas*. Atlanta, GA: Rodopi, 21–33.
Chang, D. 2001a: NBC courts Spanish-language viewers for daytime soaps. *Miami Herald* 9 July.
Chang, D. 2001b: Univisión snatches rights to rival's biggest television hit. *Miami Herald* 19 June.
Cherniavsky, E. 1996: Subaltern studies in a US frame. *boundary* 2, 23, 2, 85–110.
Chunovie, L. 2001: Telemundo schedule high on humor. *Electronic Media* 14 May.
Cisneros, S. 1996: Guadalupe, the sex goddess. In A. Castillo (ed.), *Goddess of the Americas*. New York: Riverhead Books, 46–51.
Coe, S. D. 1994: *America's First Cuisines*. Austin, TX: University of Texas Press.
Colás, S. 1994: *Postmodernity in Latin America: The Argentine Paradigm*. Durham, NC: Duke University Press.
Colina, E. and Díaz Torres, D. 1978: Ideology of melodrama in the old Latin American cinema. In Z. M. Pick (ed.), *Latin American Film Makers and the Third Cinema*. Ottawa: Carleton University, 50–3.
Contreras, S. 1998: César Aira lee a Manuel Puig. In J. A. and G. Speranza (eds), *Encuentro Internacional Manuel Puig*. Rosario: Beatriz Viterbo, 307–12.
Convenio Andrés Bello – Ministerio de Cultura de Colombia 1999: Un estudio sobre el aporte de las industrias culturales y del entretenimiento al desempeño económico de los países de la Comunidad Andina (Informe preliminar: definiciones básicas pautas metodológicas y primeros resultados en Colombia). Bogotá: Convenio Andrés Bello – Ministerio de Cultura de Colombia.
Cooper Alarcón, D. 1988–90: The Aztec palimpsest: Toward a new understanding of Aztlán, cultural identity and history. *Aztlán* 19, 2, 30–68.

Copi 1990: *Textes rassemblés par Jorge Damonte*. Paris: C. Bourgeois.
Copi 2000: *Eva Perón*, translated by J. Monteleone. Buenos Aires: Adriana Hidalgo Editora.
Cornejo Polar, A. 1982a: *Literatura y Sociedad en el Perú: narración y poesía, un debate*. Lima: Hueso Húmero Ediciones.
Cornejo Polar, A. 1982b: Unidad, pluralidad, totalidad: el corpus de la literatura latinoamericana. In *Sobre literatura y crítica latinoamericanas*. Caracas: Universidad Central de Venezuela, 43–50.
Cornejo Polar, A. 1993: Ensayo sobre el sujeto y la representación en la literatura latinoamericana: algunas hipótesis. *Hispamérica* 66, 3–15.
Cornejo Polar, A. 1994: *Escribir en el aire: ensayo sobre la heterogeneidad sociocultural en las literaturas andinas*. Lima: Editorial Horizonte.
Cornejo Polar, A. 1997: Mestizaje e hibridez: los riesgos de las metáforas. *Revista Iberoamericana* 63, 341–4.
Cornejo Polar, A. et al. 1984: *Vigencia y universalidad de José María Arguedas*. Lima: Horizonte.
Cortázar, J. 1966: *Hopscotch*, translated by G. Rabassa. New York: Pantheon.
Cortázar, J. 1973: *All Fires: The Fire and Other Stories*, translated by S. J. Levine. New York: Pantheon.
Cortés Rocca, P. and Kohan, M. 1998: *Imágenes de vida, relatos de muerte: Eva Perón – cuerpo y política*. Rosario: Beatriz Viterbo.
Cottle, M. 2001: Color TV: How soaps are integrating America. *The New Republic* 27 August–3 September, 25.
Crystal, D. 1992: *A Dictionary of Language*, 2nd edn. Chicago: University of Chicago Press.
Cuche, D. 1975: *Poder blanco y resistencia negra en el Perú*. Lima: Instituto Nacional de Cultura.
D'Allemand, P. 2000: *Latin American Cultural Criticism: Re-Interpreting a Continent*. Lewiston, NY: Edwin Mellen Press.
Damatta, R. 1982: Esporte na soiedade: um ensaio sobre o futebol bresileiro. In R. DaMatta et al., *Universo do futebol: esporte e sociedade brasileira*. Rio de Janeiro: Edicões Pinakotheke, 19–42.
Dardel, J. 1965: The mythic. In T. Sebeok (ed.), *Myth Symposium*. Bloomington: Indiana University Press, 25–64.
Davies, C. 2000: Fernando Ortiz's transculturation: The postcolonial intellectual and the politics of cultural representation. In R. Fiddian (ed.), *Postcolonial Perspectives on the Cultures of Latin America and Lusophone America*. Liverpool: Liverpool University Press, 141–68.
Dávila, A. 2001: *Latinos, Inc.: The Marketing and Making of a People*. Berkeley, CA: University of California Press.
Dávila, A. 2002: Talking back: Spanish media and US Latinidad. In M. Habell-Pallán and M. Romero (eds), *Latino/a Popular Culture*. New York: New York University Press, 25–37.
Davis, M. 1990: *City of Quartz: Excavating the Future in Los Angeles*. London: Verso.
Davis, M. 1999: *Ecology of Fear: Los Angeles and the Imagination of Disaster*. New York: Vintage Books.
Davis, R. H. 1897: *Soldiers of Fortune*, illustrated by C. Gibson. New York: Scribner's Sons.

Dear, M. J. 2000: *The Postmodern Urban Condition*. Oxford: Blackwell.
De Certeau, M. 1984: *The Practice of Everyday Life*, translated by S. Rendel. Berkeley, CA: University of California Press.
Decordova, R. 1990: *Picture Personalities: The Emergence of the Star System in America*. Urbana, IL: University of Illinois Press.
De Grandis, R. 1993: *Polémica y estrategias narrativas en América Latina*. Rosario: Beatriz Viterbo.
Degregori, C. I., Blondet, C. and Lynch, N. 1986: *Conquistadores de un nuevo mundo: de invasores a ciudadanos en San Martín de Porres*. Lima: IEP.
De la Campa, R. 1995: Postmodernism and revolution: A Central American case study. In R. de la Campa, E. A. Kaplan and M. Sprinkler (eds), *Late Imperial Culture*. London: Verso, 122–48.
Del Castillo, A. 1977: Malintzin Tenépal: A preliminary look into a new perspective. In R. Sanchez and R. M. Cruz (eds), *Essays on La Mujer*. Los Angeles: Chicano Studies Center, 124–49.
Deleuze, G. 1987: *Dialogues*. London: Athlone.
Delpar, H. 1992: *The Enormous Vogue of Things Mexican: Cultural Relations between the United States and Mexico, 1920–1935*. Tuscaloosa: University of Alabama Press.
Del Pino, J. M. and La Rubia Prado, F. (eds) 1999: *El hispanismo en los Estados Unidos: discursos críticos / prácticas textuales*. Mexico City: Visor.
De Man, P. 1983: *Blindness and Insight: Essays in the Rhetoric of Contemporary Criticism*. Minneapolis: University of Minnesota Press.
Denegri, F. 2000: *Soy Señora: testimonio de Irene Jara*. Lima: Flora Tristán, IEP, El Santo Oficio.
Derrida, J. 1974: *Of Grammatology*, translated by G. C. Spivak. Baltimore, MD: Johns Hopkins University Press.
Derrida, J. 1976: *Living on: Borderlands*. In J. Derrida, P. De Man, J. Hillis Miller, H. Bloom and G. Hartman (eds), *Deconstruction and Criticism*. London: Routledge and Kegan Paul.
Derrida, J. 1978: *Writing and Difference*, translated by A. Bass. London: Routledge.
Deusta Carvallo, J., Stein, S. and Stokes, S. C. 1984: Soccer and social change in early twentieth-century Peru. *Studies in Latin American Popular Culture* 3, 17–21.
Dobyns, H. and Doughty, P. 1976: *Peru: A Cultural History*. New York: Oxford University Press.
Dorfman, A. and Mattelart, A. 1973: *Para leer al Pato Donald*, introduction by H. Schmucler, 5th edn. Buenos Aires: Siglo XXI.
Dorfman, A. and Mattelart, A. 1975: *How to Read Donald Duck: Imperialist Ideology in the Disney Comic*, translated by and with introduction by D. Kunzle. New York: International General.
Dossar, K. 1992: Capoeira Angola: Dancing between two worlds. *Afro-Hispanic Review* 11, 1–3, 5–10.
Doty, A. 1993: *Making Things Perfectly Queer: Interpreting Mass Culture*. Minneapolis: University of Minnesota Press.
Doty, A. 2000: *Flaming Classics: Queering the Film Canon*. New York: Routledge.
Drewal, H. 1996: Sign, substance, and subversion in Afro-Brazilian Art. In A. Lindsay (ed.), *Santería Aesthetics in Contemporary Latin American Art*. Washington, DC: Smithsonian Institute.
D'Souza, D. 1991: *Illiberal Education*. New York: Free Press.

Dueñas, P. and Flores y Escalante, J. 1995: *XEW, 65 aniversario: los 65 mejores boleros de todos los tiempos*. Mexico City: Sistema Radiópolis.

Dueñas, P. and Flores y Escalante, J. 2000: *XEW, 70 aniversario: la catedral de la radio*. Special edition of *Somos* 191 (January).

Dueñas Herrera, P. 1990: *Bolero: historia documental del bolero mexicano*. Mexico City: Asociación Mexicana de Estudios Fonográficos.

During, S. 1999: *The Cultural Studies Reader*. London: Routledge.

Dyer, R. 1990: *Now You See It: Studies on Lesbian and Gay Film*. New York: Routledge.

Dyer, R. 1992: *Only Entertainment*. New York: Routledge.

Dyer, R. 1998: *Stars*, new edition with a supplementary chapter and bibliography by P. McDonald. London: British Film Institute.

Echevarren, R. 1997: Prólogo: un fervor neobarroco. In N. Perlongher, *Poemas completos (1980–1992)*. Buenos Aires: Seix Barral, 7–16.

Eco, U. 1979: *Role of the Reader*. Bloomington, IN: Indiana University Press.

Elmore, P. 1993: '*Los muros invisibles*': *Lima y la modernidad en la novela peruana del siglo XX*. Lima: Mosca Azul.

England, C. R. (no date): A look at the Indian health service policy of sterilization, 1972–1976. http://www.dickshovel.com/IHSSTerPol.html (accessed 1 August 2002)

Esquivel, L. 1989: *Como agua para chocolate*. Mexico City: Planeta.

Esquivel, L. 1993: *Like Water for Chocolate*, translated by C. Christensen and T. Christensen. New York: Doubleday.

Estill, A. 2001: The Mexican telenovela and its foundational fictions. In E. Paz-Soldán and D. A. Castillo (eds), *Latin American Literature and Mass Media*. New York: Garland, 169–89.

Evans, P. W. 1995: *Los olvidados* and the 'uncanny'. In *The Films of Luis Buñuel: Subjectivity and Desire*. Oxford: Clarendon, 72–89.

Fábregas Puig, A. 2001: *Lo sagrado del rebaño: el fútbol como integrador de identidades*. Guadalajara: El Colegio de Jalisco.

Fanon, F. 1963: *The Wretched of the Earth*, translated by C. Farrington. New York: Grove Press.

Feinmann, J. P. 1998: *La sangre derramada: ensayo sobre la violencia política*. Buenos Aires: Ariel.

Feinmann, J. P. 1999: Eva Perón (Guión cinematográfico). In *Dos destinos sudamericanos*. Barcelona: Norma, 10–145.

Fernández Retamar, R. 1971: *Calibán*. Havana: Casa de las Américas.

Fernández Retamar, R. 1975: *Para una teoría de la literatura hispanoamericana y otras aproximaciones*. Havana: Casa de las Américas.

Fernández Retamar, R. 1989: *Caliban and Other Essays*, translated by E. Baker. Minneapolis: Minnesota University Press.

Ferré, P. 1997: Artistas y artesanos. *Brecha*, 616 (19 September). http://www.brecha.com.uy/numeros/n616/apertura.htm (accessed 17 August 1999, 3 pp.).

Fine, S. 1999: From collaboration to containment. In J. Hershfield and D. Maciel (eds), *Mexico's Cinema: A Century of Film and Filmmaking*. Wilmington, DE: Scholarly Resources, 123–63.

Finkielkraut, A. 1987: *La Défaite de la pensée*. Paris: Gallimard.

Flores Galindo, A. 1986: *Buscando un Inca: identidad y utopía en los Andes*. Havana: Casa de Las Américas.

Flores Galindo, A. 1994: *La agonía de Mariátegui*. In *Obras completas*, II. Lima: Sur.
Fogwill, R. E. 1998: *Vivir afuera*. Buenos Aires: Editorial Sudamericana.
Foster, D. W. 1985: The demythification of Buenos Aires in the Argentine novel of the seventies. In *Alternative Voices in the Contemporary Latin American Narrative*. Columbia: University of Missouri Press, 60–106.
Foster, D. W. 1989a: Fontanarrosa's gauchomanía and gauchophobia in *Las aventuras de Inodoro Pereyra*. In Mafalda *to* Los supermachos: *Latin American Graphic Humor as Popular Culture*. Boulder, CO: Lynne Rienner, 37–51.
Foster, D. W. 1989b: *Mafalda*: The ironic bemusement. In Mafalda *to* Los supermachos: *Latin American Graphic Humor as Popular Culture*. Boulder, CO: Lynne Rienner, 53–63.
Foster, D. W. 1992: On expanding the base of Latin American studies. *Latin American Literary Review* 20, 34–7.
Foster, D. W. 1998a: *Mafalda*: From hearth to plaza. In *Buenos Aires: Perspectives on the City and Cultural Production*. Gainesville, FL: University Press of Florida, 17–33.
Foster, D. W. 1998b: *Buenos Aires: Perspectives on the City and Cultural Production*. Gainesville, FL: University of Florida Press.
Foster, D. W. 2000: *Producción cultural e identidades homoeróticas: teoría y aplicaciones*. San José: Editorial de la Universidad de Costa Rica.
Foster, N. and Cordell, L. S. 1992: *Chilies to Chocolate: Food the Americas Gave the World*. Tucson, AZ: University of Arizona Press.
Foucault, M. 1980: *Power/Knowledge: Selected Interviews and Other Writings 1972–1977*, edited by C. Gordon. New York: Pantheon.
Foucault, M. 1986: Of other spaces. *Diacritics* Spring, 22–7.
Foucault, M. 1997: Panopticism (extract). In N. Leach (ed.), *Rethinking Architecture: A Reader in Cultural Theory*. London: Routledge.
Franco, J. 1989: *Plotting Women: Gender and Representation*. London: Verso.
Franco, J. 1999: *Jean Franco: Critical Passions: Selected Essays*, edited by and with introduction by M. L. Pratt and K. Newman. Durham, NC: Duke University Press.
Franco, J. 2002: *The Decline and Fall of the Lettered City: Latin America in the Cold War*. Cambridge, MA: Harvard University Press.
Frank, L. and Smith, P. 1993: *Madonnarama: Essays on Sex and Popular Culture*. Pittsburgh, PA: Cleis Press.
Fraser, N. and Navarro, M. 1981: *Eva Perón*. New York: Norton.
Freeman, M. 2000: Telemundo gains new ground. *Electronic Media* 11 December.
Freeman, M. 2002: ABC soap takes a page from telenovela playbook. *Electronic Media* 11 February.
Fuentes, C. 1989: Gabriel García Márquez and the invention of America. In *Myself with Others: Selected Essays*. London: Pan, 180–95.
Galeano, E. 1998: *Patas arriba*. Barcelona: Siglo XXI.
Gamio, M. 1960: *Forjando Patria*. Mexico City: Porrúa.
García, G. 1995: Melodrama: The passion machine. In Paranaguá, P. A. (ed.) *Mexican Cinema*, translated by A. M. López. London: British Film Institute, 153–62.
García Canclini, N. 1990: *Culturas híbridas: estrategias para entrar y salir de la modernidad*. Mexico City: Editorial Grijalbo.
García Canclini, N. 1993: *Transforming Modernity: Popular Culture in Mexico*, translated by L. Lozano. Austin, TX: University of Texas Press.

García Canclini, N. 1995: *Hybrid Cultures: Strategies for Entering and Leaving Modernity*, translated by C. L. Chiappari and S. L. López. Minneapolis: University of Minnesota Press.
García Canclini, N. 1996: Políticas culturales e integración norteamericana: una perspectiva desde México. In N. García Canclini, *Culturas en globalización: América Latina – Europa – Estados Unidos: libre comercio e integración*. Caracas: CNCA, 13–40.
García Canclini, N. 1999a: *La globalización imaginada*. Mexico City: Paidós.
García Canclini, N. 1999b: Así es y no de otra manera. In *El cine de Jorge Sanjinés*. Santa Cruz, Bolivia: Festival Iberoamericano de Cine de Santa Cruz, 81–9.
García Canclini, N. and Moneta, C. J. (eds) 1994: *Las industrias culturales en la integración latinoamericana*. Mexico City: Grijalbo.
García Canclini, N. and Moneta, C. (eds) 1999: *Las industrias culturales en la integración latinoamericana*, Buenos Aires: EUDEBA; Mexico City: Grijalbo / SELA – UNESCO.
García Márquez, G. 1995 (1967): *One Hundred Years of Solitude*, translated by G. Rabassa. London: David Campbell.
García Rubio, C. 1994: *Lo que el cable nos dejó: televisión para abonados, comunicación y democracia en el Uruguay*. Montevideo: Ediciones de la pluma.
Garrido, J. S. 1981: *Historia de la música popular en México*. Mexico City: Extemporáneos.
Gastaldo, E. 2002: *Pátria, chuteiras e propaganda*. São Paulo: Editora Unisinos.
Gaviria, V. 1989: Un ojo de nadie (reflexiones en torno a 'No futuro'). *Gaceta cine* (Medellín) 1, 3–4.
Gaviria, V. 1998b: Los días de la noche. *Kinetoscopio* (Medellín) 9, 45, 37–42.
Gelpí, J. 1998: El bolero en Ciudad de México: poesía popular y procesos de modernización. *Cuadernos de Literatura* 4, 7–8, 197–212.
Getino, O. 1983: Towards a third cinema. In Michael Chanan (ed.), *Twenty-Five Years of the New Latin American Cinema*. London: BFI, 17-27.
Godsland, S. and White, A. M. (eds) 2002: *Cultura popular: Studies in Spanish and Latin American Popular Culture*. Oxford: Lang.
Goldman, S. 2001: Mexican muralism: Its social-educative roles in Latin America and the United States. In C. A. Noriega *et al.* (ed.), *The Chicano Studies Reader: An Anthology of Aztlán*. Los Angeles: Chicano Studies Research Center, 281–300.
Gollnick, B. 2003: Approaches to Latin American literature. In P. Swanson (ed.), *The Companion to Latin American Studies*. London: Arnold, 107–21.
González, G. G. 1974: A critique of the internal colony model. *Latin America Perspectives* 1, 1 (Spring), 154–61.
González, H. 1999: *Fragmentos pampeanos*. Buenos Aires: Colihue.
González Bermejo, E. 1979: *Revelaciones de un cronopio: conversaciones con Cortázar*. Buenos Aires: Editorial Contrapunto.
González Echevarría, R. 1985: *The Voice of the Masters: Writing and Autobiography in Modern Latin American Literature*. Austin, TX: University of Texas Press.
González Echevarría, R. 2000: *Mito y archivo: una teoría de la narrativa latinoamericana*. Mexico City: Fondo de Cultura Económica.
González Stephan, B. 1985: *Contribución al estudio de la historiografía literaria hispanoamericana*. Caracas: Biblioteca de la Academia Nacional de la Historia.

González Stephan, B. 1993: Sujeto criollo/conciencia histórica: la historiografía literaria en el período colonial. In J. Anadón (ed.), *Ruptura de la conciencia hispanoamericana*. Mexico City: Fondo de Cultura Económica, 15–57.
Goody, J. 1982: *Cooking, Cuisine and Class*. Cambridge: Cambridge University Press.
Green, L. 1994: Fear as a way of life. *Cultural Anthropology* 9, 2, 227–56.
Green, M. 1995: Cultural studies questionnaire. *Journal of Latin American Cultural Studies* 4, 225–9.
Greenblatt, S. 1991: *Marvelous Possessions: The Wonder of the New World*. Chicago: University of Chicago Press.
Greene, A. 2001: Cablevision (nation) in rural Yucatán: Performing modernity and *Mexicanidad* in the early 1990s. In G. M. Joseph, A. Rubenstein and E. Zolov (eds), *Fragments of a Golden Age: The Politics of Culture in Mexico Since the 1940s*. Durham, NC: Duke University Press.
Gregory, D. 1994: *Geographical Imaginations*. Cambridge, MA: Blackwell.
Gubern, R. 1988: *Mensajes icónicos de la cultura de masas*, 2nd edn. Barcelona: Lumen.
Guedes, S. L. 1998: *O Brasil no campo de futebol: estudos antropológicos sobre os significados do futebol brasileiro*. Rio de Janeiro: Editora da Universidade Federal Fluminense.
Gugelberger, G. (ed.) 1996: *The Real Thing: Testimonial Discourse and Latin America*. Durham, NC: Duke University Press.
Habermas, J. 1987: *The Philosophical Discourse of Modernity*, translated by F. Lawrence. Cambridge, MA: MIT Press.
Hall, S. and Jefferson, T. (eds) 1975: *Resistance Through Rituals: Youth Sub-Culture in Post-War Britain*. Birmingham: Centre for Contemporary Cultural Studies.
Hannigan, J. 1998: *Fantasy City: Pleasure and Profit in the Postmodern Metropolis*. London: Routledge.
Hanson, E. (ed.) 1999: *Out Takes: Essays on Queer Theory and Film*. Durham, NC: Duke University Press.
Hardt, M. and Negri, A. 2000: *Empire*. Cambridge, MA: Harvard University Press.
Harlow, B. 1987: *Resistance Literature*. New York: Methuen.
Hart, S. M. 1993: 'Mientras que en mi casa soy, rey soy': More on the politics of Hispanism. *Journal of Hispanic Research* 1, 3, 415–23.
Hart, S. M. 1999: Signs of the subaltern: Notes on nineteenth-century Spanish American literature. *Journal of Iberian and Latin American Studies* 5, 1, 27–35.
Hart, S. M. 2002: The art of invasion in Jorge Sanjinés's *Para recibir el canto de los pájaros* (1995). *Hispanic Research Journal* 3, 71–81.
Harvey, D. 1989a *The Condition of Postmodernity*. Oxford: Blackwell.
Harvey, D. 1989b: *The Urban Experience*. Oxford: Blackwell.
Hasenberg, C. and Valle Silva, N. Do 1988: As Imagens do negro na publicidade. In *Estrutura social, mobilidade, e raça*. São Paulo: Vértice, 185–8.
Hayles, K. 1990: *Chaos Bound: Orderly Disorder in Contemporary Literature and Science*. New York: Cornell University Press.
Hegel, G. W. 1956: *The Philosophy of History*, translated by J. Sibree. New York: Dover.
Helal, R., Soares, A. J. and Lovisolo, H. 2001: *A invenção do país futebol: mídia, raça e idolotria*. Rio de Janeiro: Mauad Editora.
Hernández, O. and McAnany, E. 2001: Cultural industries in the free trade age: A look

at Mexican television. In G. M. Joseph, A. Rubenstein and E. Zolov (eds), *Fragments of a Golden Age: The Politics of Culture in Mexico Since the 1940s*. Durham, NC: Duke University Press.

Hernández, P. J. 1975: *Para leer a Mafalda*. Buenos Aires: Ediciones Meridiano.

Hershfield, J. 1996: *Mexican Cinema/Mexican Woman, 1940–1950*. Tucson, AZ: University of Arizona Press.

Hershfield, J. 2000: *The Invention of Dolores del Río*. Minneapolis: University of Minnesota Press.

Hess, J. 1993: Neo-realism and new Latin American cinema: *Bicycle Thieves* and *Blood of the Condor*. In J. King, A. M. López and M. Alvarado (eds), *Mediating Two Worlds: Cinematic Encounters in the Americas*. London: BFI, 104–8.

Higgins, J. (ed.) 2003: *Heterogeneidad y literatura en el Perú*. Lima: Centro de Estudios Literarios Antonio Cornejo Polar.

Highmore, B. (ed.) 2002: *The Everyday Life Reader*. London: Routledge.

Hopenhaym, M. 1996: *Ni apocalípticos ni integrados: aventuras de la modernidad en América Latina*. Santiago de Chile: Fondo de Cultura Económica.

Hulme, P. 1996: La teoría poscolonial y la representación de la cultura en las Américas. *Casa de las Américas* 25, 3–8.

Huntington, S. 1993: The clash of civilizations? *Foreign Affairs* 72, 3 (Summer), 22–49.

Israel, S. 1997: El precio del poder. *Brecha* 601 (6 June). http://www.brecha.com.uy/numeros/n601/apertura.htm (accessed 28 November 2000, 4 pp.).

Jameson, F. 1992: *The Geopolitical Æsthetic: Cinema and Space in the World System*. London: British Film Institute.

Jameson, F. 1994: *The Seeds of Time*. New York: Columbia University Press.

Jameson, F. 1996: Literary import substitution. In G. Gugelberger (ed.), *The Real Thing*. Durham, NC: Duke University Press, 172–91.

Janik, D. 1988: Desde la literatura hasta las *bellas letras*: los principios de una literatura nacional en Nueva Granada (Colombia) al final de la época colonial y en el primer período de la independencia, reflejados en los periódicos (1791–1859). In D. Janik (ed.), *La literatura en la formación de los Estados hispanoamericanos (1800–1860)*. Madrid: Iberoamericana, 117–217.

Jauretche, A. 1957: *Los profetas del odio*. Buenos Aires: Ediciones Trafac.

Jenkins, H. 1992: *Textual Poachers: Television Film Fans and Participatory Culture*. New York: Routledge.

Jiménez, D. 1992: *Historia de la crítica literaria en Colombia*. Bogotá: Universidad Nacional de Colombia.

Johnson, R. 1987: *The Film Industry in Brazil: Culture and the State*. Pittsburgh, PA: University of Pittsburgh Press.

Johnson, R. and Stam, R. (eds) 1995: *Brazilian Cinema*, expanded edition. New York: Columbia University Press.

Jopling, D. A. 2000: *Self-Knowledge and the Self*. New York: Routledge.

Jordan, B. 1990: *British Hispanism and the Challenge of Literary Theory*. Warminster: Aris and Phillips.

Jordan, B. and Morgan-Tamosunas, R. (eds) 2000: *Contemporary Spanish Cultural Studies*. London: Arnold.

Judd, D. R. and Fainstein, S. S. (eds) 1999: *The Tourist City*. New Haven, CT: Yale University Press.

Katz, J. 1995: *The Invention of Heterosexuality*. New York: Dutton.

Keeling, D. J. 1996: *Buenos Aires: Global Dreams, Local Crisis*. Chichester: John Wiley & Sons.
King, J. (ed.) 1987: *Modern Latin American Fiction: A Survey*. London: Faber and Faber.
King, J. 1990: *Magical Reels: A History of Cinema in Latin America*. London: Verso.
King, J., Bosch, R. and Whitaker, S. (eds) 2000: *An Argentine Passion: The Life and Work of María Luisa Bemberg*. London: Verso.
Kirklighter, C. 2002: *Traversing the Democratic Borders of the Essay*. New York: State University of New York Press.
Kleinhans, C. 1994: Camp and the politics of parody. In M. Mayer (ed.), *The Politics and Poetics of Camp*. London: Routledge, 182–201.
Klor de Alva, J. J. 1989: Aztlán, Borinquen and Hispanic nationalism in the United States. In R. Anaya and R. Lomeli (eds), *Aztlán: Essays on Chicano Homeland*. Albuquerque, NM: El Norte Publications, 135–71.
Klor de Alva, J. J. 1992: Colonialism and postcolonialism as (Latin) American mirages. *Colonial Latin American Review* 1, 1–2, 3–23.
Klor de Alva, J. J. 1995: The postcolonization of the (Latin) American experience: A reconsideration of 'colonialism', 'postcolonialism', and 'mestizaje'. In G. Prakash (ed.), *After Colonialism: Imperial Histories and Postcolonial Displacements*. Princeton, NJ: Princeton University Press, 241–75.
Knight, A. 1990: Racism, revolution, and *indigenismo*: Mexico, 1910–1940. In R. Graham (ed.), *The Idea of Race in Latin America, 1870–1940*. Austin, TX: University of Texas Press, 71–113.
Knights, V. 2001: (De)constructing gender: The bolero in Ángeles Mastretta's *Arráncame la vida*. *Journal of Romance Studies* 1, 1, 69–84.
Konig, H. J. 1994: *En el camino hacia la nación: nacionalismo en el proceso de formación del Estado y de la Nación de la Nueva Granada, 1750–1856*. Bogotá: Banco de la República.
Kraniauskas, J. 2000: Hybridity in a transnational frame: Latin-Americanist and postcolonial perspectives on cultural studies. In A. Brah and A. E. Coombes (eds), *Hybridity and its Discontents: Politics, Science, Culture*. London: Routledge, 235–56.
Kraus, K. 1976: *In these Great Times: A Karl Kraus Reader*, edited by H. Zohn, translated by J. Fabry *et al.* Montreal: Engendra Press.
Kubik, G. 1979: Angolan traits in black music, games and dances of Brazil: A study of African cultural extensions overseas. *Estudos de Antropologia Cultural* 10, 7–55.
Kuri-Aldana, M. and Mendoza Martínez, V. 1992: *Cancionero popular mexicano*. Mexico City: Dirección General de Culturas Populares del Consejo Nacional para la Cultura y Artes.
Labourdette, S. D. 1987: *Mito y política*. Buenos Aires: Troquel.
Lambert Ortiz, E. 1985: *The Book of Latin American Cooking*. London: Penguin.
Lambert Ortiz, E. 1998: *The Flavour of Latin America*. London: Latin American Bureau.
Lamborghini, O. 1988: El fiord. In *Novelas y cuentos*. Barcelona: Serbal, 18–34.
Lancaster, R. 1992: *Life is Hard: Machismo, Danger and Intimacy of Power in Nicaragua*. Berkeley, CA: University of California Press.
Langleib, M. 1997: Si hubiera tenido más dinero y más tiempo, todo hubiera quedado perfecto. *El Observador* 27 January, 21–2.

Larsen, N. 1995: *Reading North by South: On Latin American Literature, Culture and Politics*. Minneapolis: University of Minnesota Press.
Lauer, M. 1989: *El sitio de la literatura: escritores y política en el Perú del siglo XX*. Lima: Mosca Azul.
Lavador, J. S. (Quino) 1983: *Déjenme inventar*. Buenos Aires: Ediciones de la Flor.
Lavador, J. S. (Quino) 1993: *Toda Mafalda*. Buenos Aires: Ediciones de la Flor.
Lavador, J. S. (Quino) 1994: *¡Yo no fui!* Buenos Aires: Ediciones de la Flor.
Lavador, J. S. (Quino) 1995 (c.1991): *Humano se nace*, 4th edn. Buenos Aires: Ediciones de la Flor.
Lavador, J. S. (Quino) 1996: *¡Qué mala es la gente!* Buenos Aires: Ediciones de la Flor.
Leal, N. 1992: *Boleros: la canción romántica del Caribe (1930–60)*. Caracas: Grijalbo.
Lechner, N. 1998: Nuestros miedos. *Perfiles latinoamericanos* (Mexico City) 13, 179–98.
Lefebvre, H. 1991: *The Production of Space*, translated by D. Nicholson-Smith. Cambridge, MA: Blackwell.
Leite Lopes, J. S. 1992: A morte da 'alegria do povo'. *Revista Brasileira de Ciencias Sociais* 7, 114–34.
Leite Lopes, J. S. 1997: Successes and contradiction in 'multiracial' Brazilian football. In G. Armstrong and R. Giulianotti (eds), *Entering the Field: New Perspectives in World Football*. Oxford: Berg, 53–86.
Leite Lopes, J. S. 1999: The Brazilian style of football and its dilemmas. In G. Armstrong and R. Giulianotti (eds), *Football Cultures and Identities*. London: Macmillan, 86–95.
Leite Lopes, J. S. and Faguer, J. P. 1994: L'invention du style brésilien: sport, journalisme et politique au Brésil. *Actes de la Recherche en Sciences Sociales* 103, 27–35.
Leite Lopes, J. S. and Maresca, S. 1989: La disparition de la 'joie du peuple'. *Actes de la Recherche en Sciences Sociales* 79, 27–35.
León, A. 1984: *Del canto y el tiempo*. Havana: Letras Cubanas.
Lever, J. 1983: *Soccer Madness: Sport and Social Integration in Brazil*. Chicago: University of Chicago Press.
Levine, E. 2001: Constructing a market, constructing an ethnicity: US Spanish-language media and the formation of a syncretic Latino/a identity. *Studies in Latin American Popular Culture* 20, 33–50.
Levinson, B. 1996: Neopatriarchy and after: *I, Rigoberta Menchú* as allegory of death. *Journal of Latin American Cultural Studies* 5, 33–50.
Lewis, J. L. 1992: *Ring of Liberation: Deceptive Discourse in Brazilian Capoeira*. Chicago: University of Chicago Press.
Lewis, O. 1964: *The Children of Sánchez: Autobiography of a Mexican Family*. Harmondsworth: Penguin.
Lienhard, M. 1981: *Cultura popular andina y forma novelesca: zorros y danzantes en la última novela de Arguedas*. Lima: Latinoamericana.
Lienhard, M. 1991: *La voz y su huella: escritura y conflicto étnico-social en América latina 1492–1988*. Hanover, NH: Ediciones del Norte.
Lienhard, M. 1992: *Testimonios, cartas y manifiestos indígenas*. Caracas: Biblioteca Ayacucho.
Lienhard, M. 1996: De mestizajes, heterogeneidades, hibridismos y otras quimeras. In J. A. Mazzotti, U. J. Zevallos Aguilar et al. (eds), *Asedios a la heterogeneidad*

cultural: libro de homenaje a Antonio Cornejo Polar. Philadelphia, PA: International Association of Peruvianists, 57–80.

Lipsitz, G. 1998: Their America and ours: Intercultural communication in the context of 'Our America'. In J. Belnap and R. Fernández (eds), *José Martí's 'Our America': From National to Hemispheric Cultural Studies*. Durham, NC: Duke University Press, 293–316.

López, A. M. 1991a: Celluloid tears: Melodrama in the 'old' Mexican cinema. *IRIS: A Journal of Theory on Image and Sound* 13, 29–51.

López, A. M. 1991b: The melodrama in Latin America: Films, telenovelas, and the currency of the popular form. In M. Landy (ed.), *Imitations of Life: A Reader on Film and Television Melodrama*. Detroit: Wayne State University Press, 596–606.

López, A. M. 1995: Our welcomed guests: Telenovelas in Latin America. In R. Allen, (ed.), *To Be Continued: Soap Operas around the World*. London: Routledge, 256–75.

López, A. M. 2000: Tears and desire: Women and melodrama in the 'old' Mexican cinema. In E. A. Kaplan (ed.), *Feminism and Film*. Oxford: Oxford University Press, 505–20.

López Austin, A. 1998: *Hombre-dios: religión y política en el mundo náhuatl*. Mexico City: Universidad Nacional Autónoma de México.

Loyola Fernández, J. 1997: *En ritmo de bolero*. Havana: Ediciones Unión.

Luciano, J. C. 1993: Comida afroperuana: resistencia y aporte. In R. O. Weston (ed.), *Cultura, identidad y cocina en el Perú*. Lima: Escuela Profesional de Turismo y Hotelería, Facultad de Ciencias de la Comunicación, Turismo y Sicología, Universidad San Martín de Porres, 169–75.

Luciano, J. C. 1995: The African presence in Peru. In C. Moore (ed.), *The African Presence in the Americas*. Trenton, NJ: Africa World Press, 119–30.

Luciano, J. C. and Rodríguez, H. 1995: Peru. In *No Longer Invisible: Afro-Latin Americans Today*. London: Minority Rights Publications, 271–86.

Ludmer, J. 1984: Las tretas del débil. In E. G. and E. Ortega (eds), *La sartén por el mango*. Río Piedras, PR: Huracan, 47–54.

Ludmer, J. 1999: *El cuerpo del delito*. Buenos Aires: Libros Perfil.

Lukács, G. 1962: *The Historical Novel*, translated by H. and S. Mitchell. London: Merlin.

Lyotard, J.-F. 1984: *The Postmodern Condition: A Report on Knowledge*, translated by G. Bennington and B. Massumi. Minneapolis: University of Minnesota Press.

MacDougall, D. 1998: *Transcultural Cinema*. Princeton, NJ: Princeton University Press.

Magazine, R. 2001: 'The colours make me sick': America FC and upward mobility in Mexico. In G. Armstrong and R. Giulianotti (eds), *Fear and Loathing in World Football*. Oxford: Berg.

Manrique, N. 1989: Clorinda Matto y el nacimiento del indigenismo literario. *Debate Agrario*, 6, 81–100.

Margulis, M. 1994: *La cultura de la noche: la vida nocturna de los jóvenes en Buenos Aires*. Buenos Aires: Editorial Biblos.

Mariátegui, J. C. 1964a: *El alma matinal*. Lima: Editorial Amauta.

Mariátegui, J. C. 1964b: *7 ensayos de interpretación de la realidad peruana*. Lima: Editorial Amauta.

Mariátegui, J. C. 1971: *Seven Interpretative Essays on Peruvian Reality*, translated by M. Urquidi. Austin, TX: University of Texas Press.

Maríñez, P. A. 1993: Entrevista con Nicomedes Santa Cruz, poeta afroamericano. *Cuadernos Americanos* 7, 110–24.
Maríñez, P. A. 2000: *Nicomedes Santa Cruz: decimista, poeta y folklorista afroperuano.* Mexico: Instituto de Cultura San Luis de Potosí.
Maristany, J. J. 2000: *Narraciones peligrosas: resistencia y adhesión en la época del proceso.* Buenos Aires: Biblos.
Martí, J. 1972: *Antología mínima*, vol. 1. Havana: Instituto cubano del libro.
Martí, J. 1999: *José Martí Reader: Writings on the Americas*, edited by D. Schnookal and M. Muñiz. Melbourne: Ocean Press.
Martín-Barbero, J. 1993: *Communication, Culture and Hegemony: From the Media to Mediations.* London: Sage.
Martín-Barbero, J. 1995: Memory and form in the Latin America soap opera. In R. Allen (ed.), *To Be Continued: Soap Operas Around the World.* London: Routledge, 276–84.
Martín-Barbero, J. 1998: *De los medios a las mediaciones: comunicación, cultura y hegemonía.* Santa Fe de Bogotá: Convenio Andrés Bello.
Martín-Barbero, J. 2000: Modernidad y medios masivos en América Latina: perspectivas comunicativas del análisis cultural. In J. Martín Barbero and H. Herlinghaus, *Contemporaneidad latinoamericana y análisis cultural: conversaciones al encuentro de Walter Benjamin.* Madrid: Iberoamericana, 63–83.
Martín Posadas, J. 1992: El papel del estado con respecto a la televisión en el Uruguay. In C. Rama (ed.), *Industrias culturales en Uruguay.* Montevideo: Arca, 31–6.
Martínez, G. and Jarque, F. 1995: Program and biographical notes. In David Byrne (ed.), *The Soul of Black Peru* (CD recording). Burbank, CA: Luaka Bop/Warner Bros.
Martínez, T. E. 1995: *Santa Evita.* Buenos Aires: Planeta.
Masiello, F. 2001: *The Art of Transition: Latin American Culture and Neoliberal Crisis.* Durham, NC: Duke University Press.
Mason, T. 1995: *Passion of the People? Football in South America.* London: Verso.
Massey, D. 1994: *Space, Place and Gender.* Cambridge: Polity Press.
Matias da Silva, J. G. ('Mestre Tigrão') 1994: *Capoeira: herdeiros do cativerio.* Salvador, Brazil: Art-Contemp.
Mato, D. 1998: The transnational making of representations of gender, ethnicity and culture: indigenous peoples' organizations at the Smithsonian Institution's Festival. *Cultural Studies* 12, 2, 193–209.
Mato, D. 1999: Telenovelas: transnacionalización de la industria y transformación del gusto. In N. García Canclini and C. J. Moneta (eds), *Las industrias culturales en la integración latinoameriana.* Mexico City: Grijalbo, 245–81.
Maturana, H. and Varela, F. 1996: *El árbol del conocimiento.* Madrid: Editorial Debate.
Mazzotti, J. A. and Zevallos, U. J. (eds) 1996: *Asedios a la heterogeneidad cultural: libro de homenaje a Antonio Cornejo Polar.* Philadelphia, PA: Asociación Internacional de Peruanistas.
McAnany, E. G. and Wilkinson, K. T. (eds) 1996: *Mass Media and Free Trade: NAFTA and the Cultural Industries.* Austin, TX: University of Texas.
McDonald, P. 1998: Reconceptualising stardom. In R. Dyer, *Stars.* London: British Film Institute, 174–200.
McGuire, J. W. 1997: *Peronism without Perón.* Stanford, CA: Stanford University Press.

McLean y Estenós, R. 1948: *Negros en el nuevo mundo*. Lima: PTCM.
Melhuus, M. 1996: Power, value and the ambiguous meanings of gender. In M. Melhuus and K. A. Stølen (eds), *Machos, Mistresses and Madonnas: Contesting the Power of Gender Imagery in Latin America*. London: Verso, 230–59.
Menchú, R. 1983: *Me llamo Rigoberta Menchú y así me nació la conciencia*. Mexico City: Siglo XXI; Havana: Casa de las Américas.
Messinger Cypess, S. 1997: *La Malinche in Mexican Literature: From History to Myth*. Austin, TX: University of Texas Press.
Metz, C. 1982: *Psychoanalysis and Cinema: The Imaginary Signifier*, translated by C. Britton. London: Macmillan.
Mignolo, W. 1995: *The Darker Side of the Renaissance: Literacy, Territoriality and Colonization*. Ann Arbor, MI: University of Michigan Press.
Miller, N. 1999: *In the Shadow of the State: Intellectuals and the Quest for National Identity in Twentieth-Century Spanish America*. London: Verso.
Mistral, G. 1993: *A Gabriela Mistral Reader*, translated by M. Giachetti, edited by M. Agosin. Fredonia, NY: White Pine Press.
Modleski, T. 1982: *Loving with a Vengeance: Mass-Produced Fantasies for Women*. Hamden, CT: Archon Books.
Molloy, S. 1991: *At Face Value: Autobiographical Writing in Spanish America*. Cambridge: Cambridge University Press.
Monsiváis, C. 1970: *Días de guardar*. Mexico City: Biblioteca Era.
Monsiváis, C. 1988: *Escenas de pudor y liviandad*. Mexico City: Grijalbo.
Monsiváis, C. 1993: *Rostros del cine mexicano*. Mexico City: IMCINE.
Monsiváis, C. 1994: Se sufre pero se aprende (El melodrama y las reglas de la falta de límites). In C. Monsiváis and C. Bonfil (eds), *A través del espejo: el cine mexicano y su público*. Mexico City: Ediciones del Milagro/Instituto Mexicano de Cinematografía, 99–224.
Monsiváis, C. 1995a. Mythologies. In Paranaguá, P. A. (ed.) *Mexican Cinema*, translated by A. M. López. London: British Film Institute, 117–27.
Monsiváis, C. 1995b. All the people came and did not fit onto the screen: Notes on the cinema audience in Mexico. In Paranaguá, P. A. (ed.) *Mexican Cinema*, translated by A. M. López. London: British Film Institute, 145–51.
Monsiváis, C. 1997a: *Mexican Postcards*, translated by J. Kraniauskas. London: Verso.
Monsiváis, C. 1997b: Mexico 1890–1976: High contrast, still life. In *Mexican Postcards*. London: Verso, 1–30.
Monsiváis, C. 2000: De las versiones de lo popular. In *Aires de familia: cultura y sociedad en América Latina*. Barcelona: Anagrama, 13–49.
Monsiváis, C. 2001a: *Amor perdido*. Mexico City: Biblioteca Era.
Monsiváis, C. 2001b: *Los rituales del caos*. Mexico City: Biblioteca Era.
Montalbetti, M. 1997: *Fin desierto*. Lima: Mosca Azul.
Montecinos, S. 1993: *Madres y huachos: alegorías del mestizaje chileno*. Santiago de Chile: Editorial Cuarto Propio.
Montiel, E. 1995: Negros en el Perú: De la conquista a la identidad nacional. In *Presencia africana en sudamérica*. Mexico City: Consejo nacional para la cultura y las artes, 213–75.
Moore, Z. 1988: Reflections on blacks in contemporary Brazilian popular culture in the 1980s. *Studies in Latin American Popular Culture* 7, 213–26.

Moraga, C. 1983: A long line of vendidas. In *Loving in the War Years*. Boston: South End Press, 90–144.
Moraga, C. 1993: Art in América con Acento. In *The Last Generation*. Boston: South End Press, 52–64.
Moraga, C. 1994: Giving up the ghost. In *Heroes and Saints and Other Plays*. Albuquerque, NM: West End Press.
Moraga, C. 1996: El mito Azteca. In A. Castillo (ed.), *Goddess of the Americas*. New York: Riverhead Books, 68–71.
Moraga, C. and Anzaldúa, G. (eds) 2000: *This Bridge Called My Back: Writings by Radical Women of Color*. New York: Third Women Press.
Morales, E. 1995: *The Guinea Pig: Healing, Food and Ritual in the Andes*. Tucson, AZ, University of Arizona Press.
Morales, M. R. 1998: Cuestión étnica y debate interétnico: ¿Qué ha pasado y qué pasa ahora en Guatemala? In M. Moraña (ed.), *Indigenismo hacia el fin del milenio*. Pittsburgh: Instituto Internacional de Literatura Iberoamericana, Biblioteca de América, 299–330.
Moraña, M. 1995: Escribir en el aire: heterogeneidad y estudios culturales. *Revista Iberoamericana* 170–1, 279–86.
Moraña, M. 1997a: El boom del subalterno. *Revista de Crítica Cultural* 14, 48–53.
Moraña, M. (ed.) 1997b: *Ángel Rama y los estudios latinamericanos*. Pittsburgh, PA: Instituto Internacional de Literatura Iboeramericana.
Moraña, M. (ed.) 2002a: *Nuevas perspectives desde/sobre América Latina: el desafío de los estudios culturales*. Pittsburgh, PA: Instituto Internacional de Literatura Iberoamericana.
Moraña, M. (ed.) 2002b: *Espacio urbano, comunicación y violencia en América Latina*. Pittsburgh, PA: Instituto Internacional de Literatura Iberoamericana.
Moreiras, A. 2000: Hegemonía y subalternidad. In M. Moraña (ed.), *Nuevas perspectives desde/sobre América Latina*. Pittsburgh, PA: Instituto Internacional de Literatura Iberoamericana, 157–71.
Moreiras, A. 2001: *The Exhaustion of Difference: The Politics of Latin American Cultural Studies*. Durham, NC: Duke University Press.
Morello-Frosch, M. 1985: Significación e historia en *Respiración artificial* de Ricardo Piglia. In H. Vidal (ed.), *Fascismo y experiencia literaria: reflexiones para una recanonización*. Minneapolis, Minnesota: Institute for the Study of Ideologies and Literatures, 489–500.
Moreno Rivas, Y. 1979: *Historia de la música popular mexicana*. Mexico City: Editorial Patria.
Morley, D. 1996: EurAm, modernity, reason and alterity or, postmodernism, the highest stage of cultural imperialism? In D. Morley and Kuan-Hsing Chen (eds), *Stuart Hall: Critical Dialogues in Cultural Studies*. London: Routledge, 326–60.
Mottram, E. 1978: The documentation of American studies. In *Essays by Eric Mottram and Philip Davies*. London: Polytechnic of Central London, 38–45.
Mumford, L. 1934: *Technics and Civilization*. New York: Harcourt, Brace.
Naremore, J. 1998: *More than Night: Film Noir and its Contexts*. Berkeley, CA: University of California Press.
Nascimento, A. de 1978: *O genocídio do negro brasileiro*. Rio de Janeiro: Paz e Terra.
Navarro, M. 1981: *Evita*. Buenos Aires: Corregidor.
Neves Flores, L. F. B. 1982: Na zona de agrião: algumas mensagens ideológicas do

futebol. In R. DaMatta et al., *Universo do futebol: esporte e sociedade brasileira*. Rio de Janeiro: Edicões Pinakotheke, 43–56.
Nieto Gomez, A. 1997: La Chicana: Legacy of suffering and self-denial. In A. M. Garcia (ed.), *Chicana Feminist Thought: The Basic Historical Writings*. New York: Routlege, 48–50.
Noble, A. 2003: Latin American visual cultures. In P. Swanson (ed.), *The Companion to Latin American Studies*. London: Arnold, 154–71.
Noriega, G. 2001: Historia de una búsqueda. (*El amante cine*). http://www.elamante.com/nota/1/1436.shtm (accessed 3 May 2002).
Ocampo, S. 1959: *La furia y otros cuentos*. Buenos Aires: Sur.
Ocampo, S. 1961: *Las invitadas*. Buenos Aires: Losada.
Ojeda, M. 2003: *Nicomedes Santa Cruz: Ecos de Africa en Perú*. London, England: Tamesis Books.
Ojeda, M. 1999: 'Nicomedes Santa Cruz: Cronología y bibliografía reciente.' *Afro-Hispanic Review*, 18:1, 25–8.
Olson, C. 1997: *Collected Prose*. Berkeley, CA: University of California Press.
Ordoñez, E. 1984: The concept of cultural identity in Chicana poetry. *Third Woman* 2, 1, 75–82.
Ordóñez, M. 1988: Introduction. In *Soledad Acosta de Samper: una nueva lectura*. Bogotá: Ediciones Fondo Cultural Cafetero, 11–24.
Orellana, M. de 2003: *Filming Pancho Villa: How Hollywood Shaped the Mexican Revolution*. London: Verso.
Orovio, H. 1981: *Diccionario de la música cubana, bibliográfico y técnico*. Havana: Letras Cubanas.
Orovio, H. 1995: *El bolero latino*. Havana: Letras Cubanas.
Oroz, S. 1992: *Melodrama: o cinema de lagrimas na América Latina*. Rio de Janeiro: Rio Fundo.
Ortega, J. 1992: *El discurso de la abundancia*. Caracas: Monte Ávila.
Ortega, J. 1995: Cultural studies questionnaire. *Journal of Latin American Cultural Studies* 4, 223–5.
Ortiz, F. 1940: *Contrapunteo cubano del tabaco y el azúcar*. Havana: J. Montero.
Ortiz, F. 1947: *Cuban Counterpoint: Tobacco and Sugar*, translated by H. de Onís. New York: Knopf.
Ortiz, R. 1986: *Cultura brasileira e identidade nacional*, 2nd edn. São Paulo: Brasiliense.
Ortiz de Montellano, B. 1990: *Aztec Medicine, Health and Nutrition*. New Brunswick, NJ: Rutgers University Press.
Osborne, P. 2000: *Philosophy in Cultural Theory*. London: Routledge.
Oyarzún, L. 1967: *Temas de la cultura chilena*. Santiago de Chile: Editorial Universitaria.
Paranaguá, P. A. (ed.) 1987: *Le Cinéma brésilien*. Paris: Centre Georges Pompidou.
Paranaguá, P. A. (ed.) 1995: *Mexican Cinema*, translated by A. M. López. London: British Film Institute.
Paxman, A. 1996a: Trim Telenovela looks abroad. *Variety* 25–31 March, 42, 60.
Paxman, A. 1996b: Tuneful take on novelas. *Variety* 25–31 March, 44.
Payeras, M. 1980: *Días de la selva*. Havana: Casa de las Américas.
Paz, O. 1950: *El laberinto de la soledad*. Mexico City: Fondo de Cultura Económica.

Paz, O. 1985: *The Labyrinth of Solitude: Life and Thought in Mexico*, translated by L. Kemp. New York: Grove Press.
Paz, O. 1992: Razón y elogio de María Félix (Introduction to *María Félix*). Mexico: Secretaría de Gobernación, Dirección General de Radio, Televisión y Cinematografía, Cineteca Nacional, Dirección General de Comunicación Social de la Presidencia de la República.
Pedelty, M. 1999: The bolero: The birth, life and decline of Mexican modernity. *Latin American Music Review* 20, 1, 30–58.
Perez, E. 1999: The poetics of an (inter)nationalist revolution, El Partido Liberal Mexicano, Third space feminism in the United States. In *The Decolonial Imagery: Writing Chicana into History*. Bloomington, IN: Indiana University Press, 55–74.
Pérez Firmat, G. 1994: *Life on the Hyphen: The Cuban-American Way*. Austin, TX: University of Texas Press.
Pérez Monfort, R. 1998: Entre 'nacionalismo', 'regionalismo' y 'universalidad': aproximación a una controversia entre Manuel M. Ponce y Alfredo Tamayo Marín en 1920–1921. *Heterofonía* 118–19, 41–51.
Pérez-Torres, R. 1995: *Movements in Chicano Poetry: Against Myths, Against Margins*. New York: Cambridge University Press.
Pérez-Torres, R. 1997: Refiguring Aztán. *Aztlán* 22, 2, 16–41.
Perlongher, N. 1989: Evita vive en cada hotel organizado. *El porteño* 88, 41–3.
Perlongher, N. 1997: *Poemas completas (1980–1992)*, edited by R. Echevarren. Buenos Aires: Seix Barral.
Picher, J. 2002: *Cantinflas and the Chaos of Mexican Modernity*. Wilmington, DE: Scholarly Resources.
Pick, Z. 1993: *The New Latin American Cinema: A Continental Project*. Austin, TX: University of Texas Press.
Piglia, R. 1993: Sarmiento's vision. In J. T. Criscenti (ed.), *Sarmiento and His Argentina*. Boulder, CO: Lynne Rienner, 71–6.
Piglia, R. 1994: *Artificial Respiration*, translated by D. Balderston. Durham, NC: Duke University Press.
Pineda, A. 1989: El bolero cubano y su transculturación a México en el caso de Agustín Lara. Thesis presented to Departamento de Filosofía y Letras, Universidad de las Américas, Puebla, Mexico.
Pineda, A. 1990: La evolución del bolero urbano en Agustín Lara. *Heterofonía* 102–3, 4–23.
Pizarro, A. 1994: *De ostras y caníbales: ensayos sobre la cultura latinoamericana*. Santiago de Chile: Editorial Universidad de Santiago.
Podalsky, L. 1993: Disjointed frames: Melodrama, nationalism, and representation in 1940s Mexico. *Studies in Latin American Popular Culture* 12, 57-73.
Poniatowska, E. 1969: *Hasta no verte Jesús mío*. Mexico City: Era.
Pons, M. C. 1998: *Más allá de las fronteras del lenguaje: un análisis crítico de* Respiración artificial *de Ricardo Piglia*. Mexico City: Universidad Nacional Autónoma de México.
Pozas, R. A. 1952: *Juan Pérez Jolote: biografía de un Tzotzil*. Mexico City: Fondo de Cultura Económica.
Pozas Horcasitas, R. 2002: El laberinto de los tiempos: la modernidad atrapada en su horizonte. In R. Pozas (ed.), *La Modernidad atrapada en su horizonte*. Horcasitas, Mexico: Academia Mexicana de Ciencias, 9–36.

Pratt, M. L. 1992: *Imperial Eyes: Travel Writing and Transculturation*. London: Routledge.
Pratt, M. L. 1999: Overwriting Pinochet: Undoing the culture of fear in Chile. In D. Sommer (ed.), *The Places of History: Regionalism Revisited in Latin America*. Durham, NC: Duke University Press, 21–33.
Puig, M. 1980: *Maldición eterna a quien lea estas páginas*. Barcelona: Seix Barral.
Puig, M. 1982: *La traición de Rita Hayworth*. Barcelona: Seix Barral.
Puig, M. 1997: Bajo un manto de estrellas. In *Bajo un manto de estrellas*. Rosario: Beatriz Viterbo, 7–72.
Queiroz Jr., T. de 1975: *Preconceito de cor e a mulata na literatura brasileira*. São Paulo: Atica.
Quiñones, S. 1997: Telenovela taps into Mexico's anger at US. *Electronic Media* 20 October, 11–12.
Quintana, P. 1993: *A Taste of Mexico*. New York: Stewart, Tabori and Clay.
Rama, A. 1974: El área cultural andina (hispanismo, mesticismo, indigenismo). *Cuadernos Americanos* XXXIII, 197, 136–73.
Rama, A. 1982: *Transculturación narrativa en América Latina*. Mexico: Siglo XXI.
Rama, A. 1984: *La ciudad letrada*. Hanover, NH: Ediciones del Norte.
Rama, A. 1996: *The Lettered City*, edited and translated by J. Chasteen. Durham, NC: Duke University Press.
Rama, C. and Delgado, G. 1992: *El estado y la cultura en Uruguay: análisis de las relaciones entre el estado y la actividad privada en la producción de bienes y servicios culturales*. Montevideo: Fundación de Cultura Universitaria.
Ramos, J. 2001: *Divergent Modernities*. Durham, NC: Duke University Press.
Randall, M. 1991: Reclaiming voices: Notes on a new female practice of journalism. *Latin American Perspectives* 18, 15–31.
Reed, J. 1991: The many masks of Aztán. *New York Times* 6 March.
Reed, M. K. 1992: *Language, Text, Subject: A Critique of Hispanism*. West Fayette, IN: Purdue University Press.
Rego, W. 1968: *Capoeira Angola: ensaio socio-etnográfico*. Salvador, Brazil: Itapuã.
Restrepo, O. 1999: Un imaginario de la nación: lectura de láminas y descripción de la Comisión Corográfica. *Anuario Colombiano de Historia Social y de la Cultura* 26, 30–58.
Restrepo Duque, H. 1992: *Lo que cuentan los boleros*. Santafé de Bogotá: Centro Editorial de Estudios Musicales.
Richard, N. 1991: Periferias culturales y descentramientos posmodernos (marginalidad latinoamericana y recompaginación de los márgenes). *Punto de Vista* 40, 5–6.
Richard, N. 1995: Cultural peripheries: Latin America and postmodern de-centering. In *The Postmodernism Debate in Latin America*. Durham, NC: Duke University Press, 217–22.
Richard, N. 1998: *Residuos y metáforas (ensayos de crítica cultural sobre el Chile de la transición)*. Santiago de Chile: Cuarto Propio.
Richard, N. 2001: Globalización académica, estudios culturales y crítica latinoamericana. *Revista de Crítica Cultural* (Santiago de Chile) 18, 185–99.
Rico Salazar, J. 2000: *Cien años de boleros*. Bogotá: Panamericana.
Rifkin, J. 2001: La venta del siglo. *El País* 5 May, 9.
Rivera, D. with Wolfe, B. 1937: *Portrait of Mexico*. London: Allen & Unwin.
Rivera, D. with March, G. 1991 (1960): *My Art, My Life: An Autobiography*. New York: Dover Publications.

Roberts, J. S. 1972: *Black Music of Two Worlds*. London: Allen Lane.
Robertson, P. 1996: *Guilty Pleasures: Feminist Camp from Mae West to Madonna*. Durham, NC: Duke University Press.
Rodó, J. E. 1988: *Ariel*, translated by M. Sayers Peden, with prologue by C. Fuentes. Austin, TX: University of Texas Press.
Rodrigues Filho, M. 1964: *O negror no futebol brasileiro*. Rio de Janeiro: Civilização Brasileira.
Rodríguez, I. (ed.) 2000: *The Latin American Subaltern Studies Reader*. Durham, NC: Duke University Press.
Romero, F. 1987: *El negro en el Perú y su transculturación lingüística*. Lima: Editorial Milla Batres.
Romero, F. 1988: *Quimba, fa, malambo, ñeque: afronegrismos en el Perú*. Lima: Instituto de Estudios Peruanos.
Romero, F. 1993: Afronegrismos en la cocina peruana. In R. O. Weston (ed.), *Cultura, identidad y cocina en el Peru*. Lima: Escuela Profesional de Turismo y Hotelería, Facultad de Ciencias de la Comunicación, Turismo y Sicología, Universidad San Martín de Porres, 177–88.
Romero, R. 1994: Black music and identity in Peru: Reconstruction and revival of Afro-Peruvian musical traditions. In G. H. Béhague (ed.), *Music and Black Ethnicity: The Caribbean and South America*. Gainesville, FL: University of Miami, 307–30.
Rosenfeld, A. 1993: *Negro, macumba e futebol*. São Paulo: Perspectiva.
Rotker, S. (ed.) 2002: *Citizens of Fear: Urban Violence in Latin America*. New Brunswick, NJ: Rutgers University Press.
Rowe, W. 1996: *Hacia una poética radical: ensayos de hermenéutica cultural*. Rosario and Lima: Beatriz Viterbo and Mosca Azul.
Rowe, W. 2000: La regionalidad de los conceptos en el estudio de la cultura y la experienca en JALLA. *Márgenes* XIV, 17, 143–54.
Rowe, W. and Schelling, V. 1989: *Memory and Modernity: Culture in Latin America*. London: Verso.
Ruiz Quevedo, R. 1988: Presencia y vigencia del bolero cubano en el cancionero latinoamericano. Paper presented to the Coloquio Internacional del Bolero; copy kept in CIDMUC, Havana.
Rutenberg, J. 2002: Univisión buys big holder of Hispanic radio stations. *New York Times* 13 June.
Safford, F. 1991: Race, integration, and progress: Elite attitudes and the Indian in Colombia, 1750–1870. *Hispanic American Historical Review* 71, 1, 1–33.
Said, E. W. 1975: *Beginnings: Intention and Method*. New York: Columbia University Press.
Saldívar, J. D. 1991: *Dialectics of Our America: Genealogy, Cultural Critique, and Literary History*. Durham, NC: Duke University Press.
Saldívar, J. D. 1997: *Border Matters: Remapping American Cultural Studies*. Berkeley, CA: University of California Press.
Saldívar-Hull, S. 2000: *Feminism on the Border*. Berkeley, CA: University of California Press.
Salinas, J. J. 1989: El peronismo como vendaval erótico: ¿qué quedó del sex-appeal del Potro? *El Porteño* 88, 37–40.
Sánchez, E. 1998: *Gobierno y geografía: Agustín Codazzi y la Comisión Corográfica de la Nueva Granada*. Bogotá: Banco de la República/El Ancora Editores.

Sánchez León, A. 1993: *La balada del gol perdido*. Lima: Ediciones noviembre trece.
Sander Damo, A. 2002: *Futebol e identidade social: una leitura antropológica das rivalidades entre torcedores e clubes*. Porto Alegre: Editora de Universidade.
Sanjinés, J. 1983: Problems of form and content in revolutionary cinema. In M. Chanan (ed.), *Twenty-Five Years of the New Latin American Cinema*. London: BFI, 34–8.
Sanjinés, J. 1996: Beyond testimonial discourse. In G. Gugelberger (ed.), *The Real Thing*. Durham, NC: Duke University Press, 254–65.
Santa Cruz, N. 1964a: *Cumanana*. Lima: Librería Editorial Juan Mejía Baca.
Santa Cruz, N. 1964b: El festejo. *Expreso* 26 January, 7.
Santa Cruz, N. 1964c: Folklore peruano: Cumanana. *Expreso* 24 May, 5.
Santa Cruz, N. 1965: El negro en el Perú. *Expreso* 21 March, 13.
Santa Cruz, N. 1966a: *Canto a mi Perú*. Lima: Librería Studium.
Santa Cruz, N. 1966b: *Décimas*, 2nd edn. Lima: Librería Studium.
Santa Cruz, N. 1967a: Mariátegui y su preconcepto del negro. *Revista Oiga*, 252 (15 December), 23–4, 26
Santa Cruz, N. 1967b: Racismo en el Perú. *Expreso* 24 September, 12.
Santa Cruz, N. 1970: *Cumanana: antología afroperuana*, 3rd edn. Lima: Editorial Luz.
Santa Cruz, N. 1971: *Antología: décimas y poemas*. Lima: Campodónico Ediciones.
Santa Cruz, N. 1972: *Rimactampu: rimas al Rimac*. Lima: Ciba-Geigy Peruana.
Santa Cruz, N. 1973a: *Ritmos negros del Perú*, edited by J. Lafforgue, 2nd edn. Buenos Aires: Losada.
Santa Cruz, N. 1973b: *Tondero y marinera*. Lima: Universidad Mayor de San Marcos.
Santa Cruz, N. 1973c: De Senegal y Malambo. *Caretas* 21 June, 22–4.
Santa Cruz, N. 1980: Racismo, discriminación racial y etnocentrismo. In *¿Cómo enfrentar el racismo en la década de los 80?: consulta de las iglesias latinoamericanas*. Lima: Celadec, 41–54.
Santa Cruz, N. 1982: *La décima en el Perú*. Lima: Instituto de Estudios Peruanos.
Santa Cruz, N. 1988: El negro en Iberoamérica. *Cuadernos Hispanoamericanos* 451–2, 7–46.
Santos, L. 1998: Kitsch y cultura de masas en la poética de la narrativa neobarroca latinoamericana. In P. Schumm (ed.), *Barrocos y modernos*. Frankfurt am Main: Vervuert, 337–51.
Santos, L. 2001: *Kitsch tropical: los medios en la literatura y el arte de América Latina*. Frankfurt am Main: Vervuert.
Saragoza, A. M. 1988–90: Recent Chicano historiography: An interpretative essay. *Aztlán* 19, 1, 1–52.
Sarlo, B. 1988: *Una modernidad periférica: Buenos Aires, 1920 y 1930*. Buenos Aires: Ediciones Nueva Visión.
Sarlo, B. 1994: *Escenas de la vida posmoderna: intelectuales, arte y videocultura en la Argentina*. Buenos Aires: Ariel.
Sarlo, B. 1997a: Los estudios culturales y la crítica literaria en la encrucijada valorativa. *Revista de Crítica Cultural* 15, 32–8. Translated into English in this volume at pp. 24–36.
Sarlo, B. 1997b: Cultural studies questionnaire. *Journal of Latin American Cultural Studies* 6, 85–92.
Sarlo, B. 2000: Raymond Williams: una relectura. In M. Moraña (ed.), *Nuevas perspectivas sobre/desde América Latina: el desafío de los estudios culturales*. Santiago de Chile: Cuarto Propio/IILI, 309–18.

Sarlo, B. 2001: *Scenes from Postmodern Life*, translated by J. Beasley-Murray. Minneapolis: University of Minnesota Press.

Sarmiento, D. F. 1970: *Facundo: Civilización y barbarie*. Madrid: Alianza Editorial.

Schelling, V. 1996: Latin America and other models of modernity. In T. Salaman (ed.), *The Legacy of the Disinherited: Popular Culture in Latin America – Modernity, Globalization, Hybridity and Authenticity*. Amsterdam: Centre for Latin American Research and Documentation, 249–62.

Schelling, V. (ed.) 2000: *Through the Kaleidoscope: The Experience of Modernity in Latin America*. London: Verso.

Schmidt-Welle, F. (ed.) 2002: *Antonio Cornejo Polar y los estudios latinoamericanos*. Pittsburgh: Instituto Internacional de Literatura Iberoamericana.

Schnitman, J. 1984: *Film Industries in Latin America: Dependency and Development*. Norwood, NJ: Ablex Publishing Corp.

Schwarz, R. 1992: *Misplaced Ideas: Essays in Brazilian Culture*, edited and with an introduction by J. Gledson. London: Verso.

Scobie, J. R. 1974: *Buenos Aires: Plaza to Suburb, 1870–1910*. Oxford: Oxford University Press.

Scorza, M. 1956: Prólogo. In J. C. Mariátegui, *Ensayos escogidos*. Lima: Patronato del libro peruano, 9–13.

Segura, D. and Pesquera, B. 1988–90. Beyond indifference and antipathy: The Chicana movement and Chicana feminist discourse. *Aztlán* 19, 2, 69–92.

Serra, O. 1995: *Águas do rei*. Florianópolis, Brazil: Vozes.

Shohat, E. and Stam, R. 1994: *Unthinking Eurocentrism: Multiculturalism and the Media*. London: Routledge.

Shua, A. M. 1997: *La muerte como efecto secundario*. Buenos Aires: Editorial Sudamericana.

Shumway, N. 1991: *The Invention of Argentina*. Berkeley, CA: University of California Press.

Sigal, C., Taymor, J. and Sunshine, L. (eds) 2002: *Frida: Bringing Frida Kahlo's Life and Art to Film*. New York: Simon and Schuster.

Simpson, A. 1993: *Xuxa: The Mega-Marketing of Gender, Race and Modernity*. Philadelphia, PA: Temple University Press.

Sklodowska, E. 1994: Spanish American testimonial novel: Some afterthoughts. *New Novel Review* 1, 2, 32–41.

Sklodowska, E. 2003: Latin American literatures. In P. Swanson (ed.), *The Companion to Latin American Studies*. London: Arnold, 86–106.

Smith, P. J. 1989: *The Body Hispanic: Gender and Sexuality in Spanish and Spanish American Literature*. Oxford: Clarendon.

Smith Duquesne, G. 1996: *Yo soy el chef, los mejores platos del maestro*. Mexico City: Diana.

Sodré, M. 1977: Mulata da melhor mulataria? *Isto É* 23 November, 46.

Solanas, F. and Getino, O. 1997: Towards a Third Cinema: Notes and experiences for the development of a cinema of liberation in the Third World. In M. Martin (ed.), *New Latin American Cinemas*, vol. 1: *Theory, Practices, and Transcontinental Articulations*. Detroit: Wayne State University Press, 35–58.

Sommer, D. 1991: *Foundational Fictions: The National Romances of Latin America*. Berkeley, CA: University of California Press.

Sommer, D. 1996: No secrets. In G. Gugelberg (ed.), *The Real Thing*. Durham, NC: Duke University Press.

Sontag, S. 1966: Notes on camp. In *Against Interpretation*. New York: Nonday, 275–92.
Spivak, G. C. 1987: *In Other Worlds: Essays in Cultural Politics*. London: Methuen.
Spivak, G. C. [1988] 1997: Can the subaltern speak? In W. Ashcroft, G. Griffiths and H. Tiffin (eds), *The Post-Colonial Studies Reader*. London: Routledge, 24–8.
Stacey, J. 1994: *Star Gazing: Hollywood Cinema and Female Spectatorship*. London: Routledge
Stam, R. 1989: *Subversive Pleasures: Bakhtin, Cultural Criticism and Film*. Baltimore, MD: Johns Hopkins University Press.
Stam, R. and Shohat, E. 1987: *Zelig* and contemporary theory: Meditation on the chameleon text. *Enclitic* 9, 102, 176–93.
Standish, P. (ed.) 1995–6: *Dictionary of Twentieth-Century Culture* (2 vols: *Hispanic Culture of South America* and *Hispanic Culture of the Caribbean*). Detroit: Gale Research Ltd.
Stoll, D. 1998: *Rigoberta Menchú and the Story of All Poor Guatemalans*. Boulder, CO: Westview.
Storey, J. (ed.) 1988: *What is Cultural Studies? A Reader*. London: Arnold.
Storey, J. 1996: *Cultural Studies and the Study of Popular Culture: Theories and Methods*. Athens, GA: University of Georgia Press.
Straayer, C. (ed.) 1996: *Deviant Eyes, Deviant Bodies: Sexual Re-Orientations in Film and Video*. New York: Columbia University Press.
Subercaseaux, B. 1999: Elite ilustrada, intelectuales y espacio cultural. In M. A. Garretón (ed.), *América Latina: un espacio cultural en el mundo globalizado*. Bogotá: Convenio Andrés Bello, 174–94.
Super, J. C. and Wright, T. C. (eds) 1985: *Food, Politics and Society in Latin America*. Lincoln, NE: University of Nebraska.
Sussekind, F. 1982: *O negro como Arlequim: teatro e discriminacão*. Rio de Janeiro: Achiame.
Sutter, M. 2002: Border crossing. *Variety* 1–7 April, A11–12, 20.
Swanson, P. (ed.) 2003: *The Companion to Latin American Studies*. London: Arnold.
Taibo I, P. 1984: *La música de Agustín Lara en el cine*. Mexico City: Filmoteca de la UNAM.
Taylor, C. 1994: *Multiculturalism*, edited by A. Gutman. Princeton, NJ: Princeton University Press.
Taylor, C. 1998: *The Beautiful Game: A Journey Through Latin American Football*. London: Victor Gollancz.
Taylor, J. M. 1979: *Eva Perón: The Myths of a Woman*. Chicago: University of Chicago Press.
Teitelboim, V. 1991: *Gabriela Mistral pública y secreta*. Santiago de Chile: Ediciones BAT.
Terry-Azios, D. 2002: Tuned in. *Hispanic* October, 54–7.
Thacker, J. 1999: Rethinking Golden-Age drama: The *Comedia* and its contexts. *Paragraph: A Journal of Modern Critical Theory* 16, 14–34.
Toro, C. M. 1995: *Historia de la literatura peruana*, vol. IV: *costumbrismo y literatura negra del Perú*. Lima: AFA Editores.
Trejo Delabre, R. 1999: La internet en América Latina. In N. García Canclini and C. J. Moneta (eds), *Las industrias culturales en la integración latinoameriana*. Mexico City: Grijalbo.

Trillo, C. and Saccomanno, G. 1980: *Historia de la historieta argentina*. Buenos Aires: Ediciones Record.
Tuan, F. 1975: *Landscapes of Fear*. New York: Pantheon Books.
UNESCO 1998: *World Culture Report 1998: Culture, Creativity and Markets*. Paris: UNESCO Publishing.
Valderrama, R. and Escalante, C. 1977: *Gregorio Condori Mamani: autobiografía (Biblioteca de la Tradición Oral Andina)*. Cuzco: Centro Bartolomé de las Casas.
Van Bottenburg, M. 2001: *Global Games*. Urbana, IL: University of Illinois Press.
Vasconcelos, J. 1961 [1925]: *La raza cósmica*. Mexico City: Fondo de Cultura Económica.
Vasconcelos, J. 1963 [1935]: *A Mexican Ulysses: An Autobiography*, translated and abridged by W. R. Crawford. Bloomington, IN: Indiana University Press.
Vasconcelos, J. 1979: *The Cosmic Race*, translated by D. T. Jaén. Los Angeles: Centro de Publicaciones, Department of Chicano Studies, California State University.
Vega Alfaro, E. de la 1995: Origins, development and crisis of the sound cinema (1929–64). In Paranaguá, P. A. (ed.) *Mexican Cinema*, translated by A. M. López. London: British Film Institute, 79–93.
Vergara y Vergara, J. M. 1974: *Historia de la literatura en Nueva Granada*, 2 vols. Bogotá: Banco Popular. Original publication (1867): *Historia de la literatura en Nueva Granada: Parte primera: desde la conquista hasta la independencia, 1538–1820*. Bogotá: Echeverría.
Vidal, H. (ed.) 1985: *Fascismo y experiencia literaria: reflexiones para una recanonización*. Minneapolis: Institute for the Study of Ideologies and Literatures.
Vieira, L. R. 1996: *O jogo de capoeira: cultura popular no Brasil*. Rio de Janeiro: Sprint.
Villena Fiengo, S. 2000: Imaginando la nación a través del fútbol: el discurso de la prensa costarricense sobre la hazaña mundialista de Italia 90. In P. Alabarces (ed.), *Peligro de gol: estudios sobre deporte y sociedad en América Latina*. Buenos Aires: CLACSO, 145–68.
Villoro, L. 1996: *Los grandes momentos del indigenismo en México*. Mexico City: Fondo de Cultura Económica.
Viñas, D. 1963: La señora muerta. In *Las malas costumbres*. Buenos Aires: Jamcana, 63–72.
Vincendeau, G. 2000: *Stars and Stardom in French Cinema*. London: Continuum.
Virno, P. and Hardt, M. 1996: Virtuosity and revolution: The political theory of exodus. In *Radical Thought in Italy*. Minneapolis: University of Minneapolis Press, 188–209.
Vogel, A. 1982: O momento feliz: reflexões sobre o futebol e o ethos nacional. In R. DaMatta et al., *Universo do futebol: esporte e sociedade brasileira*. Rio de Janeiro: Edicões Pinakotheque, 75–116.
Wade, P. 1993: *Blackness and Race Mixture: The Dynamics of Racial Identity in Colombia*. Baltimore, MD: Johns Hopkins University Press.
Wade, P. 2000: *Music, Race and Nation: Música Tropical in Colombia*. Chicago: University of Chicago Press.
Waisbord, S. 2002a Status of media in Argentina, Uruguay and Paraguay. http://www.scils.rutgers.edu/~waisbord/ENCYCLOP.html (accessed 7 September 2002).
Waisbord, S. 2002b: TV in the age of globalization, from the viewpoint of promoting

mutual understanding. 11th JAMCO Symposium. http://www.jamco.or.jp/2002_symposium/en/paper/silvio_waisbord.html (accessed 14 September 2002).
Walsh, R. 1981: Esa mujer. In J. Tula (ed.), *Obra literaria completa*. Mexico City: Siglo XXI, 163–71.
Warner, M. 1993: Introduction. In *Fear of a Queer Planet: Queer Politics and Social Theory*. Minneapolis: University of Minnesota Press, vii–xxxi.
Weismantel, M. J. 1988: *Food, Gender and Poverty in the Ecuadorian Andes*. Pittsburgh, PA: University of Pennsylvania Press.
White, H. 1973: *Metahistory: The Historical Imagination in Nineteenth Century Europe*. Baltimore, MD: Johns Hopkins University Press.
Whitefield, M. 2001: Telemundo to produce telenovelas in joint venture. *Miami Herald* 21 March.
Williams, G. 1996: Fantasies of cultural exchange in Latin American subaltern studies. In G. Gugelberger (ed.), *The Real Thing: Testimonial Discourse in Latin America*. Durham, NC: Duke University Press, 225–53.
Williams, R. 1961: The analysis of culture. In *The Long Revolution*. London: Chatto and Windus, 57–88.
Williams, R. 1981: *Culture*. London: Collins.
Williams, R. 1989: *The Politics of Modernism*, edited by A. Pinkney. London: Verso.
Woodward, K. L. 1990: *Making Saints: How the Catholic Church Determines Who Becomes a Saint, Who Doesn't, and Why*. New York: Simon and Schuster.
Xavier, I. 1982: Allegories of underdevelopment: From the 'aesthetics of hunger' to the 'aesthetics of garbage'. PhD dissertation, New York University.
Young, R. (ed.) 1997: *Latin American Postmodernisms (Postmodern Studies, 22)*. Amsterdam: Rodopi.
Young, R. 1999: Textualizing Evita: 'Oh what a circus! Oh, what a show!' *Canadian Journal of Latin American and Caribbean Studies* 24, 215–32.
Yúdice, G. 1991: *Testimonio* and postmodernism. *Latin American Perspectives* 18, 3, 15–31.
Yúdice, G. 1994: Estudios culturales y sociedad civil. *Revista de Crítica Cultural* 8, 44–53.
Yúdice, G. 1995: Civil society, consumption, and governmentality in an age of global restructuring. *Social Text* 45, 1–25.
Yúdice, G. 1997: Cultural studies questionnaire. *Journal of Latin American Cultural Studies* 6, 217–22.
Yúdice, G. 1999: La industria de la música en la integración de América Latina-Estados Unidos. In N. García Canclini and C. J. Moneta (eds), *Las industrias culturales en la integración latinoameriana*. Mexico City: Grijalbo, 181–244.
Yúdice, G., Franco, J. and Flores, J. (eds) 1992: *On Edge: The Crisis of Contemporary Latin American Culture*. Minneapolis: University of Minnesota Press.
Zavala, I. M. 1990: De héroes y heroínas en lo imaginario social: el discurso amoroso del bolero. *Casa de las Américas* 179, 123–9.
Zavala, I. M. 1991: *El bolero: historia de un amor*. Madrid: Alianza.
Zimmerman, M. 1991: *Testimonio* in Guatemala: Payeras, Rigoberta and beyond. *Latin American Perspectives* 18, 4, 22–47.

Index

Achugar, Hugo 17, 49, 56, 59, 228
Adán, Martín 45
Adorno, Rolena 46
Adorno, Theodor 29, 35
advertising 156, 159, 171
African origins 203, 242
Afro-Brazilians, portrayal of 204–10
Agger, Ben 244
Aira, César 103, 108, 301–3
Altamirano, Carlos 3
Amalia (novel by Mármol) 95
Amauta 67, 197
American Popular Revolutionary
  Alliance (APRA) 67–8
Amerindian culture 76–8
Ancízar, Manuel 218, 220–2
Anderson, Benedict 139
Anzaldúa, Gloria 80, 84–9
Archetti, Eduardo P. 116–26
architecture 35, 70, 300–11
Area studies 49–60
Arendt, Hannah 32, 35
Argentina
  cinema 183–4
  culture 90–101, 102–14
  Dirty War 94, 97, 257
  fiction 300–11
  football 119–21
  icons 102–14, 122–4
Arguedas, José María 42–3, 196–9, 232, 241
Ariel / arielismo 54, 58, 60, 65, 80, 88, 98
Arlt, Roberto 104, 300
Aronna, Michael 6, 60
AT&T 19, 21, 159
Auden, W.H. 34, 36
Auerbach, Erich 29, 35

Aztlán 77–84

Babenco, Héctor
  Pixote 181–2
Bakhtin, Mikhail 28–9, 35
Balderston, Dan 8
Barnet, Miguel 229, 233
Barrico, Alessandro 23
Barthes, Roland 12, 29, 34–5, 102
Bartra, Roger 14, 138
Baudrillard, Jean 103
Bazin, André 180
Beardsell, Peter 5
Beasley-Murray, Jon 5
Bello, Andrés 5
Bemberg, María Luisa 148
Benítez, Agustín Basave 193–4
Benítez Rojo, Antonio 7
Benjamin, Walter 27, 29, 34–5, 41, 56
Berger, John 16
Bergmann, Emilie 4
Bermúdez, Sylvia 4
Bernal, Gustavo 148
Beverley, John 4–7, 17, 42, 48–60, 231, 234, 236–7
Bhabha, Homi 14, 293
Birmingham Group 16, 27, 35, 41
black population
  in Brazil 203–10
  in Peru 239–41
Blade Runner 307
Blaine, James 64
bolero 127–39
Borges, Jorge Luis 7, 45, 97, 99, 103–4, 109, 300
Bourdieu, Pierre 27, 35, 41–2
Brazil
  cinema 181–2

Brazil – *continued*
  dance 278–89
  attitude towards race 119, 203–10
  portrayal of street violence 181–2
Brotherston, Gordon 4
Bueno, Eva T. 4
Buenos Aires 13, 183, 300–11
Buñuel, Luis 185, 189
  Los olvidados 179–81, 186

Cacciari, Massimo 27, 35
Caesar, Terry 4
Caetano, Adrián
  Pizza, birra, faso 178, 183
Caliban 1–2, 49–50, 60, 65, 98
Callois, Roger 88
cannibalism 80, 275
Capoeira 278–89
Cárdenas, Guty 130
Carpentier, Alejo 1
Casas, Bartolomé de las 5, 228
Castellanos, Rosario 274
Castells, Manuel 177, 182
Castillo, Adelaida del 89, n. 7
camp 254
  and artifice 107
  and Eva Perón's myth 107–10
  and transvestism 107–8
cartoons 261–5
Castro, Fidel 64, 229
Catholic Church 62, 224, 247
Chanady, Amaryll 192–202
Che Guevara 7
Chicano culture 76–89
Chicano literature 79, 84
Chingada, La 85
cinema
  in Argentina 147, 183
  in Bolivia 290–9
  in Brazil 147, 181–2
  in Colombia 184–6
  in France 140
  in Mexico 128, 179–81
cinema industry 135, 141–2, 146–8, 290
Cinema Novo 203, 205, 208
Cisneros, Sandra 85
class 54–5, 218, 243, 271

CNN 13, 18–19, 22
Colás, Santiago 7, 100
Cold War 12, 58
Colombia 22, 129, 158, 163, 215–27
colonial discourse 215–28
colonization 193, 203, 228, 241, 270–1, 291
collective memory 81–4, 128–9, 220–1
Comisión Corográfica de Colombia 221, 227
Commodification 16, 156–7
Communist International (Comintern) 67
consumerism 146
consumption 268–77, 300
Copi 107–8, 110–11
Cornejo Polar, Antonio 2, 5, 10, 46, 49, 59l, 88, 219, 241
Cortázar, Julio 33, 35, 301
Costa Rica 12
criminality 177–89
criollo 251, 271, 272
culture
  cross-fertilization 137, 248–9
  high 31
  mass 6, 114 n. 14, 127–38, 151–66, 167–76
  popular 5, 178, 226, 253–65
cultural identity 6, 24–5
cultural memory 54, 218, 247–8
cultural myths 76–89
cultural studies defined 3, 7, 8, 13, 15
culture, meanings 8–9
Cunha, Euclides da 228–9

D'Allemand, Patricia 2, 215–27
dance 239, 278–89
Davis, Mike 307
David, Richard H. 51–4
De Certeau, Michel 31, 35, 303
De Grandis, Rita 90, 90–101
De La Campa, Ramón 7
De Man, Paul 54
Dear, Michael 304
décima 239–40
Deleuze, Gilles 12, 38
Denegri, Francisca 4, 228–38
Derrida, Jacques 12, 14, 35, 237
Díaz, Porfirio 69

Don Quijote 58
Dorfman, Ariel 145
During, Simon 2

Echenique, Alfredo Bryce 46
Eco, Umberto 99
Eguino, Antonio 296
El matadero (short story by Esteban Echeverría) 95, 97
El sueño 301–4, 310
Elmore, Peter 46
Empson, William 40
Esquivel, Laura 33–4, 36
ethnic minorities 1, 57, 119, 205–10, 222, 243, 291
Eurocentrism 33, 59 n. 4, 198, 204, 221, 230
'exotic' 6, 73

fandom 124–6
Fanon, Frantz 239
Feinmann, José Pablo 90–101
Félix, María 140, 145, 149
feminism 3–4, 54, 80, 84–8, 193, 254
Fernández Retamar, Roberto 1–2, 98
film noir 173–4, 255
film stars 140–50
Flores Galindo, Alberto 40, 44, 46
Fogwill, Enrique Rodolfo 304–6
food 242, 251, 268–77
football
　British influence 119–20
　black players 119
　identities 121–4
　globalisation 125
　masculine ideals 125
　miscegenation 118–19
　nationalism 125
　national styles 117–21
　race 119
　supporters' culture 124–6
　violence 125
Foster, David William 3, 253–65, 310
Foucault, Michel 31, 35, 58
　and heterotopical spaces 105
foundational myths 76–89, 90–101
Franco, Jean 3–4, 15
Freud, Sigmund 81, 254

Fuentes, Carlos 65–6, 73, 149

Gallegos, Rómulo 52, 230
garbage aesthetic 210–12
García Canclini, Néstor 6, 12–23, 42, 199, 212, 244, 251–2, 298
García Márquez, Gabriel 73–4
Garcilaso de la Vega, El Inca 5
Garrincha 121–2
Gaviria, Víctor Manuel 56
　Rodrigo D. No futuro 184
　La vendedora de rosas 184–6
gay sexuality 107
gender 84–9, 107–10
gendered identities 84–9, 258–65
gendered roles 84–9, 181–2, 258–65
genetic assimilation 83, 219
global culture 13, 30; *see* globalization
globalization 13, 20, 54, 60, n. 10, 152, 154, 161, 167, 173, 182, 277, 290
Globo 13, 167
Godsland, Shelly 4
González Mike, 268–77
González Echeverría, Roberto 7, 90, 229–30, 233
González Iñárritu, Alejandro
　Amores perros 186–9
Gramsci, Antonio 54
Green, Michael 3
Greenblatt, Stephen 230
Gregory, Derek 310
Guha, Ranajit 57
Guillénh, Nicolás 79, 244
Guimaraes Rosa, João 42

Habermas, Jürgen 30, 35, 48, 50, 59
Hall, Stuart 16, 27, 35, 59
Hart, Stephen M. 1–10, 34, 290–9
Harvey, David 161, 189
Haya de la Torre, Víctor Raúl 66
Hegel, G.W. 50–1, 94, 96
Henríquez Ureña, Pedro 43
heterogeneity 5, 10, 226
Higgins, James 10
Historia de la literatura en Nueva Granada 215–27
Hoggart, Richard 27, 34–5

Hollywood 22, 128, 140–50, 173, 180, 255, 290
homosexuality 60, 107, 205, 253–65
Hulme, Peter 7
Huntingdon, Samuel 51, 59
hybridity 39, 56, 211, 251–2, 270

icons, characteristics of 8
identity and identities
   multiple 91, 102–3
   national 24–5, 132, 164, 173
   performative 103–5
   and double 111
   and mask 106
Indianism 81
indigenismo 43–4, 82, 88
indigenous peoples 86, 204, 222, 284
indigenous written production 5
interdisciplinarity 7, 14, 17, 21, 27–9, 44, 46, 48–50
Internet 18, 20–1, 26, 98
Isle of Flowers 210–11

Jameson, Fredric 183, 185, 187, 228, 234
Jordan, Barry 8, 10
Journal of Latin American Cultural Studies 8
Joyce, James 73

Kahlo, Frida 68, 141–2, 148
Kant, Immanuel 94
Kantaris, Geoffrey 177–89
Keeling, David 310 n. 2
King, John 6, 140–50
Klor de Alva, J. Jorge 59, 192
Knights, Vanessa 127–39
Kraniauskas, John 7–8, 199

La muerte como efecto secundario 307–10
La raza cósmica 77–84, 195–7
Lacan, Jacques 12
ladino 230
Lamborghini, Oswaldo 111–13
language
   and dialects 304–5
   and politics 231–2

Lara, Agustín 130–5, 145, 150
Larsen, Neil 7
Latin American Cultural Studies 3–8, 14, 16–17, 41, 46–7
Latin American Studies 9, 16–17, 58
Latin Americanism 49–50, 237–8
latinity 21
latinization 21, 277
latinos, portrayal of 152–63
latino criticism 56, 57
Lauer, Mirko 46
Lavador, J.S. (QUINO) 256–65
Lechner, Norbert 16
Lefebvre, Henri 302
Lenin, depiction of 70
lesbianism 84–8
Levinson, Brett 4
Lewis, Oscar 229
Lienhard, Martin 10, 42, 46, 192, 219
literacy-power relation 31–2
literary criticism 25–6, 28–30, 54
literary studies 26–7, 31–4
literature 15, 43–7, 51–3
   and loss of prestige 41–2
   and value 29–33
Losada, Alejandro 2
Louis, Anja 10
Ludmer, Josefina 38, 57
Lukács, Georg 29, 35
Lyotard, Jean-François 24, 34

Machado de Assis, Joaquim Maria 7
Madonna 254
Mafalda 256–65
magical realism 22
Malinche, La 3, 85, 89, 136, 150, 164
Mallea, Eduardo 93
Manrique, Nelson 46
Manzano, Francisco 229
Maradona 122–4
Mariátegui, José Carlos 1–2, 43–4, 66–8, 241
marketing 13, 18, 20, 159
Martí, José 63–4, 192, 194, 201
Martínez, Tomás Eloy
Martínez Estrada, Ezequiel 93, 96
Martín-Barbero, Jesús 6, 14–15, 43, 56, 128, 160

Marx, Karl 56, 94
Marxism 12, 54, 66–8, 106
masculinity 108, 258–65
Masiello, Francine 4
mass media 6, 18–20, 25–6, 127
master narratives 77
Mato, Daniel 17
McLuhan 40
Medellín 184–5
melodrama 114, 143, 161
Menchú, Rigoberta 7, 48–50, 59, 230, 233, 235–7
Merrell, Floyd 278–89
mesticismo 82
mestiço 204–5, 212
mestizo 39, 80, 82–3, 193, 196–7, 199–202, 222, 272, 292
mestizaje 56, 192–202, 221, 226, 270
Mexico
  bolero 127–39
  cancionero 132
  dance halls 133
  film industry 135–6
  mass media 129–30
  melodrama 135–6, 147
  modernity 81
  popular culture 131–2
  radio 132
  recording industry 129–30
Mexico City 13, 133, 155, 160–1, 182, 276
Mignolo, Walter 5, 17
Miller, Nicola 7, 62–75
miscegenation 56, 193, 195, 221, 270
Mistral, Gabriela 71–3
modernity 5–6, 81, 138, 145
  and Brazil 6
modernization 30, 127–39
modernising project 193; *see* modernity and modernization
Molina Enríquez, Andrés 193–4
Moneta, Juan Carlos 6
Monsiváis, Carlos 6, 84–5, 128, 133, 135, 144–6, 149
Montalbetti, Mario 45
montoneros 104, 113
Moraga, Cherríe 79, 84–9
Moraña, Mabel 4, 10, 50, 59

Moreiras, Alberto 4, 10, 17
Morely, David 15
Morgan-Tamosunas, Rikki 8
Morrison, Toni 73
Mottram, Eric 37
Mulhearn, Francis 3
multiculturalism 29, 34, 59 n. 2
multitude 40
  and Paolo Virno 106
  and lumpen 106
Mumford, Lewis 41
museums 110
music 127–39, 157, 242
myth 102
  Eva Perón's myth 102–3
  in semiology 102
  and literature 76–7
  political myth

NAFTA 6, 21, 154–6, 276
nation 127, 40, 53, 84–8, 90, 127, 215–16, 226, 230
national culture 18, 127, 132, 275
national identity 24–5, 132, 164, 173
national literature 24–5, 39, 43–7, 51–4, 84–9, 90–3, 215–27
negrismo 241–2
Neo-baroque 56, 109, 111
  and Néstor Perlongher 106
Neo-Realism
  Italian 179–80, 184
  Latin American 180
Neruda, Pablo 72
New Latin America Cinema 180
newspapers *see* press
Noble, Andrea 6

Ocampo, Silvina 33–4, 36
Ocampo, Victoria 4, 72
Ojeda, Martha 239–52
Olson, Charles 38, 41
oral culture 44–5, 230–4, 236
organisations 13, 18, 21, 27, 41, 141, 152, 157, 159, 164 n. 9, 167–8, 170, 243, 248, 252 n. 3, 252 n. 7, 284–5
Ortega, Julio 3, 46
Ortiz, Fernando 1, 43

otherness 6, 33
Oviedo, José 6

Panofsky, Erwin 75
past, remodelling of the 79, 91, 219
Paz, Octavio 17, 79, 85, 89, 140, 149–50
Para recibir el canto de los pájaros 296–9
Peregrinación de Alpha 221
Pérez Firmat, Gustavo 56
Perlongher, Néstor 102, 105, 109
Perón
  Administration 93
  Eva 102–14
  Juan Domingo 103–4
  Peronism 105, 109
  Peronista Youth 104–5
  and *montoneros* 104–5
  and populism 104–5
  as monster 97
Peru
  cultural studies in 43–7
  Afro-Peruvian issues
  icons 66–8
  mestizaje 197–9
philology 2
Piglia, Ricardo 91–2, 100
Pino, José M. 2
Pizarro, Ana 5
Podalsky, Laura 151–66
political contexts 53–8
political issues 48–50, 69, 90–2, 290–9
Poniatowska, Elena 229, 233
Pons, María Cristina 76–89, 100
postcolonial theory 42, 54, 194
postmodern 28, 48, 193, 194, 210
postmodernism 6–7, 12, 110
Pozas, Ricardo 229
Prado, Franciso la Rubia 2
press 25, 92, 131
publishing companies 13, 18
Puig, Manuel 107–8, 145

Quechua 5, 143, 197, 232–3, 291
queer 253–65; *see also* homosexuality
Quino *see* Lavado, Salvador Joaquín

race 77–81, 192–202, 203–14, 239–52
race relations 193, 247

radio 128, 132, 240
  radio melodramas 110
Rainha Diaba 205–6
Rama, Ángel 2, 5, 8, 42–3, 54, 56, 82, 199, 219, 230
Ramos, Julio 92
Reed, Malcolm 10
regional identity 37, 39–40, 45–7
regionalism 60, n. 10
religion 72, 239
representation
  in film 204–10
  politics of 231–2
resistance movements 17
Revista de Crítica Cultural 8, 60
Revista de Crítica Literaria Latinoamericana 8
Revista Iberoamericana 8
Richard, Nelly 6, 17, 34, 49, 59–60
Rifkin, Jeremy 18
Rivera, Diego 68–70
Rocha, Glauber 143
Rockefeller Foundation 60, 70
Rodó, José Enrique 55, 60, 65–6
Rosas, Juan Manuel de 91, 95
Rowe, William 4, 7, 10, 37–47
Ruétalo, Victoria 167–76
Ruiz, Raúl 33, 36
Rushdie, Salman 69

Said, Edward 91
Saint Teresa of Avila 71
Saldívar, José David 56
Sanjinés, Jorge 143–4, 231, 237–8, 290–9
Santa Cruz, Nicolás 239–52
  'A la hermandad de cargadores' 249
  'Dios perdone a mis abuelos' 246–7
  Marinera, La 239, 244, 251
  Our Lord of Miracles 239, 248
  'Panalivio' 244–6
  Ritmos Negros del Perú 240
  San Martín de Porres 249–50
  'Saña' 247
  'Santo de mi devoción' 250
Santería 248–50
Santiago, Hugo 33
Santos, Lidia 102–14

Sarlo, Beatriz 2–3, 5, 10, 14–15, 24–36, 41–2, 47, 50, 59, 307
Sarmiento, Domingo Faustino 55, 91–2, 94, 99, 228, 230
Sartre, Jean-Paul 94
Schelling, Vivian 4, 6
Shumway, Nicolás 77
Schwarz, Roberto 7
Scobie, James 310
Sevilla, Ninón 136
sexuality and sexualities 84–9, 106–14, 259–65
Shining Path (*Sendero Luminoso*) 68
Shua, Ana María 307–9
simulacrum
  and Baudrillard 103
  and Borges 103, 105
  and copy/original 103–5
  and Eva Perón's myth 103
Sklodowska, Elzbieta 4
Smith, Paul Julian 10
Smith Duquesne, Gilberto 336
soap operas *see telenovela*
soccer *see* football
Solanas, Fernando 142–3
Sommer, Doris 7, 134, 233–5
Sor Juana Inés de la Cruz 3–4, 83
Sorel, Georges 67
spectacle, culture of 115–89
Spivak, Gayatri Chakravorty 32, 35, 230, 233, 299
sports heroes 121–4
Stagnaro, Bruno
  Pizza, birra, faso 183–4
Stalin 69
Stam, Robert 203–14
Standish, Peter 8
sterilization 291
Stoll, David 48–50, 58–9, 235
Storey, John 2
Storni, Alfonsina 4
street children in cinema 177–89
studies, resistance to 3, 53–8
subaltern studies 5, 31, 42, 49–50, 56–7, 60, n. 10, 230–4
SUBTERRÁNEOS: LA IMAGEN 170–6
Swanson, Philip 9

tango 5, 104
Tasfuri, Manfredo 27
Taylor, Chris 4
Telefónica de España 13, 18–19, 21
telenovelas 151–66, 167
Televisa 13, 152–4, 156, 160, 167
television 6, 20–1, 24, 29, 31, 41, 182, 188
  in Uruguay 167–76
testimonio 4–5, 48–50, 228–38
Thacker, Jonathan 10
Time Warner 13, 18
Tottenham Hotspur 119
transculturation 9 n. 1, 56, 76–89, 137, 248–9
transnational groups 13, 18–19, 20, 156
Trans-Atlantic Studies 8
trauma 90–101
Trotsky 69
trova 128–9
Tuan, Fu-yi 311 n. 11

UNESCO 20, 169, 291
urban landscapes 177–89, 185
urban life 2, 181
urban spaces 300–11
United States of America 13–14, 19, 44, 50–8, 62, 64–5, 68, 129, 132, 137, 142, 152, 155, 158, 164, 195, 203, 276
University Reform Movement 66

Vargas Llosa, Mario 38, 45–6
Vasconcelos, José 72, 78–81, 194–6
Veloso, Caetano 33
Vergara y Vergara, José María 215–27
video-space (Sarlo's term) 26, 27, 29
Villa, Pancho 141–2
Viñas, David 104
Violence
  representations of 90–101, 177–89
Virgin of Guadalupe 85, 135–6, 150, 164
visual culture 6, 67, 68–70
Vivir afuera 304–6, 310

Walker, Alice 69
Walsh, Rodolfo 93, 112
White, Anne M. 4
White, Hayden 101

whitening 54, 80, 192, 222, 243
Wilde, Oscar 63
Williams, Raymond 9, 12, 15, 22, 27–8, 34–5, 40–2, 59
women
  construction of 102–12
  lesbian 84–8
  black 205–6
World Wide Web, access to 20

Xica da Silva 158, 206, 208–9

Yawar Mallku 290–6
Young, Richard 1–10, 23, 300–11
Yúdice, George 1, 4, 6, 16, 228, 234

Zapata, Emiliano 69, 78
zapatismo, *zapatistas* 17, 57